Naval Warfare in the English Channel 1939-1945

Naval Warfare in the English Channel 1939-1945

Peter C. Smith

Pen & Sword
MARITIME

First published in Great Britain in 2007 by
Pen & Sword Maritime
an imprint of
Pen & Sword Books Ltd
47 Church Street
Barnsley
South Yorkshire
S70 2AS

ISBN 978 1 844155 804

A CIP catalogue record for this book is available from the British Library

First edition published in 1984 as 'Hold the Narrow Sea' by Moorland Publishing, Ashbourne.

Typeset in Sabon by Lamorna Publishing Services.
Printed and bound in England by CPI UK

Pen & Sword Books Ltd incorporates the imprints of Pen & Sword Aviation, Pen & Sword maritime, Pen & Sword Military, Wharncliffe Local History, Pen & Sword Select, Pen & Sword Military Classics and Leo Cooper.

For a complete list of Pen & Sword titles please contact
PEN & SWORD BOOKS LIMITED
47 Church Street, Barnsley, South Yorkshire, S70 2AS, England
E-mail: enquiries@pen-and-sword.co.uk
Website: www.pen-and-sword.co.uk
A complete list of books written by Peter C. Smith can be found at
www.dive-bombers.co.uk

For

Alfred Horstead, HMS *Narwhal*

Contents

Glossary

AA	Anti-aircraft
ABU	Automatic Barrage Unit
AC	Aircraft
AOC	Air Officer Commanding
A/S	Anti-submarine
ASV	Aircraft/Surface Vessel
BEF	British Expeditionary Force
BNLO	British Naval Liaison Officer
CE	Channel East (convoy designation)
CIGS	Chief of Imperial General Staff
CN	Channel North (convoy designation)
CPC	Common Projectile, Capped
CSE	Chloro-Sulphonic Smoke Emitter
CW	Channel West (convoy designation)
DCAS	Deputy Controller Anti-submarine Warfare
DDOD(M)	Deputy Director Operations Division (Mine warfare)
DF	Direction Finding
DTSD	Director of Training and Staff duties
DTS	Director Training and Staff
E-boat	German motor torpedo boat (E=enemy; the German term was S-boot (*Schnelleboot* or Fast boat)
HA	High Angle
HE	High Explosive
HF/DF	High Frequency/Direction Finding
HG	Home to Gibraltar (convoy designation)
HMCS	His Majesty's Canadian Ship
IFF	Identification, Friend or Foe
LA	Low Angle
LCI	Landing Craft, Infantry
LCT	Landing Craft, Tank
LSI	Landing Ship, Infantry
LST	Landing Ship, Tank
MASB	Motor Anti-Submarine Boat
MD	Doctor

MGB	Motor Gun Boat
ML	Motor Launch
MMS	Motor Minesweeper
M/S	Minesweeper
MTB	Motor Torpedo Boat
OA	Outward Atlantic (convoy designation)
OG	Outward from Gibraltar (convoy designation)
OP	Observation Post
QZS	All minefields had a QZ designation, with further letter to identify them on a reference map.
R/A	Rear Admiral
RDF	Radio Direction Finding (Radar)
RNR	Royal Naval Reserve
RNVR	Royal Naval Volunteer Reserve
RTO	Railway Transport Officer
SAP	Semi-Armour Piercing
SGB	Steam Gunboat
S/O	Senior Officer
SOO	Senior Officer, Operations
TT	Torpedo Tubes
V/A	Vice Admiral
VC/VF	Auto-Recognition System
WP	Weatherproof
W/T	Wireless Telegraphy

Signals: 'AAA' = Answer immediately
'P' = Please
'Q' = Query
'R' = Repeat

Introduction

Perhaps it is best to start by identifying the area which I have called 'The Narrow Sea', in order to avoid confusion or indignation over any omission. The western boundary can be defined by drawing a line from north to south, from the Scilly Isles past Land's End to the Isle of Ushant and the great French naval base of Brest. To the east of this line, the bulk of the English Channel can be found, narrowing to the funnel of the Straits of Dover and then abruptly opening out into the wide Thames Estuary and the southern North Sea. North of this, beyond the shifting Goodwin Sands and the maze of tiny creeks and mudflats that is the Essex coastline, is Harwich, the famous British naval base at the juncture of the Rivers Stour and Orwell. A second line, drawn almost due east of this port across to the Dutch coast at Rotterdam, marks the other boundary of the 'Narrow Sea'.

The waters encompassed by these boundaries are of immense significance in English history. They sever Britain from Europe and in those days, happily, he who controlled the sea controlled our destiny. This isolation forced England to develop a mercantile marine and, more importantly for our story, a Navy to protect it and guard our shores. In these days, when anyone with good or evil intent, can seemingly enter at will unchallenged and unimpeded, sixty years ago the Channel was the great barrier to all such undesirable influences, and that, in 1940, was the *Wehrmacht* of Nazi Germany. These waters formed what still remains the world's busiest shipping lane. Those same waters also, fortunately for us, formed 'the largest anti-tank ditch' and were wide-enough to prevent the Germans crossing them 'on the run' as it were, as they had spectacularly done with the Maas, the Meuse and the Seine. On innumerable occasions in England's long history, invasion had been foiled by the existence of this stretch of water and the fact that the Royal Navy dominated it. London was built on maritime commerce and the peripheral naval bases of Harwich, Dover, Chatham, Portsmouth, Portland and even Plymouth ensured it stayed inviolate for most of that period. Only when our maritime defences waned though neglect, as during the Dutch Wars, was that barrier pierced and our population exposed. All these ancient ports were again to play their parts in the new threat to the nations safety, one of the greatest ever, that suddenly materialized in 1940 after two decades of similar political neglect and the successive inter-war Governments' failure then, as today, to heed the wise stricture, 'Look to your moat'.

For all its seemingly obvious importance to the nations well-being, however, this area of naval warfare has hitherto received little coverage. The war between E-boat and convoy, destroyer and dive bomber, made more hazardous by the ever-present concealed dangers of mines and submarines, remained largely unrecorded. Many of the stirring little battles, many heroic exploits and harsh, needless losses, had not appeared in much detail prior the first edition of this book, although many have appeared covering the same ground since. But, other than the military-tinged incidents, Dunkirk, Dieppe, Normandy, and the disasters, the Channel Dash and sinking of the *Lancastria,* the day-to-day warfare is hardly known. It is also fair to say that some of the Royal Navy's harshest defeats and biggest blunders, as well as their greatest moments of achievement, were to occur almost within sight of the southern coast of England. These too, find a place in this book.

Finally, it must be pointed out that this book is principally a history of the surface warships of the Royal Navy; I have covered some of the air aspects in my book *Impact! – the dive bomber pilots speak* and the mine warfare aspect was covered in my *Into the Minefields*, both volumes being part of this same publisher's Maritime series. Submarine operations were minimal, but a few are noted. Also, this book makes no attempt to re-record the battles, gallant though they were, fought by the small craft, which came under the heading of Coastal Forces. By this I mean the motor torpedo boats, motor gun boats, motor launches, motor minesweepers and the like that toiled from the first day to the last. Their deeds have been covered extensively in volumes like Peter Scott's *Battle of the Narrow Seas* and Gordon Holman's *The Little Ships*, as well as numerous lesser variations of the same theme. Nor is any attempt made to describe in depth more than a few episodes in the humdrum but equally dangerous, and even more essential work of the minesweeping flotillas. The role of the minesweepers was vital, but has been chronicled by others, notably in books like Lund and Ludlam's *Out Sweeps* and similar. Likewise the landing craft, which were trialled at Dieppe and came into their own at Normandy, have their own dedicated story in Lampton Burn's *Down Ramps*. All these ships played their full part in keeping open the Narrow Sea, but in this volume that part is reduced, due mainly to lack of space, to a backdrop of sustained effort against which other subject played their more spectacular roles.

The heroines of this book, therefore, are the destroyers of the Royal Navy, about their many and varied duties. These were endless and included escorting convoys of merchantmen and guarding them against submarines, E-boats and bombers; laying smoke screens to guard their charges against long-range artillery fire and air attack; patrolling to intercept enemy minelaying and invasion forces; suffering harshly at the hands of German mines and torpedoes from out of the darkness; fighting almost in the old tradition of broadside-to-broadside with their opposite numbers in fast, confused destroyer battles; taking heavy losses from dive bombers but always fighting back; evacuating exhausted troops in the face of the advancing enemy without air protection; engaging in vicious duels over open sights with German tanks in French harbours; taking foreign Royalty to safety and exile; bombarding enemy positions ashore in support of both evacuation and, eventually, re-invasion, all with varying degrees of success.

Other 'stars' will appear in the leading or supporting roles; great battleships thundering out their salvoes of one-ton projectiles to rend the night and pound the enemy ashore; lithe cruisers lending the weight of their multiple batteries to the destroyer patrols, some intervening with spectacular success, others with tragic results. Broad-beamed monitors, waddling into position to send their great missiles into dockyards in the old tradition of Admiral Reginald Bacon and the Dover Patrol of the Great War; and all manner of enemy craft will make their appearance on our stage; from mighty battlecruiser squadron to the tiny *Marder* craft, and 'human torpedoes'. But, in the main, this book is the story of the surface ships of the Royal Navy, when it was a Navy, and their part in controlling or disputing the 'Narrow Seas' when, once again, as so often in the past this moat of England was under siege.

Acknowledgements

As always, I have based my book principally upon official documents held at the various archives, but these have been interwoven with eyewitness accounts (with the leeway one should always allow for memory fallibility) from survivors. My grateful thanks are due to all those who either allowed themselves to be interviewed by me in their homes, or who wrote to me, and who allowed me to quote from personal diaries and papers. For their patience and understanding, and for the great contributions they have made to our freedom and this history, my deepest thanks. Many who have helped in these ways, have asked to remain anonymous and, much though it goes against the grain, I have respected such wishes; my gratitude is no less. Of the many others I would wish to thank and acknowledge the debt of gratitude due to my good friend and fellow researcher of many decades, Edwin R. Walker, of Great Bookham, Surrey, especially valuable is his unique and absolutely unrivalled knowledge of British destroyer operations. Edwin knows more about the movements of British destroyers in the Second World War than anyone else in the world, and much more than most who claim such authority – I am fortunate to be his friend and to be able to share that special store of knowledge. Pierre Hervieux, of Sainte Adresse, France, especially for his detailed knowledge of French operations and the German torpedo boat operations in the Channel. To Bernard S. Cottle, who served aboard the destroyers *Whirlwind, Vigo* and *Decoy* for his memoirs of the Harwich force; Michael Joyce who served aboard the destroyer *Wallace*; to Mr R. K. Barrett, who kindly made available his unique photographs of the wreck of the flotilla leader *Codrington* ashore at Dover in 1946; to S. Marsh at the Churchill Archives Centre, Churchill College, Cambridge, for access to the Ramsey Papers and Boxes, an invaluable source, and the Somerville Papers and Boxes; to the late Douglas Clare (*Albrighton*) and to the members of the First Destroyer Flotilla Association he led. Their detailed notes and records, and their permission to use many of their huge collection of photographs is much appreciated; Doug now lies buried in Portsmouth Naval Dockyard, and his grave commemorates all these gallant men, among those who I met at the reunions and after were Commander J. Wallace (*Penylan*); John Tuttlebee (*La Combattante*); Dennis Varley (*Fernie*); George Drewett (*Brocklesby*); Arthur Renshaw (*Stevenstone*); Ted Leather (*Fernie*);

Wilf Lawson (*Codrington*); W Hammond (*Fernie*) and Mrs P. Devarney for permission to quote from her father-in-law's diary of the time.

I am equally indebted to Mr A. L. M. Black and the members of the *Beagle, Boadicea* and *Bulldog* Association, both for inviting me to their reunions and for the many stories related to me there and in interviews and through correspondence. Thanks also, for permission to quote from parts of their detailed newsletter. In particular to Commander F. J. C. Hewitt (*Bulldog*); Commander Sir Michael Culme-Seymour (*Brazen*); Commander C. T. D. Williams (*Beagle*); Captain R. C. Medley (*Beagle)*; Lieutenant Commander J. Aitkin (*Gypsy* and *Bulldog*); Lieutenant H. E. Howting (*Boadicea*); A. J. B. Randall (*Boadicea*).

Also sincere thanks are due to S. E. Keane (*Codrington*) for permission to quote from his diary; to Richard Seddon, RWS, PhD, ARCA, for permission to reproduce his charcoal drawings; the late Captain C. S. B. Swinley, for permission to quote from his personal papers, and to reproduced some of his photographs; Captain Basil Jones (*Tartar*) for permission to quote from his biography, *And So to Battle* and for photographs; Ken Pritchforth (MTB *219*); Bernard Brotheridge (*Impulsive*). To Miss M. W. Thirkettle of the old Naval Historical Branch when it was the old Admiralty in Whitehall, for statistical data. To Roderick Suddaby, of the Imperial War Museum, Lambeth, London, for guidance on special papers held therein.

The author would also like to acknowledge his gratitude to the following who granted permission to quote brief extracts from books under their copyright: Commander William Donald, DSC for *Stand by for Action*, published by William Kimber, London, 1956; George Mack and William Kimber Ltd, London, for *H.M.S. Intrepid*, which I recommended to them and edited for publication in 1980; The Controller of Her Majesty's Stationery Office for Captain S. W. Roskill, *The War at Sea, Vols 1-3* (in four volumes) published by HMSO, London, 1954-63; Lieutenant Commander G. Stitt and George Allen & Unwin Ltd, for *H.M.S. Wideawake* (a fictionalized account of the destroyer *Wakeful*) published by George, Allen & Unwin , London, 1943; Basil Jones for *And So the Battle*, self-published 1976; David Highams Associates Limited for A. D. Divine, DSM, *Dunkirk* published by Faber & Faber in 1945, and the later, less-detailed from the naval point of view, *The Nine Days of Dunkirk*, published by Faber, London, 1959.

Finally, one problem with a book of this nature, is that most of the episodes described took place at night, action photographs are therefore, obviously, scarce or non-existent. Nevertheless it is hoped that the illustrations provided do at least give a good record of the ships that participated in the actions which took place.

Peter C. Smith,
Riseley, Bedfordshire.
February 2007

CHAPTER ONE

First Operations in the Channel

At the start of the Second World War, on 3 September 1939, many naval experts anticipated that the general pattern of the war would resemble that of the 1914-1918 conflict, but perhaps on a lesser scale and with the largely unknown factor of air power as the wild card. The Royal Navy was but a pale shadow of its former self, and the great days of the fleets of 1918, or even 1914, were but a fading memory. The German fleet was also much smaller and seemed to offer little threat. Its squadrons were, on the whole, composed of ships which were more modern, more heavily armed and faster than their British counterparts, but their qualities were unknown other than that they appeared to have a greater awareness of the necessity for heavy anti-aircraft armaments than did the British. It was not thought that their cruisers, battlecruisers or battleships would influence events in the Channel area (one of many false predictions); their air force was expected to be a new facet in convoy defence. The greatest threat to the Narrow Seas was anticipated from destroyer raids, submarines and mines.

Initially, this indeed was the case, but the Germans proved themselves far bolder in the deployment of their surface units, particularly their destroyer forces, than had been imagined. Indeed, no provision was at first made to intercept such forces, despite the lessons of the Dover Patrol in the previous war. As no immediate advance was made on land toward the Channel ports, the enemy lacked the advance bases to harass the huge concentrations of British and neutral shipping which assembled off such points as Southend and the Downs, and so it was considered that they were relatively immune from surface attack. And so it proved, but this did not stop losses, for the Germans boldly used their destroyer flotillas to lay mines right up the Channel, to the very doorstop of the major British naval bases in fact, undetected, and with considerable success. The U-boats were not so successful, as they were few and their usage expected. Countermeasures, such as patrols, laying of defensive minefields and the like, soon took a toll of the U-boats and brought their activities to an early pause. Likewise, the activities of the *Luftwaffe* were strictly limited during the first months, although they showed that their methods had not been satisfactorily countered in the pre-war planning. The RAF was experiencing difficulties of its own, and for the first three years of the war, its contribution to the defence of British shipping, or attacks on enemy shipping, tended to be intermittent.

Organization of Convoys

The Admiralty had already decided to introduce the convoy system on the outbreak of war, despite the crippling lack of sufficient escort vessels to offer more than a token defence. Convoys crossing the Narrow Sea were the Coastal series, those running westward from Southend to Falmouth being coded CW, those in the opposite direction, CE. These did not commence until July 1940. In the beginning the OA convoys from the Thames out into the Atlantic via the English Channel and the FN series from the Thames to Methil and back, commanded most of the Royal Navy's attention. These all commenced running from 6 September 1939.

Disposition of Forces

The surface forces available to the Royal Navy in the Channel area at the outbreak of the war consisted of the Channel Force based at Portland; the battleships *Resolution* and *Revenge*, the aircraft carriers *Courageous* and *Hermes*, the light cruisers *Cairo, Caradoc* and *Ceres* and the 18th Destroyer Flotilla (DF): *Veteran, Whitshed, Wild Swan, Windsor* and *Wren*. Also at Portland was the 12th DF: *Echo, Eclipse, Electra, Encounter*, *Escapade* and *Escort*. These were part of the Western Approaches command, as were the two flotillas of destroyers based at Plymouth, the 11th DF: *Mackay, Vanoc, Vanquisher, Versatile, Vimy, Walker, Warwick, Whirlwind* and *Winchelsea* and the 17th DF: *Keppel, Vanessa, Viscount, Vivacious, Vortigern, Wakeful* and *Wessex*. At Portsmouth lay the 16th DF: *Malcolm, Venomous* and *Wivern*, while at Dover was the 19th DF, which was composed of the Beagle class destroyers, less the *Bulldog*.

Coastal Submarine Offensive

The Germans sailed every available U-boat to British waters on the outbreak of war, but this concentration achieved very little in the waters of the Nore and the Channel. *U-26* laid a minefield off Portland, which claimed three small merchant vessels and damaged the coastal corvette *Kittiwake*. *U-17* laid magnetic mines in the Downs and these caused more problems as, although the British had invented this weapon in the First World War and had methods of sweeping prepared, nothing could be done until they discovered the method of activation used by the Germans. In addition, *U-31* sank two ships, *U-35* four, and *U-53* two, by conventional torpedo attack.

British Defensive Minefields Laid

To counter the threat of German submarines working close inshore and penetrating the Straits of Dover in order to reach the south-western approaches, the Admiralty had long prepared to lay mine barrages in the Straits of Dover and this was very quickly implemented, much to the surprise of the Germans. Both deep and shallow minefields had been planned in the Straits with a deep field in the Folkestone-Cap Gris Nez area. To catch the U-boats, anti-submarine fields were put down between the Goodwin Sands and the Dyck Shoal by the cruiser-minelayer *Adventure*, the coastal minelayer *Plover* and two converted train ferries, *Hampton* and *Shepperton*. The laying commenced on 11 September and was completed five days later, some 3,000 of the old HII type mines being laid, while protection was given to the layers by the anti-aircraft cruiser *Cairo* and the 19th Destroyer Flotilla. A further operation by the *Hampton* and *Shepperton*, laid the second field with a further 636 mines by the end of the month.

This defensive measure quickly produced results for the *U-12* was sunk on 8 October, *U-40* on 13 October and *U-16* on 24 October. This swiftly controlled and subsequently stopped, the passage of U-boats through the Channel, although not before *U-19* had lain a magnetic minefield off the Inner Dowsing and *U-33* yet further mines of the same type off North Foreland at the end of October, which sank two merchant ships and the auxiliary minesweeper *Ray of Hope*.

If the U-boats were speedily brought under a measure of control, the unforeseen threat of minelaying by German destroyers quickly brought the enemy a large measure of revenge. On the night of 12-13 November a flotilla, under the command of Captain F. Bönte, and consisting of the destroyers *Karl Galster, Wilhelm Heidkamp, Hermann Künne* and *Hans Lüdemann*, sailed from their home ports and passed close to the Noord-Hinder light-vessel and then on a bearing to the North Foreland. The three deepwater channels of the Thames Estuary were their targets and some 288 magnetic mines were sown in the 'South' and 'Edinburgh' channels. The German flotilla was completely undetected and remained so for a long time. This, their first sortie of many, was soon to reap a rich reward for their audacity.

Mining of *Adventure*; loss of *Blanche*

The German destroyers' plans were aided partly by fate and partly by the weather. The *Adventure* had been under orders to sail for Portsmouth from the Humber but had been delayed for twenty hours due to the non-arrival of her escorts; two ships of the 19th Flotilla, *Basilisk* and *Blanche* from Dover. On 10 November they had been ordered to proceed to the Humber, but their passage was delayed by thick fog, which forced them to anchor at 1115 hours on 11 November in the Outer Dowsing Channel. They weighted at 1710 hours the same day, but had to anchor once more at 2006 hours due to weather conditions. They weighed at 0700 hours on 12 November and anchored in Grimsby Roads at 0900 hours. Half an hour later they sailed back for Portsmouth escorting the *Adventure* (Captain A. R. Halfhide).

The same thick weather, shielding the work of Bönte's ships, continued to delay the British squadron, which was forced to anchor in the Barrow Deep at 2057 hours on 12 November. Not until 0300 hours next morning could they once again set sail and, two hours later, they passed the Tongue light-vessel. Six and a half minutes later they ran into the German minefield and a large explosion occurred just before the minelayer's bridge structure. Captain Halfhide immediately surmised that his ship had been mined, rather than torpedoed, and at once ordered *Basilisk* alongside to transfer wounded and burned men, while he tried to effect repairs. The rescue of the injured had been completed by 0715. Meanwhile, on seeing *Adventure* hit, the destroyer *Blanche* (Lieutenant Commander R. N. Aubrey) had at once gone full speed astern and was ordered to keep clear, but to send her boats to aid the rescue work. She then carried out an anti-submarine sweep, while *Basilisk* (Commander M. Richard) went alongside the damaged minelayer.

Good work below, resulted in *Adventure* being able to get under way under her own power at 0715, using her after steering position. *Basilisk* was ordered to lead her into the Edinburgh Channel, giving as wide a berth as possible to the position in which she had been mined. By 0725 she was making four knots, which was gradually increased to eight knots. Alas, this splendid progress had to be abandoned twenty-two minutes later when it was discovered that the oil fuel being fed to the boilers had become contaminated with seawater as a result of the explosion. *Adventure* therefore stopped engines and *Basilisk* prepared to take her in tow. However, once again thanks to the indefatigable engineering party below, she managed to clear the oil fuel system by 0807 and the cruiser once again got under way, first at six and then at eight knots. Things were looking good when, at 0810, came another blow.

Blanche was stationed on the cruiser's starboard bow when she too, fell foul of a magnetic mine. There was a large explosion in the after part of the ship and all steam for the main engines was lost. The upper deck of the destroyer was split forward of the after superstructure, the after engine room bulkhead was buckled and the engine rooms, tiller flat and spirit room were all making water. Luckily, the after magazine and shell room were intact, otherwise loss of life would have been heavy. She was still afloat, but the one remaining undamaged vessel, *Basilisk*, was not sent to her aid in case she, too, fell victim.

The various shore commands had been continuously kept in touch with these developments and, at 0910, the tug *Fabia* sailed from Ramsgate to assist *Adventure*. *Basilisk* was detached at 0952 to land the sixty-two wounded at Chatham. The cruiser seemed to have everything under control and when the tug arrived she was sent instead to help *Blanche* and took her in tow. At slow speed the crippled destroyer headed for Sheerness but, by this time, her quarterdeck was awash. It was a race against time and the salvage ships lost. At 0950 the little destroyer heeled hard over to port and did not recover. The crew took to the water and were picked up by the host of small craft now around her, which included *Fabia*, another tug, *Lady Brassey*, the trawler *Kestrel* and the smaller *Golden Spray*. These vessels between them landed *Blanche*'s crew at Ramsgate. Only two men had been killed and another twelve were injured.

Meanwhile, *Adventure* was making her way to safety, and anchored at the

Nore at 1128. The Captain Superintendent of Sheerness Dockyard went aboard her later that day and reported on her damage. She had been holed by the explosion below the waterline on the port side and flooded between fifty-four and seventy-eight frames. The adjacent compartments between forty-six and ninety frames had also been affected by the blast. The cruiser had a list of two or three degrees to port and a draught of 20½ft aft. The foremost mess decks and upper deck fittings had received considerable damage; the mess decks being rendered uninhabitable and the galleys unusable. The bridge had been wrecked and compasses, telegraphs, etc., put out of action. Wireless telegraphy transmission and all signal lamps and semaphores were out of action and the foretop mast was fractured. He ordered her to be brought into Sheerness harbour by the dockyard tugs. She remained out of commission for a long time under repair, but lived to fight again.

Continuation of German Minelaying.

This early victory only spurred the Germans to greater efforts by both submarine and destroyer. They also developed a new tactic; dropping magnetic mines from aircraft. In this, they overreached themselves, for aircraft lacked the precision of warships, and there were soon reports of mines descending onto the Thames mudflats. Lieutenant Commander John Ouvry from the mining school HMS *Vernon* at Portsmouth was successful, after some heart-stopping work, in defusing one of these mines located off Shoeburyness and from that time it was a matter of dedication and application to find ways to nullify this serious threat. Until that was done, however, ships were sunk and lives lost, including two of the Harwich destroyers, *Gipsy*, sunk on 21 November 1939, and *Grenville*, sunk on 19 January 1940.

Final Elimination of the Channel U-Boats.

The third and final stage of barring the Channel to German submarines was undertaken on completion of the minefields, by placing a double system of indicator loops between the two fields, which recorded the passage of any submarines by inducting a small electrical current through a cable on the seabed.

All these measures forced the U-boats away from the Narrow Sea and into the south-west approaches where, under the lee of a benevolent neutral, Eire, they hoped to operate with little hindrance as the Chamberlain Government had allowed itself to be pressured into giving up its naval bases there just prior to the war. However, even this potential haven was denied to the U-boats. After bad weather had somewhat dispersed the Thames section of convoy OA80, the *U-55* thought she saw her chance of easy pickings at the western end of the Channel. Only a single escort was with the convoy at the time, the sloop *Fowey*. Two merchantmen were quickly sunk, one a neutral Greek ship, the other the 5,026-ton *Vaclite*, which went down in 49° 20' N, 07° 04'W. The *Fowey* counter-attacked but lost contact;

fortunately the destroyers *Whitshed, Acasta* and *Ardent* from the 16th DF at Portsmouth, were not far away, escorting the homeward-bound light cruiser *Ajax*, fresh from her triumph off the River Plate. They found *Fowey* picking up survivors from the Greek vessel and contact with the enemy submarine was immediately made by *Whitshed* (Commander E. R. Conder).

This proved to be the final undoing of *U-55* which, it transpired, had already been damaged by *Fowey*'s earlier attack. After some time she was forced to surface and was scuttled. While she was picking up survivors the *Fowey* was shelled by a French destroyer, but luckily *Whitshed* intervened before any harm was done. With the loss of this submarine, all German U-boat activity anywhere near the Channel ceased until May, by which time vastly different circumstances prevailed.

Continued Activity of German Destroyer Flotillas

Whatever the feelings of relief and pleasure experienced by the Royal Navy on clearing one type of enemy from the Narrow Sea, another was in operation on a regular basis completely unimpeded. The German destroyer flotillas continued their daring sorties throughout the winter months unabated. On the night of 17-18 November, the German 5th Flotilla under Commander H. Hartman, with the destroyers *Hermann Künne, Bernd von Arnim* and *Wilhelm Heidkamp*, laid a field in the 'Sunk' Channel, close to their earlier success, which had accounted for the *Gipsy* and the minesweeping trawler *Mastiff*, as well as seven merchant ships. They then moved north, not returning to the Thames Estuary until the night of 6-7 January 1940 when a field, laid by their 1st Flotilla, *Friedrich Eckoldt, Erich Steinbrinck* and *Friedrich Ihn* under Commander F Berger, accounted for the *Grenville* and another six merchantmen. On the night of 9-10 February 1940, they returned under the same commander. *Frederick Eckoldt, Richard Beitzen* and *Max Schultz* laid another field in the Shipwash area, north of Harwich off Ordfordness, which claimed a further six victims.

Bernard C.S. Cottle told the author:

> As a Boy Seaman at Naval Training Establishment *Ganges* [Shotley], I saw the wreck of *Gipsy* many times, just off Felixstowe. And two quite incredible coincidences. A survivor from *Gipsy* married my sister in 1946, so I knew of the ship even before I joined. Then, when I shipped on the destroyer *Vigo*, post-war, I discovered that her captain, Commander Franks, had been First Lieutenant on the *Gipsy* when she went down. He received the DSO or DSC for swimming from the wreck to *Ganges* pier with the codes and papers in a bag round his neck. I have a framed photo of *Gipsy* (H63) issued to commemorate the 31 who died in her sinking.

First Air Attacks in the Channel Area

Although mines were the chief hazard at this time, one of the earliest indications of another arm of attack manifested itself on the night of 1-2 March 1940. An aircraft from *Kampfgruppen 26* was reported to be operating repeatedly over the Channel and made a deliberate attack on the passenger ship *Domala* (8,441 tons) which was set on fire off the Isle of Wight, some thirty miles east of St Catherine's Point. The naval authorities ashore complained that, despite repeated requests, no RAF aircraft even attempted to intercept the enemy either before or after the ship had been attacked.

Table 1: British warships sunk in the Narrow Sea September 1939 to March 1941

Name	Type	Date of Loss	Cause and Area
Blanche	Destroyer	13-11-39	Mined, Thames Estuary
Mastiff	Trawler	20-11-39	Mined, Thames Estuary
Gipsy	Destroyer	21-11-39	Mined, off Harwich
Aragonite	Trawler	22-11-39	Mined, off Deal
Napia	Tug	20-12-39	Mined, off Ramsgate
Ray of Hope	Drifter	10-12-39	Mined, Thames Estuary
Grenville	Destroyer	19-1-40	Mined, off Harwich

It was not long before the *Luftwaffe* repeated the operation and, on 20 March, the 5,439-ton freighter *Barn Hill* was sunk by bombers, three miles SSW of Beachy Head. Despite this, aircraft still remained a minor hazard in the Narrow Sea in the opening phase, although this was to change rapidly. An analysis of warship losses in the area for the first six months of the war, in Table 1, gives the general trend.

Routine Duties of Dover Patrol 1939-40

The opening months of the war in the Narrow Sea reflected, in the main, the general low level of activity in most areas. Very few of the warships involved actually caught sight of an enemy and, once the submarine menace had been eradicated, bad weather and the ever-present hazard of mines remained the main problems.

For the rest, it was a case of ceaseless patrolling, strengthening further the British minefields in the area and the constant reinforcement of the British Expeditionary Force (BEF) in France, while a whole succession of VIPs took passage in the ships of the 19th DF from Dover across to Boulogne and back. One of the earliest such dignitaries was HM King George VI, who took passage aboard the flotilla leader *Codrington* on 10 December 1939. The Captain of D19 at this time was Casper S. B. Swinley, DSO, DSC, RN, and he later recounted to the author a particular incident of that trip:

> Taking the King to France we had a submarine scare and His Majesty, who was with me on the bridge, turned and asked, 'What's this all about?' I replied that they had reported a submarine contact. 'Well',

> replied the King, 'can we not go and look for it?' This was not to be because those ashore in the Castle had got the wind up and so we proceeded at twenty-five knots with five other B-class destroyers as close escorts.

When *Codrington* entered Dover harbour on her return she was proudly flying the Royal Standard; a unique event.

His Majesty was not the only distinguished guest of the 19th Flotilla. The First Lord of the Admiralty, Winston S. Churchill, took passage on 4 January 1940, and again Captain Swinley was his host aboard *Codrington*:

> In my cabin Mr Churchill noticed a quotation from Alston's *Seamanship Manual*, circa 1865, and asked me to read it to him: 'Remember then, that your life's vocation, deliberately chosen, is *war*...*war*, as I have said as the means of peace; but still *war*; and in singleness of purpose for England's fame, prepare for....' The First Lord rose from his chair, cigar in hand, and said: 'A fine piece of English: now I should like to go on the bridge and see you take the ship out of harbour.' The cigar caused a sort of minor fog until the First Lord left the bridge to go below to do some work. On arrival at Boulogne I shall always remember the scene in my cabin, full of people and cigar smoke. At the end of the tables sat Mr Churchill, with a French Admiral on his right. The table was covered with articles such as indiarubbers, inkpots etc, and I saw Mr Churchill take up one of these and say: '*Now*, Admiral, this is the mistake the *Graf Spee* made!' We were witnessing a demonstration of the Battle of River Plate!

Such routine work continued to occupy the flotilla's time during February and March, despite the fact that the continued patrolling and escorting through one of the worst winters of the decade meant that the destroyers were in port for refitting more often than usual. The increasing demands for vessels of that type, due to the increased predacity of the U-Boats in easier fields, also led to a reduction the flotilla's strength, as did much-needed refits and periodic boiler-cleans. On 1 February, for example, both *Boreas* and *Brazen* were withdrawn from Dover and detached to Rosyth for anti-submarine duties in the north. Flag Officer (Dover), Vice Admiral Bertram Ramsay, protested the next day at the shortage of destroyers, for he was at that time reduced to just four such ships operational. Captain Swinley had left the station before this time. Heavy losses among the valuable flotilla leaders (*Exmouth* had been sunk by a submarine earlier) led to *Codrington* being replaced by *Keith* (the correct leader of the Beagle Class destroyers), while *Codrington*, in turn took the sunken *Grenville*'s place at Harwich leading the 1st Flotilla. *Keith* arrived on station to take her proper place with her flotilla on 15 February and Captain D. J. R. Simson took over command of the Dover destroyers.

Loss of *Grenville*

The 1st DF, working out of Harwich, consisted of seven ships of the Gallant class, later joined by three Polish destroyers, which had escaped from the Baltic during the German invasion of their homeland the previous September, according to a prearranged plan. Captain (D) was Captain G. E. Creasy; a fine officer.

The flotilla was returning from a sweep across to the boundary of Dutch territorial waters on 19 January when it ran into a minefield. The sea was flat calm when the explosion took place and *Grenville*, the leading ship of the line, quickly heeled over and sank, stern first. There was no time to lower boats; some men ran down her turning hull into the sea. Within a very short time only the bows of the destroyer remained visible above the shallow water as she rested a while, balanced on her stern, with the very last survivor photographed clinging dramatically to her anchor hawser, before she took her final plunge. The water was very shallow in that part of the estuary. Two of her flotilla came in close to her, disregarding their own danger, and lowered boats and rafts which managed to rescue 118 officers and men, who were landed at Harwich. Four officers and seventy-three men lost their lives in seconds. Just two days later, another leader, *Exmouth*, was sunk with all hands in the Moray Firth by the *U-22*, leaving the destroyer flotillas seriously short of modern flotilla leaders. Captain Creasy took over *Codrington* and *Keith* finally rejoined her true flotilla at Dover.

Allied Forces

As well as the three Polish destroyers attached to the 1st Flotilla, *Blyskawica, Burza* and *Grom*, other Allied forces, mainly French warships, were attached to Dover and similar commands from time to time. Captain Swinley remembered that, although well-armed and fast, attitudes were somewhat different:

> *Brestois* was, like most French ships, very dirty – the sanitary arrangements were almost non-existent. However, the ship's company was brave enough, though lacking in discipline. The Captain seemed above average intelligence, but excitable, and a stream of orders used to pour down the voice- pipe, such as '*à gauche quinze,*' ' *à droit vingt.*' ' *cinq en arrière,*' '*zéro*' which is of course the equivalent of our 'midships, but I felt like saying '*rien ne va plus*' when the bombs were falling all round us!

Dover Command War Diary February-March 1940

One excellent way to show the many and varied duties that came the way of the Dover-based destroyer flotilla during this 'quiet' period of the war in the Narrow Sea, is to print a typical extract from the War Diary of the Command:

1 Feb

Basilisk [destroyer] sailed for Boulogne with Lord Gort, retuned with

Chief of Naval Staff, Chief of Imperial General Staff, etc.

4 Feb

Basilisk and *Brilliant* [destroyer], former with Prime Minister, War Cabinet and Chiefs of Staff embarked, crossed to Boulogne.

6 Feb

Boadicea [destroyer], with Captain D19 as temporary acting leader, embarked, with Prime Minister, First Lord, First Sea Lord etc. escorted by *Beagle* [destroyer] sailed from Boulogne to Dover. En route the *Boadicea* dropped three depth charges and exploded a floating mine to entertain guests.

18 Feb

Teviot Bank (minelayer), *Esk* and *Express* (minelaying destroyers) laid Deep Line S, nine miles east of Outer Gabbard as part of the East Coast Mine Barrier, Operation DML8. *Keith* and *Boadicea* acted as escorts. On completion minelaying ships proceeded to Immingham. *Brilliant* on patrol in Straits picked up tail wheel from He111 shot down in the sea.

20 Feb

Keith alongside *Sandhurst* [destroyer depot ship] after being rammed by *Gulzar* [armed yacht] in harbour.

21 Feb

Admiralty informs that *Bulldog* [destroyer] to be brought home from Mediterranean [where she had been acting as tender to the aircraft carrier *Glorious*] to have seven days' leave and then join 19th Flotilla.

22 Feb

Keith to Chatham for repairs

24 Feb

Boadicea withdrawn from patrol due to damage to port shafting, speed limited to twelve knots except in emergencies.

26 Feb

Basilisk to Chatham for refit

27 Feb

Beagle from Dover to Boulogne with CIGS

2 March

Beagle alongside *Sandhurst* in Submarine Basin for boiler cleaning and degaussing [fitted with protection against magnetic mines].

4 March

Convoy HX20 with *Fowey* as escort had the tanker *Charles F. Mayer*, full of petroleum spirit, damaged by mine. *Brilliant, Boadicea* and later *Keith*, sailed to her help.

5 March

All three destroyers joined the crippled tanker and she was taken under tow by *Boadicea*. Later, tugs from Portsmouth joined them and they reached Sandown Bay, Isle of Wight, and subsequently Cowes Bay, in sinking condition.

7 March
Beagle completed boiler cleaning and replaced in dock by *Brilliant*. Minelayer *Hampton* (Captain G. Freyburg) laid minefield DML9 escorted by Polish destroyers *Burza* and *Blyskawica* from Harwich and *Keith* and *Boadicea* from Dover.

9 March
The collier *Ashley* went aground on the Goodwins. *Beagle* sent to help and later tugs arrived, but collier broke up *in situ*.

12 March
Brilliant finished refit, *Boadicea* taken in hand.

15 March
Keith to Chatham for docking and Asdic repairs after running aground on 13 March near SW Goodwin buoy.

18 March
Admiralty informs *Bulldog* to be held in Mediterranean for a further period

20 March
Dutch vessel *Phobos* mined five miles east of North Goodwin light-vessel. *Brilliant* standing by until crew taken off by tugs.

21 March
CIGS took passage *Boadicea* to Boulogne. *Beagle* guarding minesweeping flotilla operations.

This, then was the daily grind of just one flotilla. Already they were at full stretch, but the coming of spring meant that over the sea, the Nazi war machine was getting ready to go into action, and the tempo was to change abruptly with the invasion of Norway, and with the opening of the blitzkreig proper on 10 May1940, the war swiftly moved closer to home and intensified. Even before the Panzers and Stukas crashed over the borders to subjugate an entire continent with a few weeks, news of pending operations had filtered through to the Admiralty and the warships of the Narrow Sea were already taking precautions against the worst eventualities; eventualities which became only too real very quickly.

Calm before the Storm: March-May 1940

During this period, the Germans renewed their probing. U-boats reappeared in the southern part of the North Sea and sinkings again began to rise; aircraft attacks grew more numerous and bolder; and, despite the lighter nights, surface minelayers continued to penetrate British coastal waters with relative impunity.

On 9 March, for example, the auxiliary minelayer *Schiff II*, laid a minefield east of North Foreland, which, over the next few days, claimed the sinking of the coasters *Chevychase* (2,719 tons), *Borthwick* (1,097 tons), *Akeld* (643 tons), *Gardenia* (3,745 tons) and *Melrose* (1,585 tons). While the bulk of both nations' forces were engaged in Norwegian waters, seaplanes dropped two dozen mines in the Edinburgh Channel and in the

Downs on the night of 17 April, which sank the *Hawnby* (5, 380 tons) and the *Mersey* (1,037 tons). They repeated the operation on 21 April in the King's Channel and off Ramsgate, and again the next night, sixty mines being laid in all, sinking another five ships: *Lulworth* (1,969 tons), *Stokesley* (1,149 tons), *Rydal Force* (1,101 tons), *Margam Abbey* (2,470 tons) and *Brighton* (5,359 tons). On 30 April, significantly, the same aircraft laid a pair of mines in the sea approaches to Dunkirk.

Typical Convoy Escort Work, April 1940

Commander W. J. Phipps tells what a typical convoy operation in the Narrow Sea was like, just before the blitzkreig. He was, at that period, commanding the destroyer *Woolston*, one of the old V & W class of destroyers that had been completed around the end of the First World War, but taken out of reserve and modernized into a handy anti-aircraft destroyer. She mounted two twin 4-inch Mk. XVI guns fore and aft and had two 4-barrelled machine guns 0.5-inch calibre. Her conversion had been completed in October 1939. On 22 April 1940, she sailed from Sheerness as escort for convoy FN52. Let Commander Phipps take up the story in his inimitable way:

> Left Sheerness in nice weather, but blowing pretty fresh at 1345. Tide just turned to the ebb and should have got down quite quickly, but the Commodore made a great mistake in not rattling them on down the Channel and so got further and further behind until we were an hour late at position 'X' when the tide turned and we had it foul til midnight, when we had just got to 'Z' going four-and-a-half knots.
>
> At 2250, heard and saw a German Heinkel 115 seaplane off to lay more bloody mines. 0.5s against could not be got off though they were on target, and, determined to get something off, I fired three rounds of 4-inch at him, but I think were very short. Reported him. He looked as though he was going to Humber or Lowestoft. Never expected to see him again and went down below at 0130. At 0215 we sighted him machine-gunning convoy. They were firing back at him. Shot up to the bridge and he appeared on the port quarter and we let him have a burst of 0.5s and turned the ship, before he went off to have a look at *Hastings* [sloop] in the rear. She let him have a burst of 4-inch and 0.5s and drove him off, and he had the effrontery to come and have another look at me. Fired 0.5s at him like hell as he banked across the stern and close up the starboard side at 500ft. As he banked over both 0.5s let fly about 300 rounds at him and why he didn't come down I cannot think. Rear gunner machine-gunned us on the way up and I was standing by to duck as he got to the bridge when he stopped, so we may have killed him. No casualties, and only a few holes in the after funnel. Gave him two salvoes with the 4-inch as he went away. A marvellous target and the gunner's mate firing so why he didn't come down I don't know.
>
> Very slow and only got to Smiths Knoll at 0415. Then bucked up and

made up leeway to Dowsing at 1300 and Flamborough at 1800. *Breda* (Convoy Commodore's ship) was told to report the time of arrival of convoy at 20D buoy and, not knowing the ropes, and the speed they always pull out on the run north of Dowsing, replied 0515, when it was obvious that 0215 was nearer the mark, and sure enough it was. The result was the ships from Tyne were not going to be there until three hours after us. I was told to remain behind and bring them on. When I heard this I tried to get *Breda* to amend the time of arrival at 20D at 2230, but he did nothing, so I shot into Tyne and waved them up and got them away from there at 0245, so saved about two hours anyway. *Breda* waited and we joined our party up at 0530. Most of the night on the bridge, Longstone at 0900 and May Island at 1315 when I left them for degaussing runs which had to be done again. Did them at 12 which made it much quicker and got finished in an hour and berthed by 1615. Beastly wet day and cold.

Meanwhile, on 17 April, the destroyers *Whitshed, Verity* and *Wild Swan* reinforced Dover Command's slender flotilla. Just in time.

Chapter Two

Germany Invades the Low Countries

As far back as October 1939, the Admiralty, not expecting any German attack on the Low Countries to meet with very prolonged resistance, had laid contingency plans. They intended to delay the enemy advance as long as possible by laying a minefield off the Dutch coast, north of Ijmuiden, while naval demolition parties were to be sent to that port and to the Hook and Flushing, so ensuring that they did not fall, intact, into German hands. It was accepted that Antwerp might go the same way and similar plans were in hand for that port, although the Belgian coast came under the command of the French admiral based at Dunkirk, 'Admiral Nord', who at that time, was Vice Admiral Abrial. Since the French Navy had no suitable ships equipped to fight aircraft, four of the British destroyers so converted were to be loaned to him should the plan come into operation. In the event he received six such ships.

Although in early May the eyes of the world were on Norway, where things were going badly for the Allies, and although the bulk of the Home Fleet was tied up there, early indications of German intentions had been received which initiated a whole chain of events in the Narrow Sea prior to the actual German invasion. The C.-in-C., Nore, Admiral Sir Reginald Plunkett-Ernle-Erle-Drax, received substantial reinforcements; the light cruisers *Arethusa* and *Galatea* of the 2nd Cruiser Squadron sailed from Scapa on 8 May to join him and the light cruiser *Birmingham*, four destroyers of 2nd DF and four of 5th DF, were all ordered to concentrate at Harwich. To liaise with Admiral Abrial off Belgium, Admiral Ramsay at Dover was given responsibility for most demolition parties, but command of ships working off Holland and Belgium remained under Admiral Drax. This allowed for a great deal of confusion but, in the event, worked very well considering the enormous stress quickly placed upon it. Further reinforcements of ships and men came from time to time from adjacent commands, from Admiral Forbes's Home Fleet, and the Portsmouth and Plymouth commands. By 1 May the preliminary moves were under way at Dover to carry out the demolition of Dutch and Belgian ports should they seem likely to fall, and to save as much shipping as was possible at the time.

The First Warnings: Dover 1 May 1940

The Dover Command War Diary for 1 May records a string of small events. Any one them, looked at separately, means little; taken as a whole they signify how early the Royal Navy was preparing for the next German move.

The three French anti-submarine trawlers *La Cancalaise, La Nantaise*, and *L'Oritentaise*, sailed from Dover for Dunkirk in the morning, the later under tow of the French tug *Barfleur* following damage she had received. One was not to see home again: later in the day a report was received that *La Cancalaise* had struck a mine close to the Dyck Shoal and had sunk with the loss of more than twelve of her crew.

Casualties from the war in the northern waters passed by early in the same morning, the light cruiser *Curacoa* and destroyer *Hotspur*, both damaged, sailed through the Straits after being held up by thick fog off Dungeness, as did the crippled submarine *Cachalot*, escorted by the sloop *Foxglove*. So thick was the fog that no minesweeping was possible all that day.

At Dover Castle, reports were received from the Admiralty, originated by the British Naval Attaché at The Hague, which indicated possible developments in that area. In other words, the arrival of spring was making the neutral countries, terrified as they were of provoking Hitler into doing the inevitable, mesmerized to such a degree that they refused to coordinate plans with the British while the German build-up on their borders continued. For even though these nations had witnessed the fate of Denmark and Norway, they remained totally uncooperative until they were actually invaded and then screamed loudly for Allied help. The Royal Navy, at least, was prepared. Captain Simson aboard *Keith* was recalled from patrol in order to take charge of destroyer forces in case of further developments and was relieved on patrol by *Wild Swan*.[1]

Other reinforcements included the Motor Torpedo Boats *22, 24* and *25*, which arrived from Portsmouth that evening. Things were stirring. Enemy aircraft were also afoot, for it was reported that, on the night of 30 April-1 May, they were operating extensively over the Thames Estuary, the Downs, along the south coast as far west as Dungeness and off Dunkirk. The British defensive minefields, so long planned, were got under way as soon as by so doing, Dutch neutrality was no longer being contravened, but this meant waiting until the Germans crashed over the border on 10 May. Prior to that, the *Luftwaffe* again dropped 100 mines off Dutch and Belgian ports, as they were not bound by the same scruples as the Royal Navy. On that day also, the German bombers struck hard at Holland, Heinkel 111s of KG4 sinking the Dutch destroyer *Van Galen* and the passenger ships *Statendam* (28,291 tons) and *Veendam* (15,450 tons) in Rotterdam harbour.

British Minelaying off Holland

Plans had been made by the Admiralty to lay a minefield off the Dutch coast as soon as there was any firm indication of a German invasion. The series of false alarms between January and May 1940 had caused several false starts and postponements and when the invasion did come, half the ships of the 20th (Minelaying) Flotilla were in harbour, boiler cleaning. Luckily the former train ferry converted into a minelayer, *Princess Victoria*, had been held in reserve in readiness and she was at once pressed into service.

The minelaying destroyers *Express* (Captain J. G. Bickford, DSO, DSC), *Esk* (Lieutenant Commander R. J. H. Couch) and *Intrepid* (Commander R. G. Gordon) were already at sea that night carrying out Operation *XMG*, the laying of 180 mines in the enemy's swept channels off Heligoland.[2] While on their way back to the Humber they received orders to take over the escort of the *Princess Victoria* (Captain J. B. E. Hall) from the coastal corvettes *Puffin, Sheldrake* and *Widgeon* and escort her immediately to the Dutch coast. This they did and, during the forenoon of 10 May, the minelayer reported her planned movements, stating that she intended to commence laying at 2115 that night. That was duly passed on by the Admiralty to the British Naval Attaché at The Hague so that Dutch shore batteries would not open fire on her. She actually commenced laying her mines at 2107 and there were no interruptions; the whole force returned to Immingham by 0930 on 11 May after laying 236 mines off Egmond.

With the Low Countries falling to the German onslaught, it was obvious that further such work lay ahead for the 20th DF. On 12 May, the same three destroyers were out again, returning that same night. Operation *BS4* was carried out on the night of 14-15 May, again with the same team and *Princess Victoria*. By this time the destroyers *Impulsive* (Lieutenant Commander M. S. Thomas) and *Ivanhoe* (Commander P. H. Hadow) had finished refitting and were soon ready to join them. One of their crew members, Bernard Brotheridge, gave the author this account of those hectic days and nights:

> I joined HMS *Impulsive* in early May 1940. Three of us left Portsmouth Barracks and, after travelling to Scapa, we were told the *Impulsive* was now at Immingham near Grimsby, so we retraced our steps and eventually arrived at Immingham Dock. HMS *Impulsive* was lying alongside the jetty being loaded on her upper deck with sea mines and we found, on going on board, that she was engaged in laying mines anywhere in the North Sea. We were the first 'Hostilities Only' ratings to join the ship, the rest of the crew being regulars. The Commanding Officer at that time was Lieutenant Commander Thomas, and with his black beard and undoubted qualities he reminded me of Sir Francis Drake and *Impulsive* was a happy and efficient ship.
>
> Immingham Dock seemed a desolate place, all the ships berthed in the inner basin, which was connected to the Humber by a lock. The sheds were full of mines, for apart from the six destroyers of the 20th Flotilla, there were two large converted merchant ships, *Princess Victoria* and *Teviot Bank*, who we were to escort at various times to lay the East Coast Mine Barrier and other fields.

> We sailed next day on my first trip, to lay mines at night on the other side of the North Sea, and this pattern continued during the next three weeks. Usually, the destroyers left the Humber in daylight, at times we were delayed because the Humber Estuary had been subjected to German air minelaying operations and we had to wait for the minesweepers to perform their functions. There were a few wrecks at the mouth of the Humber where previous German mines had proved effective. We were always alert during daylight hours and it was quite unnerving to come across lone German aircraft as nobody looked forward to a bombing attack when carrying sixty mines!
>
> As we approached our dropping zone at night, action stations were sounded, as there was always the chance of coming across German E-boats. The mining party unshackled the mines and they were dropped one by one by each destroyer; five destroyers usually operated together as one often remained behind each week for boiler cleaning.
>
> For defence, we had our 'B' and 'X' guns only, plus two multiple 0.5 machine-guns, a Lewis gun on the searchlight platform and, after July 1940, a 3-inch anti-aircraft duel-purpose gun amidships. I remember at times helping to unshackle the mines as we approached the dropping area. It seemed to me to be quietly done and I cannot recall any undue noise, the mines seemed to glide down the rails very easily. We concentrated on our own minelaying and the other ships with us, as far as I was concerned, seemed very remote. During all the minelaying I did from *Impulsive*, we never once encountered any German opposition. We had no radar at that time and probably the Germans hadn't either so I guess we were lucky not to have been suddenly discovered.

On 5 May, the *Express, Esk, Impulsive, Intrepid* and *Ivanhoe*, sailed from Immingham for the coast of Holland. While *Intrepid* added her sixty mines to the Egmond field, guarded by *Impulsive*, the other three destroyers laid a new field of 164 mines off the Hook. All the ships returned safely to port next morning. It is now known that the Germans lost no less than three modern minesweepers, the *M-16, M-89* and *M-136*, in this particular field. All were lost on 26 July 1940, providing a most rewarding night's work for the 20th Flotilla.

Their next sortie to Holland proved less fortunate. They were again accompanied by *Princess Victoria* for this operation, *BS5*, and *Express, Esk, Intrepid, Impulsive* and *Ivanhoe* sailed with her on 18 May. George Mack, then serving aboard *Intrepid*, described the operation thus:

> At dawn we found ourselves almost alongside the sea wall which runs along the coast of Holland and watched *Princess Victoria* steam almost up to the wall before turning westward. As she started to lay her mines one of our flotilla turned with her and laid a parallel line. As each destroyer completed dropping her quota, another took her place so we finished up with two long lines of mines from the sea wall out to sea for

several miles.

When it was all completed and the mines laid, the destroyers formed a screen round the *PV* and we hurried to get back to safer waters before the German Air Force came after us; but in fact they were very busy with the invasion of the Low Countries and battering the Allied Armies. When we reached the Cromer Light and swung round to steam northwards up the swept channel, it was decided to send two of the escorts on ahead so that we could get through the locks at Immingham before the rest arrived.

So *Impulsive* and *Intrepid* increased to thirty knots and soon reached the Humber and were through the lock and in the basin by 0630. No sooner had we completed securing alongside, than the call came for 'All hands to stations for leaving harbour', and the buzz went round that the *Princess Victoria* had blown up! Within five minutes the order was cancelled and we heard that the *PV* had indeed sunk.[3]

The *Princess Victoria* had, in fact, been mined one mile south-east of the Humber light-vessel and was resting on the bottom. She lost four officers, including her captain, and thirty-three men; the rest were picked up by the destroyers and landed safely. But her loss caused no slackening of effort on the part of the 20th Flotilla. Europe was falling rapidly to the Germans and, as the friendly shoreline shrank, the calls to lay minefields off the newly-lost territory facing the British coast increased. A whole series of operations took place in the week that followed. *Express, Esk, Intrepid, Impulsive* and *Ivanhoe* were once more joined by *Icarus* for these operations and, on the night of 21-22 May they laid mines in Operation *BS6*, followed by *BS7* on 23-24th, *BS8* on 25th-26th and *BS9* on 27th-28th, all off the Dutch coast. Then more pressing demands were made on their services.

Intensification of German Air Minelaying

The German response was to renew air minelaying on a much greater scale than hitherto. The greater part of the German surface fleet had been sunk or damaged off Norway, but they had ample aircraft at their disposal at this time, despite commitments ashore. On 12 May some thirty-two mines were dropped in and around Belgian and Dutch ports and harbours. On 17 May and successive nights, the French Channel ports, Calais, Dieppe, Dunkirk, Boulogne and Le Havre, were similarly treated. From 25 May, the targets were switched to England and mines were dropped at Dover, Folkestone, Newhaven and Southampton, as well as Portsmouth. A total of 575 mines were delivered by air at night during this period.

Operations off the Dutch Coast 10-14 May

While the 20th DF was engaged in its initial laying on 10 May, other moves had been put in train by C.-in-C. Nore. Admiral Forbes, commanding the Home Fleet at Scapa Flow, sent down south the heavy cruiser *York* and light cruisers *Manchester* and *Southampton* to reinforce Nore

Command's resources on 12 May. They joined the light cruiser *Birmingham* and the eight destroyers of the 2nd Flotilla (Hero Class) and 5th Flotilla (Javelin and Kelly classes) at Harwich, the majority of these destroyers coming under command of Captain (D) 1st Flotilla, aboard *Codrington*. The five new ships of the 5th Flotilla, *Jackal, Jaguar, Javelin, Jupiter* and *Kelvin*, led by Mountbatten, did not initially become involved in the increasing chaos further south, although that respite did not last long.

On 10 May, the light cruisers *Arethusa* (Captain G. D. Graham) and *Galatea* (Captain B. B. Schofield) sailed for Ijmuiden under command of Vice Admiral G. F. B. Edward-Collins, to bring back to England the Dutch gold reserves and help to clear all merchant shipping from the port. Two merchant ships were laden with the reserves and escorted back on 11 May by *Arethusa* and two destroyers.

Four further destroyers sailed from Dover to the principal Dutch ports to prepare for their evacuation and demolition. In a rapidly deteriorating situation the destroyer commanders had to rely on their own good sense and performed wonders, despite the fact that on several occasions the demoralized Dutch port authorities proved far from cooperative. On 12 May Captain Creasey aboard *Codrington*, embarked the Dutch Crown Princess and her family at Ijmuiden and brought them to safety in England. Next day Queen Wilhelmina was also taken to safety aboard the destroyer *Hereward* (Lieutenant Commander C. W. Greening). At the same time the destroyer *Windsor* (Lieutenant Commander P. D. H. R. Pelly) embarked the Dutch Government and Allied legation staffs and brought them back to England the same night.

Also at Ijmuiden was the destroyer *Whitshed*, with 122 naval ratings and thirty-six sappers of the demolition party embarked, under Commander Goode. She had sailed from Dover on 10 May and had been subjected to severe synchronized air attack off the Hook, both high level and dive bombing being brought to bear against her. Three attacks had produced nothing but near misses, but one bomb of a stick exploded in mid-air abreast of 'X' 4.7-inch gun mountings, detonating a second bomb of the stick as it did so. Six men – one still holding a 4.7-inch shell ready to load – were blown over the side by the blast, two were killed outright and many others were badly wounded, including the captain on the bridge. Shrapnel holed the ship's bridge and superstructure, and the hull was perforated. Worse still, the cordite in the cases around 'X' gun had ignited in a searing burst of flame, burning the surviving crew members on that mounting and penetrating down to a lobby in which was stacked three and a half tons of TNT to be used for the demolitions. Subsequent fires disrupted the electrical circuits, putting all the destroyer's guns out of action for a time, save for a solitary pom-pom.

This attack had taken place three miles offshore and, by the time she reached the entrance to the harbour, *Whitshed* was undergoing yet further air attacks. A near miss drenched the ship with mud from the harbour as she entered the breakwaters, but she berthed safely and disembarked the demolition parties for both Ijmuiden and Antwerp. As the Dutch seemed to be holding out at that time, preparation work only was undertaken before *Whitshed* returned to Dover, where she arrived at 0550 next morning. She was quickly taken alongside *Sandhurst* where temporary repairs to her hull and upperworks were effected and her guns made ready again. Her crew was made up by reserves and she embarked ammunition, shells and cordite for the ships operating from Dunkirk. She duly delivered and disembarked these on 12 May, returning from Dunkirk to Dover on the same day. A second such run was then made, sailing from Dover at 0100 on 13 May and reaching Dunkirk at 0330, again taking ammunition to be transferred to another destroyer. This duty completed, she was ordered to a rendezvous near the Maas Lightship off the Hook. When Commander Conder berthed at The Hook things had deteriorated considerably and evacuation was ordered. Some 320 officers and men of the Irish Guards and other personnel, some RAF, were taken aboard and *Whitshed* was back at Dover at 1845 the same night. Her intensive activity, despite damage in action, was typical of the way the British destroyers were run at that period; a level of activity inconceivable to modern operations.

Brilliant (Lieutenant Commander F. C. Brodrick) lived up to her name at Antwerp as the fighting moved down the coast. She arrived at that port on the evening of 10 May and succeeded in getting to safety a huge fleet that would otherwise have fallen into German hands. By 12 May twenty-six merchantmen and fifty invaluable tugs, followed two days later by no less than 600 barges, dredgers and floating cranes, were got away from the approaching Germans; an incredible achievement. At The Hook, meanwhile, the demolition party was obstructed by the Dutch authorities, but nonetheless managed to carry out their work by 13 May. To protect these parties Royal Marines were dispatched on the night of 11-12 May, and troops of the Irish and Welsh Guards followed. The whole operation was controlled by Captain T. E Halsey, Captain (D16) aboard the flotilla leader *Malcolm* with eight destroyers from Dover under his orders. When the Dutch Army capitulated, as many troops and refugees as possible were brought out on 14 May, despite delays caused by fog. The Dutch still steadfastly refused to cooperate in the demolition even with the Nazis at the gate, and also rejected offers to take off their troops to safely. Many of their lesser warships, however, sailed for English ports, under heavy air bombardment. That day saw the loss of the passenger ship *Ville de Bruges* (13,869 tons), but Dutch fighting ships reached Portsmouth, including the minelayers *Jan Van Brakel* and *Nautilus*, the tug *Amsterdam*, armed yacht *De Mok*, torpedo boats *G-13, G-15, Z-5* and *Z-8*, armed trawlers *BV-42* and *BV-45*. A second group, comprising the minelayers *Medusa* and *Dowe Aukes* and torpedo boats *Z-6* and *Z-7*, also got away to England as did the light cruiser *Jacob van Heemskerck*, destroyers *G13* and *G-15* and even some submarines.

Work of Destroyers in Operation '*FA*'

It was early agreed that, to supplement his own destroyer forces, the French Admiral based at Dunkirk was to be loaned six British destroyers with a good anti-aircraft capability. This was known as Operation '*FA*' [for 'French Assist' and *not* the degree of cooperation ultimately received!] The six British destroyers assigned were the *Valentine* (Commander H. J. Buchanan), *Vimiera* (Lieutenant Commander R. B. N. Hicks), *Westminster* (Lieutenant Commander A. A. C. Ouvry), *Whitley* (Lieutenant Commander G. N. Rolfe), *Winchester* (Lieutenant Commander S. E. Crew-Read) and *Wolsey* (Lieutenant Commander C. H. Campbell). They were soon in the thick of it and the demand for the skyward-pointing 4-inch guns was endless. In the event, these six old destroyers were swamped by the sheer scale of air attack that the *Luftwaffe* was able to deploy, with little or no opposition in the air.

Between 10 May and 1815 on 19 May, when the Admiralty withdrew the survivors, they were constantly in action. Not surprisingly, they suffered heavily. On 15 May *Valentine* was the first to be lost, operating in the Scheldt, near Terneusen, and escorting one of the large passenger ferries when a severe bombing attack developed. *Valentine* gallantly interposed herself between the ferry and the dive bombers and received two direct hits. Her thin decks were unable to withstand such a blow and one bomb penetrated right through to her boiler room. One boiler blew up, wrecking the ship, and she was beached with an enormous hole in her hull, her back broken. Twenty of her crew were killed and another twenty wounded in this attack.

While operating off the Dutch coast, *Winchester* was also bombed and, although she was not hit, a very near miss severely damaged her hull under water. Early on 15 May, she sailed from Dover, to which she had struggled, to Liverpool to carry out comprehensive repairs. *Westminster*, which had not been damaged, had escorted her home with *Keith* and *Vimiera* and, after hasty refuelling and ammunitioning, the latter two destroyers sailed again from Dover to rejoin the French at Dunkirk on the same day. During the night of 15-16 May, while sailing through the west approach channel to Dunkirk, about 0209, *Westminster* struck an unreported wreck and sustained considerable underwater damage. She was towed into Dunkirk and put into dry-dock there for further examination.

On 19 May it was the turn of the *Whitley*. While operating off Nieuport, she was attacked by Ju87 Stukas and heavily damaged. Arrangements were made immediately for tugs to be sent to her assistance from Dunkirk and the salvage tug *Lady Brassey* was sent out from Dover. Captain Simson (D19) in *Keith* was also ordered to go to her aid. He soon reported that *Whitley* was ashore between Nieuport and Ostend with both her boiler rooms flooded and her back broken. After her survivors had been taken off, the wreck was shelled by *Keith* to prevent it from falling intact into enemy hands. *Vimiera* was then ordered to proceed to Portsmouth with the ship's company of *Whitley*, who had just four men killed in the attack, and with the crew of *Westminster* also, who were not required while she was docked. Embarking all these, as well as a demolition party for Flushing, *Vimiera* sailed from Dunkirk at 1700 on the same evening.

Lady Brassey was kept at anchor at Dunkirk ready to tow *Westminster* home under the protection of *Wolsey* and this was, in fact, done on 20 May. On arrival at Dover, *Westminster* reported being able to steam safely at nine knots on one engine and, as the weather was fine, she was allowed to continue on her way west in this manner, *Wolsey* providing an escort as far as the Nab Tower. Thus ended this brief period of Anglo-French cooperation.

Organization for Further Withdrawals Prepared

For a brief time the Dutch held out in Zeeland and on Walcheren Island, and as long as they were resisting, the Allies gave them support. The French destroyers from Dunkirk were heavily engaged in providing gunfire cover at this time. Like their British counterparts, they soon began to take losses from the unremitting and unopposed air attacks.

When *Keith* returned to Dover on 15 May she brought with her twenty naval and military officers and other ranks and two Dutch civilians. *Venomous* (Lieutenant Commander J. E. H. McBeath) arrived at 1825 on the same day with fifty British and Dutch service personnel (including some of the demolition party) and about fifty civilians of various nationalities, picked up from a tug and a motor launch in which they had escaped from Ijmuiden. The Commanding Officer of that party then reported that all demolitions had been carried out there, and at Amsterdam, and that they had also blown up an iron foundry and lock gates for good measure! He also stated that the south channel was blocked by a merchant ship and a tug and that the main entrance by a large line and a trawler, though in each case it was possible for small craft to get past in fine weather.

Two notable movements took place on 16 May. The French destroyers *Cyclone* and *Sirocco* sailed from Dover carrying Prince Bernhard of the Netherlands and the Chief of the Dutch Naval Staff to join the remains of the Dutch Army. During the following days they, and the destroyers *Fougueux* and *Frondeur*, with two squadrons of French Navy Vought 156V dive bombers, supported fully the Dutch troops fighting on Zuid Beveland and Walcheren Island, but in vain.

The other movement that day reflected the growing crisis. The *Whitshed* was relieved by destroyer *Verity* (Lieutenant Commander A. R. M. Black) on the North Goodwin Patrol, and dispatched to Ostend with the British Expeditionary Force's leave boat *Mona's Queen*, in order to bring back as many British refugees as possible. *Whitshed* was heavily bombed as she approached Ostend, but finally managed to embark some fourteen passengers, including four RAF personnel. *Mona's Queen* returned with her at 2100, with some 1,500 passengers aboard, hardly any of whom were British. She was sent into Folkestone to disembark them. Three large Belgian

Mail steamers also arrived in the Downs late at night, their capacious holds almost empty with only 200 refugees between them. As the official report put it, 'The reason for the small number brought appears to have been the anxiety of the ships to escape from air attacks in Ostende'.

Whitshed was attacked yet again between 1600 and 1700 on Sunday 19 May, while conducting the North Goodwin Patrol; she was not hit and claimed to have destroyed one attacker. Further air attacks on her and *Venomous* followed, again without damage to the destroyers, and one seaplane was shot down by *Venomous*. *Whitshed* had, by this time, expended all her ammunition and had to be withdrawn to the Downs. *Keith* returned to Dover, refuelled and then proceeded to Boulogne with the Chief of the Imperial General Staff, before proceeding to Sheerness for hasty repairs. During the course of the day, the other destroyer available, *Wild Swan* (Lieutenant Commander J. L. Younghusband) was engaged in a protracted hunt for a submarine reported by French trawlers, but with no result; she returned to Dover on 20 May.

Heavy Air Attacks Lead to Further Withdrawals

Although the situation on land was grim and getting grimmer, and although plans were being laid for the withdrawal of 'useless mouths', no decision had yet been made on the final evacuation of the Allied armies now cut off and falling back on the Channel ports. It was still hoped that the situation would stabilize. Meanwhile the rapid German advance was beginning to threaten, not just the French and Belgian ports, but the supply lines of the BEF itself. Some rearranging of both the British and French supply convoys and ports was, therefore, put in hand, but these plans were continually overtaken by events and compromised by the non-stop bombing carried out by the *Luftwaffe* with little apparent hindrance. So severe had the bombing become at Dunkirk by 20 May that Admiral Abrial took the decision to evacuate all large French ships from that port. The first group got clear but the second, which sailed at midnight, was less fortunate as the *Luftwaffe* struck at once. The tanker *Salomé* (20,000 tons) was under tow but had to be abandoned. The merchantman *Pavon* with 1,500 Dutch soldiers aboard was bombed, damaged and beached between Calais and Gravelines; the minesweeper *Niger* was hit, set afire and finally burnt out and sank; and the destroyer *L'Adriot* received a hit, was also run aground, and written off at Malo-les-Bains.

British ships in the Channel were also subjected to non-stop air attacks on 20 May. While sweeping for magnetic mines between Dunkirk and Ostend the 'LL' trawlers *Lord Inchcape* and *Rifness* were attacked almost continually and the latter was sunk. Likewise the 'LL' trawler *Our Bairns* was set upon some eight miles from Cap Gris Nez and near-missed by four bombs, without casualties. The flotilla leader *Malcolm* was on the North Goodwin patrol when three enemy aircraft attacked just after 1900. They registered three near misses which, although they caused very little damage to the ship, killed three ratings and seriously wounded ten others by splinters. She later sailed for Portsmouth for repairs. The A/S trawlers *Lady Philomena* and *Kingston Olivina* left as well. There was no let-up. The French destroyers *Cyclone, Mistral, Sirocco, Fougueux* and *Frondeur* left Dunkirk and took refuge in the Downs on 21 May. In the words of the official report: 'These destroyers were brought over from Dunkirk to give them some respite from the constant bombing to which they had been subjected for several days.'

The 21 May was no different. Evacuation of the refugees continued, as did the supply of the BEF ashore, and preparations for much worse conditions. The Admiralty ordered three more destroyers down to Dover from the Nore, to take the places of the growing number under repair: *Vimy* (Lieutenant Commander C. G. W. Donald), *Windsor* (Lieutenant Commander P. D. H. R. Pelly) and *Venetia* (Lieutenant F. Bruen, DSC). Several troop-carrying transports and supply ships were escorted to French ports, and refugees and some service personnel were brought back by warships. *Keith* sailed to Dunkirk and returned with 150 British civilians, *Wild Swan* went to Boulogne and brought back another 150, as did *Whitshed*, which took over anti-tank guns, personnel and ammunition. *Venomous* sailed to Calais and brought back 200 British refugees and the apparatus and instruments of the Sangatte Indicator Loop Station, which was being abandoned. *Wolsey* escorted transports to Cherbourg while the armed yachts *Grey Mist* and *Gulzar* sailed to Boulogne and Calais respectively to act, if necessary, as W/T links.

The *Luftwaffe*, despite its commitments ashore, did not neglect them. The minesweeping trawler *Burke* suffered near misses of the North Foreland, as did the destroyer *Venomous* at Calais. *Keith* was bombed at Dunkirk, *Wild Swan* on the North Goodwin patrol and *Grey Mist* at Boulogne. All of these ships escaped without damage fortunately.

At the same time a conference was held at Dover Castle, chaired by Vice Admiral Ramsay, which, *for the first time*, considered an emergency evacuation of very large forces back across the Channel. This meeting continued at the War Office the following day. The decisions reached were, not surprisingly, rendered null and void by the rapidly-deteriorating situation in France, but they did lead to the next phase of the story. The conclusions reached were that 10,000 men could be brought out from each of the three ports of Boulogne, Calais and Dunkirk, every twenty-four hours, if there was only 'moderate' opposition from the enemy! Consequently sixteen large passenger vessels were assembled at Dover and Southampton with a further sixteen in readiness as a reserve. Twelve drifters and six coasters were also made ready. Forty of the flat-bottomed Dutch *schuits* ['skoots' as the RN ratings christened them] which had reached England, were also given Royal Navy crews to aid the lift, while Sea Transport officers in the south, started to make a record of all small ships up to 1,000 tons available for possible future naval use. At the same time a sub-organization was set up in the Dynamo Room under Dover Castle to coordinate the assembly of such a diverse amount of shipping, 'should the need arise'.

Casualties continued to mount on 22 May. The strain of constant and unremitting aerial assault without any compensating aerial protection in defence, was already placing some skippers under unbearable pressure. The French steamer *Tlemcen* for example, sailed from Dunkirk to escape the air raids and, on her way across, stopped to pick up survivors from another French ship, *Portieux*, which had been bombed and sunk off Gravelines. It was a clear, fine day and yet, in full daylight, about one mile south of the western entrance to Dover harbour, *Tlemcen* collided with the British coaster *Efford*. The latter rapidly sank, but all her crew were saved. Eyewitnesses stated the French steamer's actions were 'absolutely inexcusable'.

The fully-laden supply ship *Firth Fisher* (574 tons) was mined and sunk half-a-mile from Boulogne Pier the same day, and only four of her eleven crew were rescued. The MV *Sodality* was shelled by German coastal guns near Calais, the first time that this had occurred and a clear indication of just how close the enemy now were. Another heavy loss was the French destroyer *Jaguar*, torpedoed by the German E-boats *S-21* and *S-23* while approaching Dunkirk with demolition parties aboard.

The Germans reached the Channel coast around midnight on 20 May. After some indecision [they seemed amazed at the ease of their own victories and lack of opposition and sensed a trap] they began to probe north. The first major port in their path was Boulogne. Here the French naval commander ordered the port to be evacuated on 21 May. This panicky reaction was cancelled by a more resolute subordinate, and a hasty improvement in morale seemed very desirable by the British, which led to the dispatch of the 20 Guards Brigade via Dover, aboard the Channel steamers *Biarritz* and *Queen of the Channel* escorted by the destroyers *Vimiera* and *Whitshed*, which arrived on the morning of 22 May. The destroyers had also embarked anti-tanks guns, as recorded. The destroyers *Wild Swan*, *Venomous* and *Vimy* (Lieutenant Commander C. G. W. Donald) were meanwhile detailed to carry demolition parties to Boulogne, Calais and Dunkirk respectively to cover every option.

Notes

1. The *Wild Swan* was to be very heavily involved in all these subsequent events in both Holland and Belgium. For the full detailed story see Peter C. Smith, *H.M.S. Wild Swan*, William Kimber, London, 1985.
2. The full story of British destroyer minelaying operations in both World Wars is told in Peter C. Smith, *Into the Minefields*, Pen & Sword, Barnsley, 2005.
3. See George Mack, *H.M.S. Intrepid*, William Kimber, London, 1980, edited for publishing by Peter C. Smith.

Chapter Three

Evacuation of Boulogne and the Fall of Calais

At Dover, the whole of the preceding twenty-four hours had been given to supplying the BEF with necessary stores and material, and replacing those from which they had been cut off by the enemy advance toward the coast. The transportation of the Guards had been in addition to that commitment, but did not delay it. There was a continued demand to evacuate, under repeated air attack, the growing flood of civilians and service personnel, the flotsam and jetsam of war, from the dwindling number of French and Belgian outlet ports back to the UK. Although working at a high pitch, no untoward emergency was felt, although it was generally recognized that the situation was rapidly deteriorating. Then late on Wednesday evening, 22 May, the position was suddenly changed, as the Dover War Diary reports:

> Apart from repeated bombing, work continued according to plan at the ports and there was nothing alarming in the situation until at 2000 *Grey Mist* signalled from Boulogne that enemy tanks were two miles south of the town. This was followed by another signal to say that she had been asked to bring away refugees, this being the start of a general evacuation by base staffs, both naval and military. Some hundreds of men were brought to Dover by destroyers, *Grey Mist* and drifters before the night was out.

When the Guards arrived, their naval escorts found what the official historian has termed 'a difficult state of affairs'. Contemporary reports, as in the Dover War Diary, not constrained by post-war Whitehall concerns for the prickliness of post-war allies, were more down to earth in calling a spade a spade:

> The situation in the vicinity of the French ports continued to be obscure and in varying degrees, serious, the gravity of the position being accentuated by an apparent demoralization of the personnel, both British and French. At Dunkirk, all confidential papers were burnt, an example followed by the BNLO; in regard to Calais the military authorities began considering complete evacuation and both service and civil

> refugees began to arrive; while at Boulogne evacuation continued and amongst other things the French coastal defence batteries were abandoned and troops were picked up from beaches outside the town and even in open boats away from the coast.

The Welsh Guards advanced into this madhouse with calm reassurance and started to dig in. When the German attack came, at 1700, it was repulsed. A second attack at dawn on 23 May, using tanks, artillery and dive bombers, was more successful. Back at the harbour the Commanding Officers of the two destroyers managed to bring some organization to the chaos and then, their decks packed with demoralized civilians and military, French and Belgian, they returned to Dover. The destroyer *Verity* (Lieutenant Commander A. R. M. Black) guard ship at Boulogne, also arrived early that morning with General Brownrigg (Adjutant General of the BEF) and his staff embarked.

Destroyer Bombardments at Boulogne

Early on 23 May, *Vimy* took a party of 200 armed Royal Marines and sailors to help clear the Boulogne dock area, blocked by a seething mass of people frantic to escape. She was joined again by *Keith* and *Whitshed*, after they had covered the passage of the Rifle Brigade to Calais to fulfil a similar function. In the interim, Admiral Abrail had sent down a flotilla of his destroyers under Captain Urvoy de Portzamparc in the *Cyclone*, with the *Chacal, Bourrasque, Frondeur, Foudroyant, Fougueux, Mistal, Orage* and *Sirocco*, which carried out bombardments of the advancing German units around the fortifications known as Tour de'Ordre until it fell to the Germans during the afternoon. *Vimy* and her two companions joined in, firing on German armoured and motorized columns as they approached the town from the south.

When *Keith* and *Whitshed* arrived, the perimeter held by the Irish and Welsh Guards had shrunk significantly. These two destroyers berthed abreast at the Quai Chanzy to the sound of machine-gun fire. The transport *Mona's Queen*, the bulk of her urgent supplies and stores still not offloaded, also lay in the harbour.

No orders had been received to evacuate the port, so *Whitshed* embarked seventy-two stretcher cases while awaiting a decision. She then backed out of the harbour, shelling a German machine-gun post in a warehouse at point-blank range with her 4.7-inch guns as she did so. Three more such positions were blasted at a range of 100 yards as she left the entrance. As *Whitshed* came out, *Vimy* entered and took her place alongside *Keith*. Once out at sea, *Whitshed* proceeded to engage *Fort de la Crèche*, by now in German hands, and several salvoes produced a satisfactory explosion. She then engaged columns of German tanks and transports. She picked up a swimmer and came under direct fire from the shore, to which she replied with zeal; in all, three German tanks were certainly destroyed by her main armament in this strange and unexpected duel. Meanwhile, Ramsay had ordered over reinforcements and the destroyers *Venetia, Vimiera* and *Venomous* had all arrived late in the afternoon. *Whitshed* was ordered to return home and land her wounded, but before she had gone far, the final evacuation signal, ordering the carrying out of Operation *Bungalow*, was received and she turned back to assist in this. She was joined later by the *Wild Swan*.

British Destroyers versus Tanks, Artillery and Dive Bombers

It was now 1730 on 23 May. *Keith* and *Vimy* began embarking troops on receipt of the evacuation order, but, as they did so, heavy dive bombing attacks commenced in conjunction with an all-out frontal land assault by the German army against the slender defences, manned by the Guards and a gallant company of French soldiers under General Lanquetot. About sixty Junkers Ju87s concentrated on the harbour area and the destroyers working just outside. Machine-gun, rifle and mortar fire also rained down upon the two destroyers alongside the quay. The whole of the dockyard erupted in a sheet of flame and smoke.

Miraculously, neither destroyer inside the harbour received a direct hit, but near misses on the quay alongside *Keith* caused considerable damage to her upperworks. A mortar shell landed on her forecastle and machine-gun fire ripped through her exposed bridge, killing Captain Simson instantly. Aboard *Vimy*, Lieutenant Commander Donald was also seriously wounded. Seven ratings were killed and twenty-eight wounded aboard *Keith* and one other officer killed and several more wounded aboard *Vimy*.

The destroyers, out to sea, were also heavily attacked at this time. *Whitshed*, with Commander Conder now the senior officer on the death of Captain Simson, was bracketed time and time again, by bombs dropped by the Stukas. However, one near miss was all that they managed to achieve, which killed *Whitshed*'s gunner and wounded one other officer and ten ratings. 'X' mounting's elevating gear was severed, 'A' and 'B' mounts would only train by the crews' shoulder power. The French destroyers did not fare so well: *Orage* was hit fair and square, set on fire and sunk after survivors had been removed and the *Frondeur* was seriously damaged.

Once this vicious attack had died away, Commander Conder took *Whitshed* back to the harbour mouth and met *Vimy* backing out astern, on fire aft and with a slight list. She was followed by *Keith*; the destroyer's guns still in action against shore targets. *Whitshed* joined in the bombardment until all three ships came clear, then *Keith* and *Vimy* were sent back to Dover. On the way back *Keith* buried her dead at sea, off the Varne.

Meanwhile Commander Conder had signalled to the Admiralty that he would require some air cover before making a further attempt at evacuation. Some fifty minutes later nine Spitfires appeared high over the port for a few brief minutes before vanishing again but not before their visitation had encouraged Conder to signal 'Going in.' By the time the destroyers returned it was low water and the same difficulties of navigation faced them as before. Nonetheless, both *Whitshed* and *Vimiera* berthed, the leading ship firing on shore targets once more, but receiving no response this time. The demolition party came aboard and reported that not all of their tasks had been accomplished, so various parties were sent off to complete the work. The Welsh Guards were hailed by megaphone and marched to the harbour in immaculate order. Due to the shallowness of the water only 500 or so men could be taken aboard each destroyer before they pulled out. Once they had done so, their places were at once taken by *Wild Swan* and *Venomous*.

Again, both ships got in without attracting any response from the Germans, and it was decided to speed up the process by sending in a third destroyer. As this ship, *Venetia*, closed the breakwaters, the evening sky was lit up with gun flashes as the German artillery, including some mobile batteries on the hills north of the town, opened a sustained bombardment in an obviously planned attempt to sink her in the harbour mouth and so trap the whole force. Direct hits wiped out 'B' mounting and its entire crew, and caused severe casualties among the bridge personnel, among the badly wounded being her Captain, Lieutenant Commander B. H. de C. Mellor. The *Venetia*'s engines stopped and, out of control, ran aground but, by heroic efforts directed by Sub Lieutenant D. H. Jones, RNR, the only officer not incapacitated, she managed to back out of harbour again. The shells, which did the damage, came from the French coastal battery which had been abandoned to the enemy earlier. In total, *Venetia* suffered twenty ratings killed and eleven of all ranks wounded.

Final Evacuation of Boulogne

The artillery bombardment coincided with another frontal attack by the German army, which by now held most of the town. Tanks clattered down side streets leading to the harbour and *Wild Swan*, by now alongside the quay, opened fire with her after 4.7-inch mountings, scoring a direct hit on one panzer, which was blown asunder. A motorcycle column was seen debouching from the main street onto the quay and was at once wiped out by pom-pom fire from *Venomous* as she secured alongside *Wild Swan*. Loading of troops commenced immediately, notwithstanding the continuous shell, machine-gun and rifle fire, to which the destroyers replied when and as they could locate targets amid the rubble.

Again, only about 500 men per ship could be embarked; even so, *Wild Swan* grounded on her way out, but managed to get clear. *Venomous*'s steering gear jammed once more but, steering by her engines alone, she too came clear of the harbour and, with the crippled *Venetia*, they set course for Dover. The time was 2130. Admiral Ramsay meanwhile, ordered the destroyer *Windsor*, which was off Calais, to Boulogne and she arrived about an hour after the others had departed. Despite the confusion, she managed to get alongside and took aboard some 600 troops, as well as the wounded and the rest of the demolition party, without any damage to herself. There were still British troops ashore and so Ramsay ordered two further destroyers over, *Vimiera* and *Wessex*, but on the way across the latter was diverted to Calais.

Vimiera alone entered Boulogne for the second time, early on 24 May, to an eerie silence, securing to the outer jetty, as, by now, any attempt to reach the inner harbour was suicidal. Her captain, Lieutenant Commander R. B. N. Hicks, hailed the shore without eliciting any response for some time, and it was thought that the port had been totally evacuated. She was about to cast off when she was rushed by a disorganized rabble of refugees, civilians and French and British soldiers who had been hiding in a dockside building. At the same time an officer from the Guards made his appearance aboard and informed Hicks that about 1,000 of his troops still remained ashore. By the time she sailed, at 0245, *Vimiera* was dangerously overloaded. She had some 1,400 people aboard, crammed into every nook and cranny of the ship, so that only the spaces around her guns and engines remained clear. Fortunately, the Germans' renewed attempts to stop her with heavy shelling and another bombing attack, failed in their purpose, or else loss of life would have been considerable. Regrettably, some 300 Welsh Guards had to be left behind, as there was simply no further room for them aboard.

So Boulogne fell, although in the ruins some French troops at least continued to hold out, to their lasting credit. The French destroyers tried to give what help they could to these courageous few, but, once again, paid heavily for their efforts. Stuka bombs hit *Fougueux*, which was severely damaged, and *Chacal*, was brought to a halt and shelled by coastal guns until she sank. After this mauling Admiral Abrial withdrew the few surviving ships of his battered flotilla.

Hot Work off Calais

Seen from Dover, the situation at Calais was no less obscure. The first moves were designed to reinforce the garrison there and to provide them with all possible support from the sea. *Venomous* had earlier landed her demolition party there and, also on 23 May, *Vimiera* had escorted two transports, *Kohisan* and *Benlawers*, filled with tanks and motor transport for the troops ashore. She remained off the port to bombard any enemy units seen approaching the town. The 30 Brigade, under Brigadier Nicholson, also arrived at Calais in the troopships *Archangel* and *Royal Daffodil*, escorted by the destroyer *Windsor*, which also remained in the vicinity to give gunfire support if required. When *Venetia* arrived from the Nore, she also was sent over to join them. Later that day the destroyer *Verity* (Lieutenant Commander A. R. M. Black) transported General MacNaughton, he being the Commanding Officer of the Canadian Division, for it had been decided to throw in last reserves into the battle. There was no question of pulling troops out yet; indeed, the Cabinet had decided that Calais must be held at all costs. What was not at first clear, was whether more reinforcements would be supplied or, as events worsened, whether this order would be rescinded in time to save some of the garrison. It was not, but Admiral Ramsay had to plan for all these possibilities with his dwindling resources. The W/T link yacht *Gulzar* brought back some evacuated troops from that port on 23 May, along with the War Graves Commission staff.

On 24 May events began to move with some speed. In the early hours, Ramsay was told by London that the evacuation of Calais had been decided in principle and that as soon as the unloading of the ships with motor transport had been completed, embarkation of all personnel not required to cover the final evacuation was to start. At 0630, the first ship left Calais with some 400 wounded aboard. Later that morning the order for evacuation was countermanded except for non-essential non-fighting troops. Instructions had to be sent to the warships off Calais to stop all vessels not fulfilling this condition and to ensure that all fighting troops remained in Calais or returned there. Just how the overstretched destroyers were to perform this task is unclear and one senses political machinations behind such an order, with Churchill's hasty and imperious stamp all over it. Despite this confusion, *Kohistan* was got away with a large number of troops and wounded, and returned safely to Dover.

Further reinforcements had arrived from Harwich to bolster the Dover Flotilla, which had been reduced to only two active ships. The Admiralty signalled that the damaged *Keith, Wild Swan, Whitshed, Venomous* and *Venetia* could be taken in hand for repairs at their home ports and were to be sailed at the first opportunity. For most, the opportunity did not arise for some time. The destroyers *Greyhound* (Commander W. R. Marshall A'Deane), *Grafton* (Commander C. E. C. Robinson), *Wolfhound* (Lieutenant Commander J. W. McCoy) and the Polish *Burza* all from the 1st DF transferred south. At the same time the demolition parties for Le Havre were dispatched aboard *Wolsey* (Lieutenant Commander C. H. Campbell) and *Windsor*. Meanwhile *Wessex* was sailed at 0700 to give all possible support to Calais, being followed by *Wolfhound* and *Vimiera* at 1000; their principal objectives being the bombardment of the road approaches and enemy batteries if located, and any enemy units, which might be seen. One German battery had been seen shelling Calais from the west. To add to the destroyer gunfire, the light cruisers *Arethusa* and *Galatea* sailed from Portsmouth that day, but returned when it was found that they could not reach Calais before dark, which would prevent accurate gunfire.

To prevent a repetition of the disgraceful scenes at Boulogne, *Wolfhound* was told at 1339 to enter Calais to act as guardship and to prepare for close action against the enemy. A party of Royal Marines was also to be landed to control embarkation should it be decided that this was, after all, to take place.

The destroyers were in action all that day and, at 1430 *Burza* was sent over to add her support. So successful had they been that it was inevitable that they would invite retaliation. The Stuka forces which had wreaked havoc with the Boulogne ships, and which had been pounding the Calais Citadel defences, now turned their baleful attentions to them.

First to go was *Wessex*, which reported herself under attack at 1642. At the time she was closing the shore to recommence her bombardment with *Vimiera* and *Burza*. As they turned, a force of twenty-one aircraft, quickly identified as Ju87s, was spotted, which immediately split into three groups and began their dives on the destroyers. *Wessex* increased speed to twenty-eight knots and started to zigzag, at the same time opening fire with her main armament in barrage fire, the pom-pom and two single Lewis guns. The first two dive bomber attacks were successfully evaded but the third aircraft planted all three of her bombs on target. The largest of these bombs, one 550-lb and two 110-lb, hit between the funnels and penetrated to both boilers which were wrecked. Widespread damage was done to the ship's bottom and sides and the bulkhead protecting the foremost engine room was perforated and started to flood. The boats, deck fittings and fore funnel 'disappeared' and the after funnel was brought down. The ship started to settle by the head although 'A', 'X' and 'Y' guns continued firing as she sank. *Burza* was also hit by two bombs forward and badly damaged. Luckily her engine rooms were intact, although shaken and, at three knots, she limped back to Dover with her bows low in the water. The third destroyer, *Vimiera*, was narrowly missed and her speed was reduced, but she was able to take survivors off the *Wessex*.

Verity and the tug *Lady Brassey* were dispatched to help *Burza*, but she made it under her own power and next day was towed away to Portsmouth by two tugs escorted by the trawler *Kingston Olivine*. The drifters *Yorkshire Lass* and *Golden Sunbeam* had been sent to Calais with ammunition and the trawler *John Catting* was also sent, to act as a wireless link.

Adventures of the Calais Demolition Party

The demolition party taken to France aboard *Venomous* was commanded by Captain Swinley, back on his old 'patch' after serving with a French destroyer off Norway. He had two RNVR officers, thirty-four ratings, eleven sappers and two tons of explosives to blow up bridges and lock gates. Captain Swinley recalled to that:

> I was given £250 in notes to assist in our getaway, if necessary, and this I distributed amongst the party. Before leaving, a signal was received telling me on no account to blow up anything without approval. We arrived, and having found the French authorities, who showed very little interest in our activities, we began to dig ourselves in, and set about putting our fireworks together. To our horror, we found that we had been given the wrong detonators and primers, so we couldn't blow up anything! I telephoned from the Pier to the Admiralty, and to Dover to tell them of our situation and I asked General MacNaughton, who commanded the Canadians and who arrived at midnight, to explain our requirements when he returned to Dover. At four in the morning, however, I was shown a signal from DMO at the War Office – 'Evacuation of Calais approved in principle; covering forces to remain behind.' What were we to do? We were certainly not the covering force – if we stayed behind we could not carry out the job we were sent to do – and anyway, nobody cared two pins about us. So we disposed of the det-

onators, embarked our stores and personnel in the drifter *Ut Prosim* and after an adventurous trip, arrived at Dover.

Here we struggled to obtain the correct detonators and primers, and eventually got them.

Meanwhile we heard that the oil tanks at Calais had been bombed by the Germans. These oil tanks had been the sappers' objective, but although this had been dealt with by the enemy, the eleven sappers volunteered to return with us and lend a hand with our various jobs. Hardly any of us had had experience of demolition work except the sappers and at Chatham Barracks we had been given only three days' instruction. The biggest thing we blew up was a small piece of railway line, for which we used an eight-ounce charge. However, that evening we returned in the drifter *Forecast*, and the wicket had become stickier. In fact, it was nothing less than bodyline bowling. There was not much time to lose, and at four in the morning charges were laid at various key points and later we blew them up. One of the sailors, during a particularly heavy air raid, took the detonators out of the fitted charges and put them in his pocket until the raid was over. Another RNVR seaman, who had only been in the Navy five weeks, climbed a crane and covered the embarkation in the drifter by means of his borrowed Bren gun. My Sub blew up a crane opposite to me, and I was anxious for his safety until the smoke cleared away and I saw him still alive. But it was not the crane we had selected, and his reply to my question was, 'Well, Sir, the one next to it was bigger.'

Mr Brown, the skipper of the *Forecast*, and his crew were magnificent, and they had an awful time. On reaching the entrance to Calais Harbour the little ship was at Action Stations, the twelve pounder and the two Lewis guns being manned. At this time, two motor torpedo boats, identity unknown, were sighted, steaming at high speed on a parallel course, aircraft were sighted coming up astern, a submarine was reported on the surface, and a salvo from a shore battery fell 150 yards over. But at that moment Mr Brown, the Skipper, cared for none of these things, as he had just realized the loss of his dentures. Otherwise the passage to Dover was made without incident, and the ship proceeded at full speed, eight knots. I often wondered whether Mr Brown got a new set of dentures out of My Lords. He was certainly very angry at losing them, but I was delighted to get a Greetings Telegram at Christmas from the gallant little skipper. He had recovered his teeth!

Evacuation and Demolition of Belgian Ports

The main responsibility for the blocking of Ostend and Zeebrugee initially rested with the French, but great resistance to their plans was encountered from the Belgians themselves. By 25 May the block ships, which had been held in readiness for such an eventuality at Sheerness, were sailed under the command of the destroyer *Vega* (Captain G. A. Garnon-Williams). There were two ships destined for Zeebrugge and three for Ostend, but shortly after they had sailed, the Ostend part of the plan was cancelled by the Admiralty in the hope that some troops might yet be taken away via that harbour before the Germans entered it. Under attack by bombers during their passage, the rest of the force survived intact but, on arrival at Zeebrugge, were fired upon by French troops! Under this fire, the leading blockship veered off course and sank outside the main channel, the second ship followed her in and sank nearby. *Vega* returned to Sheerness, her mission unaccomplished.

A second attempt was immediately mounted, *Vega* taking over two of the Ostend blockships for the job on 26 May. This time, despite E-boat attack and bombing, the two ships were scuttled in the correct position and Zeebrugge harbour was blocked. Ostend still remained open, however, but when the Admiralty sailed a further force to complete the task three weeks later, the RAF informed them that they could [would] not provide any air cover! The Admiralty was therefore forced to abandon the attempt and no further opportunity presented itself.

With Ostend remaining open, several ships tried to evacuate refugees and service personnel, under heavy air attack the whole time. The French had planned to take off some 350,000 civilians via this port, but this, like most plans in this frenzied period, proved to be totally unrealistic. As late as 27 May the steamer *Aboukir* had embarked 220 civilians and parts of the three British Military Missions and sailed from Ostend at 2300. At 0130 next morning, she was attacked by a U-boat and then torpedoed by E-boats. Only thirty-three survivors were picked up by *Codrington* and other destroyers at 0800.

News was received from several sources of submarines moving into the southern North Sea to take their share of easy pickings off the Belgian and northern French coasts and, as harbours fell into German hands, the E-boat flotillas were not slow in moving in, like jackals, to harass the night waters as well. The establishment of coastal gun positions, at first with light field pieces, and then with heavier batteries, also began to have an effect on the inshore routes to Calais and Dunkirk and added to the easy dominance of the *Luftwaffe*.

There was an almost total absence of air cover from the RAF which, as it meant that the *Luftwaffe* could carry out raids unopposed, added very considerably to the difficulties of the ships. The skies were never free of German bombers except when the weather closed in, and this was a rare event during in the days that followed.

At Dover on 25 May, the situation regarding Calais was still far from clear:

> Although plans were completed for evacuation, [it was] ordered that they were not to be put into effect, and that the defence must hold on, since every hour was of the greatest help to the BEF. Continued bombardment of the town showed that enemy batteries were firmly established and more batteries to the westward of the town in the

direction of Sangatte and Gris Nez disclosed their presence by opening fire on the minesweeping trawlers off the coast and hospital ships proceeding to Dunkirk.

Other moves gave further indications of the way things were rapidly going. For example, a signal arrived from the Admiralty ordering a preliminary survey, pending the arrival of a reconnaissance part, of the possibilities of shore torpedo tubes for harbour defence at Dover and Ramsgate, amongst other places. Another signal picked up was for all fishing vessels with 12-pounder guns to bunker and proceed to Dover.

The smaller ships were still busy off the coast north of Boulogne: the A/S trawlers and drifters picked up further batches of British troops all along the coast this day and landed them at Dover. The drifters *Lord Howe* and *Golden Gift* were sent over to Calais at midday with ammunition and medical supplies. The former managed to enter and unload part of her cargo before air attacks drove her out, while the latter could not get inside at all. Both returned to Dover later. In case the War Office relented, Ramsay sailed a force consisting of minesweeping trawlers and drifters under the protection of the destroyers *Verity* and *Windsor*, but they returned at dawn in the absence of further orders.

At 1032, the destroyer *Greyhound* was on patrol between Dover and Calais and two hours later she conducted a bombardment of an anti-aircraft battery, which had engaged a British aircraft. She also bombarded St Pierre's les Calais, in enemy hands. After appeals from Calais itself, she was joined by her sister ship, *Grafton*, and they both conducted bombardments until poor visibility prevented observation and their ammunition became almost expended. Both destroyers received damage to their directors from return fire and returned to Dover shortly before midnight with some casualties. One of the unused evacuation force, the trawler *Maretta* was also bombed heavily and had to be towed in by the trawler *Kingston Galena*.

The relighting of the North Goodwin, Gull and Wreck was authorized at this time, for the need for sea markers at night was about to become essential, in view of developments ashore. During the afternoon of 26 May, the Fleet minesweepers *Halcyon* and *Skipjack* arrived at Dover, sole survivors of the 6th M/S Flotilla, the other three ships being out of action, two with bomb damage and the third with engine defects. The 4th M/S Flotilla was ordered to Dover as soon as possible to take their place. And, almost hourly, the casualties continued to mount.

By dawn of 26 May, the garrison at Calais, having delivered its stirring rejection of the German ultimatum, was fighting its last heroic battle, and later the fortress fell. Before it did so, every attempt was made by the surface forces of the Royal Navy to assist them.

Final Hours off Calais

Between 0700 and 1000 the light cruiser *Galatea*, escorted by *Grafton*, carried out a bombardment of Calais and enemy positions in the vicinity with her 6-inch guns. Spotter aircraft were utilized. Two hospital ships were sent over to evacuate the wounded, but the Germans opened a merciless hail of fire on them each time they sought to enter the port and the attempt had to be abandoned. Then the destroyers *Wolsey* and *Wolfhound* carried out bombardments in the area while the light cruiser *Arethusa* relieved *Galatea* with A/S escort again being provided by *Grafton*. They carried on the gunfire with spotter planes directing, until poor visibility due to fog stopped it at 2030, after some seven salvoes of 6-inch shell had been pumped into one target.

After darkness fell, the armed yachts *Grey Mist* and *Gulzar* made their respective ways into the harbour to evacuate the wounded. The Germans now controlled the town and the yachts were fortunate to accomplish this without damage. *Gulzar* brought back fifty unwounded officers and other ranks from out of the jaws of the enemy.

Aircraft spotters reported that an estimated forty guns of up to 7.5-inch calibre were now in position between Sangatte and Calais, in addition to numerous AA batteries. Air attacks shifted back to Dunkirk, with the end of resistance at Calais, and *Wolsey* was sent there to act as W/T link. Despite this, hospital ships and troopships continued to make their way to Dunkirk, and evacuated many wounded and non-combatant troops and unloaded stores and supplies during 26 May.

The final events of the day marked the end of one chapter of heroism and the beginning of another, for, at 1857, Admiral Ramsay receive the signal from the Admiralty to 'Commence Operation *Dynamo*'. The epic of Dunkirk was about to begin.

CHAPTER FOUR

Dunkirk: The Evacuation Commences

It must be remembered that, although the order to commence Operation *Dynamo* was timed at 1857 on Sunday 26 May, by midnight on that same day, some 27,936 men had already been brought back to Dover. Running the gauntlet of bombers, magnetic mines, E-boats and the inevitable dive-bombers, several hospital ships, personnel ships and all manner of light craft, had made the journey across the Straits and back again with cargoes of casualties or rear-area troops. Thus that day the hospital ships *Isle of Thanet, Isle of Guernsey* and *Worthing*, all brought back wounded, while *Mona's Queen, Maid of Orleans, Canterbury* and the French *Rouen*, also got in and out with difficulty, despite repeated attacks, although some ships had to make more than a single attempt before succeeding.

It must also be restated that, even before *Dynamo* proper got under way, the warships at Dover had suffered heavy casualties, had been in action almost continuously for several days and nights, and nearly all those not sunk or badly damaged, had been under some form of attack, some many times, and had taken casualties and damage to some degree. Although a constant flow of reinforcements was fed in from other commands, there was never sufficient destroyers or minesweepers, and those available had to go back time and time again. Little wonder then that, even before Dunkirk proper began, crews were suffering from exhaustion. As time went by without any such rest, some crew members were pushed beyond their limits. It is no shame that some broke down; the wonder is that most did not. As early as 24 May this exhaustion was manifesting itself. Two of the destroyers, which had returned from Boulogne, *Vimy* and *Whitshed*, lay at Admiralty Pier and, in the early hours it was decided to shift them to buoys in the harbour. The Master of the tug *Simla* recalled that: '...the crews of the destroyers were so tired and exhausted from their recent experience at Boulogne, that we let them sleep on, and shifted the destroyers without them. I expect that when they turned out from their much-needed sleep they were surprised to find their ship in a different position, but were all fresh to got to sea again, and carry on the good work.'

They were ready all right, but hardly fresh, and they went on with the good work, not once, but again and again. The only time they stopped was when they were hit and damaged seriously enough to require docking. *Vimy*, for example, went back to Dunkirk, returned and was sent over yet again at 2238 on 27 May. At about 2355 the Captain left the bridge and, as he had not returned by 0015, the ship was searched from bow to stern without result. At no time was the destroyer halted and her First Lieutenant took command and carried on to Dunkirk.

They carried on, as did almost everyone else. But the going got tougher with each trip. It was therefore rather unfortunate that, around about this time, Brigadier Sir Oliver Leese should comment to Admiral Wake-Walker on the 'ineptitude of the Navy' in getting the Army away safely and that General Brooke should write in his diary on 29 May that he found 'arrangements quite inadequate and of a most Heath-Robinson nature'. The truth is contained in the Dover War Diary entry for 26 May, three days before this comment. On receipt of the go-ahead for the evacuation, Ramsay was able to record: 'These craft had been in course of assembly at various ports for some days and many were ready at four hours' notice.'

Weariness was not restricted to the Royal Navy, although they were driven, and driving themselves, harder. The courage of the merchant seamen and their willingness to face the carnage across the water to rescue the soldiers, is worthy of note. Not surprisingly, accidents began to increase as tiredness and numbness took its toll and the waters of the Narrow Sea became congested with ships, many damaged, and wrecks. Early on 27 May, for example, the MD ship *Corfield* at anchor in the Downs, reported a ship making an SOS. She proved to be a French patrol boat, which had struck a submerged wreck near the Deal Bank Buoy. She was towed to Dover by the drifter *Comfort*. At 0312 *Isle of Thanet* was approaching Dover Harbour with her cargo of wounded when she was in collision with the Examination Steamer *Ocean Reward*. The drifter sank like a stone and there were no survivors.

With Operation *Dynamo* now officially under way, yet more reinforcements were thrown into the fray, for it was expected that not more than a few days remained and only 45,000 men at most would be lifted. The anti-aircraft cruiser *Calcutta* (Captain D. M. Lees), the flotilla leaders *Mackay* (Commander G. H. Stokes) and *Montrose* (Commander C. R. L. Parry) and destroyers *Wakeful* (Commander R. L. Fisher) and *Worcester* (Commander J. H. Allison) joined Ramsay's forces this day from the Western Approaches Command and the destroyer *Impulsive* was also added at short notice.

Three other developments influenced the outcome of that day. Firstly, the abandoning of the shorter of the sea routes which passed Calais, due to the menace posed by the German shore batteries established there. These sank the store ship *Sequacity* and damaged several personnel ships. Secondly, every available destroyer and troop transports were sent over during the daylight hours with the lifting taking place mainly via their ships' boats from the beaches north of La Panne. But once dusk had fallen, these vessels were supplemented by the growing fleet of paddle minesweepers, drifters, schuits and coasting ships, both from Dunkirk and the Nore. Finally, and most importantly, Captain W. G. Tennant, (to later command the battlecruiser *Repulse* off Malaya), had volunteered to help the evacuation and was appointed Senior Naval Officer, Dunkirk, to take care of the naval shore embarkation parties. The two or three motor torpedo boats available were found useful for maintaining communication with vessels outside the harbour and spreading these vessels along the beaches from which the troops were embarked.

Condition of the Harbour at the Start of the Evacuation

Calais had a superior harbour, which had not been fully utilized, although it was much closer and larger than that of Dunkirk. However, when the decision was finally made to try and save at least a part of the BEF, the more distant port of Dunkirk was chosen, even though its facilities were not so good. As we have seen, Dunkirk itself, as the main French naval base in the north, had been pounded by the *Luftwaffe* and made untenable long before the evacuation commenced. On 24 May this port was at the extreme limits of the short range Junkers Ju87s (the aircraft that did the most damage to ships because of their precision attacks), but, as they jumped forward to closer airstrips, so the attacks increased in frequency. The need to crush Calais and the British resistance took some of the pressure off Dunkirk, for a short time, but there were sufficient long range Junkers Ju88s, Heinkel He111s and Dornier Do17s to make matters extremely difficult, long before the evacuation proper commenced and the harbour itself was wrecked. The lock gates leading to the inner harbour were smashed in a precision raid by Stukas that same day. The rail marshalling yards were torn up, ships sunk in the dock and, on the following day, further heavy raids started fresh fires and sank the freighter *Aden* (8,000 tons). Junkers Ju87s then took up the attack and hit ships offshore heavily; *Côte d'Azur*, a large French cross channel steamer, being one such victim.

There was never any suggestion, therefore, of using the harbour and all efforts concentrated this day on the beaches; as a result, lifting was slow. Captain Tennant's discovery that the fragile outer mole, not built to moor ships against, could be, with care, so used made a vast difference to the success of the operation. He had sailed aboard the destroyer *Wolfhound* early that afternoon, with twelve officers and 160 ratings to organize the beach embarkations. The destroyer was bombed continuously on her way over, but escaped unscathed. Tennant retained her at Dunkirk to act as communication ship but, instead, she was sent in to pick up troops, so urgent did the need seem at the time. The old destroyer *Sabre* (Commander B. Dean), which had sped from Portsmouth, was already there and these two were joined by a further seven destroyers, four minesweepers, two transports and seventeen drifters before the day was out. One destroyer, *Verity*, came under shellfire from the Calais guns and suffered casualties, but no ships were sunk this day. There were other casualties though, principally from the air.

The personnel ship *Queen of the Channel* lifted 2,000 men but was bombed at 0425 and sunk. The drifters *Paxton* and *Rob Roy* were badly damaged and beached, while an A/S trawler was mined and sunk with the loss of all but four of her crew. To give extra protection against the intervention by E-boats, which was daily expected, and from surfaced U-boat attack (many sightings had been made) the light cruiser *Galatea* and three destroyers from the Nore were patrolling south of the Inner Gabbard to the South Falls Buoy. Two Dover destroyers patrolled from there to Kwinte Bank and three more Nore destroyers from North Goodwin to the Wandelaar Searched Channel. By midnight, 7,669 soldiers were landed in England, despite many handicaps.

Loading Starts from the East Mole

The 28 May began with gloomy news. Due to a misunderstanding, a minesweeping force had been searching for magnetic mines off Calais and had run into a shallow British minefield laid there, with the result that the trawler *Thomas Bartlett* was sunk with the loss of eight of her crew. Ostend was reported to be in German hands and later it was learned that the King of the Belgians, in an action which caused a great deal of bitterness, and in spite of the support most of his troops had been getting from the BEF and French Allies fighting alongside them, had ordered the capitulation of his entire Army, leaving a huge gap in the Allied line which was only plugged with great difficulty. This selfish deed was a cruel blow to the hopes of the Allies.[1] As the official report phased it at the time:

> The effect of this could only be to make the situation of the British Expeditionary Force in Belgium perilous in the extreme, and reduce considerably the percentage, which it might be expected to evacuate successfully.
>
> Every effort was accordingly made to accelerate the rate of embarkation and many more vessels were allocated to the operations....

Among the many vessels added were the destroyers of the 1st Flotilla from Harwich, led by *Codrington* which had been operating off Norway and made the journey from Scapa Flow to Dover in record time, reinforcing her boast to be the fastest destroyer in the fleet. The ships concerned were 1st DF, *Gallant* (Lieutenant Commander C. P. F. Brown), *Grenade* (Commander C. R. Boyle), *Grafton* (Commander C. E. C. Robinson) and *Greyhound* (Commander W. R. Marshall A'Deane), 5th DF, *Jaguar* (Lieutenant Commander J. F. W. Hine) and *Javelin* (Commander A. F. Pugsley); 20th DF, *Express, Esk, Intrepid, Impulsive, Ivanhoe* and *Icarus* (Lieutenant Commander E. G. Roper) and the Portsmouth Local Defence Flotilla destroyers *Anthony* (Lieutenant Commander N. J. V Thew), *Harvester* (Lieutenant Commander M Thornton), *Havant* (Lieutenant Commander A. F. Burnell-Nugent), *Sabre, Saladin* (Lieutenant Commander L. J. Dover), *Scimitar* (Lieutenant R. D. Franks) and *Shikari* (Commander H N. A. Richardson) as well as others brought in from the Western Approaches;

thirty destroyers in all by 28 May, some of them like the two ex-Brazilian Havant class vessels, brand new ships straight from the builders' yards. In addition, lesser warships were sent in; the coastal corvettes *Guillemot* (Lieutenant Commander H. M. Darrel-Brown), *Kingfisher* (Lieutenant Commander D. R. Mallinson), *Mallard* (Commander The Hon. V. Wyndham-Quinn), *Shearwater* (Lieutenant Commander C. F. Powlett), *Sheldrake* (Lieutenant Commander A. E. T. Christie) and *Widgeon* (Lieutenant Commander R Fredrick); two old Chinese river gunboats, *Locust* (Lieutenant Commander A. N. P. Costabdie) and later *Mosquito*; the minesweepers of the 4th, 5th, 6th, 10th and 12th Flotillas and twelve large transports. Later, the minesweepers of the 7th and 8th Flotillas joined in, while many small boats were towed across to help. The disembarkation was no less carefully planned than the load: the *Calcutta* landed her troops at Sheerness, the destroyers at Dover, and they often made two trips a day if undamaged or until exhaustion caught up with their crews. The drifters, schuits, coasters and trawlers used Margate or Ramsgate, the bigger personnel steamers, Folkestone or Dover.

The one piece of good fortune on 28 May, was the weather. It was moderate, with rain in the afternoon at Dover. Over the *Luftwaffe*'s forward airfield at St Quentin, where the Stukas stood ready to take off, it was worse. A German historian glumly noted that, 'On May 28th, the weather worsened from hour to hour. Though individual Bomber *Gruppen* attacked Ostend and Nieuport, hardly any bombs dropped on Dunkirk. Low cloud, fusing with all that smoke and dust, blotted out the whole area.'

The weather, in fact, saved the day. Even so, there were some casualties, even from aircraft. The destroyer *Windsor* returning from Dunkirk, was attacked in the Downs. She had several hundred troops aboard, which made violent alterations of course precarious. She managed to avoid all the bombs aimed at her, but a near miss caused some damage in her boiler room and also caused between twenty and thirty casualties among the soldiers on her crowded decks.

Wakeful (Commander R. L. Fisher) and *Grafton*, had both been loading troops from the area of the Bray Dunes, and sailed for home within minutes of each other, using the most northerly and longest route via the Kwinte Buoy and North Goodwin lightship and then south inside the Goodwins, a total length of eight-seven sea miles. The first stage of this long journey, made necessary by the establishment of heavy guns off Calais, involved a leg to the north, up the coast through the sandbars off Nieuport and Ostend; into the heart of enemy-controlled waters, in fact, for the E-boats and U-boats were quick to move into the newly-surrendered Belgian ports and lurk on the northern fringes of the evacuation routes looking for easy kills without too much risk to themselves. At night, the small silhouette of a surfaced U-boat or an E-boat is much like a small ships' indistinct blur, and the sea was full of such craft, making identification very difficult. Thus it was that the destroyer *Wakeful* was surprised, in restricted waters, and unable to manoeuvre. Her Commanding Officer left this account of what then ensued:

> During some eight hours we got about 640 troops on board and sailed after dark. Wisely – or perhaps unwisely as it turned out – I had insisted that all troops should be stowed as low as possible so as to preserve stability in case we should have to manoeuvre at high speed to avoid bombs. At fifteen men to the ton 600 men constituted a serious top-weight consideration in a ship the size of *Wakeful*. Accordingly they were stuffed into engine room, boiler rooms and store rooms. The route this time was by Zuydcootte Pass, where I felt our propellers hitting the sand and then up to the Kwinte Buoy where one would turn west for Dover. So as not to reveal ourselves to aircraft by a bright wake we went at only twelve knots until we neared the Kwinte Buoy where any enemy might be lurking and then increased to twenty knots with a wide zig-zag. Phosphorescence was very bright.
>
> The buoy was brightly flashing once a second and when it was about a quarter of a mile on our starboard bow I saw two tacks like white swords coming towards us from that direction. We avoided one but the other torpedo hit us in the forward boiler room with, I remember, a brilliant white flash. It transpired after the war that these torpedoes were fired by Lieutenant Zimmerman from E-boat *S-30* hiding behind the brightly flashing buoy. A well planned attack and a good shot. *Wakeful* was cut in two and the halves sank immediately until their broken ends grounded on the bottom. The fore part rolled over to starboard and it cannot have been more than fifteen seconds before I found myself swimming off the bridge.
>
> There were perhaps fifty of my men, probably gun crews, in a group in the water with me. All my engine room people had been killed and all except ten of the soldiers trapped inside the ship tragically drowned. The tide was quickly sweeping our group away from the grounded wreck and we must have been a mile or two down-tide when two Scottish wooden fishing boats on their way to Dunkirk came amongst us. The *Nautilus* picked up six, including my First Lieutenant and the *Comfort* sixteen, including myself. We tried for about half an hour to pick up others we could hear shouting in the dark but it was terribly slow work hauling out sodden, half-drowned men. Eventually the shouting stopped. The *Nautilus* went on to Dunkirk and I directed the skipper of the *Comfort* to go up-tide to the wreck, where I had last seen men sitting on the stern portion some forty feet above the water. When we got there we found the destroyer *Grafton* lying stopped with her boat over at the wreck. The *Grafton*'s deck was solid with soldiers and I went alongside her starboard quarter to tell her captain to get out of it, as there were enemy about. At that moment some sort of grenade exploded on her bridge and he was killed. Nobody seems to know what this was. At the same time there was a large explosion as a torpedo hit the *Grafton* on

> the opposite side from where *Comfort* was lying. I found myself in the water and clutched a rope's end hanging over the drifter's side. I tried to climb up it but found that the *Comfort*, apparently unharmed, was steaming away at some seven knots. I yelled to them to stop and haul me in but answer came there none; everyone on her deck had been blown overboard. As she appeared to be going in the direction of enemy-occupied Belgium it seemed best to let go and I did so – after all there was still half the *Grafton* afloat not far away.[2]

The minesweeper *Gossamer* (Senior officer, 5th Minesweeping Flotilla) was also on the scene reporting the tragedy at 0136 on 29 May. Both she and the *Grafton* had commenced searching for survivors, along with the drifter *Nautilus* and the minelayer *Comfort*. They were joined by the minesweeper *Lydd* that lowered boats. Commander Fisher, as he related, had only just shouted to *Grafton*'s Commanding Officer that he was in danger of being torpedoed himself, when a torpedo slammed into her.

The attacker was, at the time, thought to be another E-boat, but was, in fact, the submarine *U-62* (*Leutnant* Michalowski). The time of the attack was 0309 and in fact the heavy explosion was caused by *two* torpedoes hitting at the same time. *Grafton* was also packed with troops and, in the resulting confusion, yet another tragedy occurred. Thinking it was an E-boat attack, *Lydd* and the sinking destroyer both opened heavy fire on a fast-moving small shape in the vicinity. The *Lydd* went full speed ahead and rammed the intruder amidships, sending her to the bottom with her crew of dead and dying. It was, however not an E-boat but the *Comfort* running out of control, and four of her crew of six were killed, along with all but four of the survivors she had picked up from *Wakeful*. Commander Fisher had been washed overboard when she tipped up in the wake of the explosions, which wrecked *Grafton*, and so survived the carnage. He was much later rescued by the Norwegian steamer *Hird* filled with French colonial troops on their way to Cherbourg.

Aboard the *Grafton* the devastation was equally great; thirty-five Army officers asleep in her wardroom were killed instantly by one torpedo, which hit just below them, and her Captain was killed on his bridge. While she remained afloat, the very few survivors from these torpedo hits and the first afterward, were taken off by the destroyer *Ivanhoe* which, notwithstanding the dangers as witnessed by the loss of her two sisters, gallantly closed *Grafton* and took them off. This double blow was a heavy loss. The conclusion at Dover was that:

> ...there was little doubt as to what had been the cause of the sinking of HMS *Wakeful* and *Grafton* and in view of the recent reports of MTBs and submarines two of the 5th M/S Flotilla were diverted from troop carrying and ordered to search along Q.Z.S. 60 from the Middlekirk buoy 3200 to a position north of the Dyck buoy. *Vega* and the ships with her were ordered, as from daylight, to carry out an A/S search between

the South Falls and the Whistle buoy near the Kwinte Bank.

Vega later reported that she was in contact and attacking a submarine in position 510 22' North, 020 45' East, but this contact evaded her and *U-62* regrettably, made good her escape.

Accidents were the cause of most of the other casualties this day and night; the flotilla leader *Montrose* was badly damaged forward, with her stem broken and some ten feet of bow plating ripped out completely, when she was in collision with a tug, towing boats to Dunkirk near No. 2 buoy. She was forced to return to Dover with the help of a tug. The tug involved sailed back to Ramsgate safely. Another leader, *Mackay*, grounded at low water around 0136 on 29 May while on her way out through the Zuydcootte Pass. Her propeller was damaged but she made her way back to Dover after refloating on the tide. She had to go into the dockyard for repair, however. Yet a further destroyer, *Wolsey*, also suffered damaged propellers, as did *Wolfhound*, the latter again requiring docking to fix them. The drifter *Nautilus*, after her rescue mission earlier, was another casualty. The sloop *Pangbourne* (Commander F. Douglas-Watson) sighted a U-boat the next day, but was loading troops and therefore unable to attack.

Withdrawal of the Modern Destroyers

A statement occasionally found in certain post-war histories runs as follows: 'The modern destroyers were all withdrawn from the evacuation and sent to hunt E-boats off Holland.' This is totally untrue; the only destroyers sent on anti-E-boat patrol at this time were the old *Vega* joined later by the Polish *Blyskawica*. The order to withdraw the more modern destroyers was issued by the Admiralty when it seemed that there would be little further opportunity for any more lifting. Should that prove to be the case, then it was essential to provide for future national insurance by reserving an efficient force of the modern ships to bar the passage of any future German invasion force. It was also necessary to preserve the best ships for future naval battles; the war would not end with Dunkirk, but it might be jeopardized later if all Britain's modern destroyers were sunk or disabled. So it was that *Javelin, Impulsive, Havant, Harvester, Icarus, Ivanhoe* and *Intrepid* sailed, not for the Dutch coast as misreported, which would only have invited their destruction, but for Sheerness. Two other modern destroyers, *Jaguar* and *Intrepid*, had already been damaged. Two old flotilla leaders, *Mackay* and *Montrose*, both accidentally damaged as we have seen, were sailed for docking and repair in the Thames at the same time. The other destroyers left to Admiral Ramsay just carried on.

Before the order, the modern ships had indeed been hazarded; *Javelin* made two trips into the inferno. Some destroyers made two journeys each day and still kept going back for more. But the weariness was growing. Some skippers saw it coming and sensibly admitted it; the Commanding Officer of the destroyer *Vanquisher*, for example, asked to be relieved after making three trips to Dunkirk. Others just kept going to perform their duty even beyond the limits of endurance. The destroyer *Verity* had trouble with her crew and there were mumblings that they just could not go again. Her Commanding Officer reported to Admiral Ramsay, and Admiral Somerville dealt with the matter. He had earlier been over to Calais in the same ship and knew just what she had endured since that time. He quickly went aboard her in his capacity as Admiral Ramsay's deputy, and restored the situation.

Further Heavy Losses on 29 May

To aid Captain Tennant and his team ashore, and to organize the ships off the beaches, Admiral Wake-Walker was appointed at 1748 on 29 May by the Admiralty, to take command of all seagoing vessels off the Belgian coast. Wake-Walker lost no time. Embarking aboard the destroyer *Esk*, he crossed the Channel and transferred his flag to the minesweeper *Hebe* (Lieutenant Commander J. B. G. Temple) anchored offshore. With him was Commodore T. J. Hallett, charged with the direction of operations off La Panne and Bray Dunes, and a beach control party of lieutenants and senior petty officers, about eighty in total. *Hebe*, already acting as an HQ ship for some time, now became Wake-Walker's new flagship and so had no chance of any return to the comparative safely of Dover.

The temporary respite from intense dive bombing caused by the weather lasted only until midday. Then the weather brightened, and back came the *Luftwaffe*. At the time the RAF claimed to have gained local superiority over the beaches, and to have shot down sixty-seven German aircraft on 29 May for the loss of nineteen of their own. A post-war detailed study of the returns of the Quartermaster-General of the *Luftwaffe* reveals just what fantasy this was, for the Germans in reality, lost only eighteen aircraft *over the whole of France* that day! Several aircraft brought down over Dunkirk that day were destroyed by the warships' AA fire. The RAF were unable to offer the sort of air cover required by the urgency of the situation; losses were heavy.

The destoyer *Gallant* was damaged by a near miss at 1211 on 29 May, but managed to reach Dover at slow speed. The modern *Jaguar*, with a full load of troops, was hit by a bomb at 1600 and had one boiler room put out of action. Her hull was holed, and damage to her oil tanks, engine room and elsewhere, left her dead in the water. Her deck load of soldiers was taken off by other ships and *Express*, in a magnificent feat of seamanship, took her larger brethren in tow and brought her back to Dover.

Jaguar had already suffered slight damage in an earlier attack when, with *Gallant* and *Grenade*, she had been sent to try out the new swept channel route, 'Y' and engage the Calais batteries. In this earlier attack, as we have seen *Gallant* was badly hit. The worst carnage came in the late afternoon, when a Stuka attack on the crowded Mole caught a whole huddle of ships busily embarking troops. *Jaguar* was relatively lucky. *Grenade* alongside her, received a direct hit in this attack at 1602. She was packed with troops and the loss of life was enormous. Raging fires turned her into an inferno and with dead and burning men all over the ship, she drifted out of control into the harbour entrance, threatening to sink and block it at any moment. Despite the flames and further bombing, a line was got aboard her and she was towed clear just in time. As she came sway, the flames reached her magazines, both of which exploded. She sank with very few survivors.

Three French destroyers had arrived and they also took heavy damage. A bomb exploding on the quay alongside one, blasted her upperworks to shreds. *Cyclone* and *Sirocco* managed to get clear, each with 500 men aboard. *Verity* was caught up in this attack. As she cleared the harbour, she hit the submerged wreckage of a sunken drifter but managed to struggle clear. The paddle-steamer *Fenella* took a bomb through her passenger deck which scythed down many of the 600 soldiers embarked. A near miss blew in the hull beneath the waterline. Listing and sinking, her master, Captain W. Cubbon, had to abandon her. Close by, another paddle-steamer, *Crested Eagle*, took off many of her soldiers, including wounded and stretcher cases, and tried to come clear of the devastation. She had just cleared the end of the Mole when a dive bomber hit her also. Heavily on fire, with her decks covered with dead and dying, she was beached off Malo-les-Bains and burned down to sea level by 1809.

Other ships that went down beneath the Stukas' bombs at this time were the minesweeping trawler *Calvi*, which took a direct hit; another minesweeping trawler *Polly Johnson*, which was so badly damaged that she had to be sunk as she could not be saved, and the transport *King Orry*. This ship, an armed boarding vessel, had been hit on the way over and set afire, but had pluckily carried on and eventually reached the Mole, only to be hit again in the main attack. She was so full of holes that there was no question of saving her, so all efforts concentrated on getting her out of the harbour before she went down. After long and dangerous work, she was got clear and finally went down half a mile north of the entrance at about 0300 the next morning.

There were other ship casualties from air attacks that afternoon. *Intrepid*, as have seen, was one. She was hit by a bomb off La Panne at 1330, one boiler room being wrecked and the other damaged, but she made it back under her own power to Dover and then on to Sheerness. The destroyer *Saladin* was near missed and had to return to Dover, damaged. The paddle minesweeper *Gracie Fields* was lost while being towed by the minesweeper *Pangbourne* after being damaged by bombs late on 29 May, and *Kellett* was also near missed and leaking. In an attack lasting one and a half hours the sloop *Bideford* was hit in the stern and beached. The old gunboat *Locust* took her in tow for Dover.

The drifter *Girl Pamela* was already lost, being in a collision at 2330 on 28 May when passing the harbour mouth on the way to the beaches. Another drifter, *Yorkshire Lass*, was caught in a mine explosion, which wrecked another ship and had to be escorted back to Dover in an unseaworthy condition. The largest ship to take part in the Dunkirk evacuation was the 6,900-ton *Clan MacAlister* (Captain R. W. Mackie). She was sent over by the War Office with a cargo of motor landing craft to help in the evacuation. Because of her deep draught she had difficulty getting close enough to the beaches to launch these craft and some were damaged. Nonetheless, the others started ferrying troops out to her in good numbers. But she was too good a target for the Stukas to ignore. In short order she was hit by several bombs and set on fire. The flotilla leader *Malcolm* came alongside and took off the soldiers and the wounded that were on board, but the rest of the crew fought the blaze and tried to save her. Alas, to no avail. A second direct hit rekindled the fire and she had to be abandoned, and was a total loss.

Despite all this, some 55,000 men were rescued this day. It could have been more, but an alarming report from Dunkirk to Dover conveyed the impression that the outer harbour was out of action due to the wrecks from the devastating air attacks. It was some time before this error was rectified; meanwhile many ships were sent back to the less effective beach loading. It was not until the destroyer *Vanquisher* (Lieutenant Commander C. B. Alers-Hankey) had crossed to make an on the spot evaluation, that Admiral Ramsay was again confident enough to divert ships back to the harbour. The order was sent at 0600, but the whole night had been wasted.

The Triumph of the Destroyers, 30 May 1940

With the renewal of embarkations from the Mole, the lifting totals rapidly went up again. By now the slender hulls of the destroyers were being crammed even more in an all out effort to lift every man before it was too late. There was a desperate air of finality about this day, which was reflected in the number of men embarked. One historian of the campaign who was there, recorded the deeds of the destroyers thus:

> On this day seven of them landed more than 1,000 men at Dover. The ancient *Sabre*, though she had come under fire from the shore batteries, lifted 1,700 men in two trips; *Wolsey*, making amazingly quick 'turn rounds' in Dover, made three trips, lifting 1,677; *Vimy* lifted 1,472, *Express* 1,431, *Whitehall* 1,248, *Vanquisher* 1,204, *Vivacious* 1,203. The work of the destroyers throughout the day is beyond all praise. Their tasks were by no means confined to the lifting of men. Patrols were operated up to the latitude of the coast of Holland. A screen was maintained against the E-boats that had caused the heavy loss of the previous night, and anti-submarine patrols were extended. On either flank of the perimeter off Nieuport and off Mardyck, destroyers carried out counter battery fire; as the German guns opened on the shipping, they engaged them singly or in groups, fighting a strange, independent war of their own. All through the day in the reports of the masters and the skippers of the little ships their names recur – rescuing men from the water, towing broken-down craft out of danger zones, covering shipping in the anchorage and in the channels with anti-aircraft fire.

That enemy E-boats and U-boats were indeed lurking on the sidelines that night was evident from the numerous reports coming in from ships on patrol or on passage. A Polish destroyer spotted a periscope at 1541 four miles from the North Goodwin Light Vessel, and at 1729 the destroyer *Anthony* sighted no less than three suspected torpedo tracks in the same area, while E-boats were reported by *Icarus* off Bray and *Harvester* was near missed astern by torpedoes at Zuydcootte Pass. A third attack also missed a short time later, while *Vimy* sighted a conning tower and a periscope near the Goodwin Knoll.

The Beaches Reorganized, Modern Destroyers Sent Back In

Meanwhile, Admiral Wake-Walker was getting things organized afloat. To aid him and Captain Tennant and their various beach parties ashore, *Wolsey* was stationed off the beaches to provide a better W/T link, and *Wolfhound* took over a party of naval signallers. Many more small craft were now arriving to help in the shore-to-ship transfer work.

Wake-Walker himself was indefatigable this day. As the various ships he utilized as flagships embarked to capacity with fresh troops and were sent back to Dover in their turn, he was forced to transfer his flag a bewildering number of times in one day but, terrible handicap though this must have been, he got things done. After transferring from *Esk* to *Hebe* at 0400 on 30 May, his next move came when the minesweeper, her crew almost at the end of their tether, and with 700 soldiers embarked in her stubby little hull, was sent back home. This was at 1530 and Wake-Walker transferred all his staff to the destroyer *Windsor*, while he flew his flag in *MTB-102*, one of the smallest warships present. She proved to be just too small and had to be sent back, so Wake-Walker shifted to the minesweeper *Gossamer* (Commander R. C. V. Ross), took passage to La Panne and then transferred to the destroyer *Worcester* (Commander J. H. Allison). When that ship had, in turn, filled up with troops and sailed for home it was 0100 on 1 June and the Admiral's flag witnessed another transfer, to the *Express*.

The French were taking a greater share of the evacuation by this time, and several of their destroyers, which had survived Calais, now began to turn up at Dunkirk and embark troops. Admiral Abrail appealed for further ships from his bomb-proof bunker buried in the heart of the blitzed town, and these were by now arriving to swell the ranks of the British fleet. On this day also, orders coming over from Whitehall were that equal numbers of French should be embarked with the British soldiers. These orders were duly complied with as much as the situation would permit.

As well as the small craft, there were Belgian mail packets whose crews had refused to sail, and so were given British naval crews. There were also some RNLI lifeboats (although others to their shame, refused point blank to sail), Thames barges, and fishing boats, not all of which proved very suitable for the task. Most had RN, RNR or RNVR crews, and the popular idea, perpetuated by a myth-loving media down the decades, of a great number of civilians spontaneously taking their boats to Dunkirk on the spur of the moment to pick up the British army is, on the whole, a fantasy and misconception.

Mines continued to be a menace. Every night the *Luftwaffe* was busy assiduously laying fresh batches with little or no interference, and the vast fleet of minesweepers at Ramsay's disposal was at full stretch keeping the passages clear on both sides of the Channel. Enemy minelayers were reported off the Downs, Dunkirk and any other place where mines could be dropped. They continued to claim the odd victim among the great mass of shipping now abroad in that congested seaway. The heavily-laden French destroyer *Bourrasque* fell victim to them after being driven out of the safe channel by heavy shelling. She ran into a minefield at 0445 and, after explosions, sank by the stern, her depth-charges exploding as she went down and adding further to the casualties.

But the two biggest boosts to the evacuation's success that day were the recommencement of loading troops from the harbour, and the very brave decision made by the First Sea Lord, Admiral Sir Dudley Pound, for which he has never been given sufficient [or any] credit, to send back most of the undamaged modern destroyers of the Gallant, Hero, Intrepid, Havant and Javelin classes. Possible losses among these fine ships were accepted in the face of the need to lift as many Allied troops as possible and was in stark contrast to the Air Ministry's refusal to commit further fighters to the ships defence. This decision resulted in a large increase in the number of troops embarked, but at a heavy cost to the ships involved themselves. With hindsight, the right decision was made to send these new destroyers back in, some of which had only been in commission a few weeks, but the risk was huge.

Fortunately, at first, the weather favoured the evacuating ships for it prevented large scale air attacks from again being mounted, so a repeat of what had occurred on 29 May did not, at first anyway, take place. Casualties were, therefore, less severe this day, but still occurred. The transport *St. Julian* was slightly damaged by bombs at midday, as was the destroyer *Sabre* at 1800, but she suffered no casualties and the main damage was to her gyro-compass making for difficult navigation among the shoals and wrecks. Accidents indeed caused most of the damage throughout that day. The minesweeper *Sharpshooter* (Lieutenant A. E. Doran) was in collision with the transport *St Helier* and had to be towed back across the Channel. Another minesweeper, *Leda* (Lieutenant Commander H. Unwin) was slightly damaged in the same way and the destroyer *Wolsey* collided with the steamer *Roebuck*, but was able to proceed, albeit at slow speed. Several ships grounded or touched bottom in the shallow waters. The flotilla leader *Malcolm* collided with the pier at Dunkirk, *Worcester* grounded in Dunkirk Roads and damaged her propeller on submerged obstructions, which reduced her speed. The *Whitehall* (Lieutenant Commander A. B. Russell), also fouled her propeller on wreckage, putting one of her engines out of action, and so did *Vanquisher*. The drifters *Golden Gift* and

Shipmates, both went aground on the Goodwin Sands, but managed to float off again without serious injury, save perhaps to their pride! But the biggest loss took place around midnight.

The French destroyer *Sirocco* had some 750 soldiers on board in addition to her crew of 180. While in the vicinity of Kwinte Buoy she reduced speed to only seven knots in order not to give her position away to enemy aircraft by leaving a wake behind her. This gave the E-boats the opportunity to reprise their success against *Wakeful*. Two of them launched torpedoes, the *S-23* (*Leutnant* Christiansen) and *S-26* (*Leutnant* Fimmen) and, at 0120 the patrolling corvette *Widgeon* reported hearing heavy explosions. It was *Sirocco*. She had avoided the first attack, but a missile of the second struck her in her stern. Disabled, she was attacked by the *Luftwaffe* who found her at first light, one of the bombs aimed at her scoring a direct hit on her ready-use ammunition, while two more demolished her bridge. She quickly sank. Another French destroyer, *Cyclone*, also fell victim to the E-boats. The *S-24* (*Leutnant* Detlefsen) spotted her in the same area and attacked at 0200. Again, the first torpedo was avoided, but the second hit her in the bows. Going astern, she finally reached Dover Harbour. Meanwhile, *Widgeon* had picked up 166 survivors from the *Sirocco* at great risk to herself, while the trawlers *Stella Dorado* and *Wolves* rescued another twenty-one and fifty respectively.

Although, since the loss of *Grafton* and *Wakeful*, it had been known that this route was unsafe, rumours put out were that the French had not been advised of this; it appears this was not the case, however, and it is certain from signals that the Captain of the *Cyclone* was most definitely informed of the new route 'Y', but still opted for the more risky northern passage.

The Strain Begins to Tell Still Further

The heavy strain under which the crews of the warships had now been under for many days was increasingly manifesting itself. The official report for 30 May describes it this way:

> This time there appeared the first signs that ships' companies, and particularly officers, were beginning to suffer from the strain of the pressures at which they had been working; in some cases for nearly four days with no stand-off at all. This was most noticeable in the cases of some of the destroyers upon whom, as usual, the most arduous tasks had fallen. In anticipation and to obviate the risk of any ships being put out of commission from this cause, arrangements had been made for spare destroyers' crew and 50 additional suitable ratings as well as spare hands for small craft, to be sent to Dover in case they should be needed.

Some of the destroyers, damaged in the earlier operations off Calais and Boulogne, began to re-emerge from the dockyards to take up the fight once more. Some of the 19th Flotilla, including *Whitshed*, had now had their defects patched up and their crews given a brief respite. They were, therefore, ready to be sent back into the fray as the evacuation reached its climax, and relieve those whose crews had had no rest for many days. Nonetheless, even aboard these ships, tiredness remained, for some, overwhelming, and was mixed with acute depression at the thought of going back to face the non-stop bombing with no sign of air protection. The Medical Officer of *Whitshed* reported one such case when two ABs, both of whom had previously been '..jocular, mentally robust men' had now become '...sullen, morose, depressed, hard-faced and silent. Occasionally they wrung their hands. Their effect on their messmates was depressing...'. It was reported that both declared that they would jump over the side rather than face another night at Dunkirk. Both were eventually cured. Such depression could spread rapidly if unchecked. The same MO reported another case aboard the minesweeper *Hebe* after her ordeal. Nobody aboard her had slept for five days and, on 1 June, in Dover Harbour, crew were afflicted, including some officers, which necessitated hospitalization. The minesweeper *Hussar* suffered similarly; 'when given an order, the crew broke and wept'. She, too, was temporarily taken out of commission.

There is no need to elaborate on these episodes. They were not the only ships so affected, and there need be no censure. The most notable thing is that, in the overwhelming majority of cases, the crews continued to go back into the inferno again and again, in spite of the dangers and hardships. Those that went and those that broke are equally worthy of our admiration for their endurance under conditions inconceivable seventy years on.

Extension of the Deadline, 31 May 1940

Lord Gort had signalled that it was possible to extend the evacuation, and Admiral Ramsay had the ships available to comply as best he could. The weather had changed again; a light wind caused difficulties in the loadings from the beaches, the consequent slow liftings caused the postponement of sailings lest congestion took place. German artillery was now well established north of the beaches as well as south, so the new 'Y' route was mainly used. By this time large numbers of French troops were flooding in and British vessels had increasingly to take over their rescue. More than 9,000 French troops had already been brought out up to that date. That number was to increase by more than tenfold, and they were mainly carried in British hulls.

Notes

1. It *may* have been militarily necessary, but it was the manner in which it was done that created the ill-feeling generally, and speed with which the Belgians rounded upon those who they had been crying out to help them just days before. One young Pilot Officer in the RAF recorded how: 'The feelings against the Belgians ran very high and one lady told us at one station they had a train of Belgians and a train of Scottish in at the same time. The latter started to go for the Belgians and they had great difficulty in stopping them. Apparently, there were large numbers of Belgian civilians who turned out to be Fifth Columnists and snipers. Bob Davidson only lost four men from his platoon and they were all shot by Belgians.' See Norman Franks, *The Air Battle of Dunkirk*, William Kimber, London 1938, p 145.

2. Rear Admiral R. L. Fisher, *Salt Horse: A naval life*, Famedram, Gartocharn, 1978, pp 122

Chapter Five

Dunkirk: The Task Completed

Ramsay's report of the events of 31 May read as follows:

> Operation *Dynamo* was pressed on with all energy and by noon/31st approximately 164,000 men (including 14,000 Allied troops) had been landed in England. The day was a repetition of previous days in almost every respect except that it was thought that the night would see the conclusion of the operation, and plans were made accordingly for the greatest possible number of ships to be available for the last trip. A large additional fleet of motor and pulling boats for beach work had also been dispatched. Eventually, however, it was decided that it would be possible to continue the evacuation for another 24 hours.

In fact, the evacuation continued for much longer than this, despite the heavy losses and the need for still more ships to be sent for repairs. The destroyer *Greyhound* sailed for Sheerness, having been damaged on 31 May, and the equally battered *Gallant* and *Jaguar* left for the Humber. Nor did the casualties stop, even though the *Luftwaffe* this day was mainly busy about other matters. The bombing might have been light compared with that which had taken place the day before, and what was to come, but it was still effective from time to time. The modern destroyer *Harvester* was near missed, damaged and put out of action; the coastal corvette *Kingfisher* was also bombed and damaged; she was able to operate in fine, calm weather only. The destroyer *Anthony* had engine room and machinery damage.

Once more it was accidents, mainly collisions, that proved to be the main hazard. The shallow waters off the beaches were now littered with wrecks as well as the usual flotsam and jetsam of war, and high speed operations, such as 'jinking' to dodge bombs and the like, could lead to other dangers. The destroyers *Icarus* and *Scimitar* collided at 1147, the larger vessel *Icarus* being only slightly damaged and not put out of action, while the much smaller 'S' class vessel, a mere 900-tonner dating back to the First World War, came off far worse, reporting herself to be 'only seaworthy in calm weather and at low speed in the gravest emergency'. She was ordered back to Dover. Another destroyer, *Vimy*, was in collision with the armed yacht *Amulree* in the early hours of 1 June. The destroyer returned to Dover out of action, the yacht sank. *Venomous* had her stern knocked about while berthing at the Mole, but carried on. *Impulsive* joined the long list of ships that damaged their propellers on sunken wreckage, seriously enough for her to be withdrawn. Later that night, or in the early hours of 1 June, the E-boats came skulking back. One A/S trawler was torpedoed and sunk at 0430 1 June; another, *Argyllshire*, went down to a U-boat attack a few hours earlier, while the coastal corvette *Widgeon* was near-missed by a torpedo at 0044. British MTBs were sent over from the Nore to patrol off Nieuport in the hope of engaging the enemy, but without success.

Further Criticism of the Rescue, 31 May

Despite the resolution expressed at the conference held at Dover on 31 May for the evacuation to be pressed ahead 'with the utmost vigour' and that reinforcements of smaller ships were to help with the loading of the larger craft, the weather and sea swell did more than the enemy in slowing down the embarkation rate this day. Shore-to-ship communications were certainly vastly improved, but the freshening wind resulted in Wake-Walker having to signal that beach evacuation had become practically impossible for the time being, while the increased shelling by the growing number of German guns around the ever-shrinking perimeter was making the loading of troops from the harbour even more hazardous. This information was conveyed to Dover by Captain Tennant. On receipt of his signals it was felt in the Dynamo Room that to continue sailing these ships would only result in unnecessary congestion off the beaches without contributing to the lift. There was never any intention to do more than give a slight pause to the momentum, and loading by night was to be increased.

Luckily the weather moderated as the day wore on, and once again a host of small vessels was able to ply between the destroyers and personnel ships and the beaches in greater number. In all, 68,014 men were lifted on that day, 31 May. After this, the beaches at La Panne were abandoned and the loading continued from Bray as well as from the harbour throughout the night. Some of the smaller ships' skippers could not quite grasp all the reasons behind their deployments. Typical was the statement made by Captain N. Baxter of the Southern Railway steamer *Whitstable* which arrived off Bray Dunes at 0820 but remained empty and not approached until 1430. 'It seemed to me very unfair that we merchantmen were kept waiting in a very dangerous position while ships armed to the teeth came in, loaded up, and departed again in an hour or so.' After another hour, German shells dropping close by forced *Whitstable* even further out to sea.

The account given by Major R. L. Hutchins of the Grenadier Guards, who was master of one of the War Department launches, *Swallow*, working off the beaches, was more sympathetic:

> Each time after loading, I proceeded alongside *Impulsive*, which had a 'jumping ladder' rigged. In order to avoid waste of time in shortening in my 80-fathom towline, I passed the end of it to *Impulsive* and requested her to haul the boats alongside, which was done by part of the ship's

company doubling along her deck. After the first trip, I borrowed *Impulsive*'s Whaler and two more hands, and made a number of trips from shore to ship, towing both boats. There were at this time very few boats working between the shore and the ships, but there were some boats full of troops broached-to on the beach and unable to get off. One motor-boat belonging to a destroyer, one whaler, and a small motor-yacht were the only boats working on two or three miles of beach, and in view of the target presented to enemy aircraft by destroyers and other ships waiting to embark troops, I requested *Impulsive* to transmit a signal from me to Admiralty, repeated V-A Dover, requesting more cutters and power boats to speed up the embarkation. There was some shelling of the beaches, and a good deal of AA from the ships as German aircraft appeared overhead at frequent intervals.

At about mid-day, *Impulsive* hoisted two black shapes, and when I next came alongside she reported that she had struck some wreckage and damaged her port propeller (this happened, I think, while she was taking avoiding action during an attack by aircraft).

As *Impulsive* had to proceed for docking, I returned her whaler and the borrowed ratings who had manned my cutter, and proceeded to work with *Winchelsea*. Up to this time *Impulsive* had taken some 400 soldiers... .

In the early afternoon the wind lightened and conditions became easier. Observing that there were boats at the davits of a wreck (the Southern Railway Company's s.s. *Lorina*) close inshore, I borrowed some hands from *Winchelsea* to lower and man them, and ordered an RAF launch which was lying astern of a neighbouring vessel to take over these boats ex the wreck and embark troops.

Soon after this, on the suggestion of the captain of *Winchelsea* (Lieutenant Commander W. A. F. Hawkins, RN) I boarded *Keith* to discuss with Rear Admiral Wake-Walker the possibility of making all remaining troops march to Dunkirk for embarkation. The Admiral concurred in the suggestion and asked me to try to get in touch with the military commanders on shore and to give orders to the troops to march to the piers, in contradiction of previous orders... .

By 5.30 pm there were few troops waiting to embark at this part of the beach and the remainder were making their way along the beach to Dunkirk, and at this time *Winchelsea* signalled proposing that this should be the last trip; I concurred. In the last trip only about thirty soldiers embarked in the cutter, and I transferred them to the cabin and engine room of my boat, handing over the cutter to the RAF launch. During this last half-hour several dive-bombing attacks were made on *Winchelsea*, which appeared to be straddled by the first salvo. A transport further to the eastward was hit about this time, and enemy air activity was intense. *Swallow* was hit by a few small splinters, presumable of anti-aircraft shell, but was undamaged.

There was a grave significance in this last statement. The weather had cleared, speeding up the loading, but with the return of good weather came the Stukas. Dusk fell before they could make a big impact but come the dawn they would be ready and waiting once more.

Carnage Off the Beaches, 1 June 1940

The Royal Navy doubled its efforts next day; the RAF reduced theirs, flying just 558 sorties that day against 704 on 30 May; the results of these two decisions were predictable. Dawn found a whole mass of shipping busily engaged in rescue work. In spite of intense bombing and grievous losses, they managed to lift 64,429 soldiers on 1 June, the majority of them French, despite claims to the contrary by German and Vichy propaganda shortly afterwards. For example, the personnel ship *Prague* embarked some 3,000 French *poliu*'s, the *Scotia* 2,000 Frenchman, the old paddle steamer *Brighton Queen* 700 Moroccans. The destroyers were equally dedicated to their task, some 1,000 troops apiece being typical loads, which were often exceeded. None could have been more wholehearted in their efforts to aid our Ally *in extremis*.

By first light it was clear that the day was destined to be a fine one with regard to the weather; clear, sunny, marvellous boating weather in fact. It was, unfortunately, also marvellous dive bomber weather and, relatively unhampered by the efforts of the reduced RAF patrols, that had neither the weight of numbers, nor the continuity of effort to form an effective screen, they duly arrived over the crowded roadstead. The *Luftwaffe* threw in the Me109s of Colonel Osterkamp's JG 51, while the Me110s of Lieutenant Colonel Huth's ZG 26 were more than a match for the few British fighters they met. Heavy and repeated waves of Junkers Ju87s, supported by some of the twin-engined Junkers Ju88s, were able to inflict great damage. They faced opposition from the AA guns of the ships but, even here, they arrived just at the right time, for many destroyers and other warships had just about expended their total AA shell complement in fighting off the previous day's attacks. The paramount need to unload troops at Dover and race back for the next consignment, left no time to embark further shells, even if the dog-tired ships companies had been capable of doing so. It was a desperately slender defence that the Stuka dive bomber aircrews had to face on that brilliant June day. Among the many victims were two destroyers of the 19th Flotilla, just returned to the beaches.

Loss of HMS *Basilisk*

The destroyer *Basilisk* (Commander Maxwell Richmond) was embarking British troops at about 0815 when the first wave of dive bombers came in. A *Staffel* of nine Stukas selected *Basilisk* as their main target immediately, making their approach and final attack from dead astern. As they came wailing down, her commanding officer ordered full speed ahead and, watching astern as the first bombs were released, he ordered the destroyer's helm hard to port. Commander Richmond later wrote:

As far as I could judge each aircraft released a pattern of five bombs [actually three] one being a larger 'B' type and four smaller bombs with slight delay action. One of the latter exploded at the after end of No 1 Boiler Room on the port side and blew away the bulkhead, piercing both main and auxiliary steam lines and the main fuel oil supply. All engine room and boiler room personnel were killed.

Further dive bombers followed their leader down upon the now-crippled destroyer.

About six of the 'B' type bombs then exploded underneath the ship, flooding the after magazine and shell room and probably the gland compartments and store rooms just forward of this position. The upper deck and sides of the ship cracked right across in the vicinity of the mainmast.

In order to preserve stability, the torpedoes and depth-charges were jettisoned and the ship floated comfortably with little increase in draught. I inspected engine room and No 1 boiler room and found that a small amount of water was making its way through shrapnel holes. These were plugged and collision mats placed over the worst leaks. It was found impossible to get steam to the engines and thereafter the ship remained immobile.

Considerable efforts were made to get a message through to a tug which been attending HMS *Keith*, but she was less than helpful, as the *Basilisk*'s Chief Yeoman recalled later:

Called in direction of a tug and *Salamander* [minesweeper]. When realized it was *Salamander* called with her pennants. She was facing towards *Basilisk* but did not answer. Called for about twenty minutes with Aldis. Tug called *Basilisk* and made 'Go and sink destroyer *Keith*. *Basilisk* made 'Q' and made 'AAA-P'. Tug still made 'AAA'. *Basilisk* made 'Q'. Could see he would not read *Basilisk*, so decided to read his message. 'Proceed and sink *Keith* by gunfire by firing at water level and destroyer Asdic cabinet. D19 standing by to watch you sink her. Sorry to trouble you.' Made the following signals back and forth. *Basilisk* 'I am out of action'. Tug: 'Sink her with torpedoes.' *Basilisk*; 'I have jettisoned torpedoes.' Tug: 'Sink her with depth charges.' *Basilisk*: 'I have no depth charges, I am out of action, require immediate assistance tug.' Tug: R'. After fifteen to twenty minutes calling up made the following signal to tug: 'Pass information to VA Dover "*Basilisk* out of action require immediate assistance and tug."' 'Tug made 'R'.' After another high bombing raid tug was not seen again. Fired two white rockets.

A Belgian fishing smack under French colours was then seen, and *Basilisk*'s motor boat was dispatched to summon her to their aid. It was then that, after some effort and language difficulties, a tow was passed but hardly had this been accomplished when a second bombing attack developed, fortunately though this was a high-level attack. *Basilisk* as a stationary sitting duck proved too great a temptation to be ignored. Again the squadron concentrated their attentions upon her and her little consort. Commander Richmond commented that, 'Considering the ship was a stationary target and there was little wind these attacks were poorly carried out and no bombs hit. This may have been due to pom-pom fire of which our Gunner (T) was in charge. Unfortunately this gallant officer was killed at his post by machine-gun fire as the bombers crossed overhead.'

A second attempt had been made to get the ship towed clear of the beaches but they had not progressed very far before yet a third attack was made. This was carried out by a squadron of *Henschel* 1 [*sic*] dive bombers. By now almost all the destroyer's AA ammunition had been shot off and the main armament of 4.7-inch guns were firing SAP shells in the remote hope of keeping the enemy at a distance. The Germans, however, in Commander Richmond's words:

> ...made a determined diving attack, which was well pressed home to about 400 feet. The ship was completely smothered by hits and near misses, some of which were of the 'B' bomb type. The ship immediately began to settle and I gave the order to abandon ship. Thanks to the adequate preparations made by my First Lieutenant, Lieutenant-Commander W. G. Boake, RN, there were plenty of boats and Carley floats ready for survivors. After collecting all stray swimmers the boats and floats pulled out to sea. *Le Jolie Mascotte* picked up six officers and 71 ratings and HMS *Whitehall* two officers and 52 ratings.
>
> HMS *Basilisk* sank in about four fathoms of water with her upper deck awash. Although the Asdic and VC-VF gear and all important documents had been destroyed I was anxious to complete the destruction of the vessel. Accordingly I requested the Captain of HMS *Whitehall* to fire guns and torpedoes [into her]. This was done and the ship was left on fire forward.

Commander Richmond made the following very pertinent statement later:

> I would like to emphasize that the older destroyers with pom-poms using belted ammunition and 4.7-inch guns with only 30 degrees elevation are no match for a determined air attack. Our Lewis guns had also been recently surrendered. When ships of this type are operating within range of enemy air attack losses must be expected unless adequate fighter protection is afforded. In all, enemy launched our big air attacks at about hourly intervals during the forenoon of the 1st June. The first, second and fourth were apparently unopposed by any British aircraft...I would also like to state that from my observation the enemy aircraft, even when opposed, were always more numerous than our own and in the subsequent air battles our fighters, although outnumbered, fought most courageously and effectively, but generally lost more planes than the enemy. From our point of view the BBC Bulletins describing the

air attacks off Dunkirk *entirely misrepresent the true situation.*

These were sentiments heard time and time again, both from the ships and from ashore. While realizing and acknowledging the courage of our greatly outnumbered pilots, and in some cases appreciating the reasons for the stream of totally false MOI and BBC propaganda, the men on the spot were acutely aware of the true situation, and were often sickened by what they saw as a misleading campaign, which uncritically glorified the RAF, and which they regarded as amateurish misrepresentation of the true state of affairs. Unfortunately, this is the picture that has stuck in the history books and assumed the quality of a legend, and was to be repeated, on a far greater scale, during the Battle of Britain.

Loss of HMS *Keith*

Some of the mystery surrounding the apparent incompetence of the tug that proved herself so strangely ineffective in reading the *Basilisk*'s last signals, can be partly understood if we go back to the time of the first dive bombing attack. The Flotilla Leader *Keith* (Captain E. L. Berthon, DSC), flying the flag of Admiral Wake-Walker still, was lying close to *Basilisk* and was also selected by the Stukas of the first *Gruppen*, who made a dead-set at her. She was in the unenviable position, even before the first Stuka descended, of being down to her last thirty rounds of AA shell. Like *Basilisk*, she immediately went to full speed and zigzagged around the crowded anchorage in an effort to throw the Stuka pilots off their aim. In this, she was partially successful, but not enough to save herself. Although no bombs actually scored any direct hits on her, there were numerous very near misses, which caused her rudder to jam and left her turning in small circles until she could be brought under control.

A report from the Master of the tug *Cervia* (Captain W. H. Simmons) gives a graphic account of the first attack on *Keith*:

> A British destroyer outside of us began to fire at the enemy planes and bombs began to fall near her as she steamed about. At full speed with her helm hard to port, nine bombs fell in a line in the water, along her starboard side, and they exploded under water, heeling the destroyer over on her beam ends, but she was righted again. A sloop joined in the gunfire, also shore batteries, and as the raiders made off over the land they machine-gunned us and we returned the fire with our Lewis gun.

Eventually, the wayward *Keith* was brought under some degree of control and sped on to avoid a second wave bearing down on her. She was again turning hard to port when the first bombs of the attack thudded down, and this time, by extreme bad fortune, as well as many near misses, one bomb went straight down her after funnel. As the boiler rooms were wrecked by the detonation deep inside her, huge clouds of steam gushed up the funnel and, wreathed in this and the smoke from her guns and fires aboard, she heeled hard over to port and began to slow down. After a while Captain Berthon managed to anchor her with a twenty-degree list and only two feet of re-board. But, for a while, her riven hull seemed to hold together and she neither listed nor sank any further.

The *MTB-102* closed the stricken vessel and embarked Admiral Wake-Walker and his staff, and then went to seek some tugs to help the destroyer. Three were already on their way to her aid, the Admiralty tug *St Abbs* and the commercial tugs *Cervia* and *Vincia*, along with the *Schuit Hilda*. But, even as they drew close, a third wave of dive bombers was seen on its way down. One heavy bomb took her right under her bridge structure and she was thrown over until she capsized, going down very fast, her battered little hull unable to endure any more punishment. Many survivors were seen in the water and the scurrying tugs picked up most of them; *Hilda* fifty, *Vincia* 108 and *St Abbs* 100 respectively, including Captain Berthon. With these aboard, Captain Berthon turned to assist *Basilisk* and it was *St Abbs*, which approached that vessel as related earlier. It was while an attack was being mounted by Junkers Ju88s that *St Abbs* herself was hit and sunk in one instant explosion with very few survivors. Amazingly the redoubtable Captain D19 also survived this second sinking.

Further Casualties of the First Dive Bomber Attacks of 1 June

The loss of two invaluable destroyers was bad enough, but that was by no means the end of the enemy success in this first mass Stuka raid. The minesweeper *Skipjack* (Lieutenant Commander F. B. Proudfoot) had embarked some 275 soldiers up to the moment of the raid and had stowed them securely below. Hit by a bomb amidships, she sank very quickly indeed and few of her crew and none of the troops survived. Her sister ships *Salamander* (Lieutenant Commander L. J. S. Ede), which had to have help from tugs, and *Hebe*, which received slight bomb damage in the next big raid at 0940 were both damaged. The destroyers *Ivanhoe* and *Vivacious* (Lieutenant Commander F. W. R. Parish) were also damaged in these early raids and forced to return to Dover, the former under tow and out of action. The fine new destroyer *Havant* became another casualty at 0905. She had already made three trips to the beaches, embarking 500 French troops from Bray Dunes, 932 more on the second trip and a further 1,000 on her third, from which she had returned from Dover at 0230 on 1 June. Now she was back yet again, and had taken on board another 500 soldiers when the *Ivanhoe* was hit amidships. *Havant* moved closer to render assistance and, going alongside, took off troops and wounded crew members from that destroyer. *Havant* herself then proceeded down channel but, just off the entrance to the harbour, she was attacked again.

Stukas attacked in a power dives and two bombs exploded under her hull, while a third dropped some fifty yards ahead and detonated as she passed over it. One survivor, wounded at the time, recalled:

I remember it took quite a long time before the ship finally went down.

> I'll never forget the captain of the *Ivanhoe* shouting at us 'Get out of here or you'll end up the same as us!' As it was, within a few minutes we were hit by the bombs. It was a great pity *Havant* was sunk, but things were desperate in those days and we were doing a job. We were never idle, and we were rescuing people, so it was all worthwhile.

The minesweeper *Saltash* (Lieutenant Commander T. R. Fowke) came alongside *Havant*, and attempts were made to get a tow started, but it was all in vain and, at 1015, some five miles from 'W' buoy, she sank. Her casualties were one officer and seven ratings killed and twenty-five wounded with about the same number of troops injured or killed. She was joined on the bottom by the ancient river-gunboat *Mosquito*, a long way from the Yangtze River or Mesopotamia, the exotic habitats for which she had originally been built to fight. This little vessel was also hit by a heavy bomb, set afire and eventually had to be abandoned at 1030.

Casualties were also severe among the merchant ships and other Allied warships. The hospital ship *St David*, was properly marked and had sent signals to inform the Germans of her duties and timing, but was forced to turn back due to shelling. She anchored off Dover, but was not safe even there, for, at 0845 a magnetic mine was detonated by a speeding ship close by and the explosion badly damaged her. Off Dunkirk itself, the personnel ships came in for a hammering. *Prague* had loaded some 3,000 French soldiers and got clear of the harbour in the midst of the bedlam of the first attack, unscathed, but suffered shelling off Gravelines and then a dive bombing attack in the vicinity of 'V' Buoy at 0927. Further damage was taken which caused numerous leaks and, by 1630, her starboard engine was out of action and she was settling. Several naval vessels closed in to render assistance. First alongside was the little 900-ton destroyer *Shikari* and she took aboard 500 men while both ships were still under way. As she backed off, the paddle minesweeper *Isle of Thanet* (Captain S. P. Herival, RNVR) took her place and embarked more that 1,500. Still moving sluggishly forward, *Prague* continued to sink and the coastal corvette *Shearwater* came alongside and took off the remaining 200 troops and landed them at Sheerness. With the majority of her soldier passengers safe, her crew made every effort to save her, but eventually *Prague* had to be towed and beached off Sandwich Flats.

Second Wave of Dive Bombing Around Midday, 1 June

The German dive bombers returned in equally large numbers between 1200 and 1300 and once more found the waters studded with suitable targets, virtually undefended save for the AA guns, and with little room for them to manoeuvre. The French destroyer *Foudroyant* approaching Dunkirk at 1300 by way of Route 'X' in a narrow channel, sprang such a trap. In the graphic and unforgettable words of the official French report, she was 'submerged in a cloud of Stukas'. Several bombs were hits or very near misses, and she capsized and sank almost at once. Small vessels scurried to pick up survivors and they were also bombed. At the same time the troop transport *Scotia* went down. She had reached No 6 Buoy when twelve dive bombers selected her as their target. She was overwhelmed with hits and near misses, two early bombs striking her aft and being followed by a third which went down the ship's funnel. Mortally wounded, she heeled sharply over to starboard and began sinking by the stern. Almost all her ship's boats had been smashed and the French soldiers, in their panic oblivious to all discipline, tried to rush the remainder. Luckily, the destroyer *Esk* (Commander Couch) was quickly alongside and with great skill he placed his destroyer's bow close alongside the sinking transport's forecastle and embarked troops that way, at the same time keeping up a brisk fire upon further enemy bombers which approached them.

Scotia heeled over until her port bilge keel was out of the water, with hundreds of frightened troops huddled aboard unable to swim or to even understand shouted instructions in English from the *Esk*. The destroyer was therefore manoeuvred around to that she could get to these men. Captain Hughes was the last man to be taken off. Some thirty of the ship's company and between 200 and 300 of the French soldiers were lost, but the saving of the greater majority was due entirely to the consummate skill of the British destroyer skipper and the calmness of the old coal-burner's captain, who had to threaten the scared troops with a pistol in order to restore order, before he could save them.

In strict contrast, some 700 Moroccan troops aboard the *Brighton Queen*, were said to have behaved 'steadily and intelligently though nearly half of them were killed by the explosion' when that ship was bombed east of the narrows. The rest were taken off by the minesweeper *Saltash*. Another troop transport damaged, was *Maid of Orleans*; the drifter *Lord Cavan* was sunk, as was the yacht *Grive*, the latter by a mine; while yet another of the newer destroyers, *Icarus*, collided with a small craft in the early hours of 2 June and was damaged. At 1600, a flotilla of French small craft, naval auxiliaries, was shelled and then attacked by Stukas off No 6 Buoy, losing the *Denis Papin*, *Venus* and *Moussaillon*.

Thirteen enemy aircraft were claimed shot down by the ships during this day, despite the lack of ammunition and other difficulties. In addition to her contribution to the lift by evacuating 1,856 soldiers, the AA cruiser *Calcutta* kept up a steady stream of fire during this period. She was the only ship really capable of giving as good as she got, for she had eight 4-inch AA guns in four twin mountings, a quadruple 2-pounder pom-pom and eight 0.5-inch machine guns in two quadruple mountings. She could therefore throw up quite a respectable field of fire for the period. The only weapons carried by the majority of the destroyers were the short-range multiple machine guns, which just did not have the weight of shell and explosive power to destroy modern bomber aircraft, although they might distract or impede its attack. A few of the older Flotilla Leaders were lucky enough to still carry a single 3-inch High Angle gun, but it lacked a director so was of limited value other than to morale. These ships had been designed in 1918 but this foresight of an earlier age had not been repeated in the majority of the destroyers built for the Royal Navy after that date and none had the dual-purpose main armaments routinely carried by their counterparts in the United States or Japanese Navies. Most had elevations restricted to a mere 30 or 40 degrees, which could engage level bombers at long-range but were totally useless against the Stukas which came down almost vertically. British ordnance seemed incapable of providing weapons capable of dealing with them. It was to be many years before sufficient imported and licence-built Swiss 20-mm Oerlikon cannon became readily available and even longer before the Swedish Bofors 40-mm gun arrived along with radar prediction and gyroscopic controls to give destroyers a half-chance of fighting back.

Until then all the warships could do was go to top speed, manoeuvre and hope for the best, which, as we have seen, was too often totally inadequate. More fortunate, ironically, were some of the oldest destroyers of the 'V' and 'W' classes which had been rearmed with two twin 4-inch HA guns just prior to the war as Anti-Aircraft Convoy Escorts ('WAIRS'), but as we have seen even these were vulnerable. They were worth their weight in gold but, as recorded, four of the six sent were put out of the fight even before the Dunkirk evacuation had begun.

Night Loading Adopted 1-2 June 1940

The heavy losses taken on 1 June, coupled with the fact that German heavy guns now dominated all three approach sea routes into Dunkirk, meant that the final stages of the evacuation had to proceed mainly during the hours of darkness. It was at first hoped to complete this on the night of 1-2 June, but reports continued to be received of more and more troops, mainly French, waiting for rescue, and Admiral Ramsay continued to extend the deadline and send over more ships. At the same time, plans were put in hand to block the outer harbour, in order to deny it to the enemy once the last defenders were brought away. Unfortunately, the French estimates of the number of troops kept changing and, to the end, proved wildly inaccurate. Although, therefore, the ships sent across were always more than requested, they were never sufficient.

During the first night, the destroyers *Codrington, Sabre, Whitshed, Windsor* and *Winchelsea* all brought away large numbers of combatants. Their approach to the deserted piers was described in this manner:

> From the North Goodwin Light Vessel, Dunkirk was unmistakable. It was only necessary to trace a big black cloud, which stretched for miles below the moon, follow it along to the point where the cloud was broken by stabs of flame and there – in the centre of the flames – was Dunkirk. In that inferno, tens of thousands of our men had been waiting all day for the night of rescue, cursing and praying, dying and suffering but, above all, hoping with a gallant confidence, which has never been surpassed.

> To handle a destroyer in the narrow approach channel under the conditions prevailing, required a rare combination of skill and coolness. Many of the original buoys, which marked the track, were now out of position, wrecks had to be avoided and the danger of serious collision with other vessels was always present. There was only one thing to do; shut one's ears to the noise of gun or bomb and concentrate solely on handling the ship.

By dawn on 2 June, some 64,429 troops had been brought back to England. It was decided to make another great effort on the following night and, if that were successful, to repeat it the night after. Admiral Ramsay had banned day evacuations for most ships due to the continued heavy losses, which were still mounting. The destroyer *Worcester*, having been badly damaged by bombs off the beaches on 1 June, had been towed across the Channel before her engines were somehow restarted and she crept the rest of the way into Dover under her own power. Within sight of safety, indeed at the very entrance to Dover Harbour, she was rammed by the Personnel Ship *Maid of Orleans* at around 2040. Both ships were badly damaged and put out of action. Up to that time *Worcester* had made a total of six trips to the beaches and brought back 4,350 men. She was sailed to Tilbury for repairs on 3 June. The damaged minesweepers *Salamander* and *Sharpshooter* had left for Sheerness on 2 June, and so the melancholy procession continued. Other vessels, with no need to be there, were caught up in the congestion in the English Channel. For example, the neutral Swedish steamer *Emma*, stoically ploughing through the stream of evacuation vessels, collided with the French steamer *Hebe* east-south-east of the South Foreland lighthouse and sank. Nor did the German Air Force ever deign to cease its nightly minelaying drops off the south coast harbours. The minesweeping forces, which had suffered heavy losses as we have seen, were kept at full stretch clearing and re-clearing the safety routes.

Continued Losses in the Channel during Daylight Hours

Even the fact that the main evacuations were now proceeding during the hours of darkness did not prevent further casualties by day. One of the most callous acts carried out by the Germans had been the shelling and bombing of hospital ships. This reached a peak on 2 June when *Worthing* was damaged by bombs between 'U' and 'W' buoys while on passage to Dunkirk at 1442. This hospital ship was properly marked, and the attack took place in full daylight, so there could only have been a very small possibility of recognition error. She was forced to return to Newhaven.

A more legitimate target was the Personnel Ship *Mona's Isle*, whose engine room was damaged by near misses during that morning, but which managed to reach Dover. The troop transports *Ben-My-Cree* and *Royal Daffodil* were both damaged by collision early on 3 June. Another hospital ship was attacked on Sunday 2 June, this time with more serious consequences. The vessel concerned was the *Paris*, which had picked up reports of the attack on her sister ship earlier. She signalled for instructions and was told to continue. This she did, but met with the same fate, being bombed by two aircraft and near-missed. Damage was caused to her machinery and her captain had her lifeboats swing out and fired distress rockets. Fifty minutes later the *Luftwaffe* responded and fifteen more aircraft attacked, again scoring near misses and so adding to her damage that she was abandoned near 'W' buoy at 1915.

Enemy submarines were still about their stealthy work, and among their victims on the afternoon of 2 June was the anti-submarine trawler *Blackburn Rovers*, torpedoed and sunk near 'T' buoy at 1618. Her sister sweeper, *Westella*, immediately went to her assistance, and was stopped, picking up survivors at 1639, when the U-boat terminated this errand of mercy, slamming a torpedo into her. The U-boat in question was spotted by the trawler *Saon*, and two French destroyers were dispatched to hunt her down, but to no avail.

Collisions damaged two of the destroyers earmarked for the night's evacuation work; the Flotilla Leader *Malcolm* had her bow and propeller damaged at 1651 while *Whitshed* had, at 1435, been in collision with *Java*, but both carried on in spite of the damage received. In all, eleven destroyers, thirteen Personnel Ships and a host of lesser craft were sent over that night and between them brought out 26,256 men. The destroyers *Venomous, Winchelsea* and *Windsor*, and the Personnel Ships *King George V, Rouen, Royal Sovereign* and *St Helier*, all got out large numbers, but many ships returned almost empty when troops ashore failed to show up as prearranged. By 2330 Captain Tennant was able to send the welcome signal: 'BEF evacuated.'

The relief felt, that so much had been achieved, especially compared with the trickle that had been the most hoped for a week earlier, was reflected in the Dover Command War Diary for that day:

> Notwithstanding the continuous strain, which for a week almost all officers and ships' companies had been undergoing, they responded, practically without exception, in the affirmative to a call for information as to which ship would be available for yet another night at sea. Incidents demonstrating the magnificent spirit and determination of the naval personnel were innumerable throughout the whole period of the operation. Some idea of the conditions under which the operations had been conducted was afforded by the fact that out of over 40 destroyers involved, only 13 remained fit for service.

But it was *still* not yet over at Dunkirk.

The Lift Continues, 3-4 June 1940

With the departure of the last of the mercantile rescue ships on 3 June, the destroyer *Vivacious* (Commander E. F. V. Dechaineux, RAN) arrived off the harbour with the three blockships to sink in the entrance. In fact one of these vessels, *Holland*, ran aground in the approach channel to the port. The other two ships, *Edward Nissen* and *West Cove*, moved in for the last five miles and, at 0300 and 0310 respectively, both were scuttled. Unfortunately, the wind and tide caused them to drift out of the main airway. Commander Dechaineux had to signal: 'It is unfortunate that the block was not complete and navigation in the approach channel is still possible.' VA Dover immediately assembled a second blocking force to try again.

Other essential work was in hand at this time. The cable ship *Alert* had started to lift the cables from the seabed and cut them as far as possible from the English coasts. The following links with Nazi-held Europe were severed: Middelkoerk-Dumpton, La Panne-St Margaret's, Calais – St Margaret's, Gris Nez – Abbotscliff, Andrecelle – Seabrook, Andrecelle – Dungeness, La Portel – Dungeness. Britain was making herself ready for the lone fight that lay ahead.

Damaged ships continued to sail from Dover to places of repair. For example the sloop *Bideford* was towed to Portsmouth by the trawlers *Olvina* and *Topaze*. By now, none of the original or reinforced Dover Command destroyers remained operational and The Nore had to transfer three more such ships to Ramsay in order to provide even a semblance of a flotilla. These were *Vega* (Commander G. J. Horton), *Vesper* (Lieutenant Commander W. F. E. Hussey) and *Wanderer* (Commander J. H. Ruck-Keene) and all arrived at Dover before midnight on 3 June.

Ramsay recorded that:

> The evacuation of the British Forces from Dunkirk having been completed, and a large number of Allied troops also brought across, it was thought that there would be no further calls on the British craft. However, the French appealed for assistance in embarking the greatest possible number of the remainder of their forces, and as these troops had formed the rearguard whose tenacity and self-sacrifice had been such a substantial contributory factor in making the major operation possible, the appeal could not be ignored. Orders were therefore issued for the final effort, and the available ships dispatched in time to make the best use of the hours of darkness.

It was still not quite clear how many French troops remained in Dunkirk, but it was thought to be between 30,000 and 35,000. Speed of embarkation was on this occasion more vital than ever before, and ships were disposed as follows: – East Pier – Personnel Ships, destroyers and paddle minesweepers; West Pier and New Outer Port – other minesweepers, coastal corvettes, *schuits* and French vessels; Inner Harbour – drifters and smaller craft. The gunboat *Locust* was stationed outside the entrance to receive loads ferried out by small boats. All these vessels were to be away by 0230 on 4 June.

There was a thick fog which threatened to hamper the operations and which did indeed delay the homeward journey of some of the ships, but the whole operation proceeded without any major hitches. The only loss from enemy action was one French transport torpedoed off the North Foreland. This was the *Emile Deschamps*, which was sunk three miles from the Elbow Buoy. The *Luftwaffe* had been switched from Dunkirk to prepare for the next great land battles in the south after their attacks on 1 June, and only intermittent bombing took place. In fact, the only incident to mar the successful conclusion of the operation was the sudden final appearance of a host of non-combatants, deserters and others, who were somehow allowed to swarm aboard the ships instead of the fighting troops, whose places they usurped. Why the French authorities permitted this disgraceful action is still not clear, but it resembled the incident at Boulogne, only on a far larger scale and left the same bad taste in the mouth. Thus, despite the Royal Navy's best efforts, some 15,000 French fighting troops were left behind to surrender to the Germans.

The second blocking force then arrived, escorted by the destroyer *Shikari*, but one of the blockships, which lacked a degaussing cable, was sunk by magnetic mines. The others also drifted clear of the main channel yet again, so it remained still not properly blocked. The Personnel Ships *Autocarrier*, *Canterbury, Cote D'Argent, Princess Maud, Lady of Mann, Royal Sovereign* and *Tynwald* had loaded up and departed, so had the destroyers *Express, Malcolm, Vanquisher, Venomous* and *Sabre* and about thirty smaller warships. In all her five trips, *Venomous* had rescued 4,140 men and other ships almost as many. Last ship of all to leave was the *Shikari*, which embarked 383 French soldiers before sailing at 0340. She had the honour to be the last ship to sail away from Dunkirk.

Casualties were light. *Sabre* grounded on leaving harbour and lost her Asdic dome, while the coastal corvette *Kingfisher* collided with a trawler at 0015, and received a large hole in her bows, which reached right down to the waterline, but she was able to reach Sheerness under her own steam. The minesweeper *Leda* collided with the Belgian Personnel Ship *Marschall Foch* at 0429 and buckled her stern. Again, at 0454, just one mile from the North Goodwins, she rammed a *schuit*, which was sunk, thus becoming the very last casualty of *Dynamo*.

The End of Operation *Dynamo*

The signal from the Admiralty officially terminating the evacuation from Dunkirk was timed at 1423 on 4 June. Some 338,226 soldiers had been snatched from the enemy's claws during the nine epic days of the operation or, if the civilians taken off earlier are included, a grand total of 366,162, all except 30,000 of them in British ships. By 1030 on that morning, the great rescue fleet was being dispersed to other commands in readiness for the renewal of the struggle. Many of the less damaged warships which had been kept going for as long as possible, were now given the brief respite required to make good their many deficiencies. Their weary crews were given a little time to rest before taking up battle again with the now victorious enemy, who was soon to be joined by the Italian jackal, who had declared war in the expectation of gaining territory at little or no military cost.

The Absence of Air Cover

Since Dunkirk there have been many explanations on the lack of air protection for the fleet and the troops. None of them has been really convincing. The ridiculously optimistic claims of four German aircraft destroyed for every British aircraft lost are still repeated today, despite long ago being invalidated. In truth, as the years have gone by the myth has, if anything, grown through a nostalgic mist; but it is still untrue. Whether the RAF liked it or not, the true figures, totally checked and validated many times, are that the GAF lost a total of 156 aircraft over the whole of France during this period. At least nineteen of these were nowhere near the coast and another thirty-five were shot down by the warships' gunfire over the same period. This leaves a figure of 102 German aircraft destroyed by the RAF for the admitted loss to themselves of 106 machines!

The RAF's own figures are reproduced in Table 2. They show precisely the effort they put into the defence of the Navy and the BEF.

Table 2: No. 11 Group Fighter Patrols – Dunkirk Area				
Date	No. of Patrols	Total flying hours per day	Enemy aircraft claimed destroyed	Enemy aircraft 'driven down'
26 May	22	480	30	20
27 May	23	536	48	32
28 May	11	576	20	6
29 May	9	674	78	8
30 May	9	704	-	-
31 May	8	490	36	4
1 June	8	558	69	-
2 June	4	231	16	6
Total *Luftwaffe* aircraft lost in area.		**106**	**297**	**76**

Air Cooperation

As ever, during Dunkirk, the RAF exercised rigid control of the forces and refused to allow the needs of the other two services to influence in any way their strict allocation and usage. This paranoia over control was almost the opposite to that exercised by the *Luftwaffe* in assisting the *Wehrmacht* where Kesselring once stated that, 'The wishes of the Army are to be regarded as my orders!' The difference in attitude was to remain throughout the war, but already, the official report was expressing the frustration the Air Ministry's attitudes had caused and were to go on causing:

> The system of co-operation between the Naval and R.A.F. Commands does not permit of direct contact with the R.A.F. operational units

> allocated for duty with the Naval Command. For this reason much time appears to be lost and the needs of the ever-changing situation may not be provided for. Delays and lag occur, resulting often in the R.A.F. effort being brought to bear either in the wrong place or at the wrong time, or with inadequate force to meet the current situation.

Admiral Ramsay did not pull any punches, so angry did he feel:

> Not only did unopposed German air effort interrupt and reduce seaborne traffic, but it also prevented embarkation by suspending troop movement. To both Naval and Military observers on the coast, the situation at times was extremely disheartening. Rightly or wrongly, full air protection was expected, but instead, for hours on end the ships offshore were subjected to a murderous hail of bombs and machine gun bullets.

He added:

> Required by their duty to remain offshore waiting for the troops, who themselves were unable to move down to the water for the same reason, it required the greatest determination and sense of duty, amounting in fact to heroism, on the part of the ships' and boats' crews, to enable them to complete their mission.

Inaccuracy of BBC Reporting

On this occasion, as on so many others, the BBC standards of reporting were lamentable and highly inaccurate. This again, was to become a recurring theme, first noticed in Norway and soon repeated in North Africa and elsewhere. Dunkirk was an earlier manifestation of that unique combination of ignorance and exaggeration that typified the BBC and, indeed, still does with regard to military matters:

> ...feelings of disgust were engendered on listening in to the BBC report of the same evening, which recounted the opposite story. The more so as the gallantry of our outnumbered airmen was so obvious at the time, and was the admiration of all.

Triumph of the Navy

Whatever the failings and weaknesses of the RAF at the senior level and the BBC at every level, the Royal Navy had done its duty. As at Norway, and as was to be seen again at Greece and Crete, the sailors had not let the soldiers down, despite some petty snarling from a few Senior Army Officers, most notably the disparaging sneering from General Alan Brooke. The cost to the Navy was high, but not terminal. The major ships that took part in Operation *Dynamo* are listed in Table 3.

Table 3: Operation *Dynamo* – Major Royal Navy Vessels Involved			
Name	**Type**	**Tonnage**	**Principal Armaments**
Calcutta	Anti-Aircraft Cruiser	4,290	8 4inch HA, 4 2pdrs
Anthony	Destroyer	1,350	4 4.7inch LA
Basilisk	Destroyer	1,360	4 4.7inch LA
Codrington	Destroyer	1,540	5 4.7inch LA
Esk	Destroyer	1,375	2 4.7inch LA
Express	Destroyer	1,375	2 4.7inch LA
Gallant	Destroyer	1,335	4 4.7inch LA
Grafton	Destroyer	1,335	4 4.7inch LA
Grenade	Destroyer	1,335	4 4.7inch LA
Greyhound	Destroyer	1,335	4 4.7inch LA
Harvester	Destroyer	1,340	3 4.7inch LA
Havant	Destroyer	1,340	3 4.7inch LA
Icarus	Destroyer	1,340	2 4.7inch LA
Impulsive	Destroyer	1,340	2 4.7inch LA
Intrepid	Destroyer	1,340	2 4.7inch LA
Ivanhoe	Destroyer	1,340	2 4.7inch LA
Jaguar	Destroyer	1,670	6 4.7inch LA
Javelin	Destroyer	1,670	6 4.7inch LA
Keith	Destroyer	1,400	4 4.7inch LA
Mackay	Destroyer	1,530	3 4.7inch LA
Malcolm	Destroyer	1,530	2 4.7inch LA
Montrose	Destroyer	1,530	2 4.7inch LA
Sabre	Destroyer	905	1 4inch LA
Saladin	Destroyer	905	1 4inch LA
Scimitar	Destroyer	905	1 4inch LA
Shikari	Destroyer	905	1 4inch LA
Vanquisher	Destroyer	1,090	2 4inch LA
Venomous	Destroyer	1,120	2 4.7inch LA
Verity	Destroyer	1,120	2 4.7inch LA
Vimy	Destroyer	1,090	2 4inch LA
Vivacious	Destroyer	1,090	2 4inch LA

Wakeful	Destroyer	1,100	4 4inch HA
Whitehall	Destroyer	1,120	2 4.7inch LA
Whitshed	Destroyer	1,120	3 4.7inch LA
Winchelsea	Destroyer	1,120	2 4inch LA
Windsor	Destroyer	1,100	3 4.7inch LA
Wolfhound	Destroyer	1,120	4 4inch HA
Wolsey	Destroyer	1,120	4 4inch HA
Worcester	Destroyer	1,120	4 4inch HA
Bideford	Sloop	1,045	2 4inch LA
Guillemot	Coastal Corvette	510	1 4inch LA
Kingfisher	Coastal Corvette	510	1 4inch LA
Mallard	Coastal Corvette	510	1 4inch LA
Shearwater	Coastal Corvette	510	1 4inch LA
Sheldrake	Coastal Corvette	510	1 4inch LA
Widgeon	Coastal Corvette	510	1 4inch LA
Locust	Gunboat	585	2 4inch LA
Mosquito	Gunboat	585	2 4inch LA
Albury	Minesweeper	710	1 4inch LA
Brighton Belle	Minesweeper	320	1 12pdr
Brighton Queen	Minesweeper	519	1 12pdr
Devonia	Minesweeper	520	1 12pdr
Duchess of Fife	Minesweeper	336	1 12pdr
Dundalk	Minesweeper	710	1 4inch LA
Emperor of India	Minesweeper	534	1 12pdr
Fitzroy	Minesweeper	710	1 4inch LA
Glenavon	Minesweeper	509	1 12pdr
Glengower	Minesweeper	553	1 12pdr
Gracie Fields	Minesweeper	393	1 12pdr
Halycon	Minesweeper	815	1 4inch LA
Hebe	Minesweeper	835	1 4inch LA
Kellet	Minesweeper	n/a	n/a
Leda	Minesweeper	835	1 4inch LA
Lydd	Minesweeper	710	1 4inch LA

Marmion	Minesweeper	409	1 12pdr
Medway Queen	Minesweeper	318	1 12pdr
Niger	Minesweeper	815	1 4inch LA
Oriole	Minesweeper	441	1 12pdr
Pangbourne	Minesweeper	710	1 4 inch LA
Plinlimmon	Minesweeper	438	1 12pdr
Princess Elizabeth	Minesweeper	388	1 12pdr
Queen of Thanet	Minesweeper	792	1 12pdr
Ross	Minesweeper	710	1 4inch LA
Salamander	Minesweeper	815	1 4inch LA
Saltash	Minesweeper	710	1 4inch LA
Sandown	Minesweeper	684	1 4inch LA
Sharpshooter	Minesweeper	835	1 4inch LA
Skipjack	Minesweeper	815	1 4inch LA
Snaefell	Minesweeper	477	1 12pdr
Speedwell	Minesweeper	815	1 4inch LA
Sutton	Minesweeper	710	1 4inch LA
Waverley	Minesweeper	537	1 12pdr

Chapter Six

Final Withdrawal from Europe

It is as well to remember that, as *Dynamo* came to an end,[1] the tasks facing the Royal Navy in the Narrow Sea were by no means at an end. Indeed, if anything, they multiplied and grew ever more diverse. The distance that troops had to be transported, either as reinforcements or in a new series of evacuations and rescue operations, grew longer, but the numbers of warships available shrank due to expanding commitments elsewhere. As the tide of defeat washed over France, the British divisions still fighting had to be reinforced, supplied and then pulled out from ports more and more distant from our home bases. Although the onus of these rescues rested less and less on the men of Dover Command and more and more on Portsmouth and Plymouth (Western Approaches) Commanders, one inevitably finds the same few ships taking part, simply because they were all that were available, no matter under whose orders they were acting. Reliance on the empty promises and hollow treaties of the League of Nations had left the nation stripped of adequate means of defence to whom all these things meant less than nothing, and the empty chalice of 'Collective Security', that clap-trap phase trotted out by politicians who refused to pay for defence, rang hollow. The old lesson had to be relearnt once more, when the chips were down, as so often in the past, Britain stood alone.

In fact, so reduced had the Royal Navy been in destroyers at this time, that valuable troop and supply convoys sailed without close escorts, or with just the bare minimum. Instead, the C-in-Cs were forced to place a few ships along the general line of convoy routes out into the North Atlantic and Biscay ports and hope that they would be able to supply at least a modicum of protection for the merchant ships and their human cargo that passed along these lifeline routes. Butter not guns had been the cry in the 1920s and 1930s, but in 1940 it was discovered that, without guns, no butter, or anything else for that matter, would reach the nation.

It says a great deal about the hard drubbing that the German Navy had received off Norway in April and May, that they almost totally failed to penetrate this slender screen. It was beyond the limited range of the E-boats, and, although many of the coastal submarines, which had scored the occasional success off Dunkirk, were duly sent south in order to try and inflict similar casualties, they proved singularly ineffective. Fortunately for the

Royal Navy, the *Luftwaffe* was far more concerned with finishing off the reeling French Army than with attacks on ships. There was not the intensity or concentration of air attack as there had been at Dunkirk, but there were times when the overexposure of ships led to some isolated, but significant disasters and it is lucky that Britain's AA defences were not pressed too hard at this time. Air protection remained minimal, but this was less important and was now accepted as inevitable by most soldiers and sailors.

Before then, turning to describe the evacuations carried out under Operations *Cycle* and *Aerial*, let us first take note of the winding-up of events at Dover before that command once again stepped into the forefront of the naval war from July and August onward. Compared with what had gone before, and with what was to come, the month from early June to early July was one of relative tranquillity.

Dispersal of the *Dynamo* Surface Forces

Immediately after the last French *poilu* had disembarked on 4 June, warships started to be sent away from Dover to other commands, either in readiness or to carry out much needed refits before rejoining their original flotillas. For example, at 1140 the destroyers *Codrington* and *Shikari* left Dover for Devonport for repairs. They were followed soon afterward by *Esk, Express* and *Icarus* to rejoin the 20th (Minelaying) Flotilla at Immingham and *Vivacious, Winchelsea* and *Whitshed* to rejoin the Local Defence Flotilla.

Also on that same afternoon, *Venomous* sailed for Devonport, *Malcolm, Sabre* and *Vanquisher* for Sheerness for repairs and the gunboat *Locust* followed for the same destination. The next day the departures consisted of MTBs *102* and *105* for Portsmouth via Newhaven, the minesweepers *Dundalk, Fitzroy, Niger, Pangbourne* and *Sutton* for the Humber and *Marmion* for Harwich. The 10th Flotilla sailed to Portsmouth for reorganization; *Emperor of India, Medway Queen, Princess Elizabeth* and *Sandown*, while *Halcyon* left for Devonport dockyard on 6 June. The 11th Minesweeping Flotilla arrived to take their places on the same day: *Goatfell, Jeanie Deans, Helvellyn* and *Scafell.*

Although the running down of the Dover Command was inevitable, it did not mean that the routine duties of patrol and minesweeping were the only tasks that remained for its limited forces. It had by now been appreciated that surface minelaying by the enemy was taking place and it was expected to increase now that convenient ports had been surrendered to them. A destroyer was therefore on patrol both day and night in the area of the North Goodwin Light Vessel, supplemented by trawler patrols.

Nor was the search for odd pockets of survivors along the coastline between Calais and Dunkirk entirely given up. On 5 June, for example, Ramsay dispatched the destroyer *Wanderer* with the armed yacht *Gulzar* (Temporary Lieutenant C. V. Brammall) from Dover at 1800 to carry out Operation *MH*, which was the embarkation from a point near Boulogne of stragglers from the BEF, whose assembly there had been organized.

Unfortunately, the troops failed to show up as planned and the ships returned empty handed.

Evacuation from Le Havre, 9-11 June 1940

Ashore, events had not remained at a standstill during the preceding days. On 5 June, the German army resumed its offensive against the French who were holding a line from the mouth of the Somme across to the Maginot Line. They very quickly broke through in large numbers and soon the battle gave way to a race with the Panzers roaring into the heartland of France and meeting but sporadic and ineffectual opposition. The attacks along the coastal region toward Rouen soon threatened Le Havre and intermediate harbours like Fécamp, St Valery-en-Crux and Dieppe, and plans were hastily made to block these. But the thrusting Panzers did more than cut off this slice of coastline; isolated within their pincers British forces were still fighting there, namely the 1st Armoured Division and the 51st (Highland) Division and they were threatened with annihilation. Moreover, in keeping with the declared policy of the British Government at that time, all haste was made to reorganize and re-equip troops and return them as soon as possible to France to continue the fight. To demonstrate that this policy was not merely hollow words, another two divisions were hastily sent over in the aftermath of Dunkirk. These were the 52nd Division and the 1st Canadian Division. As the fighting men moved in, the non-combatants were removed, as many were now no longer required, some 150,000 base staff, plus large numbers of RAF ground crew with no aircraft to service, were brought out.

But, such was the speed and penetration of the German advance, that even while these moves were in train, the evacuation of the great port of Le Havre was necessitated, and this was organized by the Portsmouth C-in-C, Admiral Sir William James. After two days of heavy bombing the port and town of Le Havre were already in a shambles and, on 9 June, the order to commence the evacuation of the port, codenamed Operation *Cycle*, was given. In the, by now familiar, pattern a large number of small boats and *schuits* were sent across along with naval beach parties and senior officer to organize operations ashore. To cover them, Admiral James dispatched all available light naval forces, which included nine destroyers (two of them Canadian) under Captain (D) in *Codrington*, along with coastal corvettes and fleet minesweepers. After a twenty-four hour postponement, the embarkation proceeded as planned until stopped by continuous bombing. Some 11,059 British soldiers were rescued, and the majority, instead of being brought back to England, were sent to reinforce the units protecting Cherbourg, where a stand was expected to be made. The lift continued until the night of 12-13 June, and the only major loss was the personnel ship *Bruges* (2,949 tons) that was hit by bombs off Le Havre on 11 June and sunk. Another loss was *Train Ferry No 2*, which was beached and abandoned the following day.

Blocking of Dieppe, 10 June 1940

Meanwhile, the blocking of the important port of Dieppe had to be considered with some haste. The destroyer *Vega* had sailed from Dover on 9 June with a demolition party from Le Havre and had transferred them to a French trawler off that port as she herself was refused entry. She was on her way back, when the Admiralty diverted her with all dispatch to Portsmouth. Here she found three blockships hastily prepared for Dieppe, the *Jacobus, Kaupo* and *River Tyne*. Two MTBs accompanied them and *Vega* led the way back across the Channel that night.

In the meantime, all efforts had to be made to delay the approaching German troops until the blockships could accomplish their task, and to this end, the destroyers *Vesper* (Lieutenant Commander W. F. E. Hussey) and *Wanderer* sailed from Dover with orders to support the left flank of the Allied army in the vicinity of Le Tréport, midway between St Valery and Dieppe itself. They were to bombard any enemy troops or vehicles seen east of Dieppe, and carry out such bombardment to the west as might be required by the British Military Command in France. These ships sailed on 6 June to accomplish this task, and returned on 8 June. Meantime the old light cruiser *Cardiff* (Captain P. K. Enright), herself a doughty veteran which had led the German High Seas Fleet to surrender in 1918, armed with five 6-inch and two 3-inch guns, was sent to Dover to reinforce this bombardment squadron. She arrived on that station at 1715 and anchored to await the go-ahead. She was still there on 9 June, while the situation on land deteriorated still further. At 2100 orders were received from the Admiralty to the effect that all available ships were to be brought to immediate notice for steam, similar orders being issued to the other Commands on the East Coast. *Cardiff, Vesper* and *Wanderer* along with all the A/S and M/S trawlers were therefore brought to immediate notice to steam. On 8 June the two destroyers carried out a bombardment of the coastal road between Abbéville and Le Tréport

In the interim, the blocking of Dieppe had gone ahead but, yet again, it was not completely successful, for one of the block ships was mined just outside the approach channel. The other two were, however, scuttled in the correct position.

Trapping of the 51st Division at St Valery, 10 June 1940

The onward rush of the Panzers had cut off the 51st Highland Division, save for some elements which had managed to reach Le Havre before the trap closed. These were taken off, as related, but the greater bulk of this highly-valued fighting force was pressed back to the sea as the Germans struck northward from Rouen. By 10 June they found themselves with little room to manoeuvre at St-Valery-en-Caux, with the enemy closing in from all sides.

Admiral James had not contented himself with directing operations from a distance, but had sailed from Portsmouth in an MTB to see for himself how things stood. At Le Havre, all was going reasonably well, but it quickly became clear to him that further evacuations would have to take place from the smaller harbours to the north-east and that they would have to be improvised very quickly indeed. To see how things were there, he dispatched the destroyers *Ambuscade* (Lieutenant Commander A. O. Johnson), *Boadicea* and *Bulldog* to reconnoitre along the coast in that direction. He also made preparations to conduct evacuations from St Valery itself and signalled his intentions thus to the Admiralty. The 51st Division was now firmly boxed in and the Germans soon broke through to the coast itself on either side of the town. In the efficient manner shown earlier at Calais, they quickly established batteries of heavy guns there to dominate the seaward approaches to the port and the *Luftwaffe* was, as usual, very much in unopposed evidence. It was soon very apparent that if any evacuation were to take place, it would have to be at night, and without delay; in fact, that very night.

If any proof were required that the operation would not succeed in daylight, then it was provided by the experience of the three destroyers. *Ambuscade* pressed her reconnaissance in close to the shore, too close in fact and was engaged by the German guns and slightly damaged. She was making her way back down the coast to report her sharp reception that evening, when she come upon the other two destroyers. They, too, had suffered, far more severely than herself, not from the shore batteries but from the *Luftwaffe*. Both her companions had been very badly damaged as a result.

Damage to HMS *Bulldog*

The *Bulldog* had just finished a period in Chatham Dockyard repairing damage to her propellers, when she received orders to proceed at once to Le Havre. Commander F. J. G. Hewitt was First Lieutenant of this destroyer at that time. The story is best told in his own words:

> Dunkirk was just finished and our newspapers were full of the idea that our soldiers were going back to hammer again at the Germans. Nobody seemed to bother that almost all of the Army's stores, transport and guns had been left behind in Flanders.
>
> When *Bulldog* arrived at the bay of the Seine, the atmosphere was desolate. Oil tanks were burning on shore with huge black clouds of smoke rising further inland; there were a few small ships anchored, mostly coasters. And we began to suspect that this was not the prelude to another invasion but more likely another evacuation.
>
> Another B-class destroyer arrived, HMS *Boadicea*, and she anchored close by. Nobody from shore seemed to take much notice of our arrival and the only information we gleaned was that the Army had lost touch with its forward units.
>
> Things brightened up when, from the distant horizon across the Channel, appeared a fast-moving Motor Gunboat flying not only the White Ensign but the Admiral's flag of the Commander-in-Chief,

Portsmouth. Admiral James had come across to find out for himself what was happening.

The next thing was that the destroyers were ordered to steam along the coast on reconnaissance. So we set off, keeping about three miles offshore. We were off St Valery when we saw, some way ahead, a German aircraft carrying out shallow dives towards the water. We fired a couple of shells from 'B' gun to show our displeasure, and the plane made off.

When we got to the position we came across a small rowing-boat and in it we saw about half-a-dozen khaki figures. When we got them aboard we found they were from the 51st Highland Division. In broad Scots accents they told us that they had become separated from their unit so they had 'borrowed' a boat on the beach and were intending to row to England!

Boadicea had meanwhile seen some soldiers on the beach and went inshore to pick them up. *Bulldog* carried on until opposite Dieppe and was about to turn into the approach channel when grave doubts smote us. A lucky thing because the German tanks were already in the town.

On our way back we saw *Boadicea* having a spot of bother with some guns on shore and she was hurriedly hoisting her whaler. It was just then that we saw the enemy planes. Three Junkers dive bombers were circling above *Boadicea* and then we saw another six above us. They attacked almost immediately in threes, three from each side. They penetrated very low before releasing their bombs, because, of course, we had nothing effective to deter them.

There were many near misses on either side of the ship. One large bomb penetrated the deck on our port side, just abaft the after funnel; this glanced off a chunk of machinery in the Engine Room and passed out through the side of the ship just on the waterline. Our sailors were very nippy about rigging a collision mat over the hole.

As the bomb entered the port boiler in No 1 Boiler Room, it blew out the side casing of that boiler and the explosion vented up the fore funnel with a huge flame. As First Lieutenant, I was going round the deck looking for damage when I came across a hole in the deck on the starboard side just forward of the fore funnel; this could not be accounted for, until, it became very apparent that another bomb was still very much with us!

Both destroyers had lost steam power but in *Bulldog* the engineers got enough power back on the engines to enable us to crawl across the Channel in the direction of the Isle of Wight. *Boadicea* was met by the destroyer *Ambuscade* coming along the coast and she was towed by her into Portsmouth. Our berth was to be the Middle Slip Jetty, so called because the jetty was in two halves with a slip in between. Across this slip was a footbridge and the rail of this was lined with dockyard men watching us being pushed alongside. They were quite used to seeing damaged ships brought in after Dunkirk and the actions of the previous weeks.

While the ship was still a few yards off the jetty, a Lieutenant Commander, a Bomb and Mine disposal officer from HMS *Vernon*, walked on to the jetty and called up to the bridge, asking what was the trouble. As First Lieutenant, I was in the wing of the bridge watching the berthing wires going ashore and I called back 'We have an unexploded bomb in the boiler.'

This was something of a guess at the time, but it is worth mentioning because I don't think I have ever seen a crowd disperse so quickly!

That officer was a brave man and I regret I cannot remember his name. I understand he was killed later on doing this sort of work. He traced our bomb and, sure enough, he found it nestling among the tubes of the starboard water-tube boiler; eventually it was disposed of.

The explanation of our miraculous escape was that those aircraft had flown too low when they released their bombs and the fuses had been burred over as they passed through our steel plating; the timing devices were for the safety of the aircraft and had not had time to work off. Our ineffectual AA fire, which had encouraged the bombers to press in so close, had therefore been a blessing in disguise!

Damage to HMS *Boadicea*

A similar fate had overtaken *Boadicea*. She had stopped off the coast about a mile to the west of the village of Veulette where a small group of British soldiers and French refugees (including the war artist Richard Seddon) had congregated. They were hidden from the eyes of the advancing German army and the fleeing French soldiers alike by the overhanging cliffs. A whaler had been lowered with *Boadicea*'s First Lieutenant in charge to bring away these men and women and to try to ascertain the current situation ashore. Altogether, some eight troops and men, a woman, four children and two dogs were slowly ferried out to the waiting destroyer. Most of the remaining troops had already surrendered or been caught up by the advancing Panzers and cut to pieces. As the last boatload was taken away, the tanks ashore arrived on the cliff tops and opened fire on *Boadicea*, who duly returned fire with her main armament and drove them away. They had called up the dive bombers, however, as we have seen, and within a short time, at about 1730, a force of nine Junkers Ju87s was observed almost directly overhead, already going into their attack dives.

They attacked in *kettes* of three, as usual, and the first wave swooped on *Boadicea*, pressing in to a very low level, about 300 feet, before releasing their bombs. The first group missed by some yards to starboard, but the second Stuka made no mistakes and planted his bombs straight on target. The missiles all hit, and penetrated *Boadicea*' s thin plating, entered the engine room and the after boiler room. The bombs from the third aircraft fortunately missed completely.

Almost immediately, the planes were gone, winging their way back to base, and the stricken destroyer was left in a cloud of escaping steam and smoke, badly damaged, close inshore, with dusk coming on. The engine room and boiler room were both badly flooded, and most of their crews were casualties. The ship's W/T was put out of action and so no signal for help could be transmitted. Everything possible was done to lighten the ship by jettisoning all top weight, some shells, depth charges and torpedoes were all fired off, heavy cable was put over the side and anything else portable enough to move and heavy enough to sink was similarly disposed of. Collision mats were put in position on the threatened bulkheads and these were shored up as well as possible; even so, they bulged in an ominous manner. Arrangements were made to pass a tow should a friendly ship appear. The gun crews stood by anxiously, ready for the expected return of the enemy dive bombers to finish the job, but none came and night fell.

All the ship's boats were hung out and the floats made ready for an immediate abandon ship routine. Then the fog came down and left them in lonely isolation in their misery. It seemed almost a miracle when, later than night, *Ambuscade*, feeling her way slowly homeward, also slightly damaged, happened upon them. Thankfully, the tow was passed and the two ships began to pick their way slowly toward safety. The night hours were anxious ones, as it was by no means certain that the bulkheads would hold at any sort of speed, but hold they did. Not until the afternoon of the following day did they reach Portsmouth. Ashore, all was normal, as if peace had never ended. Silently, *Boadicea* crept into the harbour and secured alongside.

Her exhausted crew and their passengers gave thanks. The latter disembarked. No other notice was taken of her arrival. Eventually two customs officers turned up on the quay and went aboard. Did they say 'Welcome back. Well done'? No. The question that occupied their minds at this breathless moment in England's destiny was, 'what quarantine measures had they in mind for the dogs?' Although in later years the 'Dunkirk Spirit' was repeatedly cited as a symbol of the rallying of the country in the face of mortal peril, in truth it was to take much more time before many of the civilians ashore fully realized the enormity of their situation.

Loss of 51st Division

The same thick fog in the Channel which had, that night, shielded the homeward passage of the crippled destroyers had a drastic effect on the proposed evacuation of the 51st Division from St Valery. A large number of ships had gathered to take off the troops; in all some sixty-seven merchant ships and 140 smaller vessels, and they had proved impossible to control or organize in the prevailing weather conditions. Only at Veules did ships manage to embark and rescue soldiers (2,137 British and 1,184 French) but only with great difficulty and under fire. The remaining British troops spent the night waiting in hope of ships, which never arrived.

Next day, Admiral James tried to organize another attempt for the following night, but the French surrendered even as the Highlanders were counter-attacking to win themselves breathing space. Thus the British too, were forced to surrender. The loss of 6,000 of our best troops, so close to rescue, was a bitter blow and one that has never been forgiven north of the Border. That it was the only rescue attempt of a large body of troops by the Royal Navy which had failed,[2] no matter what the odds, was a fact, and it was the weather rather than the enemy which had brought it about, but this made no difference to the legacy of failure and led to endless recrimination. Many of the sailors themselves felt that, perhaps, more could have been attempted despite the conditions but, with hindsight it is possible to state too that the odds were very much against any success.

This heavy blow speeded up implementation of the decision to bring out all the final remnants of the BEF before they shared the same fate. On 15 June it was decided that Operation *Aerial* should commence at once, and that the ports of Brest, Cherbourg, La Pallice, St Malo and St Nazaire should all be utilized as fully as possible to achieve this aim. The closer ports of Cherbourg and St Malo were to be evacuated by ships under the direction of Admiral James at Portsmouth, and the rest by a similar composite fleet under the protection of Plymouth Command with warships under Admiral Dunbar-Nasmith. It was also intended to bring out guns and equipment, as well as troops this time, and it was hoped that there would be time enough for this to be done; the need for home defence was enormous. The Air Ministry was busy rejecting every suggestion of using aircraft for close support in case of invasion, stating it was not its role, and that the anti-tank gun was the answer to the Panzer. However, it seemed to forget that most anti-tank guns had been left behind in France, along with most other heavy equipment. However, the distances involved and the quantities of material meant using much larger ships than at Dunkirk, with consequent risks of exposing such vulnerable targets to unrestricted air attacks over much longer periods.

Emptying of Dover Command 11-15 June 1940

While the focus of attention moved south and west for a while, the work of Dover Command slowed down for the same period and it was largely denuded of warships, which were temporarily diverted to other commands. Of the four destroyers to which the flotilla had, for a time, been reduced at this time, *Codrington* and *Vega* had been working from Plymouth and *Wanderer* sailed for that port at 1225 on 11 June, leaving only *Vesper* on station. Similarly, the anti-submarine trawlers *Kingston Andalusite, Lady Philomena* and *Saon* sailed, two for Tilbury and one to Barry for repairs. The drifter *Torbay II* sailed to Southampton, also for repairs. The remainder were sent to patrol between North Foreland and Dungeness while *Vesper* patrolled from the South Goodwin to Dungeness. As an anti-invasion screen at this period of the war, the Royal Navy was, for a brief time, stretched very thin indeed!

The emptiness of Dover Harbour was further emphasized when the light cruiser *Cardiff* sailed at 1235 to cover the evacuation near St Valery-en-Caux with bombardment, under the orders of C-in-C Portsmouth. By the time she arrived off France at 1518 and joined the destroyer *Harvester*, it had become clear that no more troops were coming away. She therefore withdrew to some thirteen miles offshore at 1530 and, at 1700, was instructed to stay twenty miles off St Valery. At 1900 the tug *Cameo* secured alongside and put aboard six army wounded, whom *Cardiff* took back when she returned to Spithead, arriving there just before midnight.

A more serious note was struck with the arrival at Dover the next day of the steamship *Umvoti* which was intended for use as a block ship for Folkestone harbour should this ever be required in the event of a German invasion. The destroyer *Express* berthed overnight at Dover on her way from Portsmouth to Immingham, as she was unable to cross the Thames Estuary before dark; she arrived at 2205 on 13 June and sailed again at 0347 the next morning. Two of the magnetic minesweeping trawlers, *Georgette* and *Inverforth*, also left the Command for Plymouth that day, and two others, *Bervie Braes* and *Lord Grey*, left at 1736 on 15 June. This reduced Dover to one destroyer and two 'LL' trawlers, both out of action, plus a few anti-submarine trawlers and drifters. Very few people realized just how limited Britain's resources were at this period.

The Admiralty was striving, in the face of heavy casualties, to organize a strong destroyer defence of four full flotillas (thirty-two destroyers) based on Harwich, Dover, Portsmouth and Plymouth. It faced the need to provide at least minimum destroyer screens for the Home and Mediterranean Fleets (a further thirty-two destroyers), Force H at Gibraltar (at least sixteen destroyers) and yet still protect the Atlantic convoys. In mid-June 1940 those plans were more evident on paper than at sea but, on the evening of 15 June, the destroyer *Griffin* arrived at Dover, the first ship of the newly reconstructed 1st Flotilla, which, it was hoped, would join the 4th Flotilla to form a force eventually consisting of *Codrington* (D), *Beagle, Boadicea, Boreas, Brazen, Brilliant, Bulldog, Gallant, Greyhound* and *Griffin*, along with the Polish ships *Blyskawica* and *Burza*. The arrival of *Codrington* was slightly delayed due to the need for her to repair damage received off St Valery in a fog-related accident, while *Boadicea* and *Bulldog* were not expected to be ready for at least four months and one month respectively. However, things did not work out according to this plan.

Evacuation of the Biscay Ports, 15-18 June 1940

As we have already noted, the decision to implement Operation *Aerial* was made on 15 June as the French army was burst asunder by the fresh German land offensive. To avoid a repetitions of the St Valery fiasco, all available forces were mustered and dispatched to achieve the evacuation of what remained of the BEF, and as many Allied soldiers as wished to go on fighting, these being mainly Poles. With so few fighting ships available, risks were taken and accepted, the destroyers and escorts patrolled along general evacuation channels to offer some protection to the stream of craft, large and small, bringing troops away. Considering the risks, the operation proceeded remarkably well at first. Troopships, MT ships and store vessels sailed from Southampton to Cherbourg and St Malo, while the smaller vessels, coasters, *schuits* etc., sailed from Poole and Weymouth harbours. Other vessels went to Caen, covered by destroyers, where the oil tanks were fired and the installations wrecked.

By the late afternoon of 18 June, over 30,000 men had been taken off without loss and brought back to England, despite growing air attacks. The 1st Canadian Division embarked at St Malo on 16 June, and, by next day, another 21,000 plus fighting troops had been brought home unscathed. A few ships went back on 18 June in order to pick up any that remained and the port was subject to the usual demolition. All-in-all, Portsmouth Command had swiftly retrieved the situation after the initial disaster and came through hits own 'mini-Dunkirk' with remarkably light losses.

Plymouth Command was not so fortunate, although, here again, things went very well initially. There were far more troops to be brought away from the Biscay ports across far greater distances. In addition to providing protection for the host of merchant vessels crammed with soldiers, the Royal Navy had the task of escorting the French Navy from its main bases so that valuable ships did not fall into German hands. These warships included the brand-new battleship *Jean Bart* at St Nazaire and her sister, *Richelieu* from Brest, both of which were larger and more powerfully-armed than new battleships being built for the Royal Navy. Consequently, their fate was regarded as being of the highest importance. The military risks were, however, compounded by the political complications; there was great division in the French Government over the fate of these warships, and many were strongly against handing over any of their fleet to the British. Many senior French Admirals were out-and-out Anglophobes – an attitude typified by the mercurial French Navy C-in-C Darlan, who proved an arch collaborator under the Vichy regime. This meant that the Royal Navy was required to use exceptional diplomacy and tact with our prickly ally at a time of great stress and emotion.

Demolition parties and some personnel ships had already reached Brest by 16 June, when the British Cabinet ordered the operation to commence, and Admiral Dunbar-Nasmith quickly sent over the large ships held ready for such an eventuality, the *Arandora Star, Otranto* and *Strahaird*. In total, some 32,584 troops were got away from Brest by the time the embarkation ended on 18 June. Again, all the ships evaded submarines and mines, and the *Luftwaffe* did not intervene at all. Many soldiers were taken away in the Navy's cruiser and destroyers, which were equally unmolested in the main. By 1600 many of the French warships had sailed, including the battleships, and the naval demolition parties moved in to do their work the next day. With the docks wrecked, the Flotilla Leader *Broke* (Commander B. G. Scurfield) picked up the last men and sailed for home.

While this was being conducted so well, the wide estuary of the River Loire was alive with shipping making its way from Quiberon Bay (where they had been sheltering) to St Nazaire. Up-river at Nantes, 60,000 Allied troops were retreating toward that port and the evacuation plan for these was put into operation immediately by Admiral Dunbar-Nasmith. Captain D19 (Captain E. B. K. Stevens) in the destroyer *Havelock*, with the *Beagle* (Lieutenant Commander R. H. Wright) and *Wolverine* (Commander R. H. Craske) were the only major warships present to protect the liners *Batory, Duchess of York, Georgic* and *Sobieski*; and on 15 June this group was joined by the liner *Lancastria* and some cargo ships. By that same evening *Duchess of York* and the Polish ships *Batory* and *Sobeski* had taken aboard about 13,000 non-combatants with stores and transport, and had sailed for England. All was well, so far.

The small flotilla was reinforced by the destroyers *Highlander* (Commander W. A. Dallmeyer) and *Vanoc* the next day, but the *Luftwaffe* also put in an appearance for the first time and, in attacks on the Quiberon Bay shipping, gave a foretaste of what was to come, the liner *Franconia* being damaged. On 17 June the loading continued apace but, at 1535 a heavy air raid developed over the large assembly of ships. Many attacks were well pressed home against AA fire, which proved too scattered to provide an effective blanket defence for all. A Dornier Do17 bomber of KG2 pressed home its dive attack against the *Lancastria* (16,2343 tons) scoring several direct hits, which immediately set the great ship on fire.

The *Lancastria* sank in the brief time of fifteen minutes. She had more than 5,000 soldiers aboard and there were not enough lifeboats and rafts for more than a fraction of that number to be saved, even had there been time to lower them all. Air attacks were continuous as she went down and, amid the bedlam and confused situation, the demise of this ship passed almost unnoticed until too late. Many of her passengers were burned or drowned in a film of blazing fuel oil, which spread across the waters of the Loire. The myriad of dots, each one a struggling soldier, soon vanished, despite the efforts of the A/S trawler *Cambridgeshire* (Lieutenant Commander A. Blewitt, RNR), which somehow managed to haul 1,000 men from the sea onto her tiny deck. Many thousands more drowned within minutes; it was one of the greatest national disasters for loss of life in the war. The British Cabinet, to their eternal shame, seemed more concerned with hushing up this tragedy and keeping it out of the news, but such a scale of loss could not be swept under the carpet and news of it leaked out, until finally the loss of some 3,000 troops was admitted. The true total was far higher and it has been estimated that about 5,000 is nearer the true loss figure. The veil of silence imposed by Churchill has been penetrated only recently, but the full facts of the matter are still subject to speculation.

However, despite this appalling tragedy, at least 23,000 other soldiers were saved and taken away in a convoy of ten large ships at dawn on 18 June. These were followed by twelve further ships later that morning after which the whole operation was prematurely aborted as too risky. Meanwhile, Vice Admiral T. J. Hallett arrived, flying his flag in the destroyer *Vanquisher*. His job was to ensure that the French got the *Jean Bart* safely out of German clutches or, failing that, destroy her. Admiral Hallett sent in tugs to aid them in this task. After a long and tense period of waiting, the mighty, even though incomplete, battleship finally arrived at the rendezvous and *Vanquisher* escorted her away south, en route to the safety of Casablanca.

Further down the Bay of Biscay lay the great naval bases of La Pallice, La Rochelle and Rochefort behind the Ile d'Oléron. The Gironde river, leading to Bordeaux, lay to the south while, bordering the Spanish frontier, lay Bayonne, St Jean de Luz and other small ports. This was the scene of the final evacuations from France. As they lie well outside the scope of this book, it only needs to be said that the scenes were repeats of all the earlier ones. The brand new Hunt Class destroyer *Berkeley* was sent over with demolition parties for all these ports and, under the command of Lieutenant Commander H. G. Walters, her CO, proceeded up the Gironde to act as a wireless link. The light cruiser *Arethusa* sailed from Gibraltar on 16 June, and arrived at Le Verdon at the mouth of the river that same day. The First Lord of the Admiralty (Mr A.V. Alexander), the First Sea Lord (Admiral Sir Dudley Pound) and Lord Lloyd had all arrived at Bordeaux in an attempt to sway Darlan, but in vain. In the end, the British Consular parties embarked aboard *Berkeley*, which transferred them out to *Arethusa*. The British Ambassador remained until 23 June, when he embarked aboard the light cruiser *Galatea*, which was still flying the flag of Rear Admiral A. T. B. Curteis. *Arethusa* also took the president of Poland and his ministers back to Britain.

Table 4: British warship losses during May-June 1940 in the English Channel.

Name	Type	Date	Details
Valentine	Destroyer	15 May	Bombed, River Scheldt
Whitley	Destroyer	19 May	Bombed, off Ostend
Rifnes	Trawler	20 May	Bombed, off Ostend
Wessex	Destroyer	24 May	Bombed, off Calais
Brighton Belle	Minesweeper	28 May	Collision at Dover
Thomas Bartlett	Trawler	28 May	Mined, off Calais
Rob Roy	Drifter	28 May	Bombed, Dunkirk
Paxton	Drifter	28 May	Bombed, Dunkirk
Ocean Reward	Drifter	28 May	Collision, off Dover
Grafton	Destroyer	29 May	U-boat, off Dunkirk
Wakeful	Destroyer	29 May	E-boat, off Dunkirk
Grenade	Destroyer	29 May	Bombed, Dunkirk
Crested Eagle	A. A. Ship	29 May	E-boat, off Dunkirk

Gracie Fields	Minesweeper	29 May	Bombed, Dunkirk
Waverley	Minesweeper	29 May	Bombed, Dunkirk
Calvi	Trawler	29 May	Bombed, Dunkirk
Polly Johnson	Trawler	29 May	Bombed, Dunkirk
Comfort	Drifter	29 May	Collision, off Dunkirk
Girl Pamela	Drifter	29 May	Collision, off Dunkirk
Nautilus	Drifter	29 May	Bombed, Dunkirk
King Orrey	ABU	30 May	Bombed, Dunkirk
Ambeleve	Canal Boat	30 May	Grounded, Dunkirk
Devonia	Minesweeper	30 May	Bombed Dunkirk
St Achilleus	Trawler	31 May	Mined, off Dunkirk
Argyllshire	Trawler	31 May	E-boat, off Dunkirk
Stella Dorado	Trawler	31 May	E-boat, off Dunkirk
Basilisk	Destroyer	1 June	Bombed, Dunkirk
Keith	Destroyer	1 June	Bombed, Dunkirk
Havant	Destroyer	1 June	Bombed, Dunkirk
Mosquito	Gunboat	1 June	Bombed, Dunkirk
Brighton Queen	Minesweeper	1 June	Gunfire, Dunkirk
Skipjack	Minesweeper	1 June	Bombed, Dunkirk
Grive	Armed Yacht	1 June	Bombed, Dunkirk
St Abbs	Tug	1 June	Bombed, Dunkirk
St Fagan	Tug	1 June	Bombed, Dunkirk
Fair Breeze	Drifter	1 June	Wrecked, Dunkirk
Lord Vavan	Drifter	1 June	Gunfire, Dunkirk
Amultee	Armed Yacht	1 June	Collision, off Dover
Pellag II	Trawler	1 June	Wrecked, Dunkirk
Ocean Sunlight	Drifter	13 June	Mined, off Newhaven
Myrtle	Trawler	14 June	Mined, Thames Estuary
Murmansk	Trawler	17 June	Grounded at Brest
Charade	Drifter	21 June	Collision, Portsmouth
Campeador	Armed Yacht	22 June	Mined, off Portsmouth

In a similar manner, the destroyer *Beagle* conveyed Rear Admiral F Burgess-Watson upstream to Bordeaux on 20 June with a demolition party, to destroy the docks and the enormous oil tanks there. The French refused to cooperate and the Admiralty turned down a suggestion to allow *Beagle* to do the job by surprise attack. Later, they regretted their hesitation and a flotilla was readied to make a desperate last ditch attempt but this, in turn, was vetoed by the War Cabinet. The huge oil supplies thus passed intact into the hands of the pliant Vichy Government and thence on to the German war machine.

The rescue of Polish forces continued from the southern Biscay ports until 25 June. The long, and quite remarkable, sequence of evacuation without loss was not marred until the very last day, when the anti-aircraft cruiser *Calcutta*, flying the flag of Admiral Curteis, accidentally rammed and sank the Canadian destroyer *Fraser*, with severe loss of life among her crew. This, and the unhappy *Lancastria* incident were, however, the only major casualties of the whole mainly successful sequence. In total, some 191,870 soldiers were rescued, along with 310 guns and 2,292 military vehicles, as well as 1,800 tons of stores. Although not as well known as Dunkirk, Operations *Cycle* and *Aerial* were no mean achievements for the men of the Narrow Sea Commands.

Naval and mercantile losses were light. Apart from the vessels already mentioned, the trawler *Murmansk* grounded at Brest on 17 June and was abandoned; the *Ronwyn* (1,766 tons) and *Hester* (1,199 tons) were damaged and abandoned at Rochefort and the *Dido* (3,554 tons) was abandoned at Brest and taken by the Germans.

On 22 June, France lay prostrate at the feet of Hitler. He imposed severe conditions on a collaborationist Vichy Government, the most pertinent to our story being the handing over of the whole French coastline, to the enemy, so that German troops now stood guard from the North Cape of Norway to the Spanish frontier. The fight for the Narrow Sea was now really beginning.

The E-Boats Move In, June 1940

The whole of the vast Channel area was now under threat from the enemy. German heavy gun emplacements began to grow on the headlands and coastal points, while dive bombers and fighter aircraft squadrons moved into captured French coastal airfields after trouncing the last French resistance ashore, and prepared themselves for the final stage of the campaign in the West. The German Navy had been severely reduced in strength off Norway, and so could do little at first, other than gather suitable craft, barges and the like, and prepare them for invasion. They had a few cruisers, some destroyers but little else fit for battle, but there were several flotillas of E-boats which they moved down into captured ports. These slender surface forces had a wide selection of ports and harbours from which to operate and it was not long before they began to make their presence felt. On the night of 24 June, the tanker *Albuera* (3,477 tons) was torpedoed and sunk by the

S-36 (*Leutnant* Babbel) off Dungeness, and the coaster *Kingfisher* (276 tons) was sunk by *S-19* the same day.

Notes

1. The number of troops rescued by ships of all types at Dunkirk was 337,000. Numbers by type of ship with regard to largest share of lifts broke down as:

British Destroyers	91,624
Personnel Ships	69,321
British Fleet Minesweepers	30,942
Paddle Minesweepers	18,838
Navy-manned Dutch *schuits*	20,284
French Destroyers	7,623

The rest were rescued by the 'Little Ships'.

2. The 1st Canadian Division (21,474 men) from Cherbourg and a further 32,584 from Brest, as well as the 52nd Division (30,630) were all rescued by the Royal Navy without the loss of a single man while, simultaneously in Norway, Narvik and Harstad were being evacuated, but all these evacuations are not remembered while the failure at St Valery is.

Chapter Seven

Initial German Assaults on Convoys

The growth of the German surface force attacks on British convoys passing through the Straits, was initially mainly confined to one E-boat flotilla and a steady build-up of minelaying operations. There seemed to be no great urgency to counter these threats, for it was thought that they could be contained. After evacuating the bulk of the British Army safely, the main consideration seemed to be preparing to repel the expected German invasion of England. This governed the allocation of defending warships, in particular that of the British destroyer flotillas from a very early stage and it is ironic that from mid-June 1940, Hitler had not yet made any firm decision with regard to the landings and had no firm plan for an invasion. He hoped the British, seeing the hopelessness of their position, would come to an agreement without the need for invading, thus leaving him free to turn on his real enemy, his chum, ally and fellow totalitarian state, the Soviet Union. The British failed to see things the same way, however. The two opponents on either side of the English Channel, therefore had totally differing expectations and were preparing for a totally different kind of war in the Narrow Sea for the next few weeks or so.

Coupled with the British need (as they saw it) to provide powerful surface striking forces close at hand to counter an invasion attempt (the four destroyer flotillas, plus a large auxiliary back-up) was the continuation of normal coastal traffic and sailings to and from the London Docks, then as always, the hub of the Empire. The CW and CE convoys did not start until this period and at first they, somewhat surprisingly, were only lightly attacked. Offensive patrolling against the E-boats, a more obvious threat, at first met with little or no success, while they, in reply, continued to achieve only pin-prick victories against lightly-defended targets. The *Luftwaffe* was not initially as obvious a factor as had first been feared, although that soon changed. In truth, they needed a brief respite after their tremendous achievements and non-stop combat and movements since 10 May. Most of the dive bomber units were refurbishing and taking up their new dispositions while their aircrew sunbathed on the French Channel coast. The temporary lull in air activity enabled a gradual build-up again to a peak of operations, increasing in scope, weight and power from July onward and reaching its maximum (as far as the ships operating in the Narrow Sea were concerned) in July and August. Air activity then died away as the fighting moved inland and toward London, only to flare up again in November and once more in the spring of 1941. Behind all this activity, the ever-present threat of the mine remained the most enduring and, all-in-all, the most baleful arbiter of shipping losses in these confined waters.

There has, on occasion, been expressed the view that the Royal Navy in this period was inactive, 'kennelled in their ports' as one blinkered and not very perceptive historian once wrote, waiting upon events. This is totally incorrect. The flotillas of destroyers, based at Harwich, Portsmouth and Sheerness to intercept any attempted German invasion convoys, did not merely lie passively at anchor, awaiting an enemy force that was never to materialize, to come to them. Quite the opposite. Although based on these ports, they were fully utilized on other duties. Nor did the rest of the Royal Navy wait for the enemy to appear; offensive patrols, bombardments and aggressive sweeps into the enemy held coastal waters were conducted at regular intervals continually by all available forces from the very first. We have already seen how, even during the evacuation period, the Royal Navy lost no chance to take the fight to the enemy. This policy continued and none of the flotillas was 'kennelled' in 1940 any more than they were to be in 1944. In fact, this was a great influence on the enemy. Even in the waters off Boulogne and Calais, guarded by their radar sets, patrolled by their superior air force and dominated by their armies, the Germans could not venture very far from the shore without bring down on their heads the weight of the Royal Navy, and very quickly indeed. Churchill was to comment, while countering a somewhat agitated query as to how the invasion was to be repelled by our inadequate military defences ashore, that; '...we hope to drown most of them en route'.

This was clearly reflected in the Admiralty letter of intent on the matter of an invasion, which followed a signal on 28 May. In this, their Lordships stated, quite unequivocally, that the best way to defeat an invasion attempt was to hit as hard as possible, as soon as possible. That did not mean waiting for the invasion fleet to sail, but striking before they could do so or, as they put, 'attack before departure'. To achieve this the Royal Navy was not going to remain passively in Dover Harbour or elsewhere, but seize the initiative by means of offensive patrols and bombardments, as well as mining. This it did, with great élan.

Air power finally proved decisive by day, if not by night, and heavy losses forced the Dover Flotilla to be withdrawn. The *Luftwaffe*, contrary to claims which have often been made, was able to operate almost with impunity over the Channel between June and August. It proved very efficient at ship-busting up to the very end, but in 1940 was particularly deadly.[1]

Lull Before the Storm, 19 June – 3 July 1940

At Dover, this was a time of steady build-up once more, an increasing scale of air attack, steady mining attrition, and efforts, mainly unsuccessful, to grapple with the E-boat menace. It was considered too risky to allow shipping to attempt the crossing of the Thames Estuary at night, due to minelaying. Thus, on the night of 18-19 June, the destroyer *Anthony*, on passage from Portsmouth to Harwich, was held in Dover Harbour between 2053 and 0612. *Vesper* and *Vivacious* had tried to intercept an enemy E-boat force, but had failed to do so and the conclusion was that 'the proper and essential counter' to this threat was similar craft of our own on the station. A signal was sent by AOC Dover at 1810 on 18 June to this effect and MTBs were soon dispatched. In practice, they also failed to provide the answer, being much smaller than the E-boats, slower, inadequately-armed and poorly trained and coordinated (the British sailors referred to the Coastal Forces as the 'Costly Farces' at this time) and time proved that destroyers, given added close-range weapons, were the best counter.

Meanwhile destroyers continued to arrive on station for both the reconstructed 1st and 4th Flotillas, *Greyhound* on 19 June, *Boreas* the next day, *Codrington* returned the day after and so on. The Minesweeping Flotillas were also reinforced during this time. The first two ships of the 10th Flotilla rejoined after their refits at Portsmouth on 19 June, *Medway Queen* and *Princess Elizabeth*, while the ships of the 11th Flotilla, *Helvellyn*, *Goatfell*, *Jeanie Deans*, *Mercury* and *Scafell*, returned to Portland the same day.

The Admiralty had ordered the assembly of a vast number of minor patrol craft to supplement the regular naval forces on anti-invasion watch. Like the ramshackle but keen amateur Home Guard units ashore, the net was spread far and wide and, in many cases, the ships selected for active service were considered by those who had to use them to be more of a menace to themselves and everyone else who had the misfortune to come into contact with them, than to the enemy! Typical of this type of well-meaning but useless endeavour was a collection of twelve small motor yachts destined for inshore anti-invasion patrol, which sailed from Newhaven, five bound for Dover and seven for Ramsgate, on 19 June. As the official account dryly reported:

> The expedition was not a very great success, as one boat caught fire and sank before reaching Beachy Head, two others then returning to Newhaven with her crew. The remainder also turned back for Newhaven not long after passing Beachy Head owing to stress of weather and engine troubles.

Little wonder then, that the Admiralty preferred to put their trust in the regular warships built for the job. But the watch on the E-boats based at Boulogne failed to prevent them scoring several small victories in the period.

Shortly after midnight on 20 June, four E-boats made repeated attacks on the freighter *Roseburn* (3,103 tons) on her way to the Tyne after a long voyage from New Zealand with a cargo of timber. She was three miles east of Dungeness, and spotted at least four torpedoes fired at her. Three of these missed close alongside but the fourth struck her in the stern. The E-boats machine-gunned her bridge and upperworks after expending their torpedoes and the crew abandoned ship. The destroyer on night patrol, *Vesper*, made an unsuccessful attempt to intercept the retiring enemy and then, joined by the tug *Lady Brassey*, made attempts to tow the damaged ship up-Channel. The drifter *Lord Howe* had meantime rescued the fourteen crew members who had prematurely lowered the boats. After the master of the vessel had expressed himself unwilling to attempt the tow, *Roseburn* was finally beached off Denge Marsh, west of Dungeness. The Salvage Officer reported that he hoped to shore up and strengthen her bulkheads and pump her out in an effort to save her. The salvage ship *Dapper* was sent to aid him in this work but, in the event *Roseburn* became a write-off; she was a totally needless loss. The next day, the Salvage Office reported that the bulkheads had all given way and water was flooding through the hull of the wreck. Some of her cargo was got ashore by small craft.

One solution suggested to deal with the threat posed by the E-boats was similar to that attempted against submarines in the First World War. This was the rigging of nets (known as 'sausage nets') which consisted of a wire supported by floats and towed behind the drifters, each 'sausage' being a quarter-of-a-mile long. The drifters *Forecast* and *Shipmates* tried this contraption out off Dungeness the next night, but no E-boats appeared to test its efficiency. It was never to prove to be the slightest deterrent to high-speed craft. More realistic was the arrival at Dover of a flotilla of MTBs (MTB*s-18, 67, 70, 71* and *107*) on 21 June.

On the anti-invasion front, the Admiralty reported that reconnaissance on 20 June of the ports of Cherbourg, L'Havre, Boulogne, Calais, Dunkirk, Nieuport, Ostend, Zeebrugge, Flushing and Ijmuiden, revealed that all were clear of any concentrations of enemy shipping. Clearly, the Germans were having great difficulties in finding suitable craft at such short notice. If the invasion fleet did assemble, they would be in severe difficulties, even if they broke through the main defensive screen. The British trawlers were being fitted out with two depth charges each, on the assumption that they would close with the German transports and blow them up at point-blank range by this method. The Fleet Air Arm continued to attack German strongpoints ashore with its limited number of Skua dive bombers and Roc fighters acting as makeshift dive bombers; nine of these dive bombed the German heavy gun battery being established near Cap Blanc Nez on 21 June, scoring four direct hits and several near misses for the loss of one aircraft. Both Hawkinge and South Foreland radar stations were monitoring the enemy E-boats at this time. Strangely, the British never seemed to feel that the Germans might be doing the same thing to our naval forces; they *were* so doing, however, and this was soon to be made evident when their *Freya* system led to some important losses amongst the British warships in the Channel area.

There was a panic at this time caused by the return home to Germany from Norway of the battlecruiser *Scharnhorst*. With an eye to any eventuality, the destroyer *Boreas* was sailed to maintain a night patrol between the North Goodwin 'R' and 'U' buoys, while the other three destroyers and four MTBs at Dover were kept at fifteen minutes' notice to steam. It must have seemed a remote possibility that they would have to meet the mighty *Scharnhorst* off Dover in 1940 yet, less than two years later she and her sister were to steam straight by that port totally inviolate!

In a ruse to intercept the elusive E-boats, MTBs *70* and *71*, both of which had only recently arrived at Dover, were painted black and sent out to lurk in the vicinity of Dungeness around 2200 on 22 June, while *Boreas* kept to the eastward of No. 10 buoy to give support. Radar indications gave hope for an action, but nothing actually developed that night. The operation was repeated the next night, with the same result, but plans were made to persevere, under the appropriate codename *Nitwit*!

Another clandestine operation, which also ultimately proved abortive, was *Collar*. This involved the sailing of a number of fast motor boats from Dover and Ramsgate to land military parties at various points along the French coast at night for reconnaissance, demolition and harassing operations. Yet another new development was the escorting of Outward Atlantic (OA) convoys as far as Dover by destroyers from Sheerness. On the night of 22-23 June, *Vivacious* performed this duty and the old submarine *H-32* (Lieutenant J. L. Livesey) secretly provided an additional escort.

None of these activities prevented another E-boat attack from being launched successfully, the victim this time being the 3,447-ton *Albuera* on passage from Halifax, Nova Scotia, to the Tyne with a cargo of pit-props. Soon after 0100 on 24 June, she was torpedoed by E-boats some two miles south-west of the Lydd Light Floats. Twenty-nine survivors were picked up by a Dutch ship and were transferred to the A/S trawler *Grimsby Town*. It was later learned that *Albuera* had sailed from Weymouth directly contrary to strict orders that ships should only pass Dungeness by daylight.

The effectiveness of the radar watch on the Channel on the British side of the water was demonstrated on 24 June. Strong contact reports were received at about 1620 by the Dover Station, which showed a surface contact circling some 12¾ miles out; further fixes at 1625 and 1631 indicated that it was moving south slowly. *Boreas*, on patrol, was ordered to investigate and *Codrington* was sailed to lend support. She located the whale factory ship *Svend Foyn*, which was lost in thick fog off Dungeness. In that same fogbank, the ships of *Collar* returned from the adventures.

In the air, two incidents deserve mention because they gave advance warning of what was to become commonplace. They also indicated a gap in the British warning system, a gap which was not plugged and which was later to lead to further casualties. Both incidents took place early on 28 June. At around 0610 that day, three Me109 fighter aircraft swept in from the sea at very low level and machine-gunned the searchlight positions at Dover, passing low over the harbour itself. No radar warning was received due to the wave-skimming approach altitude and speed, and no guns were fired against them until it was far too late. A little later, at 0658, the Flotilla Leader *Codrington*, on patrol one mile from the Folkestone Light Vessel, was attacked by a single He111 twin-engined bomber, but escaped without damage or casualties. Vice Admiral Dover commented that:

> These two incidents, unimportant in themselves and their results, were interesting in that they were the first attacks of their kind following the occupation by the enemy of the French coast. The surprising feature was perhaps that such attacks had not occurred sooner and more frequently.

That period of immunity was now swiftly drawing to a close.

By Monday 1 July, the Destroyer Flotilla at Dover had been built up to strength of seven ships. *Gallant* arrived at 1110 and was immediately taken in hand for a quick boiler clean, and *Brazen* arrived at 0806 the next day. Two Norwegian-manned MTBs, *5* and *6*, arrived to reinforce the 11th MTB Flotilla at Dover, as did the old submarine *H-49* (Lieutenant J. C. Ogle) to operate from there while the threat of invasion loomed.

The position of air cover for the convoys, now daily plodding up and down the Narrow Sea would, one have thought, exercised the minds of the RAF considerably, now that this lifeline of the nation was, in fact, the front line. The Official Historian was to record:

> The naval view was that standing patrols should be flown over the convoys; but this would have been an extravagant use of our precious fighters. The Royal Air Force therefore preferred to extend cover to the convoys from various Sector Headquarters off whose area of responsibility a convoy might be passing. This, however, tended to result in the arrival of the fighters after the enemy bombers had done their worst and withdrawn.

One senior naval officer at the time was a little more explanatory of the results of Air Ministry inflexibility. Admiral Sir Max Horton, a submarine VC, inclined to straight-talking, put on record at the time his experience of how the various parties operated, and related how C-in-C, Nore, had asked if he could meet AOC Fighters. He was told to, 'put his points on paper and sent it to Fighter Command, with a copy to the Air Ministry'. It can therefore be seen that there were deep divisions, not to say a distinct lack of courtesy or understanding, between the two services, as to the best ways to employ our limited resources. The only certainty was those resources were desperately inadequate for the task facing them. The feeling that the Air Ministry was fighting an entirely separate war to the other two services, already strong after events in Norway and France, deepened as the summer weeks of 1940 went by.

The Destruction of Convoy OA.178, 4 July 1940

Convoy OA (Outward Atlantic) 178 left the Thames and passed Dover safely on 3 July. It consisted of fourteen heavily-laden merchantmen with valuable cargoes, and it was escorted through the Straits without loss. OA 178 was to be the last of the series, although this was not so planned at the time. The passage of these valuable convoys under their very noses, had occupied the Germans' thoughts for some time. They watched them in daylight and at night on their radar screens. They plotted their course and noted the absence of aerial protection, which almost seemed insulting! On the runways, the distinctive crank-winged, hunched forms of two *Gruppen* of Junkers Ju87s lay ready to go; beneath each fuselage a 550-lb bomb was fixed in its wing-down bomb crutch and under each wing was a 110-lb bomb. They had rested after chasing the Allies across the length and breadth of Western Europe. Now they were waiting for their chance to spearhead the German Army's attack from the Kent coast to Reading. Meanwhile, what better use of their precision and skill than millions of pounds' worth of cargoes steaming just off the ends of their runways? On 4 July they pounced. Two *Gruppen* of St G 2 under Oskar Dinort, hit OA178 hard in their screaming dives. There was little warning and no protection from the air for the massed plodding shipping; they had to rely on their guns and those of the two escorting destroyers. But this was just not sufficient.

The convoy was off Portland when the first Stukas struck at about 1300, coming down almost with no warning in waves of six at a time, continuing their attack for an hour or more. This had not been the first such attack for, just two days earlier, the 10,058-ton freighter *Aeneas* had been so hit by Ju87s in the same area. Hit by two bombs, the merchantman had been abandoned by her crew with the loss of twenty-one lives, the survivors being rescued by the destroyer *Witherington* (Lieutenant Commander J.B. Palmer). What happened to OA 178 was a rerun of this strike, but on a much larger scale.

Four ships were sunk outright on this day, all sizeable freighters, *Britsum* (5,225 tons), *Dallas City* (4, 952 tons), *Deucalion* (1,796 tons) and *Kolga* (3,526 tons). Many more were damaged, *Flimston* (4,674 tons), *Antonio* (5,225 tons), *Eastmoor* (5,812 tons), *Argos Hill* (7,178 tons), *Briarwood* (4,019 tons), and *Lifland* (2,254 tons).

The dive bombers then turned their attentions to Portland Harbour itself, where they found many more ships sheltering. They hit and sank the tug *Silverdial*, while the merchantmen *East Wales* (4,358 tons), *William Wilberforce* (5,004 tons), *City of Melbourne* (6,630 tons) were all damaged, the latter in her engine room, flooded by a near miss. As well as these civilian losses, the newly-converted anti-aircraft ship *Foylebank* (Lieutenant Commander H. V. Todd, RNR) was bombed and sunk with the loss of sixty lives in an attack by the Stukas at 0815, which her many AA guns were unable to deter.

Nor was this the end of the story, the survivors were attacked at night by E-boats which torpedoed and sank the *Elmcrest* (4,343 tons) and damaged the *British Corporal* (6,972 tons) and *Hartlepool* (5,500 tons).

Little wonder then, that Admiral Horton felt his worst fears had been fully justified.

Winston Churchill, now Premier, was moved to order that future convoys should have a six-plane escort. This was to be applied to the 'CE' and 'CW' convoys of small coastal colliers, but no more big ships were to be risked in the Narrow Sea just yet. Such convoys were re-routed or held up. In one of their first attacks, therefore, the Ju87s had achieved one of their prime objectives. Further attacks were duly planned.

Churchill, aghast, sent an 'Action This Day' memo to the Vice Chief of the Naval Staff:

> Could you let me know on one sheet of paper what arrangements you are making about the Channel convoys now that the Germans are all along the French coast? The attacks on the convoy yesterday both from the air and by E-boats, were very serious, and I should like to be assured this morning that the situation is in hand and the Air is contributing effectively.

The true answers to his questions were that the situation was *not* in hand, the Air was *not* contributing, effectively or otherwise, but this the VCNS had to spell out with some tact.

It was not only OA 178 that had been hit. Although this had proved to have been by far the most serious blow, all along the Channel the bombers had struck hard at shipping, from Plymouth to Falmouth, Portsmouth to Weymouth. At Portland for example, the bombers returned on 7 July, He111s sinking a mooring lighter and hitting the minesweeper *Mercury* forward. Four of her crew were killed and three wounded. The steamer *British Inventor* was near missed in the same attack and one man was killed. On 9 July the freighter *Aegean* was damaged by a near miss. But all this was merely the warm-up.

Also on 9 July, the *Luftwaffe* struck further down to the east when a 'CE' convoy was approaching the Downs at 1545. The coaster *Kenneth Hawksfield* was hit and suffered substantial damage, which necessitated her being beached. Luckily there were no casualties among the 1,546-ton vessel's small crew. She was patched up and refloated two days later, and subsequently proceeded to London under her own power.

That evening a Heinkel He59 Air-Sea Rescue aircraft, painted white with a red cross, was towed into shore by the tug *Vincia*. She had been shot down by several British fighter aircraft near the South Goodwin Light Vessel in breach of International Law and her crew taken prisoner. The floatplane was beached at Kingsdown and inspected. She proved to be exactly what was claimed – an unarmed rescue plane. After all the press and radio protestation at the bombing of British hospital ships, this was kept strictly under wraps with not a peep from the BBC. Moreover, a few days later, the order went out from the War Cabinet that all such aircraft were to be destroyed, despite the fact that they were rescuing British pilots as well as German ones;

a shabby and shameful act, but, in Churchill's eyes, totally justified in total war!

Commando Raids on the Channel Island, 14-15 July 1940

It was only with the greatest reluctance that Churchill had agreed to the hasty evacuation of the Channel Islands, although they had little military significance and were absolutely indefensible and certainly unsupportable once France was in German hands. He gave way on this with very bad grace, and the few troops stationed there, along with many demoralized civilians, were taken back to England aboard the merchant ships *Biarritz* and *Malines* on 20 June from Guernsey and Jersey respectively. These evacuations were organized by the skipper of the destroyer *Wild Swan*,[2] Lieutenant Commander J. L. Younghusband, RN, who received no acknowledgement, while the Governor ('who was in a considerable stew') later received a medal for it, but it was done efficiently. On 22 June the Trinity House Light Vessel *Vestal* took off lighthouse personnel and civilians from Alderney, followed by six more vessels ('mainly potato boats') the next day, including the *Isle of Sark, Alderney* and *Sheringham*, escorted to safety by the destroyer *Sabre*.

Almost as soon as the first Germans had landed on the Islands, the angry Premier was demanding action, any sort of action, to strike at them. His haste precluded any careful planning and a hasty reconnaissance by Second Lieutenant Nicolle, who was landed from the submarine *H-43* (Lieutenant G. R. Colvin) on 7 July, was followed by an equally hasty and ill-prepared landing by 140 Commandos a week later. This operation, *Ambassador*, left Dartmouth on 14 July in nine Air-Sea Rescue launches, escorted by the destroyer *Saladin* (Lieutenant Commander J. L. Dover) and various small craft of all types. Almost immediately, two of the launches were found to be unserviceable and had to be left behind.

The Commandos were put ashore on the south coast of Guernsey under Lieutenant Colonel J. F. Durnford-Slater, to attack Guernsey airport and a German machine-gun position at Telegraph Bay. One boat went to the wrong island; another group found that one of its landing boats had sprung a leak, landed at the wrong spot and returned. Only Durnford-Slater's group got ashore at the correct place, Petit Port, but they found no Germans, lost half their men re-embarking and left without achieving anything whatsoever.

Monitor Bombardment Proposed, 25 August 1940

Although it is jumping slightly ahead in our story, another example of Churchill's impatience and consequent rashness, was demonstrated in his demand that the old monitor *Erebus* should attack the German heavy guns at Calais. He minuted the First Lord and the First Sea Lord to that effect on 25 August and was demanding action be taken three days later: 'She has an armoured deck against bombing. What is being done about this? When is she going into action?' This was on a par with his suicidal idea, Operation *Catherine*, to send half the Home Fleet into the Baltic earlier in the war, where they would have all quickly been sunk by the *Luftwaffe*, and about as realistic.

Armoured deck she might have, but to put a solitary First World War monitor (top speed twelve knots flat out) against the whole might of the *Luftwaffe* in northern France showed a remarkable lack of understanding of modern warfare. Churchill totally ignored this. Another memo sped to the Admiralty about a week later: 'I trust therefore *Erebus* will not be delayed, as every day our task will become harder.' He was informed that the monitor needed time to work up her new crew and gunners in order to achieve the pinpoint degree of accuracy required, otherwise all the risk would count for little, and that many senior officers had grave reservations on the practicality or even the value of pitting warships guns against forts (as should Churchill, had he taken any cognisance of what had taken place in the Dardanelles in 1915 at his insistence!). But he came back:

> We must not simply look at dangers piling up without any attempt to forestall them. *Erebus* will have to face double the fire on the 16th that she or any other ship would have to face in the next week.
>
> I remember well that it was customary to bombard the Knocke and other German batteries on the Belgian coast very frequently during the late war. It was possible to fire most accurately by night after a buoy had been fixed and sound-ranging used. I ask for proposals for action this week.

At Scapa for working up, however, *Erebus* encountered many troubles. She had been used as a training ship for boy seamen for many years, not as a fighting unit. Due to that, her great age and the lack of essential maintenance she had received over the previous two decades due to lack of funds, (for which Churchill, as a previous Chancellor of the Exchequer was partially responsible), she needed time to be got ready. Bad weather delayed practice shoots. Not all her defects had been ironed out when she was finally sent south in September to accede to this particular bee in the Premier's bonnet.

Notes

1. For eyewitness account of how the Stuka pilots developed their skills in ship attacks see the accounts in Peter C. Smith, *The History of Dive Bombing*, Pen & Sword, Barnsley, 2007.
2. See Peter C. Smith, *H.M.S. Wild Swan*. William Kimber, London, 1985

CHAPTER EIGHT

The *Luftwaffe* Closes the Straits

From 10 July onward, for a period of about two months, the normal hazards of mines and E-boats in the Narrow Sea, were eclipsed by the activities of the *Luftwaffe* and the newly-established Coastal Heavy Gun batteries as they were brought into commission. Not that losses from the first two sources lessened, quite the contrary, but the ebb and flow of the battle to protect the convoys, guard against invasion, and maintain a strong Royal Navy force in the Channel area was mainly linked to the efforts of the German Air Force to oppose them, which were considerable for a short period. The rejection of the German peace plan initiated a burst of effort on the German side in readiness for the invasion, which, real or illusory in fact, appeared to be then a very serious proposition, as it always had been to the British. The initial steps in the German invasion plan called for the elimination of the RAF's fighter force, the laying of a corridor of mines on the flanks of the proposed invasion convoy route and the setting up of heavy guns also to guard the flanks of these routes. The Royal Navy's destroyers and lesser warships had to be driven from the ports of Dover, Sheerness and elsewhere, they had to be prevented from interfering with both the initial landings and the follow-up supply shipping required to maintain their armies once ashore. The German planners had no doubt that, once they got on shore, they would mop up the defenders very quickly with their usual Stuka/Panzer combination against troops mainly armed with little more than rifles and light guns, and even pikes, such was the state of the Nations defences.

No, it was just getting ashore was the real problem. While the main bomber force geared up the air battles, which would eventually become what was known as the Battle of Britain, the Stuka dive bomber force, which should have been kept back in readiness to support the army, was instead, sent out as bait to lure out the British fighters. At first the RAF would not commit more than a fraction of their strength, but, by turning their attentions to the essential coal convoys and inflicting heavy losses on them and on warships, the *Luftwaffe* succeeded both in eliminating for a time, the Royal Navy presence from the Dover area and in drawing out more and more RAF aircraft. This phase of the battle was a success for the German strategy. The subsequent phase did not work to plan, but, as it did not so readily affect the warships in the Narrow Sea, is not part of our story here.

For an adequate defence of these convoys, proper anti-aircraft firepower, adequate numbers of escorts, proper organization and effective air cover were all lacking, or, where they existed, as we have seen, did not mesh. The convoys were protected against submarine and E-boat attack quite well, if not perfectly. The mine menace could be dealt with, or at least contained, only by the endless and patient application of the minesweeping force, which was dedicated and skilled enough. But against bombing, and especially dive bombing, there was no answer initially. The distances were too short for the defending fighters always to reach the convoys in time to intercept, when scrambled from their own airfields, and the convoys were always at a disadvantage. Shelling by the heavy guns on the French coast was unpleasant but the number of hits scored was always tiny. The effect on morale, was, of course, bad, especially when coupled with dive bombing. Had the scale of this combination of attacks continued at the intensity of July-August, grave problems would have undoubtedly resulted.

After the first heavy losses, lessons were slowly learnt. The size of the convoys (twenty-five ships or more) made them too cumbersome and was halved, the escorts increased, the new Hunt Class destroyers were just beginning to come into service and gradually replaced the older destroyers of the Beagle and Gallant class, which, as we have seen, were mainly equipped with low-angle guns only. The Hunts had excellent, dual-purpose main armaments, and better close-range weapons. They were far more suitable for dealing with air attack, but, conversely, they lacked the hitting power of the fleet destroyers 4.7-inch guns and also lacked sufficient torpedo tubes to make them as efficient, in surface actions, as the older ships. A good mix was the idea, but there were insufficient destroyers available. To deal with E-boats, MTBs were brought in, but did not have much success. Throughout the war, the German E-boat crews always feared destroyers first and foremost for the firepower they could deliver. The fitting of extra close-range weapons, like the 'bowchaser' 6-pounder carried by some destroyers, on both the Hunts and the older ships where possible, proved most effective. Many of the older 'V' and 'W' classes were also rearmed, on the lines of those converted pre-war, mainly as anti-aircraft or anti-E-boat ships. This made them a class apart from their sister ships converted for Atlantic duties (who lost a funnel and a boiler to become slow, long-range escort destroyers for deep water operations). All this, of course, took time to develop and mature and most of the heavy casualties in the period now under review, happened before the changes could be fully implemented.

The Opening Phase, 10-19 July 1940

The first convoy to be attacked in this phase of the battle was a 'CW' convoy with thirty coasters, under the escort of the destroyer *Versatile* (Commander H. J. Jauncey). Also involved in the attack were the destroyer *Gallant*, on patrol from Dover, and the 10th Minesweeping Flotilla. The convoy was stretched out between Folkestone Gate and Dungeness around 13000 on 10 July, when the Germans were first sighted. The attacking force consisted of twenty Dornier Do17s from III/KG2. They had an escort of about twenty Me109 and Me110 fighters, and the RAF threw in thirty or so fighters from four squadrons of Hurricanes and Spitfires. This did not prevent the bombers from carrying out their attacks, albeit from a high level and in some haste. The only casualty was the Dutch *schuit*, *Bill S*, which received a direct hit and sank very quickly, although all her crew were picked up safely.

On 11 July, the Stukas returned to Portland Harbour intent on finishing off the job they had started earlier, Ju87s from both St.G 2 and St.G 77 were involved in this assault. Offshore, at 0855, the patrol ship *Warrior II* was bombed off St Abb's Head and sank quickly. Inside the harbour itself, dive bombing developed at 1155 and the *City of Melbourne* was damaged for a second time, as was the *Peru* (6,961 tons). The small tanker *Kylemount* was bombed and sunk off Dartmouth and the steamer *Eleanor Brooke* was another casualty at Portland itself. He.111s attacked Portsmouth on the same day.

There was a lull the next day as the bulk of the German air attacks were shifted north, where a convoy off Ordfordness was hit. On 13 July the dive bombers were back in force with attacks all along the southern coast, with the chief effort by Junker Ju87s of St G 1 against a convoy off Dover, but this had little effect. The following day, their aim had improved and their targets included CW6, which they caught between Dover and Eastbourne at around 1500. Stukas from IV./LG 1 made a heavy attack with twelve aircraft. The only escort was the destroyer *Vanessa* (Lieutenant Commander E. A. Stocker) on which some of the dive bombers concentrated to good effect. Near-misses disabled her main engines very quickly, although the damage to her hull was light. The *Gallant* was at Dover making ready to sail to Chatham to have her after torpedo tubes taken out and replaced by a 3-inch HA gun, she was then to sail to the Mediterranean. But when the news came in of the crippling of *Vanessa*, she was instead sent to take that ship under tow. The bombing had also put *Vanessa*'s degaussing equipment out of action and there had been reports of enemy minelaying aircraft busy the night before. Accordingly, the 'LL' trawlers *Athenian, Onetos, Rodino* and *Taipo* were sent to sweep ahead of the towing party as far as Sheerness. It was not until 0430 on 15 July that the crippled destroyer was got under way, but she was finally brought in safely.

Meanwhile, other dive bombers had selected their targets in the convoy, and the coaster *Island Queen* (779 tons) was hit. She sank soon afterwards, while being towed by the trawler *Kingston Alalite*. The coaster *Mons* (640 tons), was near missed and suffered engine room damage, but managed to reach Dover under her own power. The Norwegian ship *Dlader* was hit aft, badly damaged and set ablaze. Four of her crew were killed and one seriously injured, but the fire was eventually extinguished and she was towed into harbour by the salvage tug *Lady Brassey*. To help in the rescue work, the destroyer *Griffin* was called in from patrol, the destroyer *Boreas* sailed to re-form the convoy and escort it as far at the Portsmouth Command area and two MTBs, a trawler and two tugs were also dispatched.

There was air activity on the following three days, but little actual fighting as far as the surface ships were concerned. On 18 July, the *Luftwaffe* made a bad blunder, and delivered a concentrated attack against several old wrecks at the edge of the Goodwin Sands, apparently under the impression that they were seaworthy vessels. The East Goodwin Light Vessel was also dive bombed and sunk. This was photographed, and much was made of it but, as the Dover Command War Diary admitted, this vessel, '...had not been manned since the early days of the war'.

On 19 July, things warmed up considerably at Dover. Stukas mounted a heavy attack with fighter cover. A squadron of RAF Defiant fighters was sent up to oppose them, but lost six machines in as many minutes to the fighter escorts over Folkestone. These 'turret' fighters were totally out of their depth in such battles and were not so employed again. The Ju87s were therefore able to inflict great damage.

At about 1215 the destroyer *Beagle*, on patrol off Dover, was attacked by a whole *Gruppen* of dive bombers, it was estimated that between forty and fifty aircraft were employed, including fighter escorts. *Beagle* fought back at this mass as best she could, but it was an uneven struggle. Although her high-speed evasion tactics ensured that she was not actually hit, there were many close misses, which damaged her gyro and fan engines. Luckily there were no casualties at all. She limped back to Dover for examination and had to be sent to Devonport Dockyard for full repairs later.

Her gallant and lonely fight took some of the sting out of the dive bombers attack, but a second wave then came in at 1550. This time there were nine Do17s and they bombed the harbour itself and the ships therein in shallow dives. Twenty-two high explosive bombs fell into the harbour area, the main victim being the Admiralty oiler *War Sepoy*, which received a direct hit amidships, which broke her back and she sank in flames. The destroyer *Griffin* was near missed forward and suffered further damage which necessitated docking for attention, the drifter *Golden Gift* was near missed and badly damaged as was the tug *Simla*. Strangely enough, there were no casualties from this severe attack.

The Breaking Point, 20-27 July 1940

The increasing seriousness that these Stuka attacks were having on destroyer dispositions, especially those of the Dover flotillas, was already causing concern. Three ships had been damaged in as many days. Losses had been made good, but the limit in this war of attrition was rapidly being approached.

On 20 July came another heavy blow. Ju87s with heavy fighter protection made a massive dive bomber assault against convoy CV7. The largest clashes of rival aircraft up to that time took place, as the escorts and defenders fought overhead, but the dive bombers again got through to do their job. The main attack was preceded by a feint against Dover itself at 1330, when a small formation of nine bombers attacked, but failed to inflict any damage at all. At 1800, however, larger formations of aircraft were sighted by the convoy, which was between Dover and Folkestone. The escort consisted of the destroyers *Boreas* (Lieutenant Commander M. W. Tomkinson) and *Windsor* (Lieutenant Commander G. P. Huddart) along with the patrol destroyer *Brazen* (Lieutenant Commander Sir Michael Culme-Seymour) and the A/S trawler *Lady Philomena* (Skipper J. Hodson, RNR). They estimated the attacking force to be some thirty Junkers Ju87s escorted by many fighters.

Most of the dive bombers concentrated upon *Brazen* and she was soon surrounded by the spray of near misses. A large bomb exploded directly under her hull in the vicinity of her engine room, splitting her frames and breaking her back. She quickly settled and began to sink. Her gunners fought back to the last; no less than three Stukas fell to her gunfire as she went down, taking her last plunge at 2000. Fortunately, casualties proved light, one man was killed and four injured, but another destroyer had quickly been eliminated.

Other Ju87s had gone for the convoy. The coaster *Pulborough* (960 tons) was hit, set ablaze and sank by the stern. *Lady Philomena* was also slightly damaged, but stood by the sinking *Pulborough* and took off her crew. The coaster *Westtown* (710 tons) was damaged by a near miss and took refuge in Dover Harbour. It had been a sharp blow. The bombers ranged up and down the Channel that evening, and the damaged *Beagle* was again attacked at about 1600 while off Portland on her way to Devonport. Ten Stukas peeled off over her, but she somehow managed to avoid serious damage and shot down one of her tormentors.

Next day it became the turn of the Cherbourg-based Stukas to attack and they hit a convoy off the Isle of Wight, some ten miles west of St Catherine's Point. They hit and sank the 2,318-ton *Terlings* and the Norwegian steamer *Kollskeg*. The destroyer *Greyhound* managed to save thirty-six survivors from the latter vessel and the destroyer *Scimitar* (Lieutenant R. D. Franks) rescued seventeen seamen from the former and landed them at Portland. Both these victims were from a westbound convoy that had been badly mauled.

There were other alarms and excursions at this time. At 1540 on 24 July, for example, the army reported at that a U-boat had been sighted off the Dorset coast steering east. The trawler *Ellesmere* and an MASB were sailed from Portland to investigate, but found nothing. Later that evening, Portland Bill reported that a steamer showing navigation lights was being machine-gunned in the approximate position 500 26'N, 20 23' W, and again, *Ellesmere* put to sea with *St Modwen* and several smaller craft. Plymouth Command sailed the destroyers *Viscount* (Lieutenant Commander

M. S. Townsend) and *Wolverine* (Commander R. H. Craske) and Portsmouth sent the destroyers *Sabre* (Commander B. Dean) and *Shikari* to make a search. The victim turned out to be the French steamer *Meknes*, which had been sunk by the E-boat *S-27*. The four destroyers returned at 0100 laden with survivors; in total they rescued ninety-nine French officers and 779 French naval ratings and passengers. These were fed and provided with boots and clothing before being dispatched to Devonport, Portsmouth and Skegness after being landed ashore at Portland naval base. The persistent U-boat was again reported off St Abbs Head by the army and the coastal corvette *Kingfisher* was dispatched to search for her, but once more, with no luck.

Despite these repeated alarms, strangely enough, there was no widespread incursion of German submarines into these waters. The British minefields, although already fairly extensive, were continually being added to and the British coastal minelayer *Plover* with the Dutch *Willem van der Zaan*, fitted with British broad-gauge mine-rails, were both actively extending them. On the night of 12-13 July, for example, these two minelayers laid fields in the Dover Straits in four different locations:

51° 12.9' N, 1° 51' E
51° 08.4' N, 2° 01' E
51° 06.8' N, 1° 56.2' E
51° 10.4' N, 1° 48.2' E

The Dover-based MTBs provided the converting escort in case of E-boat intervention, but this failed to materialize.

Night attacks by the *Luftwaffe* were also commonplace at this period, but not serious. On the night of 14-15 July an aircraft dropped a stick of eight bombs across Dover town and harbour, the only casualties being two men hit by splinters when the trawler *Birch* was near missed. Minelaying continued to be the *Luftwaffe*'s main nocturnal activity. For example, on the night of 19-20 the destroyer *Vimy* (escorting a convoy northward) reported seeing mines dropped shortly after midnight near the North East Spit Buoy, and two hours later the trawler *John Catting* similarly reported low-flying aircraft, probably minelaying, in the Downs. The destroyer *Beagle* had also reported seeing a seaplane take off from the water about twelve miles south of Leathercoates.

On 22 July, Hermann Goering issued a further directive to his airmen to seal the ports of Dover, Plymouth, Portland and Portsmouth, using both minelaying and air attack. The only hindrance to their schemes was the restricted stocks of magnetic mines that they could obtain.

While all eyes were, naturally, on the air battles over the Straits during the daylight hours, there was a great contrast between these and the passage of the convoys by night. Commander W. J. Phipps of the destroyer *Woolston*, records one such passage, made on the night of 23-24 July.

> At 2040 called up for aircraft overhead and just as I got on the bridge a stick of bombs fell at the head of the convoy. No hit but not far off the Commodore and a lot of them pooped off, but I never saw him and I think he was at about 5,000 [ft] and don't believe the convoy saw him. Shots going off all over the place and they told me afterwards they were firing at the sound. Bloody fools, and I am sure the sound of gunfire attracted the others that came snooping around. There were several about but we never saw one all the time. Closed up and at 0310 another lot were flung at the convoy. The whistle of the bombs sounded as though they were going to be very close and we all dropped flat on the deck. Missed everything and were about 500 yards from us I should think. Remained closed up until daylight at 0400 but nothing more. Busy in the forenoon getting details of their actions and sinking mines. Two of the masters of the merchant ships were below throughout the night and all with a very hazy idea of the attack.

Air attacks by day continued, and, on 24 July, there were very heavy strikes off Dover and elsewhere. The Trinity House vessel *Alert* was sunk near the South Goodwin Light Ship, along with the trawlers *Kingston, Galena* and *Rodino*. But it was on the following day that another peak was reached, on what was termed by one journalist, 'Black Thursday'.

The Attacks on CW8

Convoy CW8 consisted of twenty-one coasting vessels which had left their normal assembly point in the Thames Estuary off Southend and were plodding docilely past Dover at about 1500, the rearmost ships being about two miles from the Detached Mole at that time. Two large waves of dive bombers were dispatched against these vessels, both Ju87 and some Ju88 aircraft being employed from the St.G/3 and the KG.4, about ninety aircraft in total, with fighter protection. It was the Stukas from II/St.G 1 under *Hauptmann* Hozzel, with others from the IV/LG.1 under *Hauptmann* von Brauschitsh, which led the attack and which caused the principal damage. Held in reserve, ready to swoop on any damaged laggards after the Ju87s had done their work, was the 1st E-boat Flotilla (*Käpitan zur See* Brinbacher). The second attack was made on the, by that time, disorganized remnants to the convoy at 1620.

Although an RAF patrol was overhead, it was almost totally ineffective in preventing the dive bombers from carrying out their attacks, such was the weight of the opposition. The ships had to rely, once more, on their limited AA capability. It resulted in a major defeat for the convoy. In the first attack the Stukas scored hits and sank the *Corhaven* (991 tons), *Leo* (1,140 tons) and *Polegrange* (804 tons). In the second attack, which caught the ships off Sandgate, they sent the *Henry Moon* (1,091 tons) and *Portslade* (1,091 tons) to the bottom.

In addition to these sinkings, the following ships of the convoy were damaged to a greater or lesser extent, *Hodder* (1,016 tons), *Gronland*

(1,264 tons), *Newminster* (967 tons), *Summity* (554 tons) and *Tamworth* (1,332 tons). The smallest of these ships, *Summity*, managed to survive. An official account of her exploits read as follows:

> The *Summity* (Captain E. Milton, MBE) a small motor ship carrying cement for Plymouth, was hit three times. The first bomb, on the port side abaft the bridge, blew a naval signalman off the bridge; the second, on the starboard side of the main hold, blew the second naval signalman off the bridge – the third landed right in the main hold. The last one made a mess of the ship; the master, although he and the helmsman had been severely wounded in the wreck of the wheelhouse, decided to beach her. The engines were still running, but the *Summity* could not be steered with her rudder. By manoeuvring the engines ahead and astern, dropping an anchor and sheering with the tide, she was put upon the beach under the Dover cliffs.

The two naval signalmen were among the six dead and twenty wounded suffered by the convoy's crews. While *Summity* went ashore under Shakespeare Cliff, the other four damaged ships were brought into Dover, assisted by tugs. The convoy Commodore was aboard *Gronland* and was transferred by trawler to proceed with what remained of his convoy. Several ships were hit again inside Dover Harbour and sunk.

This had been a prolonged ordeal, but, while the air raids themselves were coming and going, another facet in the drama opened with the dispatch of the E-boats to finish off the cripples. These were soon sighted from Dover and counter-measures were immediately taken. Ten or eleven of these deadly craft were reported by the Port War Signal Station to be seen putting to sea between 1330 and 1400. They were first sighted off Gris Nez steering westward. Fighter aircraft confirmed this sighting and were sent in to attack them, but they failed to do any damage or the deter them. At 1645, clearly seen from the cliff-tops, the E-boats held firm their westerly course, but now appeared to be turning in toward the remnants of the convoy seen plodding off in the direction. It seemed likely that they planned to attack the convoy off Dungeness. Dover Command decided that the time had come for more effective counter-measures. The destroyers *Boreas* and *Brilliant*, along with two MTBs were therefore sailed out at high speed in order to intercept and thwart the enemy flotilla.

The fact was that battle damage had so reduced the Dover Flotilla that these two destroyers were all that remained available, and this is confirmed by the War Diary which stated that the *Brilliant* had been at half-an-hour's notice to steam and *Boreas* at two hours. Within a very short time the two ships had got themselves within range of the E-boats and their salvoes of 4.7-inch shells soon had the desired effect. The enemy boats turned tail and fled. At 1700, one of these vessels was reported as being stopped and it was hoped that the destroyers would sink her, but she got under way again soon afterward. Some twenty-six minutes later *Brilliant* again reported that six E-boats were in sight and, at 1745 she opened fire on them.

The Germans countered by laying smoke to cover their retreat and, as the destroyers pressed home their attack, the German shore batteries, thought to be of 4-inch calibre, opened fire in their turn upon the British ships at a range of about 10,000 yards. To avoid damage to his last ships, V/A Dover ordered them to break off the action and retire forthwith, which they did at 1751. This recall signal was, however, too late to prevent an attack from the Stukas, which had returned to the scene.

The destroyers were returning to Dover at high speed when, around 1800, heavy dive bombing attacks developed over them. Both ships fired back as best they could with their limited AA weapons, but these again proved totally inadequate to prevent the Ju87s from pushing their attacks right home. The first wave scored no hit on either vessels, but there were numerous near misses and two especially close alongside, brought *Boreas* to a dead stop with her steering gear out of order. *Brilliant* closed in to her sister and stood by until she managed to get under way once more, steering 'somewhat erratically'.

They were still some two or three miles from harbour when a second wave of dive bombers struck. This time the Stukas made no mistakes at all. *Boreas* took a direct hit on her bridge wing which penetrated the thin plating and exploded in the galley flat, causing many casualties, fifteen men being killed and twenty-nine wounded, some seriously. The effect of this hit was to damage all her boiler room fans and main cooler castings, which meant that she was unable to raise steam. *Brilliant* took two bombs into her stern, both passed through her quarterdeck, through the whole of the hull and exploded beneath her. Incredibly, no casualties were caused by these hits, but her steering gear was wrecked and the steering compartment, magazine, shell rooms and spirit room were all flooded. Eventually tugs had to be sent to tow both destroyers back to Dover.

Effects of the Stuka Attacks

The consequences of the dive bomber attacks on both convoy and destroyer flotilla were far-reaching. Initially, Dover Command was left with but a single destroyer to guard against invasion at its most likely point. This ship was the Flotilla Leader *Codrington*, but even she was not operational, being moored alongside the depot ship *Sandhurst* engaged in a boiler-clean. The Admiralty immediately sent two destroyers from the Nore Command, *Vivacious* (Lieutenant Commander P. A. R. Withers) and *Walpole* (Lieutenant Commander H. G. Bowerman) to reinforce Dover until more ships allocated to that Flotilla could reach there. Both arrived in the Downs at around 0100 on 26 July and docked at Dover by daybreak.

Even now the ordeal of CW8 was still not ended. Under cover of night the E-boats ventured forth again and attacked. Only three of the enemy were able to take part, *S-19, S-20* and *S-27* but they made every torpedo count. South of Shoreham they hit and sank the *Broadhurst* (1,013 tons), *London Trader* (646 tons) and *Lulonga* (821 tons). Only ten ships of the original twenty-one reached the waters off Portland with a trawler escort. After a short pause, the survivors resumed their voyage sailing for Dartmouth at 2050 on 27 July.

The War Diary commented on this disaster thus:

> The sinking of two destroyers and the damaging to a greater or less degree of five others in 15 days, constituted a rate of loss, which could not be suffered for an indefinite period. Accordingly, arrangements were made first for the 1st Destroyer Flotilla, consisting of H. M. Ships *Bulldog* and *Fernie*, to be based on Portsmouth, leaving one sub-division at Dover, and later, when serious attacks began on the harbour itself, for the whole Flotilla to move to Portsmouth. Patrols were also modified so that destroyers should only be at sea during dark hours.

It was also decided to send the depot ship *Sandhurst* away, transferring her work to the shore. Likewise the costal convoys 'gave food for considerable thought during the period'. A meeting to examine the use of the English Channel and the Straits of Dover, which was attended by the First Lord, Alexander, and the Secretary of State for War, took place on 28 July. It was decided that henceforth the convoys would only pass the Straits at night. But with the German *Freya* radar stations ashore, even darkness could not guarantee their immunity; nonetheless, it was tried.

Destroyers Driven from Dover, 27 July 1940

The 26 July was a relatively quiet day in the Narrow Sea. Only small formations of Stukas were active around the Isle of Wight and off Portland. The sky was overcast, with heavy rain squalls. On the following day, the *Luftwaffe* returned, striking some crippling blows. As well as massed Stuka attacks on convoys in the Thames Estuary, Harwich and off Portland, two very heavy assaults were mounted against Dover itself, including, for the very first time, the Me109 *Jabo* fighter-bombers, which could penetrate any British radar or coastal defence due to their high-speed, low-level approach, armed as they were with a single 550-lb bomb under the fuselage. There was no effective counter to this new aircraft, nor to the continued attacks of the dive bombers.

At Dover the Admiralty decision to withdraw all but one division of the 1st Flotilla was received, but little could be done to implement that order as only one division, and that from the Nore, remained, except for the *Codrington*, which was being refitted. *Brilliant* had been examined, and had been sailed away in the early hours of the morning in an attempt to reach Sheerness under her own steam, but, even at ten knots, she could not make it and had to return. Plans were made to tow her across later. Little else happened during the morning hours.

However, at 1430, a surprise attack was made by four of the new Me109 *Jabo* fighter-bombers. They suddenly appeared from the *landward* side of the harbour out of low cloud and rain, crossed the harbour at high speed and released their bombs, before climbing back to safety in the cloud cover. In truth, the attack was over before it was realized that it had begun. Five bombs fell into the harbour; two were near-misses close astern of the destroyer *Walpole*, the concussion wrecking her turbine feet and damaging one of her dynamos. One day after joining Dover Command, she was out of action. There were no casualties from this attack.

Although given a foretaste of what this form of high-speed sortie was capable of achieving, the defences were again caught out when a second such bombing run was made between 1746 and 1751 by a further six Me109 *Jabos*. All these aircraft came from Experimental *Gruppe* 210 led by *Hauptman* Walther Rubensdörffer. His elite unit consisted of Messerschmitt Me109 single-engined fighters and twelve twin-engined Me110s, all capable of toting 550-lb or 1,100-lb bombs in addition to their normal fighter weapons. They were to feature prominently in the attacks of the next few weeks and caused considerable damage to shipping targets, for negligible loss to themselves. This, the second time they had been in action, proved to be one of their most successful missions.

Although some of their bombs fell outside the harbour, most were right on target. One bomb in particular, fell close alongside *Codrington*, which was moored alongside *Sandhurst* in the submarine basin. The hull of the Flotilla Leader was unable to move at all and the concussion of the 'water-hammer' effect in such a constricted area was sufficient to break her back. The centre portion of the *Codrington* collapsed and quickly settled on the bottom of the harbour. There were only three çasualties, but the ship was doomed. The effect of this one bomb at close range also almost sank the depot ship as well. The shock waves blew in her inlet casings and her boiler room, engine room and bunkers quickly flooded. This inrush of water was eventually brought under control, but with some difficulty.

To give some idea of how surprised the defences had been, the bomb, which damaged these two ships hit at 1749, at the exact time that the AA alarm was sounded. Barrage fire was ordered five minutes later and the civil 'Red' warning alarms sounded off only after another eight minutes had elapsed! By then the *Jabo* aircraft were well on their way back home. The old minesweeper *Tedworth* (Lieutenant Commander W. J. Stride) was also attacked while passing Dover en route for Portsmouth at 1640, but was undamaged. She landed her wounded at Dover before continuing her journey on at night.

There was now no longer any thought of keeping even one division of destroyers at Dover. Only one fit destroyer remained, *Vivacious*, and she was used to escort the crippled *Walpole*, able to steam at ten knots, and the damaged *Brilliant*, being towed by the tug *Lady Brassey*, to Sheerness. To maintain the Straits patrol, the oldest destroyer in the Royal Navy, the 'R' Class veteran *Skate* (Lieutenant F. P. Baker) was lent by Portsmouth Command, pending the return to service of the other ships of the 1st Flotilla, of which only *Bulldog* was still operational. Plans were in hand to re-equip the Flotilla with the new Hunt class ships as they came into service.

On Monday 29 July, the *Luftwaffe* returned to an almost empty Dover to deliver the *coup de grâce*. In truth, they had already done the assigned job. Some four dozen Junkers Ju87s were involved, with heavy fighter escort. They attacked in two waves, commencing at 0275, and it was all over in about a quarter-of-an-hour. The first wave came in from north to south and the second from north-east, both turning into the sun on leaving the target area. Each Stuka deposited one large and four small bombs (550-lb and 110-lb). At least 200 bombs fell, but they fell so rapidly in succession that it was impossible to make an accurate count. One estimate had nearly fifty bombs dropping in the submarine basin alone, where the two biggest ships, the oiler *War Sepoy* and the depot ship *Sandhurst*, both already damaged, lay.

The ancient *Sandhurst* had then suffered direct hits by two bombs, one of which caused a fire to break out in her sick quarters, which was brought under control. Eight other bombs impacted on the Eastern Arm of the harbour wall and caused severe blast damaged. *Sandhurst* began to settle by the stern. To add to her difficulties, a big bomb fell close to the armed steam yacht *Gulzar*. She was driven by diesel oil, but her auxiliary machinery was petrol driven. Diesel oil and petrol seeped out of her and two incendiary bombs hit, causing her to burst into flames and burn furiously as she sank. Oil drums on the Eastern Arm were also pierced by splinters from the bombs, which fell close by and added yet more fuel to the blazing oil slick in the basin. To compound the floating conflagration, furnace oil which had seeped out of the broken *Codrington* also ignited. A fierce wall of flame surrounded the sinking *Sandhurst*. It was brought under control at 1200, only for smouldering debris to reignite it afresh 1¼ hours later. The blaze was not finally quenched until 1500, leaving the depot ship's hull and upperworks blackened and scarred.

Another casualty of this raid was the damaged merchantman *Gronland*, which was now hit again and this time sunk. To prevent the blockship *Umvoti*, moored at Folkestone, from going the same way, she was duly scuttled at the prearranged spot. It was claimed that twenty enemy aircraft were shot down this day over Dover, but it is now known that the total *Luftwaffe* loss was only six machines from all causes, over the whole country. The RAF admitted the loss of three aircraft.

Loss of HMS *Delight*

Serious though it was, this attack on Dover Harbour was by no means the only enemy victory of 29 July. Further west, the destroyer *Delight* (Commander M. Fogg-Elliot, DSO) had sailed from Portland bound for the Clyde in daylight, in spite of Admiralty standing orders to the contrary. Just two days earlier, on 27 July, the Admiralty had issued this order, which stated that owing to damage to destroyers, Dover would no longer be used as an advanced base for the flotillas. The night patrols by the 1st DF in the Dover area, would be carried out at night from Portsmouth instead. This ruffled a few feathers; destroyers could not be manacled in this way many felt. The Admiralty later notified the C-in-C Portsmouth, Admiral James, that while they agreed with him that destroyers must be able to carry out war operations and that, consequentially risks must be accepted, the experience of the last few weeks had shown that there were grave risks to destroyers from dive bombers by day in southern waters. So serious did they view these risks that because of the critical shortage of destroyers, the greatest care had to be taken that they were not unnecessarily subjected to dive bombing attacks.

There was an ample warning of the risks for James to study. On 20 July, for example, the *Acheron* had been attacked at 1610 by a force of ten Stukas while in position 180 degrees St Catherine's Point, off the Isle of Wight. Fortunately *Acheron* escaped damage on that occasion but it was exactly the area that *Delight* was scheduled to pass through on her way down-Channel in broad daylight. The *Delight* herself had arrived at Portsmouth on 19 July for a quick refit and the re-tubing of her superheaters. She did not emerge from the dockyard on completion of this work until noon on the 28th. Meanwhile the Flag Officer, Greenock, hundreds of miles away from the seat of the action, and with no knowledge of local conditions in the English Channel, was requesting that *Delight* urgently rejoin his command, which was short of ships and was due to meet and escort in the Canadian Troop Convoy TC.6 and had to borrow the two Flotilla Leaders *Keppel* and *Inglefield* from Western Approaches Command for that job.

In order to reach the Clyde by a.m. on 29th the *Delight* just had to sail at once at twenty-five knots; she could not await nightfall before proceeding, so James gave the go-ahead, despite the Admiralty stricture to the contrary. Even then, defects developed at the last moment, and *Delight* was further delayed until midnight on 28-29th. She swung her compass that morning and then, being finally ready for her dash northward, sailed from Portsmouth alone.

She was quickly detected by the *Freya* radar station at Cherbourg. A strong force of fifteen fighter-bombers was immediately dispatched and located her at 1830 about twenty miles SSW of Portland Bill in position 500 10' 50" North, 20 27' 50" W. The lone destroyer was quickly overwhelmed by the sheer scale of the attack. The Me109s and Me110s attacked in waves of three aircraft each. The first three bombs fell close to the destroyer but had no appreciable effect, but from the second wave, one of the three bombs hit with a glancing blow of the portside at the break of the forecastle. This blow caused severe structural damage to the ship's side, but not terminal injury. More vitally, however, it caused considerable splinter damage and this was to be her nemesis.

These bomb splinters started a severe fire in the *Delight*'s lower power room and this was fuelled by the escape of oil fuel from tanks, which had also been damaged by splinter penetration. The main steam pipe was fractured and all lighting failed, while the forward magazine group serving 'A' and 'B' guns was probably flooded. This oil-fed fire rapidly spread throughout the ship. Both boiler rooms and her W/T equipment were put out of action. Warned by a report from the station at Portland Bill of what had occurred, Portland base rapidly sailed the patrol ships *Conqueror* and *Pilot*, the Motor Launches *ML-102* and *105*, and the *MASB-1* and *5* to her assistance.

When these vessels arrived at the scene of the attack, *Delight* was on fire fore and aft. The rescue flotilla was joined by the destroyers *Broke* and *Vansittart* (Lieutenant Commander W. Evershed) and, between them, they managed to rescue 147 survivors, including fifty-nine badly injured men. She lost eighteen of her crew killed, missing or died of wounds, mostly bad burns. When last seen, the destroyer was still afloat and afire, but, at 2130 there was a large explosion and she probably went down between then and 2145.

The Admiralty, losing yet another destroyer despite its direct orders, was far from pleased! The Admiralty told James, 'In the case of *Delight*, Their Lordships are of the opinion that an error of judgement was committed in sailing her by day in order to meet the wishes of an officer who could not be aware of the local conditions.'[1]

With the sinking of the *Brazen, Codrington* and *Delight*, all fairly modern ships, the destroyer loss rate kept climbing. Nor was this all, for, on 27 July, further north off the Suffolk coast near Aldeburgh, the destroyer *Wren* (Commander F. W. G. Harker) had been bombed and sunk in position 520 10' N, 20 6'E, while attempting to protect the minesweeping fleet. The Flotilla Leader *Montrose* (Commander C. R. L. Parry) and minesweeper *Halcyon* (Commander E. P. Hinton) managed to pick up four officers and ninety-nine ratings, but thirty-five men had been killed and eight injured. With the loss of yet a fourth destroyer the invasion route had been cleared by the Stukas, at least for daytime use, but the Germans still had no fleet ready to cross.

The Mining of HMS *Whitshed*, 31 July 1940

Enemy dive- and fighter-bombers were not the only factor causing a constant drain on the British flotillas at this time. The mine continued to be a major menace. As an example, on the night of 30 July, three of the Nore Flotilla were on patrol off the Thames Estuary. These destroyers were *Ambuscade*, *Wild Swan* and *Whitshed*. One description of the event read as follows:

> The sea was clam and phosphorescent, but the night was so dark that a destroyer at half a mile was invisible through night glasses. They were, therefore, reasonably secure from air attack, but a good look-out had to be kept for enemy 'E' boats or other craft creeping in under cover of darkness. The night passed peacefully and, as dawn began to break at 4 a.m., the hands – already at action stations – became more alert than ever. In the gathering daylight, visibility soon became extreme. No enemy was in sight. A few miles to the north-eastward and astern a

> coastal convoy, under the escort of other destroyers, was slowly moving to the south, silhouetted against the rising sun. There were no other ships to be seen. *Wild Swan* and *Ambuscade* were still disposed on either side in their night patrol formation.

Whitshed hoisted a signal for the other destroyers to form a line astern, but before it could be hauled down to execute the command, disaster struck.

Suddenly, there was a terrific, thumping explosion under the forecastle of *Whitshed*, and a great column of water, with what appeared to be a black core at the centre, shot into the air as the bows crumpled downwards. The ship had struck a mine! Things unpleasant to contemplate were in that column, and the intestines of one man wrapped themselves around the fore steaming light.

With the ship driving forward at eighteen knots, there was a very real danger of the foremost bulkhead collapsing under the strain... . Luckily, the ship's engines were brought to a late halt in time. The scene below was graphically described:

> Tables and other wreckage had jammed the hatch leading down to the stokers' mess deck, which had automatically shut when the explosions occurred. Instead of rushing out on deck at the order to prepare to abandon ship, a Leading Seaman, helped by two young reservists, all of whom had been knocked about by the explosion, struggled to clear the hatch in order to rescue any stokers who might still be alive. They could hear the frantic struggles from below as trapped men beat upon the hatch, while the water rose steadily in their compartment. Animated by a frenzy and superhuman strength, which only appears in moments of great emergency, the seamen had pushed and pulled, struggled with the heavy wreckage and then thrown their energies into the work of raising the hatch.

Wild Swan eventually towed her leader into Harwich, badly damaged.

A Pause for Regrouping, 30 July to 5 August 1940

The destroyers had gone from Dover, the damaged *Sandhurst* was patched up and prepared for her own escape (she was to be towed up the Thames to Blackwall dock for refitting) and the convoys had stopped, at least for the time being. Harsh lessons had been imparted, note had been taken. Time was now required to put into effect the measure which it was hoped would nullify the enemy's temporary success. Armed gunners were recruited, the 'Channel Guard', to 'ride shotgun' on the coasters. Trawlers were equipped with apparatus to fly barrage balloons to deter [it was fondly hoped] the dive bombers from closing in too much. More important, was the arrival of the new destroyers. A note in the Dover War Diary records this event on 31 July:

Shortly after dawn HMS *Fernie*, the first of the Hunt class destroyers for the

1st Destroyer Flotilla, reached Portsmouth, having passed through the Straits and down channel in darkness in accordance with Admiralty signal 1333/30/7, this bringing the flotilla up to a strength of two ships.

Fernie was soon to be joined by further of her sisters; meanwhile she and *Bulldog* had to hold the fort. On the other side of the disputed water, activity was confined to reconnaissance over the English Channel and small-scale raids inland. Minelaying activity continued unabated, but with no ships venturing out into the Channel results were negligible. The Stukas were forced to await events as 'Eagle Day' approached. It was a pronounced lull. One important victory claimed by the *Epröbungsgruppe 210* on 2 August was the sinking of the 8,006-ton *City of Brisbane* in an attack off the South Longsands Buoy in the Thames Estuary.

The Convoys Recommence: The Battle for CW9

Under the new operating regime, the first coastal convoy to move through the Straits was CE8, which sailed from Dartmouth on 2 August; it was joined by two more ships off Weymouth and sailed on to St Helen's, Isle of Wight on the next leg at 1800 the same day. The new tactic of creeping from harbour to harbour and laying up by day had appeared to work. CE8 got through with no losses and no opposition. It looked good for the return convoy, CW9, which assembled off Southend on 6 August. At the time it was not known that the Germans had carefully plotted the progress of the eastbound convoy for the whole of its tedious passage and drew up their plans accordingly. Night was really no protection from the all-seeing eye of *Freya*. CW9, consisting of twenty-five ships, passed through the Straits of Dover in the late afternoon of 7 August. By midnight it was off the southern coast of the Isle of Wight.

Also off this part of the coast, hidden in the darkness, waiting patiently just off the main swept channel for the easy, slow targets they knew to be chugging steadily toward them, were the E-boats. The German 1st Flotilla, under Birnbacher, had only four ships operational that night, *S-20, S-21, S-25* and *S-27*, but foreknowledge was everything. When the quartet struck, it was deadly. Torpedoes slammed in the *Fife Coast* (367 tons), *Holme Force* (1,216 tons), *Polly M* (380 tons), sending the first pair to the seabed. These were joined there by the *Ouse* (1,004 tons), which, in swinging wildly to avoid a torpedo track, collided with the *Rye* (1,048 tons).

Confusion was total, the merchant navy skippers were highly disorientated and the convoy's pattern quickly disintegrated into a seething, scattering mass of individual small craft trying to save themselves from the unseen assailants. The E-boats took full advantage of the confusion, of course, until *Bulldog* and *Fernie* (Lieutenant Commander R. M. P. Jonas) were hurried out from Portsmouth to restore the situation. They quickly drove off the E-boats, but there was no time to reimpose much discipline among the coasters before dawn broke and left them vulnerable to the German dive bombers, waiting bombed-up and ready.

Several mass Ju87 attacks were mounted against the 'convoy' during the following daylight hours, and, despite a few interceptions by the RAF, who claimed to have shot down thirty-one aircraft for the loss of twenty of their own, the scattered coasters inevitably took further losses. The *Coquetdale* (1,597 tons), and *Empire Crusader* (1,042 tons) were sunk outright; *Balmaha* (1,428 tons), *John M* (500 tons) and *Scheldt* (497 tons) were damaged. Five of the survivors crept into Portland Harbour, seeking refuge, some badly damaged like the *John M*, others relatively unscathed. Several foreign ships in the convoy were also damaged, the Dutch *Veenenburgh* slightly, but others such as *Omlandia, Surte* and the Norwegian *Tres*, had to be towed in, the *Tres* sinking in St Helen's Bay later as a result of her wounds. All-in-all CW9 was *not* the successful debut for which the Royal Navy had hoped to reintroduce the convoys.

Nonetheless, these convoys did continue and, never again did they suffer such losses. It was not, however, the new tactics that saved the day, nor the RAF's exaggerated claims, nor the introduction of the new destroyers. The coaster sailed through the Straits only because the dive bombers had been assigned new and different targets, naval bases, radar stations and front-line airfields, rather than ships. In other words, the battle had moved on to the second stage, which called for the elimination of the defences. Ships continued to be attacked and sunk, but only in isolated episodes which were mainly incidental to the principal task of the enemy aircraft. Unbeknown to the brave and stoical merchant seamen who commanded the little ships, their worst ordeal was over, at least from the air.

Note

1. Signal, Admiralty to C-in-C, Portsmouth, contained in ADM 199/101, (National Archives, Kew, London). I am grateful to my good friend Edwin R. Walker for this information.

Chapter Nine

The Convoys Fight Back

Before taking leave of the coastal convoys and their defence, and indeed of the trials of the Dover Command during its first year of war, an examination of one more ordeal of fire which was undergone by the little ships and their escorts is necessary. The batteries of heavy guns, emplaced by the Germans in order to lay down a defensive field of fire on both flanks of their planned invasion route, was never a practical defence. They tended to simplify matters in their own eyes by equating the crossing of the English Channel to a more complicated equivalent of crossing the River Meuse; laying on massive artillery and dive bomber support was a natural part of this to the German planners. Unfortunately, as 'an excellent anti-tank ditch', as the French politician Weygand once ruefully remarked, the Channel was much more difficulty for the Panzers to leap at a bound, no matter how well organized! Nevertheless, having established the heavy guns, and while waiting for the invasion to begin, the German artillerymen determined to make life eventful for the British convoys now that the main focus of the *Luftwaffe* had moved on and away from them.

The principal artillery batteries emplaced by the Germans from June 1940 onward along the stretch of coastline from Cap Gris Nez to Calais, were:

Batterie Lindemann	Three 16-inch guns
Batterie Todt	Four 15-inch guns
Batterie Grosse Kurfurst	Four 11-inch guns
Mobile Railway Batteries	Four 11-inch guns

All these heavy weapons could, in theory, dominate twenty-two miles of the Channel waterways, and beyond, and, at first, the British had no reply whatsoever to these colossal weapons, other than their own few heavy guns mounted aboard battleships and monitors. Dive bombing attack by Royal Navy Skua and Roc were accurate but only delayed the construction of these gun positions for a time, and once the Navy aircraft were moved back north to attack targets in Norway, there were no aircraft in the RAF with the precision to hurt them. Work was therefore pushed forward and they were soon operational. Two 14-inch guns, manned by the Royal Marine Artillery, [who christened the first one 'Winnie' out of respect for Churchill, and the second one 'Pooh' because that is the uniquely English sense of mocking humour] had been hastily established in May. From September 1940 onward, the Royal Artillery began setting up yet further gun batteries in the Dover area to respond to German shelling and attack German shipping. These were:

Fan Bay Battery	Three 6-inch guns
South Foreland Battery	Four 9.2-inch guns
Wanstone Battery	Two 15-inch guns

The first of these emplacements was not finally completed until February 1941, the second in October 1941, while the Wanstone Battery was not made ready until June 1942, when the time of greatest need had long since passed. In conjunction with the establishing of these batteries, both sides set up Coastal Radar Stations capable of tracking both surface shipping and aircraft, and these grew more sophisticated as the war continued. Already, as we have seen, trials with special CHL sets had produced good results at Dover, but not until early 1941 were they established as part of the defence proper. By contracts, the German systems were in use from late August 1940.

Bombardment by German Long-Range Guns

On 22 August 1940, the eastbound convoy CE9 was due off Dover at 0930. It consisted it just twelve coasting ships, (the reduced number of vessels being part of the new defence measures) escorted by two Hunt class destroyers, *Fernie* and *Garth* (Lieutenant Commander E. H. Dyke) along with the usual trawlers and kite vessels. The weather was fine, with light to moderate winds, the sea was fairly smooth and visibility was good, with some light cloud. As the convoy plodded past Hythe, three four-gun salvoes were fired by the Gris Nez battery, the first shell falling at about 0924. Although the *Official History* comments that the Germans began their shelling of convoys ten days earlier, the shots on 12 July were only ranging ones and not aimed at specific ships. This attack was different and the first true shelling, so 22 August actually marked this new phase in the Battle of the Narrow Sea. After this there was about an hour's uncanny silence. Indeed, so unexpected was the whole incident, that *Fernie* initially reported that they were being bombed, although no aircraft were to be seen, a mistake repeated by the coastguards ashore.

By 1040 the head of the convoy was approaching Dover, when fire was re-commenced, and it was maintained until they had passed Leathercoates. Most of the shells appeared to be directed against the head of the convoy, which was proceeding in two columns as usual. Most of the rounds fired were in salvoes of four and, when the next battery took up the attack, in salvoes of three. In total, 108 rounds were counted, several of which missed the convoy completely and fell off the Shakespeare Cliff, well inside the line of the Detached Mole of the harbour. As the little ships passed across the harbour entrance, two shells actually landed inside the harbour, close alongside an A/S trawler. Several of the coasters were near missed, but not one hit was obtained, which was just as well as these small ships would not have survived a direct strike.

Fernie and *Garth* raced up and down the convoy lanes, laying a thick smokescreen to shield their charges from observation, either on land or in the air, and this was thought to have helped matters at the time. It is, unfortunately, hardly likely to have made much difference with the radar installations the German's had at their disposal. As the convoy passed South Foreland and drew slowly out of range, the accuracy of the salvoes, itself impressive despite the lack of reward, soon began to fall off and firing finally ceased at 1215. An attack by twelve dive bombers also failed to produce the usual results. As a postscript to this event, from 1730 to 1845 the solitary 14-inch guns in position at St Margaret's opened fire on the Gris Nez battery in reply, using a spotter plane to direct fall of shot. One round was short and two were over, and fire was ceased after that. It is doubtful whether the Germans were much impressed by such a feeble response, but it was of course well played up in the British press at the time.

Continued Shelling of Coastal Convoys

An official account continues the story of the German gun batteries:

> During the following two years, approximately one out of every five of the convoys passing through the Straits was attacked, and each convoy attacked received on the average, twenty-nine rounds from the German heavy guns ashore. Then there was a lull and, in 1943, no convoy was fired at from the ashore. But shooting commenced again sporadically in 1944 and so continued until the German batteries were finally silenced. The time between the flash of the German guns and the explosion of their shells was some thirty-two seconds. Comparatively few ships of the convoys were hit by shellfire, for small ships at long range are not easy targets; but in their many passages during four years, the men of the coasters experienced 1,500 flashes and 1,500 periods of suspense – each of thirty-two seconds duration – any of which might have culminated in the destruction of their ships.

It no doubt gave another cause for grave deliberation in the German camp at this time, with invasion preparations steadily mounting, that the guns which had been expected to drive thirty-five knot destroyers away from their troops transports and supply ships, failed to hit any of the five-knot coasters after two hours' deliberate practice. In this way, it could be argued, the coasting convoys drove yet another nail into the coffin of Operation *Sealion* – the abortive German invasion of England.

Air Attack on Naval Bases Increase: August – September 1940

Having cleared the Straits, if only for a short period, most German dive bomber units were switched to attacks on main ports, airfields and military installations in the coastal region as the second stage of the Battle of Britain got under way. Although in these attacks, the warships of the Royal Navy were regarded as prime targets, actual losses, while heavy at peak times, were kept within [just] bearable limits.

One example of this took place on 11 August when a heavy raid was made on Portland and Weymouth by an estimated 150 aircraft. The destroyer *Scimitar*, lying in Portland Harbour, was slightly damaged by several near miss bombs and sustained some casualties. Motor Launch *102* had her hull damaged by splinters. Three days later, three Junkers Ju88 bombers attacked from 10,000 ft and hit the coaling pier, the MASB base, Admiralty House and other targets, including slight damage to the tug *Carbon* and the coastal corvette *Kingfisher*.

Other attacks were more serious, like the one directed against Portsmouth Naval Base on 24 August. The First Lieutenant of the destroyer *Bulldog* recalled that happened:

> After repairs *Bulldog* was expected to rejoin what was left of the 1st Flotilla at Dover but before she sailed for that port there was a very heavy air-raid (in which the Leader *Codrington* was sunk) and the order was rescinded. Instead, *Bulldog* worked with the flotilla from Portsmouth and our principal work was to patrol the Channel at night in case of invasion and to deter the E-boat attacks on our coastal convoys. Ships returned to harbour by daylight.
>
> Air raids were increasing by day and it was in August that a particularly heavy one occurred. *Bulldog* and *Acheron* were lying alongside the North-West Wall when the planes were seen coming over Portsmouth from the south-east at a low height. It was a heavy raid; it was lucky that so many bombs overshot our ship and landed in the water. But one bomb landed plumb in the centre of *Acheron*'s quarterdeck. Many were killed in the other ship and in *Bulldog* it was our captain, Lieutenant Commander Wisden, who was hit badly with splinters in the stomach. We called alongside one or two small craft afloat in the harbour and our wounded were taken as quickly as possible across to Haslar Hospital. Wisden died two days later.
>
> We were in something of a mess. Splinters from the bombs had damaged the barrels of 'X' and 'Y' guns as well as the after screen. Depth charges had been punctured and were spitting and burning, giving off acrid smoke. Presently along the road came a car and it was Admiral James, the C-in-C, driving himself and wearing his tin hat; touring round to see the damage. He was a remarkable man. He came aboard and looked over our two destroyers and told me to take charge. He appointed me in command of *Bulldog*, an appointment which was

confirmed by the Admiralty.

This raid was mounted by some forty Ju88s with Me110 escort, and produced the heaviest civilian casualty figures to date. The alert sounded at 1610 and *Acheron* (Lieutenant Commander R. W. F. Northcott) received a direct hit on her starboard quarter ten minutes later, midway between the stern and the foremost bulkheads of the tiller flat. Three other bombs burst within 100 yards. The explosion demolished the ship abaft 'Y' gun down to the level of the lower deck and killed two ratings as well as *Bulldog*'s CO. Both ships were lying alongside the north-west wall, south, with *Acheron* inside *Bulldog*, so she took most of the blast.

The Offensive Reopens – Striking Forces Operate 7-12 September 1940

On the evening of Saturday 7 September there was excellent visibility in the Channel, and large numbers of small craft, tugs, trawlers, self-propelled barges and the like, were seen from Dover to be on the move off Calais and Boulogne. There appeared to be a general movement in progress towards the south-west and plans were laid for the MTBs to strike at this mass of shipping that night. Accordingly, four MTBs, *6, 29, 71* and *72*, were dispatched from Dover at dusk; the first pair to the waters off Calais, the latter pair to Boulogne. To date, the coastal craft of the Royal Navy had not been particularly successful, especially when compared with the achievements of their German opposite numbers. In fact, so disappointing had been the results of the MTBs up to that date, that initial enthusiasm for the type had generally been replaced in the Royal Navy regular warship crews by a tolerant resignation. Not for another year or more was this poor record to be rectified to any great extent with more craft, better armed and improved training and tactics.

On the night of 7-8 September, both MTBs heading for Boulogne were soon forced to withdraw due to the weather conditions. British MTBs were much smaller than their German E-boats, and more temperamental due to their power-plants, more vulnerable thanks to being petrol-engined instead of diesel, and more lightly equipped. The two Calais boats pressed on and reported sighting a number of small vessels off that port, although they could not properly identify them. Both boats made torpedo attacks and scored one hit each, 'although it was not certain upon what', and both made machine-gun attacks at very close range on a tug or similar craft.

Something more substantial was obviously required than this type of thing. The 1st Destroyer Flotilla was already at sea: *Atherstone* (Commander H. W. S. Browning), *Beagle* (Lieutenant Commander R. H. Wright), *Bulldog* (Lieutenant F. J. C. Hewitt) and *Saladin* (Lieutenant Commander L. J. Dover) and were ordered to divert from their patrol and attack the enemy shipping concentration off Calais. The order was not given until far too late, however, and, although they complied with it, they had further orders to be well clear to the west of Dungeness by dawn. The force had no choice therefore, but to turn back when off Blanc Nez; even so *Atherstone* reported that they were shadowed by German aircraft on their way back to Portsmouth once dawn broke.

At Dover, Portsmouth and Harwich it was decided to take the offensive against the reported enemy concentrations should conditions so permit. When similar mass movements were once again observed during the daylight hours of 8 September, strong surface forces were readied and duly put to sea at dusk. The light cruiser *Galatea*, which was escorted by the destroyers *Campbell, Garth* and *Vesper* formed one striking force. Her sister cruiser, *Aurora* (Captain L. H. K. Hamilton) with the destroyers *Hambledon* (Commander H. Carlill), *Holderness* (Lieutenant Commander Deric E. Holland-Martin) and *Venetia* (Lieutenant Commander B. H. de C Mellor) was another. MTB forces from Harwich were to operate closer inshore, while ships of the 1st Destroyer Flotilla from Portsmouth – *Atherstone, Berkeley, Beagle, Bulldog* and *Fernie* – were to carry out a sweep along the French coast from Le Touquet to the south-west up to five miles north of Cap d'Antifer. To assist in navigation for the cruiser squadrons, additional lights, the South Foreland Lighthouse and the North and South Goodwin Lightships, were shone, while tugs and rescue craft were held ready in case of mishap.

The whole force sailed as planned that night but, in fact, met with little or no success, due mainly to the weather. At midnight a very violent and sustained thunderstorm broke out and low cloud and heavy rain reduced visibility to a very low level. The Portsmouth flotilla had no luck with their sweep and nothing very tangible emerged from the intermittent clashes reported by the other groups. Worse yet, *Galatea* was damaged when she exploded a mine at 0525 next morning, which put her in dockyard hands for a month. The hard fact is that, while these powerful British forces were at sea looking for German invasion craft, German torpedo boats (in effect, small destroyers) were laying minefields on the British side of the Channel. They did so under the very noses of the British, not once, but time and time again, as they had done in 1939. Even after a year of war these audacious German surface forces were still operating with impunity. On the night of 5-6 September for instance, the *T-5, T-6, T-7* and *T-8* of the German Second Torpedo Boat Flotilla, commanded by *Kapitän zur See* Riede, carried out Operation *Walther*, the laying of a minefield in the Dover Straits. Again, on the night of 8-9 September, the same ships conducted another such operation, *Hannelore*. This time they were extremely fortunate to escape both detection and annihilation; only more bad weather saved them.

Meanwhile the assembly of suitable invasion craft continued. The were four main German groups being readied:

Transport Force A – Dunkirk – *Kapitänleutant* H. Bartels. 15 Steamships, 60 tugs, 180 flat-bottomed barges, 120 motor boats
Transport Force B – Ostend – *Kapitänleutant* E. Lehman.

50 Steamships and smaller craft, 25 barges
Transport Force C – Calais – *Kapitän zur See* G. Kleikamp
400 tugs, steamers and small craft and self-propelled barges.
Transport Force D – Boulogne – *Kapitän zur See* W. Lindenau.
330 barges, 15 minesweepers and R-boats, 25 trawlers.

Despite the impressive titles and numbers of vessels assembled, there was not much enthusiasm for the enterprise from Grand Admiral Erich Raeder himself down to the humblest trooper. No one in England, however, was prepared to discount completely the threat of invasion, save for one man. The C-in-C, Home Fleet, Admiral Sir Charles Forbes, was a wise head among the panicky Whitehall Warriors, and he continually advocated the policy of allowing the Army and Air Force to withstand the first shock of any landing, not that he really believed it would occur. He felt that the correct role of the Royal Navy was to mop up and ensure that, once across, nobody in the invading force would ever get back. This was not a risk that the War Cabinet was prepared to take, and Forbes got no thanks or recognition from the politicians for having been, as events turned out, the only one to get it right.

On the night of 10-11 September, a striking force consisting of the Flotilla Leader *Malcolm* (Captain T. E. Halsey) with destroyers *Veteran* (Commander Jack E. Broome) and *Wild Swan* (Lieutenant Commander C. E. L. Sclater) patrolled off Ostend. The sea marks had been removed but these destroyers were old hands in these waters and, although the North Hinder Light was not sighted, the Kwinte Bank Whistle Buoy showed up on the expected bearing and the Ostend Bank RB, RW Whistle and Wenduyne Bank Bell Buoys were all burning correctly and on station to assist navigation. *Malcolm, Wild Swan* and *Veteran* approached Ostend in single line ahead, at a speed of twelve knots and, at about 0305, the radar plot reported four objects three miles off the squadron's starboard bow. Shortly afterwards, Captain D16 sighted a large barge on the correct bearing. At 0316, the course was altered to parallel the Dutch coast and fire was opened on the barge at 1,000 yards range, while speed was increased to twenty knots. Bombers were over Ostend at the time and light of the flares they were dropping haphazardly over the whole area was sufficient to illuminate the warships' targets. *Malcolm*'s second 4.7-inch salvo hit the target and debris flung up from it could clearly be seen. They estimated that it was slightly shorter than a destroyer, self-propelled, with a raised bow and only two or three feet of freeboard. As each of the destroyers sped past they pumped main armament salvoes into this target at close range. By the time *Veteran* had left her astern she was awash and sinking.

Already another target was in view to the north-west. This proved to be a second barge, somewhat smaller than the first, and two or three salvoes had been directed at it, with one direct hit, when yet another ship came into sight, a large trawler. Fire was promptly switched to engage this target. The

German escort fired back for a brief period, but was soon heavily hit and her guns silenced, one shell of a salvo hitting her under the bridge and producing a sheet of flame. When in turn the German escort was left astern she was heavily on fire and sinking, breaking up as she went down.

It was not twenty-five minutes since the first sighting. Ahead nothing was to be seen either visually or by radar, so course was altered to 035 degrees, and they quickly came up with a fresh target. A small tug or trawler came into sight towing yet another barge (described by *Malcolm* as ' about the size and appearance of a Thames barge without mast') to the east. Both main armament and pom-pom fire was poured into these vessels, the barge being heavily hit first; then the tug was repeatedly hit aft by the 4.7s and the pom-pom, one shell knocking the whole bridge structure over the side. When last seen, this vessel too, was very low in the water, apparently sinking. The barge had been hit once by *Malcolm* with her main battery and then by both *Wild Swan* and *Veteran* in turn.

In his summary of this brisk little action, Captain D16 thought that both the large trawler and the large barge were certainly sunk, that the small trawler was almost certainly sunk, and that the small barge might have escaped in a damaged condition. Most of the return fire from the Germans came from ashore, shells of various calibres from pom-pom and 12-pounder shells up to 4-inch and 6-inch calibre were spotted off *Malcolm*'s port quarter and *Wild Swan*'s port bow, but no hits were received on any of the British trio.

Malcolm's gyro failed at the first salvo of the action and this was not immediately observed. By the time it was noticed, the ship was steadied on a magnetic course, and it seemed certain from the evidence of the destroyers astern of her that this course was considerably closer to the enemy coast than had been anticipated. It was noted that: 'The RDF (an ASV set) has once again proved itself of immense value both for locating and ranging, and the security it gives against surprise.'

Similar operations were conducted by the various flotillas on patrol. For example, the following night the 21st Destroyer Flotilla with the Flotilla Leader *Campbell* and destroyers *Garth* and *Vesper*, operated off the Dutch coast, and the 1st Flotilla was active from Portsmouth. Occasionally it was not just the smaller German shore guns that joined in, as Commander Hewitt recalled to the author:

> One night in September *Bulldog* was last in the line of four destroyers steaming up the Channel and we had neared the Dover Strait and were expecting to be turning back when a signal arrived from the Flag Officer, Dover. It told us that enemy minelayers were thought to be operating on the other side of the Channel and we were to investigate. Our leader turned and led us round and we crossed to a short distance from the hostile coast. It was pitch dark. We were cruising along slowly, prepared to catch any enemy vessels by surprise, when suddenly, there was a

'WHOMP'. A tower of water shot up into the sky between *Bulldog* and the next ahead, the old destroyer *Sardonyx* (Lieutenant Commander R. B. S. Tennant).

It reminded me of the Nab Tower suddenly rearing up ahead. It was a very nasty shock, for there was no warning it was on its way.

Without any signals at all we did a 'Nine Blue', which at that time meant we turned to port together ninety degrees. Sparks were showering from the old *Sardonyx*'s funnels as she piled on the steam and put her foot down and we dashed back across the Channel in short order. But no matter how we weaved and turned on the run back to safety, the enemy had our exact range and plot (probably by use of radar) although he could not see us for line. The heavy shells continued to fall between us. I believe they were 11-inch shells from guns newly installed on the cliffs at Cap Gris Nez. The most interesting thing was, of course, that the sound of the projectile arriving was heard *after* sight of the splash of the shells. It was a bit unnerving at first.

Shortly after this experience, *Bulldog* met *Beagle* and *Brilliant* and the three ships carried on north to the Firth of Forth where they joined the Home Fleet and had a hard winter alternately escorting the Fleet itself and some Atlantic convoys. Their job in the Narrow Sea was done for the time being, as there were now sufficient Hunt class destroyers or converted 'V' and 'W' class destroyers to relieve most of the Fleet destroyers. However, with the arrival of four of the larger German destroyers at Cherbourg on 6 September, *Karl Galster, Hans Lody, Friedrich Ihn* and *Erich Steinbrink*, the powerful British ships of the 5th Destroyer Flotilla were moved from Harwich to Plymouth to act as counter forces. The ships of the flotilla, the new 'J' and 'K' class ships, were powerful destroyers and under the command of Captain Lord Louis Mountbatten; however, they failed to destroy their rivals and, indeed, came off very much second-best on several occasions due to his questionable leadership decisions.

Blooding of the Hunts, September 1940

The First Flotilla at Portsmouth by now had a fair leavening of the new Hunt Class ships and it soon became almost exclusively a Hunt equipped unit, and was destined to remain the case throughout most of the rest of the war. Some twenty of these little destroyers were under construction at the beginning of the war, a programme got underway through the wise decision of Roger Backhouse, appalled at the lack of British destroyers pre-war, but it had to be disguised from the politicians of the day that they were destroyers and the ruse of calling them 'Fast Escort Vessels' had to be resorted to in order to get funding![1] So handy and valuable did these ships prove themselves to be, that further orders were placed, with the result that eighty-six were finally constructed. They lacked the 'Fleet' destroyers speed, not being capable of much more than twenty-five knots in most conditions, which meant that they were also much slower than the German types. Furthermore they lacked the punch and hitting power of conventional destroyer's 4.7-inch guns and torpedo tubes. These handicaps were, however, less real than apparent. The older 'Fleets' quickly had their torpedo armaments halved, from eight to four or five, by the replacement of one mounting with an old 3-inch or 4-inch HA gun with no proper control and little value as some means of air defences. By contrast, although some of the earlier Hunts proved top-heavy and had to have one of their three twin mounts removed, reducing their main armament from six to just four 4-inch guns, these guns were dual-purpose and invaluable at this period. The Hunts did not at first carry torpedoes at all, but later groups were fitted with three 21-inch torpedo tubes, which meant they almost equalled the modified 'Fleets' in this respect. Again the German destroyer types, both large and small, retained their full outfits of torpedo tubs, much as they had been built, throughout the war, and could always outfight the British ships in this respect. The Germans had better close-range AA weapons. But the Hunts were sturdy little ships, capable of mass-production, and were eminently suitable for the rough and tumble of the war in the Narrow Sea. They earned their laurels the hard way. They were soon in the very thick of the fight, at first supporting the 'Fleets', but more and more taking over from them.

The very first Hunt to be commissioned was the *Atherstone* (Commander H. W. S. Browning) which had run her trials in Liverpool Bay only nine months after being laid down in Cammel Laird's shipyard. She touched over thirty knots and this remained the fastest speed ever recorded for a ship of her class. She joined the 1st Flotilla after working up and, like many other ships in those dangerous days, did not last long unscathed.

On 11 September 1940, *Atherstone* was Senior Officer of the escort of convoy CW11 along with *Fernie*. The convoy had formed up off Southend at 1330 and was just beginning to file its way through the channels of the Thames Estuary to commence it journey. *Atherstone* was leading it in a long single column, with *Fernie* stationed astern. The RAF Fighter Command for CW11 was *Peewit* and as they steamed between the South Edinburgh and East Tongue Buoys, the signal 'Blue Peewit' was received, indicating imminent air attack.

Almost immediately, three Messerschmitt Me109 *Jabos* appeared and attempted to bomb and machine-gun the convoy and shoot down the barrage balloons some ships were flying, but they were driven off. This sortie took place at 1820, and was obviously a preparatory strike for the main blow which swiftly materialized. Twenty minutes later, some twenty-one Junkers Ju88s appeared, escorted by two lines of Me110s. As the *Atherstone*'s skipper later wrote in his report:

> The navigation position of the attack could hardly have been better chosen as the ships had no manoeuvring room and minesweepers were

> just passing ahead of the escort in order to stream their sweeps. Convoy was in single line ahead with *Atherstone* leading and *Fernie* in the rear. In order to attack the convoy all the bombers had to pass *Atherstone*. Eleven of the twenty-one attacked *Atherstone* from the bow and right ahead, the remaining ten being held in reserve until the escort had been dealt with. During their descent two broke off to attack the minesweepers, the remaining nine synchronized their attack from right ahead and fine on both bows.

It was a clever and determined attack, executed with speed and the efficiency the Navy had come to expect from the *Luftwaffe*. Some twenty-seven bombs were dropped and most were hits or near misses. The control and barrage fire of the little destroyer appeared to have some effect on the bombers, especially when the rate of fire was increased in barrage, but the ship was overwhelmed by the size and speed of the attack. Again, the *Atherstone*'s skipper:

> In all the ship received three direct hits and five near misses within sixty yards of the ship, but the total armament was not affected and there is no doubt that the remaining bombers were dissuaded from attacking the convoy while *Atherstone*'s guns were capable of being fought. During the dive-bombers' descent Messerschmitt 110s machine-gunned the ship and possibly one or two of the ships in convoy. The sky was clear of aircraft within two minutes of the attack. During both the raids fighter assistance was asked for but was not forthcoming: the same thing occurred during convoy CW1O. The reasons for this are not known.

Two of the bombs which hit *Atherstone* passed right through the bridge, one exploding in a bunker and one in number one boiler room. The third fell on the port side at the break in the forecastle and exploded in number one boiler room, blowing in the bulkhead of number two boiler room, and blowing out the port side. These three direct hits put all the machinery, lights and W/T out of action. Both boiler rooms were flooded and the bulkhead forward of number one boiler room was leaking steadily. Both the forward and after bulkheads were quickly shored up and the leaks plugged, but had the swell been any greater, it was considered extremely doubtful that the destroyer would have made it back to port safely. Command of the convoy was handed over to *Fernie* and the tug *Turquoise* took the cripple in tow, eventually anchoring off the Nore Light Vessel at 0415 hours. The captain summed up as follows:

> The position in which HMS *Atherstone* found herself at 1850 was far from pleasant as (1) It was problematical whether the forward bulkheads of No. 1 boiler room would hold; (2) 50% of the dive-bombing aircraft had not unloaded their bombs, and *Atherstone* was a sitting bird; (3) *Atherstone* was on the German bomber route to the

South East of England; (4) There was still two hours daylight followed by a bright moon; (5) No fighter escort had yet appeared. In spite of the above, which all the ship's company had realized, the conduct of all the crew was in accordance with the highest traditions of the Service, and the one desire of the Officers and men was to get the ship home. In this connection it is submitted that it is a triumph to the Constructor Branch that, after receiving three direct hits and five near misses the ship was still capable of being brought home by the ship's company.

Big Guns go into Action: Battleship and Monitor Bombardments

One feature of the old Dover Patrol, under German occupation of the Belgian coastline in the First World War, had been the effect of the Royal Navy's heavy guns on the seaward flank of the army. Very early on in that great conflict, with German armies similarly established on the coast, one of the oldest battleships in the Royal Navy had been fitted with 'bulges' underwater to protect her from torpedoes and had her fins relined. She then crossed over the Channel, the ship was heeled over to give the guns extra range and she bombarded the Germans at 16,000 yards distant or more from a position off Westerende. Her name had been *Revenge*, but she was renamed *Redoubtable* soon afterwards when a new battleship was built called *Revenge*. By a curious coincidence, when another battleship was required to carry out this same duty in the same area in another war, it was that *Revenge*, now herself an old lady, that was selected, for she had become, by this time, the oldest battleship in the fleet!

The coincidences did not end there, for a monitor was built in the First World War and named *Erebus*. She was armed with the same 15-inch guns as the battleships. In 1940 she was still serving and was based at Portsmouth with *Revenge*. She too, as we have seen, was called into action to bombard the enemy, despite her age. The Admiral in command of the Dover Patrol during most of the Great War had been Admiral Reginald Bacon, a great gunnery expert. He had spent a great deal of time and trouble perfecting techniques and developing methods to enable the big gun monitors under his command to carry out pin-point bombardments of the lock gates at Zeebrugge, Ostend and elsewhere. As the only accurate method known of hitting back at the enemy, in view of our lack of dive bombers, the same techniques were to be tried again at Churchill's insistence, as he had been First Lord for a time in that earlier conflict. Many old ghosts must have stirred in the Narrow Sea in those days.

First Bombardment Attempt by *Erebus*, 20 September 1940

The target selected for the first attempt at Monitor bombardment by night, Operation 'MW', was against the heavy batteries at Cap Gris Nez. Even when this attack was first proposed, there had been opposition to it at the Admiralty. The old *Erebus* (Captain H. F. Nalder) had been built as long ago as 1916 (as the *M-15*), and had lain inert at Portsmouth for many years prior the war as a training establishment. She mounted one twin 15-inch turret, and also had four twin 4-inch mountings and two single 3-inch AA guns and carried a crew of over 300 officers and men. Her great broad-beamed hull with the enormous anti-torpedo bulges, coupled with her shallow draught (eleven feet) made her a cumbersome craft at the best of times. Her best speed had been about twelve knots in her heyday, but that was long since past. Captain Nalder had been appointed to command her on 1 July. Her great guns were to be utilized at last. Many felt that she would merely provide the E-boats with the best possible target; huge, vulnerable and slow, yet offering them the chance to notch up a notable 'scalp' if they could hit her. The reply to such criticism was that it was the way of the Navy to fight back at its enemies and not just suffer and endure in silence. The German big guns had been a menace, it was high time they were challenged. Even so, replied the critics, to achieve the phenomenal accuracy required needed perfect conditions and much training, as well as good reliable spotting. None of these was available in September 1940. Nor could the racing tides of the Channel assist with accurate plotting and holding her position relative to the target, vital if hits were to be achieved. Nonetheless, it was attempted, and *Erebus* duly sailed with her own escort of two destroyers to try and keep the E-boats at bay.

To shield her slow passage along the Channel by daylight, the approach of which would be long plotted and detailed in France, the old monitor sailed from Sheerness and attached herself to the westward-bound convoy CW.12. Two MTBs also added themselves to her escort for a while. MTB-*5* from Dover and MTB-*28* from Harwich. The tugs *Muria* and *Lady Brassey* were also added in case of the worse, the former to take her in tow if damaged, the latter to rescue her crew if sunk. It was thus hoped that, in company with the convoy (which consisted of seventeen coasters, two destroyers, six trawlers, two minelayers and four MASBs), this group would be assumed by the Germans to be merely taking passage to the westward. By the time the convoy reached the South Goodwin Light Vessel after nightfall, *Erebus* and her party would detach themselves to carry out their night's work. It was apparently still not fully realized that the German radar plotted each ship's position by day or by night!

The bombardment itself was to be carried out in conjunction with a second, heroically laid on by the 14-inch gun at Dover, again in the rather naive hope that the Germans would assume that coastal batteries were responsible for *all* the gunfire. This assumed a great inability on their part, to distinguish different calibre shells. Most of the success of the attack, of course, depended on good weather. The night of 28-29 September was a rough one, especially in the Thames Estuary. Before they had even reached North Foreland, the MTBs had been driven to seek shelter, at 1530. The old *Erebus* was soon in trouble, her great bulk bucketing and rolling about. After sticking at it for several hours, Captain Nalder was forced to concede. At 2016 he signalled 'MW is cancelled, weather unsuitable'. In his subsequent report he revealed that *Erebus* was totally unmanageable in the narrow waters in those prevailing conditions of weather and sea. A solitary German bomber spotted and shadowed the force for a time during its retreat, carrying out an unsuccessful attack on the monitor before finally departing.

Second Bombardment Attempt by *Erebus*, 30 September 1940

Another attempt to carry out the operation was made the following night. The tug *Lady Brassey* sailed from Dover to Sheerness to assist in managing the unwieldy monitor as the weather continued to be poor, with a fresh north-easterly wind blowing, and moderate visibility, which improved toward the evening. Unfortunately, the time of departure of *Erebus* and her escorts from Sheerness was advanced by two hours and *Lady Brassey* missed the rendezvous. The back-up tug, *Muria*, was therefore sent out to take her place but, once more, the weather was too much for the MTBs whose own sailings were cancelled. This time the target selected was the alternative to the Gris Nez guns; the barges and ships of the invasion assembly in the Calais dock area. Zero hour for the commencement of the bombardment was fixed for 0130 on the morning of 30 September. A special buoy had been laid in position 510 06' 27" N, 010 39' 42" E. (No. 2A) to assist location and *Erebus* reached this buoy at 0150. The twenty minutes' delay had been caused by the weather conditions. Fire was duly opened by the main armament after *Erebus* had waited patiently for two spotter aircraft to arrive overhead. They were late, and the whole operation was hazarded because of their tardiness.

Nonetheless, once *Erebus* opened fire, her shells were directed into the Calais area at regular intervals. Unfortunately, after seventeen rounds she was forced to cease firing. The stoppage was brought about by an error in the drill aboard ship, which resulted in a loading failure. This in itself was not serous, and fire could have been resumed, but it was compounded by a more serious error. No information had been received from either of the spotting planes over the target, as to the fall of shot. It later transpired that, of the two aircraft supposed to be present, one had failed to take off due to engine trouble and the second had delayed its own taking off, hoping the first would get airborne. When the solitary spotter did arrive, twenty minutes late, it was found that its wireless was not working correctly and that it could not communicate with *Erebus*. In addition, heavy AA fire troubled the plane. Only three of the seventeen rounds fired were actually seen to fall, and all those three were in the target area. Although she was scheduled to fire for a full thirty minutes, these failures caused *Erebus* to abort the mission and return forthwith. The 14-inch gun at St Margaret's Bay made only a token contribution, firing a solitary round at the Gris Nez Battery.

On the following day the German guns at Wissant fired on Dover between 1125 and 1150, dropping a total of seventeen shells on the town in retaliation for the *Erebus* bombarding, which they evidently did not enjoy! This tit-for-tat caused the British more inconvenience than the enemy. Together with the destroyers and *Muria*, the monitor made her way sedately back across the Channel to Dover, suffering the indignity of being straddled by eight rounds from the German batteries while in the vicinity of the South Goodwin Light Vessel.

The German destroyers *Falke, Grief, Kondor* and *Wolf* were busy that night laying mines off Dover, no doubt in an attempt either to bottle *Erebus* up, or damage her should she attempt to venture forth again. One can assume by the efforts made to hurt her, that her salvoes must have caused some consternation to the enemy, even if the results were somewhat nebulous for all the effort put in. It was on this occasion, the night of 30 September, that the Portsmouth flotilla on patrol westward of the Lydd, was ordered to investigate, as related earlier. The destroyers concerned were the *Mackay* (Commander G. H. Stokes) and *Witch* (Lieutenant Commander J. H. Barnes) which had already been sent off to probe, and *Bulldog* and *Sardonyx*, which were ordered by the Senior Officer, to accompany them for the sake of mutual support, rather than make the long journey back to Portsmouth in daylight. As we have seen, they failed to make contact with the German flotilla, though they shared the shelling that *Erebus* had experienced, and had similar comments to make about its accuracy.

Mining of Hambledon, 7 October 1940

The laying of defensive minefields to screen their attack forces was discontinued by the Germans with the abandonment of *Seeloewe*, but the British felt that they could not relax their vigil. Mines continued to exercise a constant restraint upon the movements of shipping in the Straits and the interception of the German destroyer flotillas engaged in this work continued to present a seemingly insoluble problem to the Royal Navy, despite continuing attempts to bring them to book. One of the results of this unceasing effort by the German Navy was a constant attrition of the fighting ships and merchantmen in the Narrow Sea. Indeed, mines were responsible for as many casualties in the autumn of 1940 as in the corresponding months of 1939, and no solution had been found after a year of war to the problem of enemy surface minelayers.

At 2230 on 7 October, the Hunt class destroyer *Hambledon* became the latest victim. She struck a mine in position 51° 08' N, 01° 21' E, in the very centre of the swept channel abreast South Foreland, near to No. 4 buoy. This was despite the fact that minesweepers clearing a passage for convoy CE.12 earlier in the day, had passed along the channel without mishap and without detonating any mines. *Hambledon* was badly damaged aft by the detonation and her screws were blown off and engines rendered non-operational. She was taken in tow by her accompanying destroyer, *Vesper*, which started to tow her into Sheerness. Three minesweepers were sent out to help them and they exploded further devices in the immediate vicinity.

The party around the cripple were quickly located and subjected to various attacks, the German battery at Framselle opened up with seven two-round salvoes, all of which fell short. They straddled the South Goodwin Light Vessels, however, which the radar plot may have confused with the true target. No damage was caused and there were no casualties. At the same time, the fireship in company with the destroyers had a complete engine breakdown and had to be towed into Dover by the tugs *Lady Brassey, Lady Duncannon* and *Muria*. Dive-bombers later attacked the minesweepers, but these also escaped damage. It was found later, that the minefield covered a radius of some one-and-a-quarter miles around the spot where *Hambledon* had struck.

Notes

1. Similar deception had to be employed to obtain just three of the so-termed 'Through-deck cruisers'; in reality small aircraft carriers, against similar misguided Government and RAF opposition in the 1970s.

CHAPTER TEN

Attrition in the Winter Months

As autumn passed into winter in 1940, Britain began to realize that the crisis was over. The *Luftwaffe* had switched the main focus of its attacks from RAF Fighter Command to London. This had saved the former, which was faltering, while the latter target had just too large a population to be beaten by bombing alone, no matter how severe. Londoners 'took it' as stoically and bravely as did the German civilians later in the war. The myth that victory could be achieved solely by bombing cities was exposed early, but it took a long time for that chimera to die. More importantly, it was pretty certain that, as the weather worsened in the English Channel, the enemy (who would not face the Royal Navy in fine conditions) would certainly not test them in a challenge for control of the Channel in a risky invasion gamble. Thus Britain was reasonably secure from threat of invasion, at least until the following spring. The end of September saw the phasing out of one threat and the ushering in of a new phase of siege warfare. For this, the Navy was better equipped and the transition recorded in this chapter is from the offensive bombardment and patrol to a resumption of patient convoy work and waiting. Interspaced with these activities, serious efforts were made once more to end the activities of the elusive and skilful German destroyer flotilla, whose minelaying off the British coast proved to be both daring and effective, and whose continuing success was a hushed-up blot on the Navy's pride in its achievement to date.

A Lower Deck Viewpoint, Autumn 1940

Like the majority of fighting troops and civilians, the crews of the warships in the English Channel were told very little by their leaders; very little that was accurate or meaningful that is. The official line by the misnamed Ministry of Information (MOI), aided and abetted by the compliant and, in military matters, largely ignorant, BBC, was one of almost stupefying blandness in which the 'lower ranks' were not allowed to know what, who or how they were fighting to any great degree. Anything other than our relatively few victories was concealed from them by both their own officers and the media. But the majority of these men were not stupid, they could see for themselves how things really were, both at sea, on their visits home on leave to much-bombed London, and later, on a smaller scale, some of the provincial towns and cities. There was, therefore, a considerable degree of cynicism at the 'official line' as propagated generally; some even felt that even Lord Haw-Haw was more forthcoming than their own information outlets. This stultifying blanket policy of denial was only gradually moderated as the war turned in our favour, but that was not for several years ahead. Some of the best commanders, *did* go out of their way to inform their men more openly as to what the real picture was of course, but their hands were tied to a large extent. The Government, naturally, had a vested interest in concealing from its people the mistakes they made, and would continue to make, during the war. But the sailors had eyes and brains and knew what they witnessed daily, even if it bore little resemblance to that the press and BBC broadcasters *told* them they saw!

Typical was the memoirs of one such sailor, Mr W Hammond aboard the destroyer *Fernie*. He recalls the way that his own little vessel was in the forefront of events during those desperate days, now largely forgotten, and how no amount of what would now be termed 'spin' from Churchill on down, could hide the way things *really* were.

> The English Channel is one of the busiest shipping lanes in the world and during World War II the nearest to the enemy. In occupied France they had ample land-based aircraft which often dive bombed our convoys. In fact, I have experienced shelling, dive bombing and attacks by E-boats all in the same day, so determined was the enemy to stop the Channel Convoys getting through. I would say that the 1st Destroyer Flotilla saw more action at close range than most other ships in the Royal Navy. We would expect to be bombed or attacked by E-boats six times out of ten. We were also engaged in patrols along the French coast in which we were often in action with German convoys and their escorts, heavy guns or our old friends, the E-boats. One of their favourite tricks was to tie up to a buoy in the swept channel our minesweepers had cleared for us and wait for the convoy to turn up and then select their moment to attack. But, as time went by, we got used to this and used to have all our guns trained on these buoys just in case.
>
> We had several near-misses in 1940 from both dive bombers and shells. In addition we evacuated a lot of troops from Cherbourg who had been caught up in the aftermath of the Dunkirk business, were involved in many cross-Channel raids, attacked U-boat contacts and towed home a crippled frigate as well as participating in D-Day bombardment!

The Bombardment of Cherbourg by *Revenge*, 10-11 October 1940

The first attempts at heavy naval bombardments using the monitor *Erebus* had *not* been successful, due to her lack of manoeuvrability in anything of a seaway. But the much larger battleship *Revenge* (Captain E. R. Archer) was a very different proposition. As well as mounting eight large 15-inch guns [the same weapons as those mounted outside the Imperial War Museum,

London] she was well able to look after herself and was capable of the higher speed of twenty knots. Her main task was that of Channel Guard battleship, with frequent excursions into the North Atlantic, escorting vital troop convoys from Canada and Australia. Held at Portsmouth, where she was a potent threat, one that the Germans had failed to account for when devising the invasion plans.

Great care was taken in the drawing up of the plans and the coordination of all units taking part in the planned use of her for a bombardment of an enemy invasion assembly. Operation *Medium*, as it was code-named, was one of the most noteworthy examples of such care and planning amid an avalanche of failures in the British armed services in 1940. As such, it is deserving of more than the extremely brief treatment, or total ignoring, afforded it by naval historians to date.

One of the most noteworthy aspects of these preparations was the training of the battleship's crew in precision bombardment procedure. For this, the *Revenge*'s Gunner Officer, Lieutenant Commander W. F. H. C. Rutherford, was later commended for his zeal and patience. Also singled-out for special praise by Captain Archer, was the Navigating Officer, Lieutenant Commander G. E. Bingham-Powell, who, the Captain's words: '...kept to an exact programme, and maintained a very accurate reckoning under difficult circumstances in a strong tideway; more especially as this officer is only lent to *Revenge* in lieu of an officer sick in hospital, and this was the first time he had ever been to sea in a ship'.

The battleship herself was given an intense work-up in readiness, and equally she was provided with good back-up. The RAF laid on a simultaneous bombing raid which, it was hoped, would confuse the enemy into thinking, at least for a time, that the huge concussion of one-ton HE shells from the leviathan steaming offshore were, in fact, bombs. The light cruisers *Emerald* and *Newcastle*, based at Plymouth, were sailed to cover the western end of the Channel against any surprise (thought unlikely) intervention from that quarter. For close escort, the 5th Destroyer Flotilla under Captain Lord Louis Mountbatten, was to provide a screen, while a flotilla of MGBs gave distant cover against intervention by E-boats once the alarm had been raised.

The *Revenge* Sails

The *Revenge* left Plymouth at 2000 on Thursday 10 October, screened by the seven ships of the 5th Flotilla. Mountbatten embarked in *Javelin*, [his normal Flotilla Leader, *Kelly*, being under repair at the time], while *Jackal, Jaguar, Jupiter, Kashmir, Kelvin* and *Kipling* made up the rest of the flotilla. Again, in Captain Archer's words:

> The thorough planning of the operation, supplemented by meetings of those concerned in its execution, had the happiest of results – not once during the operation was anyone in the least doubt as to how to act, and, what is more important, as to how his next ahead (or astern) would

act – in consequence no signals had to be made once the force had formed up.

The six MGBs departed from Portland and they rendezvoused as planned at 0035 on 11 October. Due to an air raid the light which should have served as a departure link on Portland Bill was extinguished, but as there was good visibility this was no handicap. Long before the force arrived off Cherbourg, the signs of the diversionary air attack being mounted by RAF Bomber Command on that port were very apparent, and heavy AA fire was seen.

Heavy fires were also observed in the bombardment target area and, exactly at the time requested, aerial flares were dropped over Cap de la Hague, so that *Revenge* could take a final precise fix. At the same time, the light cruisers *Emerald* and *Newcastle* opened fire with star shell to the west, in order to create an additional diversion for any enemy forces in the vicinity.

By 0333 *Revenge* herself was steering 096 degrees at a speed of eighteen knots on the bearing selected for the bombardment, the target being the centre of the dockyard. Right on time, the huge guns of the battleship boomed out, the destroyers joining in with their 4.7-inch weapons not to be outdone. Chart range, gyro bearings and bombardment levels were all utilized for accuracy; the fires started by the RAF, although useful as a guide, were not considered to be accurate enough to use as an aiming mark. Wisely, the German searchlights on the breakwater did not illuminate, so their beams could not be used as target guides either.

For eighteen minutes *Revenge* pounded the dockyard area at an average range of 15,700 yards, spreading for line and laddering for range to a pre-arranged plan to cover the whole target area. In total, the battleship pumped some 120 CPC 15-inch shells into the mass of enemy shipping. The seven destroyers contributed some 801 of their smaller projectiles into the inferno over a four-minute period, before reassuming their anti-E-boat patrol duties to seaward of *Revenge*.

In the words of the official report:

> There can be little doubt that surprise and mystification were effected, proof of this being the intensification and wild character of the A.A. barrages as the salvoes fell. 'Flaming onions' and multi-coloured tracers were fired in all and every direction, while the searchlights gave a display worthy of a Tattoo – the whole combining to make a veritable 'Brock's Benefit', a sight worth seeing.
>
> The fire started by the RAF died down after a while but soon a bigger and better fire was burning some little distance to the westward of it as the result of the second bombardment. The second fire burnt strongly and spread rapidly – dense volumes of smoke were observed, the flames extending several hundred feet into the air. The fire was visible up to 40 miles to seaward. Several salvoes were observed to fall into the target area, thanks to the light it provided.

Enemy Reaction and British Withdrawal

After the first wild and stunned reactions, the Germans began to retaliate more coherently, but far too late to affect the issue. The first salvoes from the German shore batteries were fired. One battery in particular, sited to the east of the town and composed of heavy guns of up to 13.5-inch calibre, shelled the British force for a period of half-an-hour as it retired on a course of 008 degrees, and many of the big projectiles fell quite close to the ships. Their accuracy continued to be good up to a distance of 36,000 yards, but thereafter it fell rapidly away. There was little doubt that the guns were radar-controlled. The Battle Group took avoiding action by the simple expedient of altering course on sighting the flash, with the destroyers acting independently. The whole force withdrew at a speed of twenty-one-and-a-half knots, which is half-a-knot faster than the old *Revenge* was officially capable of when first built a quarter of a century earlier! Captain Archer recorded that: '...*Revenge*, despite her years, steamed very steadily at this speed'. The British force sustained no casualties or damage and the *Revenge* and the 5th Flotilla arrived back at Spithead at 0800 the same morning.

The Admiralty was please enough to send an '...expression of Their Lordships' satisfaction at the highly successful execution of this operation', which from these remote and austere dignitaries, was almost hysterical praise indeed!

German Destroyers Sortie, 11-12 October 1940

Almost immediately, however, the German surface navy struck back in a brilliant raid, one that once again revealed the limitations of the 5th Flotilla and British surface forces in general in responding to such hit-and-run tactics. At 1309 on 11 October, the German 5th Flotilla sailed from Cherbourg under the command of Captain Henne. It comprised the *Greif, Kondor, Falke, Seeadler* and *Wolf*, and their orders were to attack any shipping encountered off the south coast of England. They proceeded due east at a speed of twenty-one knots and arrived in a position 50° 25' N, 01° 05' W at 2320. Two small ships were sighted at a range of about two or three miles, on a bearing to port of 345 degrees; they were identified by the Germans as being coasters. They were, in truth, the armed trawlers HMS *Listrac* and HMS *Warwick Deeping* of the anti-invasion patrol. They were heading west at a speed of five knots in line ahead, *Listrac* leading. They were caught totally by surprise by the German destroyers who immediately closed them and opened heavy fire into them at a range of 2,600 metres, at 2327. Initially, they concentrated their fire on the larger *Warwick Deeping*.

Despite the havoc the German destroyers had been creating in these waters, it was evident that the British patrol could still not believe that it was the enemy attacking them. *Listrac* switched on her identification lights and received a blistering fire in reply. She took one shell in the boiler room, which caused a large explosion, and she began to sink. A torpedo from *Greif* struck her as she was going down and she at once blew up. The few survivors were picked up the following day.

Meanwhile, her companion was on fire, having been hit two or three times by shells, She attempted to make off to the north, in the hope perhaps of beaching herself, but *Kondor* and *Falke* quickly overhauled her. A torpedo from the former missed, but the combined gunfire of the two destroyers soon overwhelmed her and she too sank with very few survivors.

The German flotilla resumed its hunting and, at 0007, was again rewarded with fresh targets. These were the former French submarine-chasers *CH-6* and *CH-7*, manned by Polish crews. At only 114 tons, and carrying just light weapons for defence, they appeared to be as easy a prey as the two trawlers earlier, and the flotilla attacked without hesitation, closing in from the port bow to within 1,000 metres. They opened fire at 0111 and soon had reduced both little vessels to floating wrecks. All this took time, however, and the expenditure of much ammunition. About forty survivors from both ships were picked up, including some of the original French crew, who were very reluctant to be 'rescued' by a German ship, knowing the fate that awaited them at the hands of their former Vichy colleagues.

The German 5th Flotilla then re-formed, and steered east at twenty-three knots until 0220, when they were due to turn back for home. Meanwhile the British 5th Flotilla had belatedly appeared and, at 0325, *Jackal, Jaguar, Jupiter, Kelvin* and *Kipling* were bearing 140 degrees at a range of 5,000 metres from the five German ships in a position 51° 10' N, 01° 25' W. Five against five, but not only were the British destroyers much larger and more powerfully armed than the Germans, but the latter were also very low on ammunition. Only four of the British ships were sighted, but even so, the odds were clearly against them and the Germans accordingly put their helms over and headed back to France.

The German vessels soon worked up to a speed of twenty-eight knots and began to lay smoke to shield their withdrawal. Initially, this was all in vain, because the British ships had intercepted on a course and bearing that could force the German ships away from the safest coasts and off to the north or west, where they must be doomed. But their skilful use of smoke and the slow reaction of the British destroyers, gave them their opportunity to escape and they gradually edged south. It was not until the British destroyers were almost dead astern in their wakes, that they opened fire on the German ships.

The gunnery action commenced at 0325, with star shell being fired by the British ships, followed by ranging salvoes, which were very accurate indeed. British shells fell between *Greif, Seeadler* and *Kondor*, but did not cause any damage, so they were not forced to slow their pace of retreat. *Kondor* was again near missed later, close off her starboard bow but, thereafter, the British fire became more ragged and the German ships were not seriously threatened again. The smokescreen effectively countered the star shell illumination, and, although the British flotilla used their searchlights, this did not aid them at all.

As was usual in such situations, the German ships refrained from replying with their own guns, which would only have revealed their positions, and instead used the flash of the British guns as aiming points for their torpedoes. *Falke* and *Wolf* each fired one with good deterrent effect. *Kondor*, with a British destroyer pressing her close, used the fact that they were crossing a known British minefield to try another ploy. She dropped three depth-charges to simulate mine explosions in the hope of discouraging further pursuit. By 0400 the Germans had thrown their pursuers off the trail. At around 0550 they altered course for Brest and steamed south with Cap de la Hague on their beam. Forty minutes later Naval Group Command West ordered them to proceed to Cherbourg, where they all arrived safely at 1025.

Second Bombardment by *Erebus*, 16 October 1940

A repeat of HMS *Erebus*'s earlier attempt to bombard the French coast in the vicinity of Calais was called for and this time carried out to better effect. Better conditions and closer cooperation with the spotter aircraft were sought and, largely, achieved. Certainly the passage of the force itself to the firing position was arrived at without incident and the sea was smooth, the sky clear and the moon full. The surface visibility was better (some four miles) and from the air the spotter aircraft sighted *Erebus* and her escorting destroyers *Garth* and *Walpole*, at a distance of some four or five miles.

The three ships left the North Goodwin Light as their departure point, sighting a large number of red flares in the sky as they approached the French shoreline, but they arrived off 'W' buoy at 1340 without incident. The squadron took up the bombarding position according to plan, and all three were ready to open fire at 2355. *Garth* and *Walpole* were then instructed by visual signal to commence laying a white smokescreen, but there was a delay of some ten minutes before this could actually be done.

At 0100, *Erebus* commenced firing, and continued until 0142, during which time she loosed off some fifty rounds of 15-inch shell, with no delays and no misfires; a very commendable performance. Once again, however, the plan was compromised by the spotter aircraft. Lieutenant C. W. B. Smith, RN, made a written report of what went awry on this occasion.

The aircraft were airborne at 2230 and in position to seaward of the target at 2320, but W/T communication was not established until fifteen minutes later, due to the range. Although the weather conditions were good, the airmen experienced difficulty in observing the bursts of the huge shells, the flash being momentary and not very large. The AA fire over the target also caused confusion. In Lieutenant Smith's opinion: '...the difficulty of seeing the bursts rendered spotting ineffective. Occasional burst were reported and two definite hits in the centre of the dock area were observed; these started fires.' He suggested that in future operations of this type, the time of splash should be reported by W/T rather than the time of fire. As far as the methods used are concerned, the scheme seems practicable. The spotting aircraft suffered no interference and could see the target. There was a large number of enemy fighter aircraft in the vicinity but they did not interfere.

Aboard *Erebus*, it was reported that no spotting signals were made by the aircraft until the fifth round had been fired, when 'not observed' was received. Thereafter, four spotting signals were received at intervals of about every ten rounds until the thirtieth salvo. The last two rounds fired were, however, seen by the flare-dropping aircraft. Although only three rounds were spotted accurately enough to provide guide for range, these all agreed. In all, some forty-five rounds were fired within 600 yards of this range, of which thirty were fired within 400 yards.

It had been planned to lay smoke-screens both across the line of fire and toward Calais itself for protection, but the direction of the Force 2 wind was about twenty degrees off and up the line of fire, which necessitated the laying of the screen some distance from *Erebus*'s engaged side. In addition, sea-room was restricted on that side because of enemy minefields. Due to the bright moonlight, it was originally decided to use only white smoke laid by *Garth* and *Walpole* (via their CSA smoke-screen laying devices and the dropping of smoke floats), but, in the end, black smoke had to be laid as well. The resulting screen was described as 'ineffective'.

Withdrawal of the Force

On this occasion, the German reaction was sluggish, indeed almost non-existent. They did not retaliate and the return passage was uneventful, except that the old *Erebus* suffered a failure of her port engine at 0632. The monitor carried on with one engine, assisted by the tug *St Clair*. Twice the massive ship, the tug and the two escorting destroyers sighted patrol trawlers, which failed to respond to the challenge. *Garth* was detailed to investigate one such case at 0330 in the vicinity of Dumpton Buoy. With the fate of the *Warwick Deeping* fresh in everyone's mind, this sloppiness was severely criticized by the Admiralty. 'The failure of the patrol vessels to keep a proper lookout is serious. If they did not see *Erebus* and her escort on this occasion, it would appear that a considerable force of enemy small craft could slip by unobserved', said one report. Of course, this was not in the least uncommon. As for the failure of the spotter aircraft once more, the Director of Training wrote that: 'There is little doubt that air observation of a night bombardment cannot be relied on.' The consensus of opinion was, however, in the words of Admiral R. Plunkett-Ernle-Erle-Drax, C-in-C, Nore, 'This was a satisfactory operation and provided useful experience which will be turned to account on the next occasion'. Unfortunately, there was to be no next occasion, and Operation *PS* remained a teasing example of what might have been achieved had not both *Revenge* and *Erebus*'s hard-earned expertise been abandoned.

Submarine Attacks on Enemy Shipping, 15 October 1940

All branches of the Navy were employed in hitting the enemy as often as possible and keeping his preparations off-balance. Battleships to MGBs had attacked the enemy, and even submarines played a limited part in holding the Narrow Sea during this critical juncture. For example, on the night of 15

October the submarine *L-27* (Lieutenant Commander C. R. E. Campbell) a twenty-year old veteran boat displacing just 890 tons, carried out a combat patrol. Although post-war reference books state that she only took part in training duties in the Second World War, this is false, and she went so far as to make an attack on a heavily escorted German convoy in the Channel, regrettably without firm result.

Another Indecisive Action with German Destroyers, 17 October 1940

Although everyone was straining to do their best, the many shortcomings in Britain's makeshift defences were revealed in yet another unsatisfactory encounter with the daring German destroyer flotillas. Once more, it was a night action at extreme range; as always, the Germans turned for home, and yet again, the action by the British force failed to stop them. Air cooperation was, yet again, to be almost non-existent and the lack of proper training in RAF Coastal Command was glaringly demonstrated. Despite these shortcomings being revealed for the umpteenth time, two years on and the escape of the German battle-fleet through these self-same waters only proved that twenty years neglect by the RAF of maritime matters in their care at their insistence, could not be remedied very quickly.

Thus it was that, on the evening of 17 October, Commander Bey took the destroyers *Hans Lody, Karl Galster, Friedrich Ihn* and *Erich Steinbrinck* to sea on another sortie against British coastal shipping off the western approaches to the Bristol Channel, despite the fact that it was known that a strong British cruiser and destroyer force was stationed there for just such an event. The big destroyers' movement was covered in turn by their smaller brethren of the 5th Flotilla, with *Greif, Falke, Kondor, Jaguar, Seeadler* and *Wolf*, but these vessels played no part in the subsequent encounter.

British Preparations and Reactions

No submarine patrols had yet been established off Brest, and the two flotillas of German destroyers were a constant worry to the C-in-C, Plymouth, upon whose bailiwick they frequently intruded. This officer was concerned lest the enemy ships fell upon one of his poorly guarded Sierre Leone or Gibraltar convoys and annihilate both escort and merchantmen alike. Fortunately, no such enterprising course of action seems to have commended itself to Bey or his skippers, who did not like venturing too far out of sight of land, and contented themselves with smaller fry in the Channel. The first news that the British had that the German flotillas were at sea was obtained quite by chance. A bomber of Coastal Command reported four enemy destroyers in position 48° 24'N, 05° 33' W, steering west, at 0835 on 17 October. All was ready for them, as some days earlier fears for the safety of convoys OG44 and HG 45, both of which would pass within striking distance of Brest, had led to the formation of battle group, Force 'F'. This consisted to the light cruisers *Emerald* (Captain F. C. Flynn) and *Newcastle* (Captain A. Aylmer) and the available destroyers of the 5th Flotilla, which at this moment were *Jackal* (Captain D embarked), *Jupiter,*

Kelvin, Kipling and *Kashmir*. This powerful squadron was immediately ordered to raise steam. The two vulnerable convoys were diverted westward until the danger passed. Finally, steps were taken for the RAF to institute comprehensive air patrols to locate and shadow the enemy destroyers.

a. A signal was sent to Sunderland D/10 Squadron at 0840 which read 'Search for and report and shadow 4 enemy destroyers (Force PL) sighted 0700/17 steaming west from 48° 24' N, 05° 33' W.' This flying boat had taken off at 0600 on Patrol SA 12 modified. At 0824 D/10 landed and reported no contact with Force PL.

b. 'Four Ansons from St Eval to carry out sweep. Report and shadow 4 enemy destroyers sighted at 0700 steering west in position 48° 21' N, 05° 33'W. Send sighting report and amplifying report and continue to shadow.' These aircraft took off at 0920-0940 and reported that they could see no enemy surface craft.

'One Sunderland from Mountbatten to search for Force PL. Cross over patrol through:

48° 10' N 11° 10' W
45° 30'N 10° 40' W
45° 40' N 9° 50' W
45° 00' N 11° 10' W

to prudent limit of endurance. Enemy force to be reported and shadowed' B/10 took off and landed at 2200, having had engine trouble. Aircraft reported that they did not contact Force PL.

After a later message from Fighter Command, an order was issued to one Anson at St Eval to investigate and shadow Force PL. This aircraft located Force 'F' but not the enemy. This report came not from Coastal Command, but was another chance sighting [similar to the Channel Dash incident two years later] from Fighter Command relayed to C-in-C, Plymouth via a telephone message from the Gun Operations Room, of enemy ships some 100 miles south-west of Land's End, steering NNW at high speed at 1345. While this signal was being coded for transmission, the Admiralty was asked whether any more accurate information was available, and gave a corrected position of 48° 20'N, 06° 10' W.

Sailing of Force 'F' and Contact with Enemy Ships

While Coastal Command was searching to no avail, the ships of Force 'F' put to sea in high hopes and full of confidence that they would at last be able to retaliate against this elusive foe, with a strong enough force to destroy them. They had the advantage of speed [or at least, it was so assumed, for in the prevailing seas, the larger British cruisers were expected to be more seaworthy] and hitting power. *Newcastle* mounted twelve 6-inch guns in four triple turrets plus ten 4-inch guns in twin mountings, while *Emerald* mounted seven 6-inch guns in one twin turret and three single mountings, while the British destroyers each carried six 4.7-inch guns apiece, against the total German broadside of twenty 5-inch guns. Torpedo armaments were also superior; both cruisers were heavily equipped with torpedo tubes and each of the five destroyers had a quadruple mounting, and thus forty-two British torpedo tubes opposed the German twenty-four. The British force was within short range of its own airfields for once; the Germans less so. There was also the added advantage of surprise, as in this instance the Germans had been located first. Spirits on board the British ships were high.

Force 'F' sailed from Plymouth at 1035 and, on clearing the twenty-fathom line, both cruisers took the standard precaution of streaming paravanes to cut any mines. They moved out to sea in line ahead and in open order, the five destroyers forming an anti-submarine screen around them. On clearing the minefield QZS at 1126, a course was set to the south-west to clear minefield QZY and the whole force began to zigzag from 1130 onwards. By 1230 in position 49° 43' N, 4° 31.5' W, course was altered to 260 degrees and *Newcastle* signalled the latest news to *Emerald* and Captain (D) 5. The weather at this time was fine, with a light northerly breeze, a calm sea, and very good visibility.

Although there were no contacts with the German ships by Coastal Command, Force 'F' was shadowed continuously by the *Luftwaffe* from midday onward, and enemy bombers were sighted by the British ships on frequent occasions throughout the afternoon. The Admiralty signalled 'Blue Force F' at 1542, indicating the proximity of the enemy, but no sighting followed. Seven minutes later the C-in-C's signal, '4 destroyers have been reported in position 048° 21' N, 006° 10' W steering NNW at high speed' was received on *Newcastle*'s bridge. Her estimated position at this time was 0490 30'N, 0060 40'W. This was at 1600 and two minutes later there appeared the welcome sight of a two-funnelled vessel, hull down, bearing 201 degrees. This was quickly identified as a German destroyer. *Newcastle* immediately turned towards this ship and increased speed to thirty knots, at the same time hoisting the signal 'Enemy in sight'.

The Action Commences

Within five minutes of sighting the enemy, *Newcastle* opened fire at extreme range; the time was 1607 and the distance some 25,000 yards. The target vessel was right ahead bearing 197 degrees. At once the target turned away and commenced zigzagging. *Emerald* tried her first ranging shot nine minutes later, but the enemy was beyond the reach of her guns. The whole force was ordered to 'Chase' and all telegraphs were put to full speed. Meanwhile, a second enemy destroyer had been sighted at 1615, bearing 201 degrees, and a third was sighted six minutes later, bearing 182 degrees. The last to come into view was the enemy flotilla leader, sighted at 1624. The first three appeared to be steering about 120 degrees, while the last was laying smoke across their sterns to cover their withdrawal. The CSA screen put down was reported to be very extensive and effective.

Meanwhile, some of the British ships were already beginning to find the pace too hot. The destroyer *Jupiter* was unable to keep up owing to a machinery defect. She formed a line of bearing 260 degrees from *Newcastle*, while *Emerald* remained on a bearing of 080 degrees, in open order. By 1630, the bulk of Force 'F' was travelling at thirty-two knots.

The *Luftwaffe* now began to engage the British ships, and continued to make largely ineffectual interventions throughout the action. At 1630 two large enemy floatplanes appeared to the west, but they were driven off by gunfire from the British destroyers. Ten minutes later, a black-painted Dornier Do17 appeared; it was engaged by *Emerald* and driven off. On the British side, efforts were made to launch the old Walrus amphibian from *Newcastle*. All major British cruisers were at this period of the war equipped with spotter aircraft, and they took up a great amount of space with their hangars and catapults, as well as presenting great fire hazards from shell and bomb splinters. In common with most cruiser COs, the *Newcastle*'s skipper was eager to be rid of the plane as soon as possible. It was hoped that she would be able to see over the smokescreen being laid down, and enable better shooting to be made. In practice, these amphibians rarely, if ever, came up with any useful results, but on this occasion the Walrus from the *Newcastle* did her job efficiently. Despite the considerable relative crosswind, the aircraft was shot off at 1651 and reported herself ready to observe just eight minutes later.

Dusk was falling at 1700. *Jupiter* had fallen out of the chase and the other destroyers were also having difficulty in keeping up, but *Newcastle* was holding her own and engaged with the only visible enemy destroyer at a range of about 23,000 yards. The rest of the German ships were totally concealed by their own smoke and were not seen again as a whole unit. Their return fire was totally ineffective. One, and rarely, two gun salvoes were fired with resulting tall, thin splashes but none of these was closer than 2,000 yards and caused *Newcastle* no inconvenience at all.

An incidence during the Battle of Jutland was recalled when, at 1720, just as during that encounter, a sailing vessel was sighted crossing the field of battle, and *Jupiter* was detached to investigate. She turned out to be a French tunny boat, and a second was seen some fifteen minutes later. *Jupiter* detained their skippers for interrogation, but meanwhile the chase sped eastward.

German Torpedo Attack

In the standard German manner when hard-pressed, the enemy flotilla turned to make a torpedo attack on the pursuing British squadron but, fortunately, their plan was observed by *Newcastle*'s Walrus, which gave ample warning of the fact. It was 1738 when Bey turned his flotilla to port and, three minutes later, the Walrus reported torpedoes approaching on the bearing 170 degrees; a second report 'Course torpedoes 016°' followed. Force 'F' therefore turned to 196 degrees to comb the tracks. At least three torpedoes passed between *Newcastle* and *Emerald* and eight more were observed by the Walrus to pass clear to port of the latter ship. From *Emerald* one of these was observed to make a full circle before sinking at the end of its run, but that was the closest they came.

The turn away had been effective in achieving its objective as far as the Germans were concerned; a hit would have been a bonus. Another time, this exact same tactic was to bring startling success. By the time that the British ships had resumed the pursuit course once more this had been changed to 150 degrees with the enemy destroyers now in full flight toward the sanctuary of Brest harbour. *Newcastle* ceased firing at 1641, but resumed again at 1750 to follow the temporarily-revealed enemy. *Emerald* had fired from time to time to test the range, but never managed to get into the action. Between 1756 and 1820, *Luftwaffe* bombers appeared in response to pleas for aid from Bey's hard-pressed squadron. Three further Dornier Do17 and Junkers Ju88 bombers, which had previously contented themselves with distant shadowing and ineffectual passes at the Walrus, now made medium-level bombing attacks. *Newcastle* was near-missed astern by one stick of bombs, while another stick fell some four cables ahead. Five attacks were made on *Emerald* and more bombs fell between *Newcastle* and the destroyers. All these aircraft were painted black; they were engaged by the ships' AA guns, which kept them at a distance.

Contact Lost and RAF Attack Wrong Ships

By 1810 the enemy destroyers were lost to sight in the gathering dusk and haze, and *Newcastle* ceased firing, By this time she had expended some 750 rounds of 6-inch LA and 300 rounds of 4-inch HA. *Emerald* had fired off some sixty-eight rounds of 6-inch LA and ten rounds of 6-inch against the aircraft in barrage fire, plus 118 rounds of 4-inch HA. She had recently been refitted and had run engine trials, but her engine revolutions on this occasion averaged fifteen above those obtained during those full power trials, while *Newcastle* developed 7,000 more horse power than the authorized 82,000 hp, with revolutions up to 292. Even so, it was felt that had it been possible for her to slip her paravanes, another one and a half knots might have been wrung out of her.

At 1807 a signal from C-in-C Plymouth, was received which warned that the RAF could not dispatch any fighters to protect the force if it continued the chase, and that ships might therefore withdraw at the SO's discretion. They were now close to German dive bomber bases and so, wisely, they withdrew at 1817, when all the enemy ships were out of sight and all firing had ceased. The pursuit was therefore broken off at 1823 and Force 'F' withdrew at twenty-five knots on a course of 310 degrees. The only *Luftwaffe* inference came when the Walrus was told to take the short route home via the Lizard, and was attacked by a Do17 and damaged, the pilot receiving a bullet wound in his chest. The plane was safely put down on the sea close to the ships and hoisted inboard. *Jupiter* was ordered at 1854 to return to Plymouth independently, while the rest of Force 'F' retired to the north-west until 2230 before also returning to Plymouth.

The detour taken by the main British force did not, however, save them from the expected air attacks. Regrettably, it was the RAF rather than the *Luftwaffe* bombers, which did their best to inflict damage on the British ships. At 1816 three Blenheims arrived over HMS *Jackal*, identified themselves and went away. Ten minutes later, two Blenheims were seen approaching in low gliding attack dives against the destroyers *Kelvin* and *Kashmir*. These aircraft were from No. 16 Group, and had not been trained in ship recognition; in spite of this fact, they had been sent off and just bombed the first ships they saw!

So firmly were these attacks pressed home that the two destroyers had no choice but to open fire in an effort to deter them. In this they were successful, and no damage was done to either ships or aircraft. This farce was the RAF's last contribution to the day's events. Although all had done the best they could, the enemy had once again shown them a clean pair of heels and made good their escape; even early warning had brought about no result. Nor was there much chance of the British ships ever catching them, as the Admiralty later commented:

> Under difficult conditions, *Newcastle* seems to have made the most of her opportunities in the action and was perhaps unlucky not to have obtained a hit. It must be admitted, however, that the chances of hitting were low.

Captain Aylmer wrote that: 'The operation was, I am sure, thoroughly enjoyed by all Officers and Men and was a valuable experience, although it was disappointing that a decisive result was not obtained.' C-in-C Plymouth, commented that: ' The Commanding Officer of *Newcastle* handled his force with skill and determination and it is unfortunate that the enemy was sighted at extreme range.'

And so the elusive flotilla escaped retribution yet again. The air experiences were to be repeated in an almost identical way eighteen months later in these same waters, when it could be seen that nothing had been learned. At the time, the feeling in Force 'F' was that the Germans had been chased home, and had been lucky to escape unscathed.

CHAPTER ELEVEN

The Convoys Win Through

With *Newcastle*'s failure to bring the bold minelaying and anti-shipping sorties of the German destroyers to an end, the most intensive period in the life of the Narrow Sea commands was brought to a close. The onset of winter meant that both surface and air actions were increasing restricted. Minelaying continued unabated, both by destroyers and from the air and British losses continued to be severe. The devoted work of the minesweeping units continued unsung and unnoticed for the most part. Many of these ships were lost and many more damaged. Apart from the Fleet Minesweepers of the regular Navy, most were converted trawlers and drifters manned by raw recruits; their role was far from glamorous and their passing but a minor incident in the main panorama of the war. Nevertheless, without their endless work, Britain would have had to capitulate no less surely than if the Germans had landed or if the U-boats had been successful in the North Atlantic. Mines continued to be the biggest menace to shipping. The winter of 1940-41 saw the end of one period and the beginning of another; from headline news to the routine and patient slog of keeping the convoys running despite all the enemy could do. With the bulk of the deadly Stukas transferring to airfields in Poland and Romania in preparation for the assault on the Soviet Union, air attacks were not as intense as they had been in the summer. The Junkers made a brief and unexpected reappearance before they were finally totally withdrawn to get ready for the Russian campaign but, thereafter, the very few that remained contented themselves with night dive bombing attacks, an unpleasant and novel idea, but one which produced few firm results. The E-boats continued to prey upon British shipping and so stretched were Allied forces at this time that there was always the chance that they would break through and score isolated victories from time to time. These were, however, kept with reasonable limits.

Loss of *Venetia*, 19 October 1940

Another squadron of destroyers was at sea from the Nore Command on the night of 18-19 October. These were the *Walpole*, *Garth* and *Venetia* (Lieutenant F. Bruen, DSC) and they patrolled the Straits of Dover throughout the dark hours, but without sight of the enemy. By daybreak they had begun to withdraw to Sheerness but, close to the East Knob Buoy, the *Venetia* was mined, and this old veteran of Boulogne was sunk.

Brief reappearance of the Stukas

Since their redeployment to the Cap de Calais airfields in September to wait out the air battles and then conduct their traditional armed support operation in *Seeloewe* should the German army manage to lodge themselves ashore, little had been seen of the Junkers Ju87 dive bombers. Their tasks had included assignments to destroy the British coastal batteries and other vital targets but, once it had become clear that the invasion was not going to take place, most of these specialized units began to be dispersed. Many went to the Mediterranean to support their faltering Italian ally; others went to prepare themselves for the forthcoming invasion of Russia. Those remaining units included some with pilots and crews with naval experience who were anxious to try out their new anti-shipping methods against live targets. Accordingly, selected strikes were mounted against convoys assembling in the Thames Estuary. These proved quite successful in their limited aims. On 1 November the dive bombers hit and sank the coaster *Letchworth* (1,317 tons) and on 8 November they returned and scored a hit, which badly damaged the *Fireglow* (1,495 tons), *Ewell* (1,350 tons) and *Catford* (1,568 tons). Another Stuka attack in the same area damaged the *Corsea* (2,764 tons), *Colonel Crompton* (1,495 tons) and *Corduff* (2,345 tons) on 11 November. These new assaults prompted the RAF to try a mass fighter interception of the next attempt. This duly took place on 14 November and enough British fighters had been assembled to swamp the dive bombers' own fighter defences and cause some losses (although nothing remotely like the numbers claimed at the time). One *Gruppe* of Stukas was switched by their Fighter Commander (who for the first, and last, occasion, was directing dive bomber operations) from the Thames Estuary to attack targets at Dover instead. However, the German pilot kept his fighters well clear of that area to avoid the heavy flak concentrations and thus the Ju87s were left to attack as best they could through AA fire, barrage balloons and heavy fighter defences.

Some twenty Stukas duly approached the port at about 1420 from a height of 10,000 feet, and they split up in the normal manner into their attack *Ketten*. These dive bombed the harbour, the radar station and the coastal batteries at Leathercoates respectively. The last two targets were relatively unscathed, but the dive bombing of the Submarine basin resulted in the total destruction of the drifter *Shipmates* from a direct hit. The *Lord Howe, Yorkshire Lass* and *Cirrus* were also all damaged, as were the buildings in the dockyard and on the Eastern Arm and the West jetty. Fortunately, casualties were light, two killed and nine wounded. One unique event was the claim that the Unrotating Projectile (UP) batteries had actually destroyed a plane! This ghastly and ineffective instrument of war, the UP, was the brainchild of Professor Lindemann, Churchill's pet scientist and was one of his more harebrained inspirations. Known also as the Naval Wire

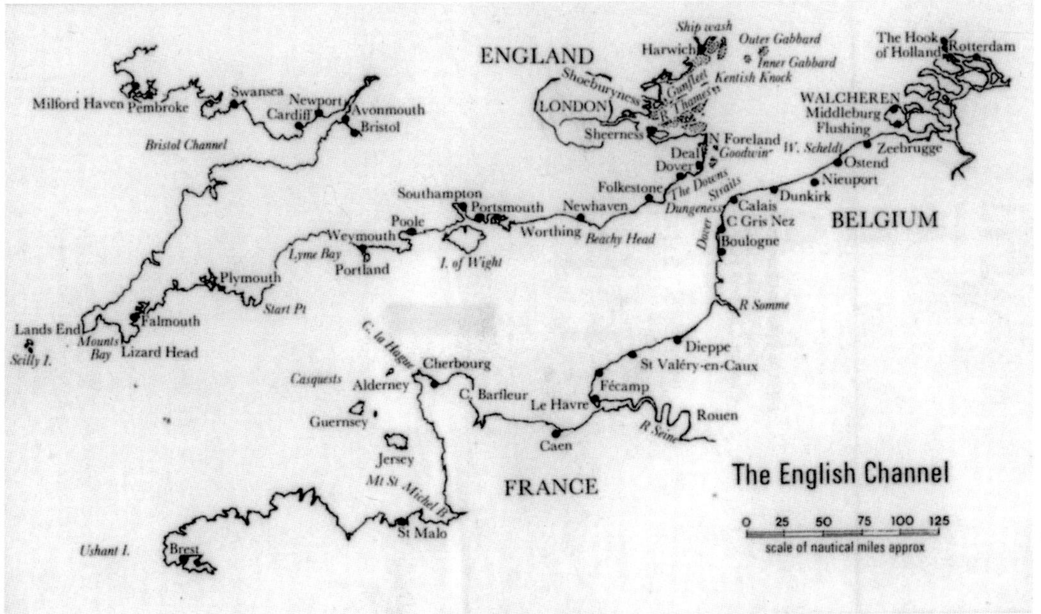

1. The English Channel.

2. The Flotilla Leader HMS *Codrington*, leader of the 19th Destroyer Flotilla in the Narrow Sea in 1939. She had the reputation of being one of the fastest ships in the Royal Navy at this time. *(Wilf Lawson)*

3. The Dover Patrol. Ships of the destroyer flotilla based at Dover on patrol, as seen astern from the after bridge of the Flotilla Leader HMS *Codrington,* early in 1940. *(Mrs P. Devarney)*

4. In the tradition of World War I, the destroyers of the 19th Flotilla took up the guardianship of the Narrow Sea on the outbreak of war. This photograph shows the Flotilla Leader HMS *Codrington* entering Dover Harbour flying the Royal Standard with HM King George VI on the bridge. *(Captain C. S. B. Swinley, DSO, DSC, RN)*

5. Captain Creasy, commanding officer of HMS *Codrington*, now leading the 1st Flotilla in place of the sunken HMS *Grenville*, holds the infant Dutch princess in his arms, as her mother, Princess Juliana, disembarks at Harwich following their dramatic rescue in May 1940. *(Mrs P. Devarney)*

6. One of the ancient 'V' and 'W' class destroyers from the First World War which served with distinction in the Narrow Sea. This is HMS *Vanquisher*, seen here in 1943 after her armament had been reduced and she was serving as a convoy escort ship. *(MOD Navy)*

7. Admiral Sir Bertram Home Ramsay, KCB, MVO, RN, 'Black Ramsey' to the destroyer crews who served under him. He organised the salvation of the BEF at Dunkirk, held Dover Command's forces together in the dark days that followed, and was the brilliant naval organiser of the victorious D-Day Normandy landings back in France in 1944. *(Imperial War Museum, London)*

8. The swept channels for the Dunkirk evacuations.

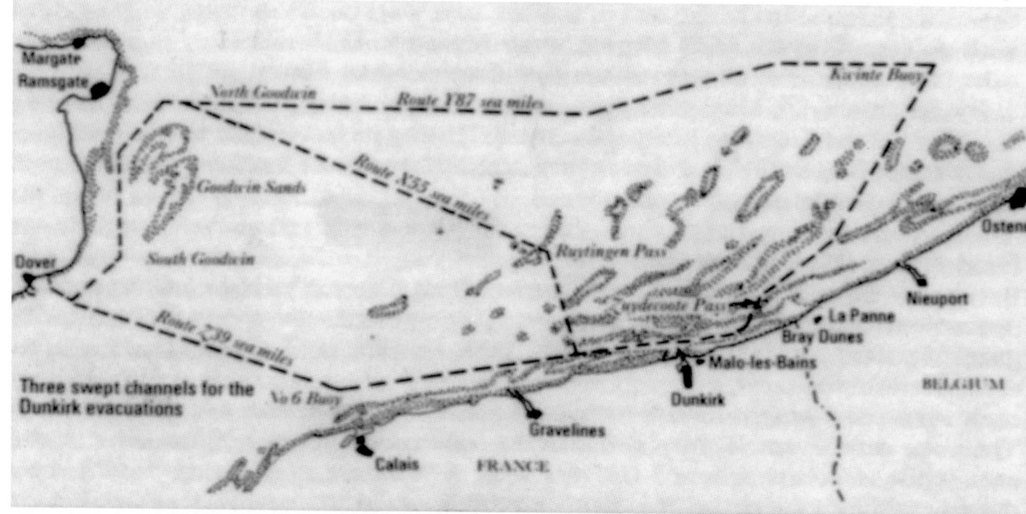

9. Farewell Europe! A very mixed collection of ships making their way back from one of the channel ports during the evacuation of France in June 1940. Freighters, tugs, small motor launches, all make their way slowly to safety. Aboard, a mixed complement of French and British troops saved from years of imprisonment.
(Imperial War Museum, London)

10. The minelaying destroyer HMS *Express*. She served in the famous 20th (Minelaying) Flotilla early in the war, but was diverted to Dunkirk where she served well in the forefront of evacuation operations. Later in the war she was handed over to Canada. *(MOD Navy)*

11. A mixed contingent climbing aboard the destroyer HMS *Boadicea* after having been taken off the beach at Veulette on 10 June 1940.
(From the painting by Richard Seddon by kind permission of the artist)

12. The destroyer HMS *Boadicea* engaging German tanks ashore with her main armament off the coast of France, 10 June 1940.
(From the painting by Richard Seddon by kind permission of the artist)

13. After being severely damaged by Stuka dive bomber attack, HMS *Boadicea* was towed home by the destroyer HMS *Ambuscade* and finally nursed into Portsmouth harbour after a voyage back through fog with many wounded men and evacuees aboard (not to mention the dog!)
(From the painting by Richard Seddon by kind permission of the artist)

14. Stuka Attack! Bombs bursting and exploding astern of a *Beagle* Class destroyer as she accelerates away, her AA guns firing. *(Imperial War Museum, London)*

15. Prior to the Battle of Britain, the German dive bomber forces were concentrated on the Channel coast of France and in heavy attacks throughout July and August caused severe losses to British coastal convoys. This film clip records a very near miss on a small coaster by a 550lb bomb. *(British Movietone News Archive)*

16. End of HMS *Brazen*. A unique set of photographs showing the last minutes of the destroyer as she sinks with a broken back after a near-miss bomb during a Stuka attack in the Channel during which she shot down no less than three of her attackers. *(Commander Sir Michael Culme-Seymour)*

17. Gun crews still man the skyward-pointing 3-inch HA gun as survivors leave the sinking ship. *(Commander Sir Michael Culme-Seymour)*

18. HMS *Brazen* settles as her flotilla mate, HMS *Boreas* takes her departure, laden with survivors, her own guns elevated awaiting the next attack. *(Commander Sir Michael Culme-Seymour)*

19. The bows of the destroyer HMS *Brazen* show for one final moment as they plunge into the Channel depths and spray boils up from her sunken stern portion.

(Commander Sir Michael Culme-Seymour)

20. The Port of Dover.

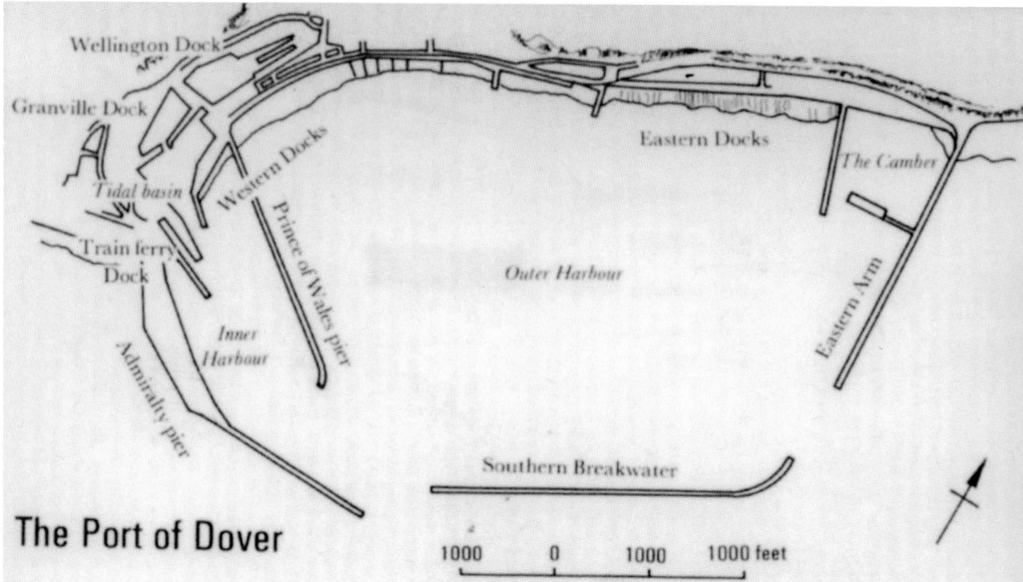

21. The target – Dover! During July 1940, a series of heavy Stuka raids were made on Dover harbour which finally caused the Navy to abandon it as an anti-invasion destroyer base. In this attack, mounted on 29 July 1940, bombs erupt between the moored merchant ships and several Ju87s can be seen pulling out of the dives at the top and right of this film still. *(Associated Press)*

22. In September 1940, the coastal convoys passing 'Hellfire Corner' (the Dover Straits) faced a new hazard, shelling by long-range German guns. Here the *Hunt* class destroyer HMS *Fernie* escorts slow-moving tramp ships as the salvoes fall close ahead and alongside. *(Douglas Clare)*

23. One of the smaller German torpedo boats (escort destroyer), the rough equivalents of the British Hunt class but with an armament focus on torpedoes rather than HA guns. They were also much faster than the British ships and were fitted for minelaying. *(Imperial War Museum, London)*

24. The destroyer flotillas maintained constant patrols off the coast of Europe between June and September 1940 presenting a floating bulwark against German invasion hopes. Here the destroyer HMS *Beagle* (H30) and HMS *Hurricane* are shown on patrol. *(Imperial War Museum, London)*

25. One-ton shells were fired at German invasion barges in September 1940. They were delivered by the battleship HMS *Revenge*, a veteran from the Great War, which fought throughout World War II. In 1940 she was the only capital ship left in the Channel area. *(Imperial War Museum, London)*

26. The only dive-bombers available to the British forces during the dark days of 1940, to do a little to the Germans what they were doing a lot of to the Allies, were a handful of Blackburn Skuas of the Fleet Air Arm, briefly seconded to Coastal Command who did not understand their capabilities. They made one brilliant attack at Nieuport and were frequently in action (with both sides attacking them!) over the Channel ports later. *(Author's collection)*

27. The German battle-cruiser *Scharnhorst*, with a screen of destroyers. She is seen here viewed from the heavy cruiser *Prinz Eugen*, making a violent turn to port at full speed during the escape of the German squadron through the Channel in February 1942. *(Imperial War Museum, London*

28. The Flotilla Leader HMS *Campbell* in which Captain Pizey led the five old destroyers from Harwich in their gallant attack on the battle-cruiser *Gneisenau* and heavy cruiser *Prinz Eugen* during Channel Dash episode, February 1942. Despite their age, they were the only torpedo-carrying destroyers available to challenge the German Navy in the 'English' Channel at the time. *(Imperial War Museum, London)*

29. The destroyer HMS *Worcester*, a veteran of World War I, which pressed in her torpedo attack against the German Battle Fleet to within suicidal range. Hit many times and shot through and through, written off by the Germans and attacked by the RAF, she survived it all to return and after being refitted, continued to carry out her duties until the war's end. *(Imperial War Museum, London)*

30. Bold dazzle camouflage patterns break up the sleek destroyer outline of HMS *Haydon*. The Type 3 Hunt class destroyers lost one twin 4-inch gun mounting in order to carry more short-range weapons and a few torpedeo tubes; this made them more suitable for the close-range night action work in the confined waters of the Channel. *(P. A. Vicary, Cromer)*

31. Destroyer Skipper – Lieutenant Commander B. J. Harrison, the commanding officer of the destroyer HMS *Albrighton* in 1942. *(Douglas Clare)*

32. HMS *Atherstone* was the first Hunt class destroyer to be completed. On only her second war voyage she took on a force of twenty German bombers to defend her convoy in the Thames Estuary and successfully drove them off, despite being hit by three bombs. She was badly damaged but, after being rebuilt, she survived the war. *(P. A. Vicary, Cromer)*

33. Seagulls and Sunset. HMS *Albrighton* returns to Portsmouth after another mission in the Narrow Sea. Note the torpedo tube amidships, radar aerials, depth charge stowage astern, bowchaser in the eyes of the ship, 'X' mounting housed forward. A typical fighting Hunt of the period. *(Douglas Clare)*

34. Dieppe 19 August 1942.

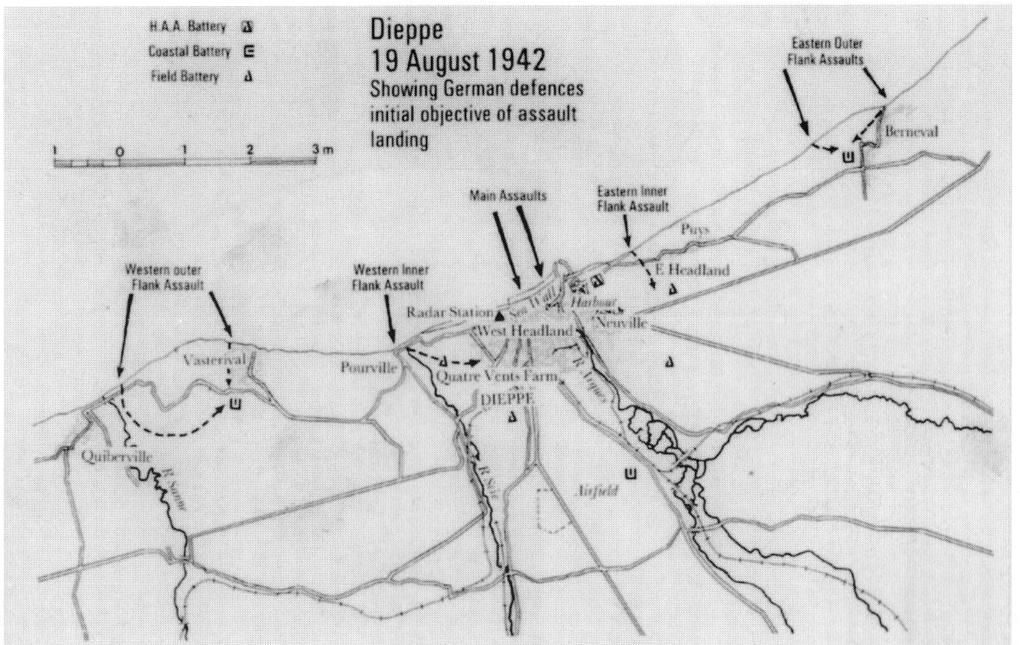

35. Landing craft of the early type, primitive by later standards, alongside the destroyer HMS *Albrighton* off Dieppe on 19 August 1942. *(Douglas Clare)*

36. Oerilkon gunners. A posed shot that nonetheless reflects the equipment and apparel of the anti-aircraft personnel in the Channel destroyers during 1942. *(Douglas Clare)*

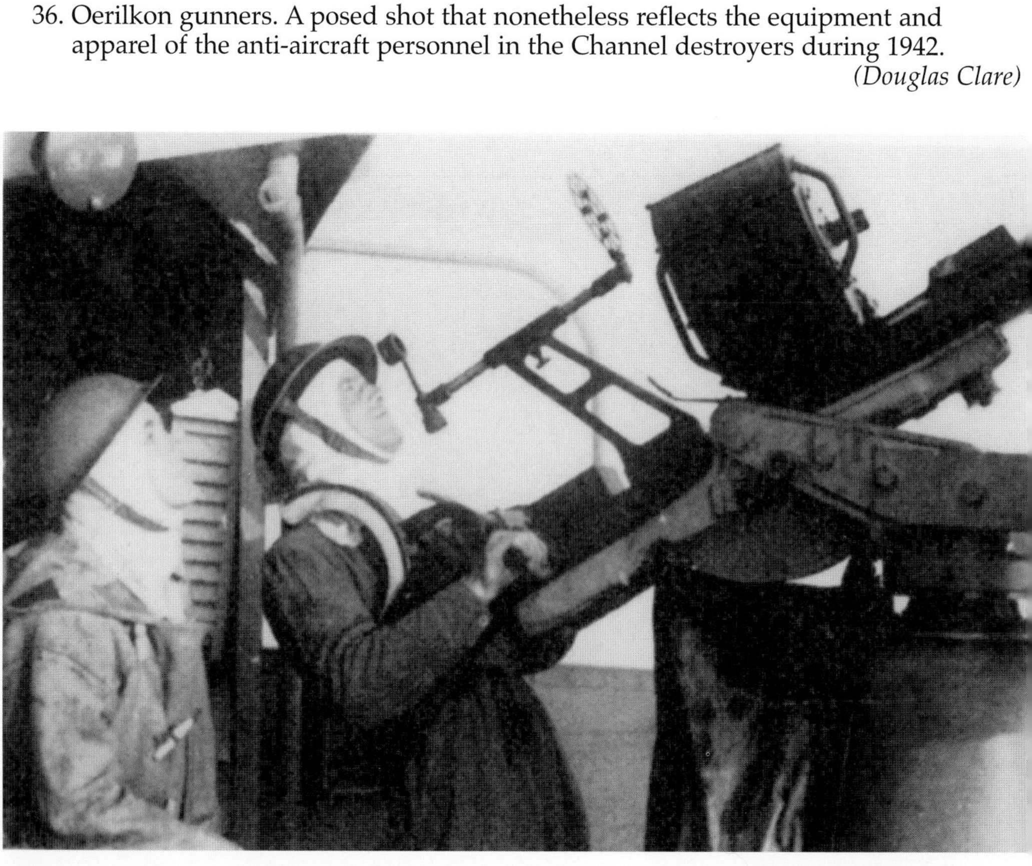

37. 2-pdr pom-pom crew closed up and ready for another attack. Note the anti-flash gear and limited protection for the crew. HMS *Albrighton* 1942. *(Douglas Clare)*

38. The last crewman is rescued from the stern of the sinking destroyer HMS *Berkeley* off Dieppe by HMS *Albrighton.* *(Douglas Clare)*

39. Death of a destroyer. HMS *Berkeley*, damaged by a random bomb shed by a Dornier bomber during air raids off Dieppe, is sent to the bottom with a 'friendly' torpedo, one of two fired by the HMS *Albrighton*. *(Douglas Clare)*

40. Ramming home a 4-inch shell into the breech of one of the twin-guns in the gun-house of the destroyer HMS *Bleasdale*. Although posed, this photgraph shows clearly the cramped conditions of such mountings, which had to be fought in pitch-blackness at high speed and short notice. *(Douglas Clare)*

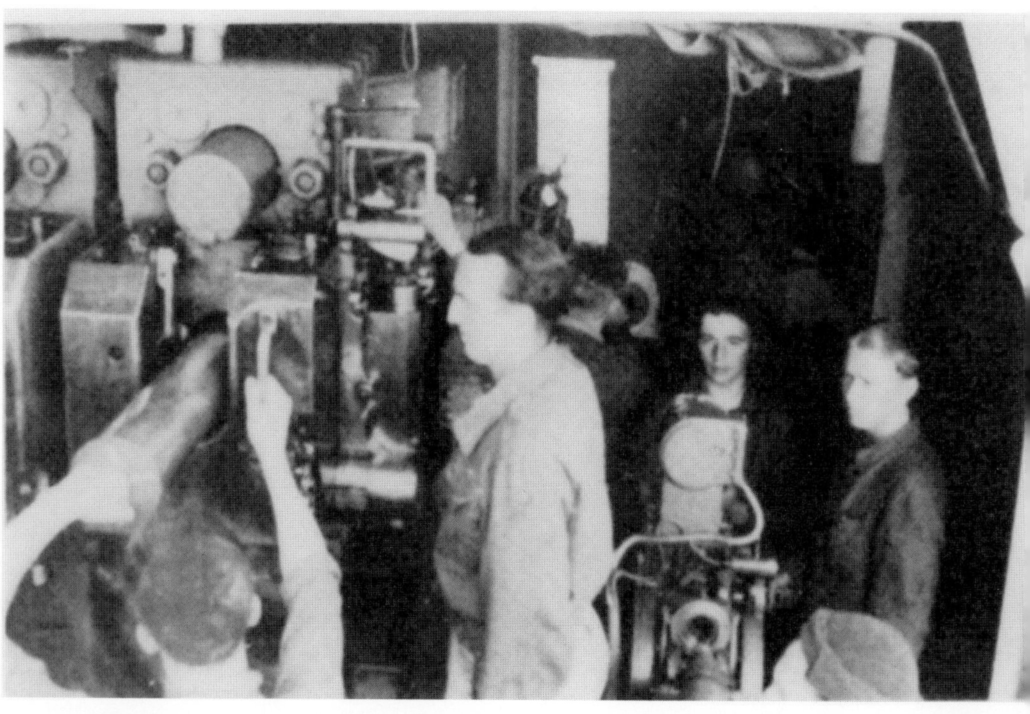

41. HMS *Stevenstone* was Type 3 Hunt class destroyer which mounted a pair of 21-inch torpedo tubes as well as the usual HA and AA gun armament. She took part in the disastrous Operation *Tunnel*, but was unable to get into the fight due to confusion in the British force. *(P. A. Vicary)*

42. Elevation. Rapid fire! The forward gun mounting of a Hunt is trained on the starboard beam to defend a convoy against yet another air raid. The single 20-mm Oerlikon gun can be seen mounted in the bridge wings, indication that this is a later stage of the war. *(Douglas Clare)*

43. The ill-fated anti-aircraft cruiser HMS *Charybdis*, chief victim of Operation Tunnel's stereotyped night sweeps in the Channel in 1943. She was one of only two of the successful Dido class cruisers which received a reduced armament of just eight 4.5-inch HA guns in four twin mountings in place of the ten 5.25-inch guns in five twin mountings due to production shortages early in the war, a fact the *Tunnel* planners appeared to have overlooked. *(Imperial War Museum, London)*

44. The crowded bridge of the destroyer HMS *Grenville* in 1943. She was the Flotilla Leader of the Ulster class destroyers, and had been named in honour of the earlier leader mined off Harwich earlier in the war. She was engaged in two fast-moving actions in the Channel at night. During the fatal Operation *Tunnel* operations, she took over command after the loss of her two senior officers. *(Imperial War Museum, London)*

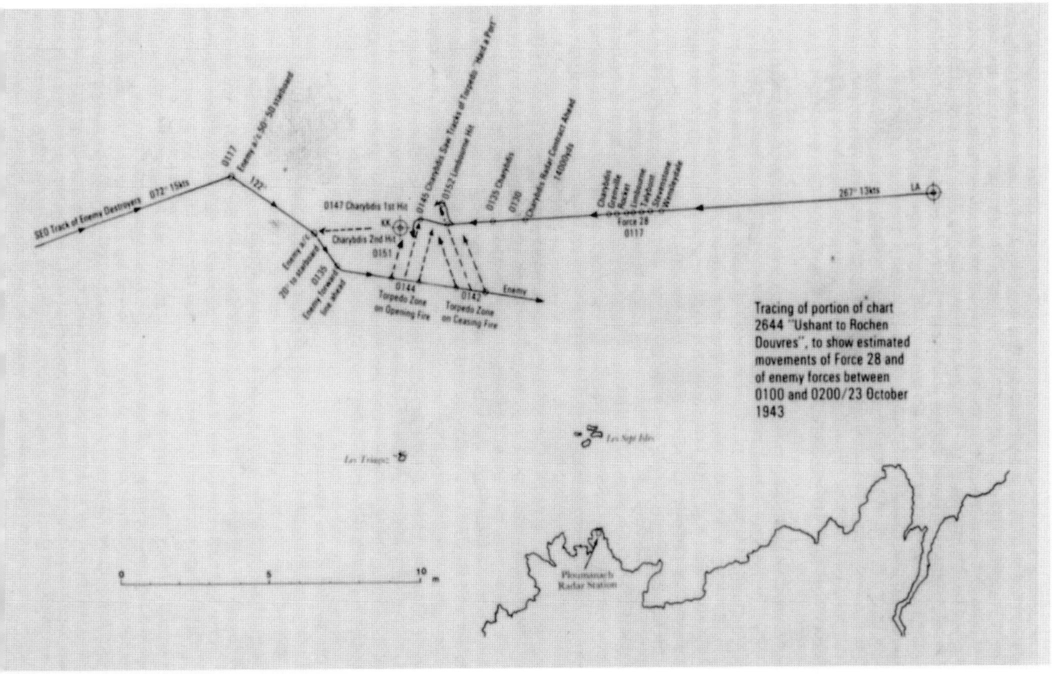

45. Operation Tunnel, 23 October 1943.

46. Normandy! The greatest amphibious landings up to that time, 6th June 1944. Here the massed ranks of the smaller landing craft pass in review prior to the actual assault. *(Imperial War Museum, London)*

47. General Charles De Gaul visits the Free French Hunt class destroyer *La Combattante.* This ship, formerly HMS *Haldon,* ha been handed over to the Free French in 1942 and she quickly built up an enviable reputation for aggressiveness in action. *(Douglas Clare)*

48. Back to Europe! British 'Tommies' wade ashore from their landing craft on the Normandy beaches on 6th June 1944 to begin the fight-back.
(Imperial War Museum, London)

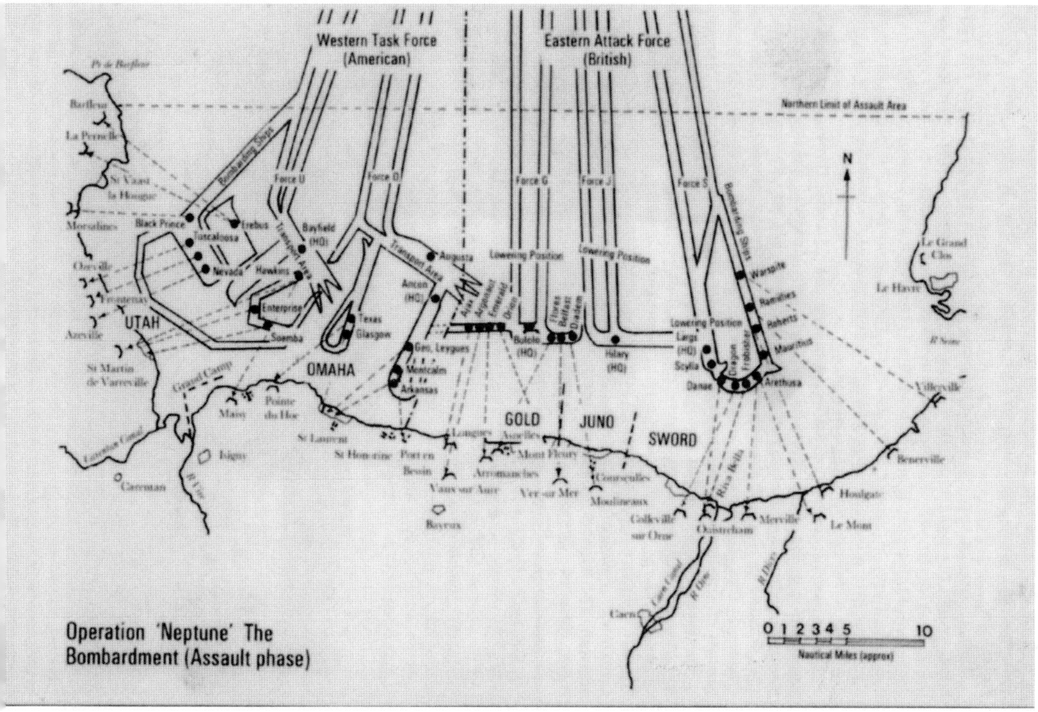

49. Operation *Neptune*. The Bombardment (Assault Phase).

50. The famous Flotilla Leader HMS *Jervis*, spent most of her war service in the Mediterranean, but she briefly returned to home waters in order to participate in the invasion of Normandy, and was one of very few Flotilla Leaders that served all through the war in the front line. *(MOD, Navy)*

51. Famous ship, still fighting almost thirty years after her first battle. The battleship HMS *Warspite*, veteran of Jutland in 1916, of Narvik and Calabria in 1940 and of Matapan in 1941, is seen here in action with three of her four 15-inch twin turrets, busy pulverizing German troop concentrations and shore batteries on 6 June 1944. She was later to give the same treatment to the enemy garrison on Walcheren Island as the fighting moved north. *(Imperial War Museum, London)*

52. The first and the last! Among the host of destroyers present at the Normandy landings were a few veterans from the original Dover Flotilla, including HMS *Beagle* herself, seen here protecting some LSTs and smaller vessels off the Normandy beachhead. *(A. L. M. Black)*

53. Mulberry harbour. The artificial harbour constructed off the Nomandy Beachhead enabled the largest transports to offload war material for the Allied armies ashore without the need to storm a major French port immediately, one of the bitter lessons of Dieppe that had to be absorbed. There were two, but, unfortunately the American one did not stand up to a typical Channel storm and the British one had to operate alone until Cherbourg was captured. *(Imperial War Museum, London)*

54. Destroyer Battle in the Channel 9 June 1944.

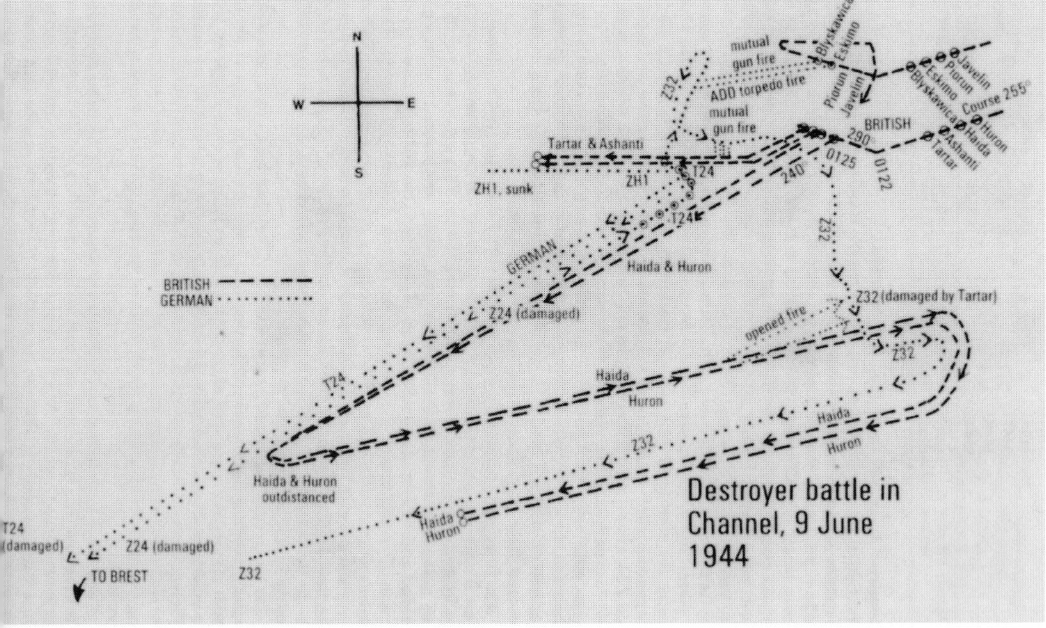

55. Heavy support for the D-day landings and for long afterward. The veteran battleship *Rodney* brings her nine 16-inch guns to the aid of the army, sending her huge projectiles twenty miles inland to break up massing Panzer formations. She later conducted bombardments of the German coastal forts in the Channel Islands.
(Imperial War Museum, London)

56. The destroyer HMS *Fury*, which had served right through the war in the front line, but was mined off Normandy and driven ashore in a gale as seen here. She was later successfully towed back intact to Portsmouth, but never repaired and written off as a 'Constructive Total Loss', and was later broken up.
(Imperial War Museum, London)

57. Duel off Cherbourg. The light cruiser HMS *Glasgow*, her twelve 6-inch guns ranged on the powerful German shore batteries on the French coast guarding this important harbour, takes a hit from a heavy shell amidships. *(Imperial War Museum, London)*

58. The Tribal Class destroyer HMS *Tartar*, leader of the 10th Destroyer Flotilla, as the thick black band around her fore-funnel indicates, in 1944. Their chief asset, heavy gun power, was finally made to pay off in some brisk night actions with German destroyers off the invasion beaches. *(Captain Basil Jones)*

59. The old destroyer HMS *Velox* saw some heavy fighting in the Narrow Seas throughout the war, but survived many adventures and finished the war in fighting trim, albeit reduced to the role of convoy escort. *(MOD Navy)*

60. The strain of comman
Captain Basil Jones
seen aboard his
destroyer HMS *Tartar*
on the morning after
night action in 1944.
(Captain Basil Jones)

61. An infantry landing ship comes ashore on Walcheren Island to embark the many wounded after the initial assault. This proved to be one of the hardest fought and bloodiest British landings of World War II. *(Imperial War Museum, London)*

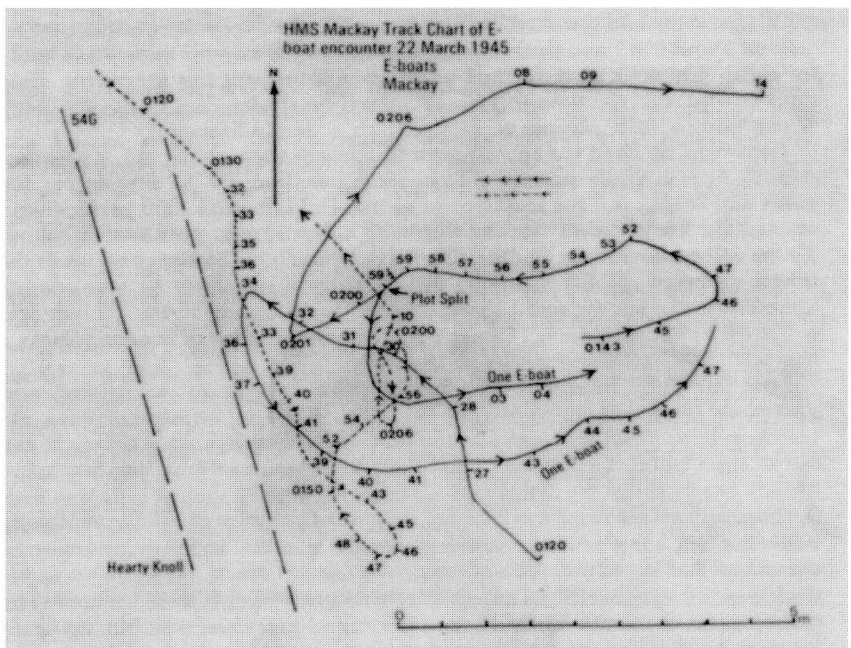

62. HMS *Mackay* – Track Chart of E-boat encounter 22 March 1945.

63. The Flotilla Leader HMS *Faulknor*, which in 1945 embarked Vice Admiral Friedrich Huffmeier, Commanding Officer of the German Occupation Forces in the Channel Islands as a prisoner of war. She also assisted in the surrender operation at Jersey from General Major Wulf, which had taken place aboard the two original Dover Flotilla veterans HMS *Beagle* and HMS *Bulldog*, which was highly fitting!
(MOD, Navy)

64 & 65. The story comes to its post-war finale. After the fighting was over, work was finally taken in hand to salvage the wreck of the Flotilla Leader HMS *Codrington,* which had lain where she sank in 1940. Why no effort had been made to salvage and repair her prior to that date is a mystery but these two photographs show her being raised in 1946 and her stern finally beached ashore at Dover for breaking up.

(Reproduced courtesy of Mr R. K. Barret © All Rights Reserved)

Barrage, it consisted of a multiple rocket launcher, which fired rockets, trailing wires behind it. They proved totally useless, and the one success (if true) was achieved this day (although aboard warships they did nothing and even possibly contributed to the loss of the battlecruiser *Hood* as an exposed fire hazard). In fact, the commanding officer of one of the Stuka units confirmed to the author that all his planes returned safely to France, although many were badly damaged.

Out at sea the German fighters located the motor launch *ML-120* and conducted strafing runs on her, which resulted in six of her crew being wounded. She had to put into harbour for repairs. After the dive bombers had departed, the German gun batteries dropped a few rounds close to the 14-inch gun at St Margaret's Bay to round things off.

Ironically, had the Stukas arrived over Dover Harbour just one day earlier they would have been presented with a greater array of choice targets to attract them. For, on 13 November, convoy CE16 was in some disarray. This convoy, which consisted of thirteen merchant ships, escorted by the destroyers *Fernie* and *Cleveland*, three A/S trawlers, four minesweeping trawlers, six balloon vessels and seven motor launches, of which *ML-120* was one, had sailed from St Helen's Bay, Isle of Wight, at 1530, and was due at Dungeness at 0245 under cover of darkness. By 2330 the Freya system had picked it up off St Leonard's.

All was thought to be well until a signal was received from *Fernie* at 0200 addressed to the convoy, ordering it to heave-to. As the delay would have ensured that the convoy crossed the most dangerous area in daylight, *Fernie* was instructed to return to Portsmouth or Newhaven. However, when dawn broke, the minesweeping trawlers could be seen plodding along past Dover! By full daylight half the ships, the sweepers and some of the M/Ls and balloon vessels were all travelling east, strung out between Hastings and the Downs, while the rest of the convoy was, presumably, following *Fernie* back to Portsmouth as instructed. Heavy fighter cover was laid on in case the *Luftwaffe* took advantage of the confusion but, as we have seen, the enemy arrived a day too late.

New German Destroyer Sorties, 24-25 November 1940

The bombardment of Cherbourg by *Revenge* had influenced the removal of the Germans' destroyers to Brest at this time. From that latter port, however, they continued their almost nightly jaunts into British coastal waters, laying mines or attacking coastal shipping, without hindrance. It seems strange that, with the whole of the south coast on the alert for any impending invasion, the German flotillas should have been able to continue their incursions unchecked.

On this occasion the destroyers under Captain Bey, consisted of the flotilla leader *Karl Galster*, with *Hans Lody* and *Richard Beitzen*, and they prowled around the Plymouth area, attacking on sight, claiming to have dispatched two ships totalling 2,156 tons, without response. In fact, the powerful ships of the 5th Destroyer Flotilla under Captain Lord Louis Mountbatten were based at Plymouth, and were frequently at sea hoping to make a more successful interception than the previous one. Finally, however, Lord Louis and his ships were given yet another opportunity.

German Destroyer Raid, 28-29 November 1940

Captain Bey led the same vessels to sea again on the evening of 28 November, and they rapidly arrived at their old hunting ground off Plymouth. In a short time, after midnight, several small vessels had been sighted and snapped up. The tug *Aid* and the self-propelled barge *BHC-10* were fired on some eight miles off Start Point, and duly dispatched, but not before they had fired off signal rockets and roused the patrols. Leaving *Hans Lody* to finish off these sinking ships, Bey quickly increased his speed and headed for home with *Karl Galster* and *Richard Beitzen*. Being equipped with fine surface-warning radar sets, Bey felt confident of avoiding any British ships, unless he was very unfortunate. On this sortie, his legendary good luck almost evaded him, but he was able to turn a potential disaster once more into a small victory, aided again, by errors on the British side.

The approach of the intercepting British force was first detected on the German ships' radar sets at a range of 7,000 metres, and a total of five ships could be distinguished. The German destroyers at once went to full speed and edged to the west to place the oncoming British ships as far astern as possible. There was still a considerable gap between the first two German ships and the *Lody* coming up from astern. In thus detecting the British flotilla, the Germans had considerable advantage, had they known it. It was not until some time later that a visual sighting only was made from the leading British destroyer, the *Javelin*. The rearmost German ships were seen from her bridge to be crossing the bows of the British line from left to right, at a range of about 5,000 yards. *Galster* and *Beitzen* were then seen some distance further off on the *Javelin*'s port bow.

The British Flotilla Intercepts

The British force was, of course, Mountbatten's 5th Flotilla with Captain (D) embarked aboard *Javelin* (Commander A. F. Pugsley) and with the *Jackal* (Commander C. L. Firth), MVO), *Kashmir* (Commander H. A. King), *Jupiter* (Commander D. B. Wyburd) and *Jersey* (Lieutenant Commander W. Evershed). With the flotilla approaching the Germans' ragged line, instant gun action against these fleeting targets might have smothered the closest German ships and scored some damaging hits. Certainly, the Javelin and Kelly class destroyers had two thirds of their main armament concentrated forward for just such an eventuality and, as the ships were en echelon, this type of fire would not have been unduly masked for a few vital moments.

In such a fast-moving scenario, snap decisions have to made very quickly, and Mountbatten made his, choosing instead to turn his force onto a course parallel with the enemy, in order to keep pace with them. He therefore gave the order 'Flotilla turn ninety degrees to port together', The *Javelin*'s director which had been tracking the enemy and locking the guns on target, at once lost sight of the target with the violent alteration of course and so, for a short, but vital time, the British gunners could do nothing at all. In that interval, the Germans played their standard card, launching a full salvo of torpedoes as they sped south. Instead of just having the bows of the British ships to aim at, they were now presented with their full lengths.

Javelin Damaged, German Ships Escape

As the British destroyers careered round onto the parallel course to the retreating enemy, they were still some distance astern of Bey's rearmost vessel. Both sides had commenced a brief gun duel at close range, Initially both sides miscalculated the gap, which had closed considerably, and both tended to overshoot. Before any fine adjustment could be made, the German torpedoes reached the head of the British line. Two of these missiles hit *Javelin* fair and square, causing devastating damage.

One torpedo blew the bows off the *Javelin*, the other her stern. This latter hit detonated her after magazine, which exploded with a huge roar. The ship heeled over to port, due to the force of the explosion, but somehow righted herself. Amazingly, the midships portion, containing her vital bridge structure, engine and boiler rooms, remained intact and the bulkheads at both extremes held, despite the violence of the blows she had taken.

The remaining ships of the British flotilla passed her by and continued with the chase for a while, but it was all in vain. Once more the German destroyers had the legs of the British and were able to make good their escape.

Javelin herself was in a sorry, and highly vulnerable, state. The entire deckhouse and forecastle forward of 'B' mounting had been blown up and 'A' mounting had vanished. The structure of the hull had been twisted up from the port side and over to starboard. All the compartments forward of the boiler room had been opened up to the sea and were flooding. Aft, everything had been destroyed up to and including the after 4-inch HA gun.

The fuel oil had been ignited by the explosions and a fierce fire raged, seemingly out of control. The whole after structure of the ship, including the propellers, was a twisted mass of metal, which hung down below the waterline until its sheer weight eventually broke it off some hours later. As the seriousness of the ship's condition would indicate, losses were heavy, three officers and forty-three ratings, mostly from the crews serving 'A' and 'Y' mountings. The mess decks had been devastated but, as the crew was at action stations, this was not as serious as it might have been; normally, they would have been crowded with men.

Jackal, which had lost touch with the enemy early on, joined *Javelin* and managed to rescue some men who had been blown into the water. She then provided an anti-submarine and anti-E-boat screen during the hours of darkness, until dawn, when the situation could be properly assessed. She also embarked many of the wounded and other, non-essential, hands to help lighten the ship, which was not expected to last the night out in her sorry state. (In truth, what remained of *Javelin* was a 155 ft midships section of a 340 ft ship!) After *Jackal* had sailed for Plymouth, word came that tugs were on their way and fighter cover was laid on in anticipation of air attacks, which later materialized. *Kashmir*, *Jupiter* and *Jersey* also took station later as further protection and, during the forenoon, the tug duly arrived from Falmouth. She jury-rigged a wire around the torpedo tubes aft and thus got a tow under way at the slow speed of two knots. Later, a second tug arrived to assist yet further, and she lashed herself alongside.

Javelin was later docked for thirteen months while her entire bows and stern were rebuilt. After that she went unscathed through the rest of the entire war, one of only two of the Javelin class to survive.

Yet another disappointing result and severe damage on a new ship was all the British had to show for yet another clash with the German destroyers. The tactics employed were examined, and found wanting, but no great changes seem to have taken place and the pattern of British action, and German response, was repeated over and over again in the Channel. It was a sterile doctrine, insisted upon by theorist and shown more than once, to be non-effective. It was, in the end, to lead to even greater disasters before any rectification of doctrine was carried out, and even then it was done in the teeth of strong opposition.

Loss of HMS *Swordfish*, 7 November 1940

One result of the continuing immunity of the German destroyers operating from Brest was the establishment of a special submarine watch set up on that port. This watch was to continue until the early days of 1942, but it was never rewarded. It was part of the anti-invasion measures and, on 7 November, the submarine *Swordfish* sailed from her base HMS *Dolphin* at Gosport to relieve the *Usk* on this duty. She then vanished and was never heard from again. It was subsequently widely believed that *Swordfish* was sunk by German destroyers off Brest when three of them attacked a contact on 16 November. Other reports claimed that she was mined on 10 November, and she is so recorded in one German reference book. But all these 'official' accounts, both German and British, were found to be so much speculation when her wreck was located off the Isle of Wight in August 1983.

A civilian diver, Martin Woodard, from Bembridge Maritime Museum, was diving for a First World War wreck in the area. He found *Swordfish* in 150 ft of water, broken in two halves, in an area known to have been mined one month before she was sunk. She had struck one of these mines within hours of sailing and had gone down with all hands, forty officers and men. The after section of the submarine was still standing upright, the fore section lay on its side on the sea bottom. The after escape hatch was open, as if an attempt had been made to escape from the wreck. The letter 'S' of her name was still attached to her coning tower, and the letter 'W' was on the bottom nearby; the whole wreck was in remarkably good condition. It was planned to make her hull a belated official war grave.

The fact that the true demise of the *Swordfish* only came to light forty-three years after the event, even though she was lost in the very home waters of the Royal Navy's premier naval base, indicated the nature of sea warfare. It is particularly poignant in waters so close to home but, with submarines, their exact fate was often hard to determine.

Even major warships could be mined, or torpedoed, and sunk within view of the populated south coast of England, and still the survivors could die from lack of attention, as witness the fate of the destroyer *Acheron* in these self-same waters at this period of the war.

Loss of HMS *Acheron*

One of the greatest tragedies of the gloomy days of the winter of 1940-41 also took place within a stone's throw of Britain's premier naval port and with the friendly shore of the Isle of Wight almost within reach. This was the setting when the destroyer *Acheron* put to sea to carry out her trials after completing comprehensive repairs necessitated by the bomb damage she had received in August. The ship had been almost totally rebuilt aft by Portsmouth Dockyard, and she had a full ship's company of 190 officers and men under the command of Lieutenant Commander R. W. F. Northcott, as well as twenty-five dockyard workers to witness the trial and judge the effects of their workmanship. It was a bitterly cold night, with a strong wind blowing from the north-east and the light had not yet brightened the eastern sky. The normally busy waters of Spithead and the Solent were almost empty and little stirred in the grey, choppy waters, save for the destroyer herself. She was due to show her paces on the measured mile trial course from St Catherine's Point Lighthouse to Ventnor Pier, known as the inshore course.

The first run passed uneventfully and a second run, to the east, was commenced to enable full power to be worked up. What happened next was later described by one of her ratings, D. E. Sleeman:

> ....I heard a muffled roar and a sudden unfamiliar hiss. The blackness of the night was transformed by a brilliant light...I was horrified to see the ship on fire, great flames were leaping skyward completely enveloping the bridge.

As he made his way aft to set the depth charges to safe, the stricken destroyer lurched and began almost at once to settle, her bows blown away, her stern cocked in the air.

> ...the deck was now tilting alarmingly, and the ship was completely submerged forward of the 3-inch gun deck, so it was an easy thing to slide down the sloping deck. 'This is the end', I though as I swam away towards the direction of land, so far off and hopelessly beyond my capacity to reach...oil fuel stank with a nauseating aroma and burnt with every mouthful of water. Looking over my shoulder some 200 yards behind me I saw the gaunt stern poised vertically above the sea,

> and then, accompanied by a tremendous gurgle it slid into the dark waters.

The sea hereabouts is some eleven fathoms deep. Initially Sleeman was taken down by the suction, but luckily he eventually surfaced again and was hauled aboard a Carley raft, which had a calcium flare, attached to it. This was just about the only life raft to be launched, so quickly did *Acheron* take her final plunge after striking the mine.

> Slowly the time passed, the silence broken at intervals with plaintive cries for help...as I stood the water was just below my waist; every now and then it would rise to my neck. The cold was intense... would the day never come? All our party were not destined to see that dawn, one by one the men holding on to the handles lost their grip. At last day was fully with us, far away ahead we could see the faint outlines of the Isle of Wight, away to port in cold mockery to our shipmates drifted an empty Carley raft...we tried to sing but our voices became harsh like the croaking of frogs. At long last a ship appeared, an escort vessel; slowly she altered course and bore down on us, we drifted alongside. One by one nineteen weary men, the sole survivors of the ship's company, climbed up the scrambling nets and fell into the arms of rescuers.

German Minelaying Continues with New and Old Types

Acheron was one tragic victim of the enemy's minelaying campaign, which continued unabated and with ever newer ploys and devices. The magnetic mine had lost its novelty but losses still continued and, in September, the introduction of an acoustic mine, long feared, was confirmed. Although acoustic sweeps were soon introduced, much work had to be done to perfect them. Delaying devices were also being fitted to magnetic mines so that they were only detonated after several ships had passed over them. Anti-sweeping devices like the explosive sweep cutter, were mixed with moored mines, which the Germans continued to sow all around the south coast, but especially in the Thames Estuary. Such a mixture of mines made the work of the minesweepers a tiring and dangerous occupation. The methods of delivery of these mines continued to be as diverse as ever; destroyers, E-boats, submarines (less frequently) and aircraft, all contributing. Once again, though, the enemy started a campaign without sufficient resources to maintain the pressure. Nonetheless, a quick glance at the losses suffered by warships alone in this period will show the baleful influence of this most impersonal of weapons. That *any* ships got through at all was due to the dedicated work of the minesweepers' crews, many of whom had little or no previous training in this work, but were simply expected to cope, so great was the expansion and so slender the resources for training during this time of crisis.

Table 5: British Warship Losses in the Channel, September – December 1940.			
Name	**Type**	**Date**	**Details**
Royalo	Trawler	1 Sept.	Mined, off South Cornwall
MTB-15	MTB	15 Sept.	Mined, Thames Estuary
Recoil	Trawler	28 Sept.	Mined, English Channel
Comet	Trawler	30 Sept.	Mined, off Falmouth
Sappho	Armed Yacht	30 Sept.	Torpedoed, off Falmouth
Kingston Sapphire	Trawler	5 Oct.	Torpedoed, Dover Straits
Scotch Thistle	Drifter	6 Oct.	Grounded, Thames Estuary
Aisha	Armed Yacht	11 Oct.	Mined, Thames Estuary
Resolvo	Trawler	12 Oct.	Mined, Thames Estuary
Warwick Deeping	Trawler	12 Oct.	Torpedoed, English Channel
Danube III	Tug	13 Oct.	Mined, Sheerness
Lord Stamp	Trawler	14 Oct.	Mined, English Channel
Kingston	Trawler	14 Oct.	Mined, English Channel
Cairngorm	Trawler	14 Oct.	Mined, English Channel
Venetia	Destroyer	19 Oct.	Mined, Thames Estuary
Hickory	Trawler	22 Oct.	Mined, English Channel
Lord Inchcape	Trawler	23 Oct.	Mined, off Plymouth
Tilbury Ness	Trawler	23 Oct.	Bombed, Thames Estuary
Torbay II	Drifter	1 Nov.	Bombed, off Dover
Rinova	Trawler	2 Nov.	Mined, off Falmouth
Swordfish	Submarine	7 Nov.	Mined, off Bembridge, IOW.
Reed	Drifter	7 Nov.	Mined, Thames Estuary
Muria	Tug	8 Nov.	Mined, off North Foreland
Kingston Aladite	Trawler	10 Nov.	Mined, off Plymouth
Stella Orion	Trawler	11 Nov.	Mined, Thames Estuary
Ristango	Boom Defence Vessel	14 Nov.	Fouled Medway boom
Shipmates	Drifter	14 Nov.	Bombed, Dover Harbour
Guardsmen	Tug	15 Nov.	Mined, off North Foreland
The Boys	Drifter	18 Nov.	Foundered in The Downs
Go Ahead	Drifter	18 Nov.	Collision, Sheerness
Xmas Rose	Drifter	21 Nov.	Mined, Thames Estuary

Amethyst	Trawler	24 Nov.	Mined, Thames Estuary
Conquistador	Trawler	25 Nov.	Collision, Thames Estuary
Kenmore	Trawler	25 Nov.	Mined, Thames Estuary
Elk	Trawler	27 Nov.	Mined, Plymouth
Chestnut	Trawler	30 Nov.	Mined, off North Foreland
Sevra	Whaler	6 Nov.	Mined, off Falmouth
AN-2	Whaler	8 Nov.	Mined, off Falmouth
Capriconrus	Trawler	7 Dec.	Mined, off S.E. Coast
Acheron	Destroyer	17 Dec.	Mined, off Isle of Wight
Thomas Connolly	Boom Defence Vessel	17 Dec.	Mined, Sheerness
Carry On	Drifter	17 Dec.	Mined, Sheerness
Lord Howard	Drifter	24 Dec.	Collision, Dover Harbour

The Minesweeping Men of the Royal Navy; An Eyewitness Viewpoint

Typical of the men and methods prevailing in 1490-41 was George Drewett, and his story was told to the author, so that it would serve both as an illustration of the problems and as a tribute to the many hundreds of men like him:

> In 1940 I was a young leading seaman in RN Barracks, Portsmouth. I was summoned to the drafting office and I was told that I would be in charge of party who were going on draft. I was not told where we were going. The following day I paraded and I was informed to pack my bag and hammock and be ready that same day to take a draft somewhere! Later that day I mustered with some thirty or forty young sailors who had only been in the Navy for a matter of weeks. No-one seemed to know what was happening. I was given some instructions and a railway warrant and told I was in charge of these sailors and I had to report with them to Portsmouth BTO on the railway
>
> From here we caught a train and much, much later, arrived at Troon in Scotland, miserable, cold and hungry. From Troon railway station we marched or ambled into a dockyard still wondering what we would commission, a battleship? – a cruiser? – or a destroyer? No, it wasn't to be; it was a brand new fleet minesweeper built for magnetic, acoustic and moored minesweeping. We also had Asdic for anti-submarine work. We were fresher than fresh to all this. We were still trying to find our way around the ship while most of my 'sailors' were still using civilian terms, such as 'upstairs', 'down the back' and one even referred to the deck as 'the floor!' We were in fact as green as grass, many of us homesick and feeling very dejected. You must remember we were all about 18 or 19 years of age. A Lieutenant RNVR, who I later found out

was a former solicitor, said, 'Leading Seaman Drewett, you are in charge of the minesweeping deck.' I could have dropped dead for I hadn't a clue about minesweeping or the gear used to do it. I was given a pile of Confidential Books and told to 'swot up' on it. This I did. Throughout the war our work never stopped and in 1946, when most others had been demobilized and sent home I, like many others now skilled at this work, was still clearing up our own and enemy mines and minefields.

Table 6: German Destroyer Operations off the English Channel Coast September 1940- July 1942			
Date	Area	German Destroyers involved	Purpose
1-2 Sept. 1940	S.W. North Sea	Minelayers *Cobra, Roland* and *Tannenberg* escorted by destroyers *Erich Steinbrinck, Karl Galster, Paul Jacobi, Falke, Iltis, Jaguar, Grief, T-5, T-6, and T-7 & T-8.*	Minefield SW3
5-6 Sept. 1940	Straits of Dover	Minelayers escorted by *T-5, T-6, T-7* and *T-8*	Operation *Walter*
6-7 Sept. 1940	SW North Sea	*Falke, Greif, Iltis, Kondor, Jaguar, T-1, T-2* and *T-3*	Minefield SWO
8-9 Sept. 1940	Straits of Dover	*T-5, T-6, T-7* and *T-8*	Operation *Hannelore*
15-16 Sept. 1940	Straits of Dover	*T-5, T-6, T-7* and *T-8*	Operation *Bernhard*
28-29 Sept, 1940	Falmouth Bay	*Hans Lody, Karl Galster, Paul Jacobi, Erich Steinbrinck, Friedrich Ihn, Friedrich Eckoldt* & *Theodor Riedel*	Minefield
30 Sept.-1 Oct. 1940	Off Dover	*Falke, Greif, Kondor, Seeadler*	Operation *Werner*
8-9 Oct. 1940	Isle of Wight	*Greif, Falke, Kondor, Jaguar, Seeadler, Wolf*	Anti-shipping sortie.
11-12 Oct. 1940	Isle of Wight	*Falke, Greif, Kondor, Seeadler, Wolf*	Anti-shipping sortie.
17-18 Oct. 1940	Bristol Channel	*Hans Lody, Karl Galster, Friedrich Ihn, Erich Steinbrinck, Falke, Greif, Kondor, Jaguar, Seeadler* & *Wolf*	Anti-shipping sortie.
29-30 Oct. 1940	Off Dover	*Iltis, Jaguar*	Operation *Alfred*
24-25 Nov. 1940	Off Plymouth	*Karl Galster, Hans Lody* & *Richard Beitzen*	Anti-shipping sortie.
28-29 Nov. 1940	Off Plymouth	*Karl Galster, Hans Lody* & *Richard Beitzen*	Anti-shipping sortie.
2-3 Dec. 1940	Off Dover	*Iltis, Jaguar*	Operation *Oskar*
3-4 Dec. 1940	Off Dover	*Falke, Greif, Kondor* & *Seealder*	Operation *Marianne*
21-22 Dec 1940	Western North Sea	*Falke, Greif* & *Seeadler*	Operation *SWa*
7-8 Jan. 1941	Thames Estuary	*Kondor, Wolf*	Operation *Renate*

23-24 Jan. 1941	South Coast	*Richard Beitzen, Iltis, Seeadler*	Operation *Weber*
25-26 Feb. 1941	Off Eastbourne	*Iltis, Jaguar*	Operation *Augsburg A*
5-6 March 1941	Off Eastbourne	*Iltis, Jaguar*	Operation *Augsburg B*
20-21 July 1942	English Channel	*T-4, T-10, T-13 & T-14*	Operation *Rhein*
21-22 July 1942	English Channel	*T-4, T-10, T-13 & T-14*	Operation *Stein*
1-2 Aug. 1942	English Channel	*T-10, T-13 & T-14*	Operation *Masuren*

German E-boats Extend their Activities

Although their proven success showed that E-boats were a potent weapon for night attacks against slow-moving and ill-defended convoys, the Germans were tardy in developing them in sufficient numbers to mount more than an insignificant number of sorties. Nevertheless, from September 1940 onward, numbers of E-boats grew slowly until some twelve or fifteen were on hand with the 1st Flotilla, and they spread their attacks to cover the east coast and the Channel areas. Their successes in the latter area were still something of a rarity. Our own MTBs and MGBs were smaller, slower and powered by petrol engines, which made them much more vulnerable than their German counterparts, a result of sounder German thinking pre-war. The answer to the E-boat therefore was ultimately, as ever, adequate destroyer screens by ships properly equipped to deal with them, but in 1940-41 this demand just could not be met with all the other commitments destroyers were called upon to fulfil. Even so, several sharp actions took place during that winter.

On the night of 23-24 December 1940, for instance, a strong attack was mounted by the German 1st Flotilla, who fielded seven boats, *S-26, S-28, S-29, S-34, S-56, S-58* and *S-59*. These hit the trawler *Pelton* and the merchantman *Stad Maastricht* (6,552 tons) from convoy FN 366. On 19 February 1941, *S-102* (*Leutnant* Töniges) after a night attack with *S-28* and *S-101* sank the freighter *Algarve* (1,335 tons) in the Thames Estuary. The E-boats had sunk a total of twenty-three ships (47,985 tons) by the end of 1940.

German Destroyer Minelaying Continues, 1941

The close brush with the 5th Destroyer Flotilla earlier had not deterred the German destroyer crews; rather, it was their unreliable machinery that proved the biggest restriction on their operations. Constant breakdowns of their temperamental turbines resulted in most of the big destroyers being sent back to Germany for refits during 1941, but they were replaced with the newer, smaller so-called 'torpedo boats', which were similar in size and armament to the British 'Fleet' destroyers in essence. Minelaying operations were resumed but more and more infrequently as these new ships became available. They also made raids on shipping.

On the night of 7-8 January 19041, *Kondor* and *Wolf* sailed to carry out

Operation *Renate*, a mine lay off Dover. This was done, without a hitch, but on their return to Dunkirk, *Wolf* (*Leutnant* Peters) herself struck a mine and sank in shallow water.

The one remaining 'heavy' destroyer, *Richard Beitzen* (*Kapitän zur See* von Davidson) led the *Iltis* (*Kapitän zur See* Jacobson) and *Seeadler* (*Kapitän zur See* Kohlauf) on a similar mission, Operation *Weber*, without detection. This took place on the night of 23-24 January, while, a month later, the *Iltis* and *Jaguar* (*Kapitän zur See* Hartenstein) laid another minefield off Eastbourne. The same mission was repeated on the night of 5-6 March, thereafter lighter nights brought about a lull in operations.

Blockade of Brest: 20th Flotilla Lays Minefield, 20 February 1941

In the meanwhile, in the larger sea war, the German destroyers were not alone in laying minefields of strategic importance. When the German battlecruisers *Scharnhorst* and *Gneisenau* were loose on the epic raiding voyage out into the Atlantic early in the new year of 1941, it was suspected that they might make for Brest rather than returning to Germany, so that they might continue operations again when ready. These suspicions were later to prove correct but, at the time, every effort was made to prevent them from reaching that haven and, among the far-reaching movements that took place, was the utilization of the destroyers of the 20th Flotilla for an attempt to block the possible approaches.

Therefore, at 1630 on 19 February, *Intrepid* (Commander R. C. Gordon), *Icarus* (Lieutenant Commander L. C. Maud) and *Impulsive* (Lieutenant Commander M. S. Thomas), sailed from Plymouth to carry out Operation *GS* [*Gneisenau-Scharnhorst*] and they duly arrived off Brest later that evening.

For support the 5th Flotilla, *Jackal, Jersey, Jupiter* and *Kashmir*, served as their escort, and took station on the three minelaying destroyers' starboard quarter.

It must be remembered that the approaches to Brest, which was one of the major ports of occupied France, and recently serving as a similar haven for the heavy cruiser *Admiral Hipper*, was one of the most heavily patrolled harbours in the Channel area. In addition, German radar stations were expected to be well established in the area to cover all the seaward approaches.

The mines were nonetheless laid to a complicated pattern in groups in the rough form of a many-angled salient to make detection and regular pattern sweeping impossible. They also laid a mixed mine load, making possible the utilization of various combinations, which were deliberately designed to make life much harder for the enemy minesweepers. It was indeed a remarkable action by the 20th Flotilla.

Continued British Minelaying off Channel Ports

These three British destroyers continued to be usefully employed for some weeks after this audacious sortie. One of *Impulsive*'s crew, Mr T.

Brotheridge, told the author that:

> We often loaded mines at Portsmouth and proceeded from there to either Dartmouth or Plymouth to await darkness for laying mines on the other side of the Channel, off Brest and the Channel Islands. Dartmouth seemed quiet, but often, when leaving Plymouth at night, we would hear the German bombers overhead and see the flames of the city in our wake. We were now supplied with moored magnetic mines and were the first to lay them off Cap d'Antifer. Another safe source of supply for our mines was Milford Haven, which was hardly ever bombed, and we used to go there often and then back to Plymouth for our operations.

Table 7: Mining Report of HMS *Icarus*, 20 February 1941		
1	Date of operation	20 Feb. 1941
2	Title of operation	GS
3	Type of mine and sinker used	Mines – Mk XVII. Sinkers – Mk XVIIxB and XVB.
4	Number of mines laid	26
5	Special fittings or arrangements	4 sinkers with grapnels. 4 sinkers with sprockets. Mines with flooders 1A
6	Identification Marks painted on mines	Nil
7	Depth set (plummet sinkers)	23 ft.
8	Depth set (hydrostatic sinkers)	Nil
9	Depth of tops of mines below Chart Datum	6 ft.
10	Charted depth of water where mines are laid	51 fathoms
11	Height of tide at time of laying	17 ft.
12	Strength and direction of current	See remarks of SO
13	State of sea	Moderate
14	Visibility	7
15	Time began laying	0058.06
16	Time finished laying	0108.34
17	Speed of ship	15 knots
18	Position of first mine of line	48° 10' 4" N, 48° 11' 48" N 5° 8' 39" W, 5° 7' o" W
19	Direction of line	015-1/2°
20	Number of groups in line	2

21	Number of mines in each group	7 6 6 7
22	Spacing of mines in groups	150 ft.
23	Interval between groups in line	650 yds. 700 yds.
24	Date and time at which flooders or delayed release devices are set to operate	on 21 March 1941
25	Date mines embarked	9 Feb. 1941
26	Tests carried out on board	As laid down in OU5302, Chapt 'X'
27	Number of mines remaining on surface	Nil
28	Number of premature locks	Nil
29	* Remarks on failures, delays, accidents	Nil
30	Number of units observed	-
* Full report of failures etc, to be rendered, *vide* Mining Drill Book, para 78(v).		

Renewal of Bombing Attacks Upon Coastal Convoys

Throughout this period, the RAF resolutely refused to allow ships under bombing attack to control the fighters sent out to protect them, a ludicrous situation brought on by the Air Ministry's continued paranoia about any sharing of 'control'. Fighter Command would permit only that ships could pass on any information they had, which the pilots would then interpret as they saw fit! Losses from bombing thus rose steeply in November whenever the Ju87 Stukas were out; eleven ships were sunk and seventeen damaged. The lull between December and February was due to the falling off of enemy sorties but, when they resumed their bombing offensive on shipping toward the end of February and again in March, the graph again began a steady climb and a large number of ships were sunk in broad daylight off Ramsgate.

Among the losses to German bombers in the spring of 1941, until the impeding invasion of the Soviet Union brought about another respite, were: *Old Charlton* (1,562 tons), *Empire Frost* (7,005 tons), *Baltistan* (6,803 tons) and *Cabenda* (534 tons).

Chapter Twelve

Escape of the German Battle Fleet

With the departure of the bulk of the *Luftwaffe* to Russia and the long summer days restricting (although never wholly curtailing) the activities of the German destroyers and E-boats, there was, if such a term can be used about the war in the English Channel, a lull during the period April-August 1941. Momentous events were taking place in the Mediterranean, and the clouds were gathering in the Far East, but while eyes were pulled elsewhere, the job of getting the convoys through the Straits had become an almost dull routine by comparison.

It should not be imagined that this meant vigilance could be relaxed one iota, or that death was not waiting for any slackening of effort between April and June 1941. In May, German bombers sank sixty-five merchant ships, totalling 146,302 tons. The reduced effort after that time was therefore very much welcomed by the British. The activities of the 4th E-boat Flotilla also eased off for a time; it was undergoing a period of reorganization, but the E-boats were still deadly when on the hunt and their confidence was still growing. On the 11th they signalled their reappearance on the scene with the sinking of the coaster *Sir Russell* (1,548 tons) in an attack upon a convoy off Dungeness.

Mines continued, as always, to be a major headache, but sweeping continued relentlessly. The full synchronization of minesweepers and convoys was now a fact. Nevertheless, the losses were remorseless and among the many ships lost during the period under review was the destroyer *Vimiera* in January 1942.

Seen as individual losses, the toll was heavy and ongoing. For instance, Nore Command had no less than sixty-nine ships sunk in their area of operations in 1941. Against that, the *Official History* reveals that over 36,000,000 tons of shipping passed in and out of the Thames that year and the loss rate for such a vast tonnage was less than ½ of a per cent. However, the British offensive arms fared little better, and the Germans continued to make full use of the Channel as they wished. No less than twenty-nine major German ships and eleven destroyers passed through the Straits between April and June 1941 without loss or hindrance.

Britain's armed service still had hardly any dive bombers, other than a few belonging to the Fleet Air Arm, which, from time-to-time were landed ashore from the carriers and operated under the orders of a totally uncomprehending Coastal Command from airfields in Cornwall. The Minister of Aircraft Production had ordered such aircraft from American manufacturers but the Air Ministry was disdainful of the type and placed them on the lowest of priorities, despite the continued evidence of their effectiveness in German hands in Greece, Crete, North Africa and Russia, and later the startling success of the Japanese and American Navies in using this method. So misused and misunderstood did the FAA Skua dive bomber crews feel that when the *Luftwaffe* made determined raids on their base at St Eval and destroyed many of these aircraft their own crews cheered! They were never to be replaced and the Royal Navy spent the rest of the war without a true dive bomber. The RAF continued, as always, to pin their faith on level bombing and their main effort, some 6,000 sorties, resulted in just fifty vessels sunk (totalling 65,352 tons) against the loss of 215 medium bombers. Nor did Bomber Command's sustained effort against the three stationary German warships at Brest achieve the desired outcome although, again, bomber losses were severe and French civilian casualties appalling.

The Tramlines

The convoy lanes, which passed between the minefields and the hazards of the coastal waters between Plymouth, on into the Thames and up the East Coast to Methil, because of their restricted width, became known to the Royal Navy crews tasked with voyaging back and forth in them, as 'The Tramlines'. Commander William Donald, at that time commanding the destroyer *Verdun* of the Rosyth Escort Force, has left us with this impression of the endless chore of convoy escort in these confined waters:

> ...the whole atmosphere of the East Coast convoys was one of standing by for action. Although on many a trip nothing happened, we also had to be ready for anything. One of the great dangers for the ship's company was boredom: at sea, day after day, night after night, they would close up on watch or at Action Stations, and nothing would happen – but, when something did, it happened quickly and the danger was to be caught napping.
>
> But at the end of each trip, it was a very satisfying sight to see the convoy entering harbour; it was something accomplished, something done. I never failed to get a thrill out of it. In *Verdun* we had a special flag of our own, not found in the official signal books. I cannot remember how we acquired it – probably just as well – but it was a large white flag with a broad green border. In the middle was a lovely glass of brown stout with a foamy white top, and underneath, in bright red letters, the words 'Guinness is good for you'!
>
> At the end of a particularly tough trip, when we had had an exasperating struggle with the enemy or the weather, or possibly both, we used to hoist that flag just before arrival in the Thames. Then we would turn and steam back past the line of ships in convoy. From every bridge

would come a cheery wave of the hand, or a toot-toot on the siren, or a signal flash: 'Meet you ashore for one tonight.'

Table 8: British Warship Losses in the Channel 1941			
Name	**Type**	**Date**	**Details**
New Spray	Drifter	3 Jan.	Foundered in gale off Sheerness.
Dusky Queen	Drifter	9 Jan.	Grounded, Dover
Desiree	Trawler	17 Jan.	Mined, Thames Estuary
Darogah	Trawler	27 Jan.	Mined, Thames Estuary
Almond	Trawler	2 Feb.	Mined, Falmouth
Arctic Trapper	Trawler	3 Feb.	Bombed, Ramsgate
Tourmaline	Trawler	5 Feb.	Bombed, North Foreland
Boy Allan	Drifter	10 Feb.	Collision, Thames Estuary
Keryado	Trawler	6 March	Mined, Channel
Gullfloss	Trawler	9 March	Mined, Channel
Asama	Trawler	21 March	Bombed, Plymouth
Roche Bonne	Trawler	7 April	Bombed, off Lizard
Wilna	Armed Yacht	24 March	Bombed, Portsmouth
Torrent	Armed Yacht	6 April	Mined, Falmouth
Jean Frederic	Trawler	1 May	Bombed, Start Point
Ash	Trawler	5 June	Mined, Thames Estuary
Devon County	Drifter	1 July	Mined, Thames Estuary
Receptive	Drifter	3 July	Mined, Thames Estuary
Lord St Vincent	Drifter	7 July	Mined, Thames Estuary
MGB-90	MGB	17 July	Fire, Portland
MGB-92	MGB	17 July	Fire, Portland
MMS-39	MMS	7 Aug.	Mined, Thames Estuary
ML-141	ML	22 Sept.	Mined, Channel
Forerunner	Drifter	14 Oct.	Collision, Thames
Monarda	Drifter	8 Nov.	Foundered, Thames
Fisher Girl	Drifter	25 Nov.	Bombed, Falmouth

The Merchant Navy Viewpoint

Although this book is written to record naval history, the viewpoint of the men of the merchant ships that the destroyers, sloops and coastal corvettes sought to protect while 'proceeding about their lawful occasions', is deserving of inclusion. Captain D. M. Mackay, MBE, the master of the coaster *Fendris*, contributed this eyewitness account of Channel convoys at this stage of the war:

> After a lifetime's experience gained in many waters and many types of ship, in war and in peace, I have come to the conclusion...that of all the many wartime conditions and activities in which merchant ships are engaged, last of all – if my personal desires only were concerned – I would serve in coastal convoys, especially East Coast convoys.
>
> Imagine a convoy leaving the Thames Estuary composed of, say, fifty ships – at least five miles in length – threading its way during the night (without lights of any kind) between sandbanks, shoals and numerous wrecks, in a narrow swept channel seldom more than six cables wide, with a strong tide erratic in direction and rate. Navigation becomes more a matter of intuition and chance than mathematical precision. Logs cannot be towed but by the leading ships. Compasses are not dependable because of degaussing or of local attraction. Navigational aids (dimly lit buoys) are difficult to discover and, during poor visibility, have to be searched for by escort vessels. The farther one is down the convoy, the more one's vision is screened by the ships in front. If, during the night, the master risks going into the chartroom to look at the chart, on return to the bridge he is almost totally blind for about five minutes.
>
> Convoys are very jerky in their speed of advance, and ships are frequently overrunning each other and bunching up. Coastal convoys are, I think, more liable to this, due to the great difference in the sizes of ships composing them...Despite the utmost care collisions frequently occur and have given rise to the coining of the new terms 'convoy stems' and 'convoy sterns'...Ships join and leave the main convoy, on its passage along the coast, from and to the several ports passed. The joinings cause some considerable anxiety, even in daylight. This anxiety becomes much more intensified during black-out.
>
> Dark nights with bad visibility and stormy weather are bad enough, but our worst enemy is fog. Imagine the convoy steaming along at eight knots on a clear night, amid the sand-banks and wrecks of the East Coast, and suddenly running into a dense fog bank. Prearranged signs are given by the Commodore's ship for such occasions and repeated down the line. After several ships have repeated the signals, the sounds simply merge into a riotous uproar without meaning. Rule-of-the-road signals, ports and starboards and full asterns mingle with fog signals. Ships crowd on to one another. Ships in the van going astern, taking way off and anchoring, to the accompaniment of fog signals from ships only beginning to feel the fog bank, who, perhaps, have not heard the reduce-speed and anchor signals and may still be steaming at eight knots. Realization soon comes to them, however, and they too are taking frantic action to keep out of the crowded mass of shipping ahead. Fog

bells are now mingling with action signals, the sound of dropping anchors and the rattle of cables being paid out. This continues until it would seem that only exhaustion brings the pandemonium to an end, and a seemingly unnatural silence ensues...Ships so crowded are an ideal target for torpedo attack. I have had the unenviable experience of having four of these happenings within twenty-four hours.

The German Viewpoint

What of the enemy in these self-same waters? On the other side of the English Channel, convoys seemed to have easier passage. Vice Admiral Ruge described the German way of operating during early 1942 in this manner:

> The passage through the Dover Strait itself was now made only by single ships, which had to receive ever-stronger protection; eventually it consisted of an inner screen, usually of trawlers or minesweepers, and another screen composed of motor minesweepers (R-boots). Despite determined attacks by British craft, losses remained within bearable limits for a considerable time. In the spring of 1942, for example, an 8,000-ton tanker, which had lost its rudder and propellers, could be towed from Boulogne to Holland despite numerous attacks. The most unpleasant feature of these journeys were the heavy batteries at Dover, which from 1942 used radar-controlled firing, steadily improving their performance...During 1942, 5.7 millions tons of ships were convoyed through this whole area. In 1942, seventeen escorted ships were lost, and forty-two escorts were sunk either while doing duty as such or while minesweeping. In 1943 the figures were twelve and forty-three respectively. Between 1942 and 1944 there were occasional skirmishes with British destroyers in the Channel and off the North Brittany coast, in which the German M boats [minesweepers] and armed trawlers put up a surprisingly successful defence against superior forces, while their losses remained reasonable.

Operation *Cerberus* – The German Plan

Much has been written of the so-called 'Channel Dash' from the Bucknill report and similar official whitewashes, to the more scathing criticisms of recent years, when some of the hitherto suppressed facts leaked out, but were subject to Court Action under the British laws of libel. It is doubtful whether the full story of the many sorry blunders which punctuated the execution of Operation *Cerbeus* will ever now come to light; there has been too much misreporting for too long. Two factors are, however, generally agreed. First, the German estimation of British reactions to such a bold move were absolutely accurate, and Hitler's reading of the situation was exactly correct. Secondly, the extreme gallantry shown by the men of the Fleet Air Arm, the MTBs and the destroyers of the Royal Navy shone like a beacon through the muddle and confusion of British air operations. Unhappily, that gallantry went unrewarded. Here we can concentrate on the facts as they affected the ships of the Royal Navy; we have not the space, or appetite to relate the whole sorry story in full.

The Germans made very detailed plans to ensure the safe passage of the battlecruisers *Scharnhorst* and *Gneisenau*, along with the heavy cruiser *Prinz Eugen*, through the English Channel from their bolthole at Brest, back home to Germany. One facts stands out above all others; the Germans preferred to face everything that the RAF could throw at them rather than risk the long sea passage back via the North Atlantic. It would seem that they were far more concerned at being cornered by British battleships from Scapa Flow than Bomber Command's much-vaunted legions closer to hand. Preparatory work included the transfer of several destroyers south through the Channel to reinforce the escorts' flotillas, and the reinforced and intensified minesweeping of a safe passage through the minefields by an increased number of minesweepers. In this vast enterprise, the ships of the German 1st, 2nd, 4th, 5th and 12th Minesweeper Flotillas with the smaller motor minesweepers [R-boots] of the 2nd, 3rd and 4th MMS Flotilla, all put in long hours of dedicated work. The only casualties from this concentrated endeavour were the destroyer *Bruno Heinemann*, lost on the night of 25 January in the Dover Straits as the 5th Flotilla moved south, and the similar mining and loss of *M-1208* on the night of 10-11 February off Barfleur while clearing the route. These casualties were the most severe suffered by the Germans in three years of warfare in the Channel, but they were a small price to pay for the success of the most daring mission of them all.

The main German units (the full composition of which is contained in Table 9) put to sea on 11 February. The two battlecruisers *Scharnhorst* (*Kapitän zur See* Hoffmann) and *Gneisenau* (*Kapitän zur See* Otto Fein), along with the heavy cruiser *Prinz Eugen* (*Kapitän zur See* Brinkmann), were under the overall command of Vice Admiral Ciliax, Commandant Battleships. As they sailed from Brest, they were given the most powerful escort ever assembled by a German naval squadron during the Second World War, led by the 5th Destroyer Flotilla, with *Z-29* (flying the flag of Commander Destroyers, Rear Admiral Bey) and *Richard Beitzen* (Commander 5th Flotilla, *Kapitän zur See* Berger). Reinforcing this screen of six powerful ships were fourteen smaller escort destroyers of the 2nd, 3rd and 5th Torpedo Boat Flotillas and no less than three E-boat flotillas.

Despite fears expressed by some German naval officers that they would have to fight all the way, they passed the most dangerous part of the voyage, the Dover Straits, without any undue hindrance save the shelling of the big guns which came too late to do any damage. Only five MTBs were available at Dover, which, along with three more from Ramsgate under Commander Pumphrey and Lieutenant Commander Long respectively, were all the ships available to offer any sort of surface challenge at this stage. The story of their attack has been recorded in detail elsewhere. The eyewitness account of one of these gallant men as told to me has, however, been included, as it has not been previously recorded.

Table 9: Operation *Cerberus*. Composition of German Battle Fleet			
Ship	Type	Tonnage (Standard)	Main Armament
Scharnhorst	Battle-Cruiser	31,800	Nine 11-inch guns.
Gneisenau			Fourteen 4.1-inch guns
Prinz Eugen	Heavy Cruiser	14,800	Eight 8-inch guns Twelve 4.1-inch guns
Z-29	Destroyer	2,603	Five 5.9-inch guns
Z-25			
Richard Beitzen	Destroyer	2,171	Five 5-inch guns
Paul Jacobi			
Frieidrich Ihn			
Hermann Schoemann			
T-2	Torpedo Boat	844	One 4.1 inch gun
T-4			
T-5			
T-11	Torpedo Boat	839	One 4.1-inch gun
T-12			
T-13	Torpedo Boat	853	One 4.1-inch gun
T-15			
T-16			
T-17			
Falke	Torpedo Boat	933	Three 4.1-inch guns
Iltis			
Jaguar			
Kondor			
Seeadler			

The British MTB Attack: An Eyewitness Account

At the time Ken Pritchforth was a nineteen-year-old seaman who, as he put it to me, 'had broken the golden rule of all sailors and "volunteered".' It was a case of out of the frying pan and into the fire, for his last ship had been the much-bombed aircraft carrier *Ark Royal*. He had joined his first Coastal Command ship, *MTB-219*, at HMS *Hornet*, the MTB base at Gosport, in June of the preceding year. She was one of Lieutenant

Commander Nigel Pumphrey's flotilla. Ken quickly saw action in the constant skirmishing that took place when the flotilla moved to Dover right on the front line. His account of the 'Channel Dash' episode is terse and to the point:

> Being daylight, no-one expected to come back, and no-one gave a damn either. There were Me's above us all the time, even while we were leaving Dover Harbour, enemy all around us in great numbers. We got fed up of being chased everywhere by German destroyers as we tried to break through the screen surrounding the heavy ships. That day, our respect for the RAF reached zero! We saw nary a one. If they had arrived they could probably have blasted a way through the screen for us, but with our own 'massive' armament of two 0.5-inch machine guns and three rifles, even our two stripped Lewis were left at Base Maintenance, we didn't stand a chance of doing so on our own. Especially so, when you remember the 11-inch and 8-inch projectiles were churning up the water around our frail hulls all the time we were in range.
>
> But the outstanding sight of the day for me was Lieutenant Gould, the skipper of *MGB-43*, shooting up the bridge of the destroyer, which was chasing us, and gaining, while bracketing us with his 5-inch bricks. He certainly saved us that day as there was no way we could have escaped. Our best speed was only eighteen knots and although we did fire our torpedoes in the general direction of the German fleet, it was a forlorn gesture. To cap everything, the rabbit stew, which the Coxswain had brought back from Birmingham the previous day, was lying all over the Galley floor when we eventually arrived back in harbour!
>
> But I must place on record that all this nonsense about the German escape through the Channel being a surprise is all a lot of rubbish. We had been at immediate notice every night for a fortnight, despite what the Brasshats claimed later. We may have stood a little more chance during a night attack. But I suppose the winners of all wars are those who make the least cock-ups, rather than those who have the best plans.

A similar forlorn hope was the attack by the Fleet Air Arm Swordfish without any fighter cover, led by Esmonde. The loss of almost the whole of No. 825 Squadron was a bitter blow. The fact that these heroic young men were expected to attack battlecruisers with biplanes during the third year of war was a scandal amongst many scandals. After the Coastal Forces, the next group of warships to take on the enemy legions were just as antiquated, they were, in fact, destroyers built during the Great War a quarter-of-a-century earlier when biplanes of the same, or better, capabilities, were all the rage. No wonder the Germans scornfully remarked during the height of the battle that the British were down to their 'Mothball Fleet'.

British Destroyer Flotillas Concentrate

There were four destroyer flotillas present in the general area of the battle, two Hunt class flotillas and two made up of First World War veterans. However, all were well under strength. Most of the Hunts, being of the earlier group, either had no torpedoes at all, or only a pair of tubes, and their top speed was, of course, at least five knots less than the old destroyers and seven or more knots slower than the German squadron. Thus it was decided that the Hunts themselves would not take part in the planned night destroyer attacks on any German surface force, as envisaged in Operation *Fuller*, the British standby plan. Instead they would be held in readiness to provide a back-up force and also to provide anti-aircraft cover for the old destroyers hopefully making their way to and from the battlefield. A daylight torpedo attack was not seriously considered! It was not thought that the Germans would risk their fleet in daylight off the southern and eastern coasts of England!

All-in-all then, the old ships of the 16th and 21st Flotillas, were insufficient in number to muster one full flotilla between them. The 21st Flotilla lay at Sheerness, but this comprised only two ships, the Flotilla Leader *Campbell* and the *Vivacious*. At Harwich was the 16th Flotilla, with the Flotilla Leader *Mackay*, and *Walpole, Whitshed* (Lieutenant Commander W. A. Juniper) and *Worcester* (Lieutenant Commander E. C. Coates) The two forces were ordered to concentrate and on 4 February Captain Pizey took his two vessels into Harwich, where he assumed overall command of the combined unit. The six destroyers were placed at short notice for the next eight days, as these were the nights with the most favourable tides to aid the passage of the German squadron. The actual signal from Admiral Ramsey at Dover stated that if the order:

> 'Proceed in execution of previous orders' is made, destroyers are to proceed forthwith at best speed to the North-West Hinder Buoy, latitude -51 degrees 33 minutes North, longitude 002 degrees 36 minutes east, via 53 buoy. You will be kept informed of the movement of enemy ships through Dover Straits and you should endeavour to intercept them in the approximate latitude 051 degrees 30 minutes North. MTBs will not operate north of latitude 051 degrees 30 minutes North. Acknowledge.

Early on the morning of 12 February, these six veterans were at sea, exercising in pairs in the wide swept channel off Harwich with an escort of six Hunts to provide AA protection. They had sailed from Harwich at 0600 as Captain Pizey felt that his ships would be more readily available in case of emergency if they were at sea, instead of inside port on this, the last day of their emergency stand-to. It proved a remarkable piece of foresight on his part.

British Destroyers Attack by Daylight

On receipt of the agreed signal from Vice Admiral, Dover, 'Enemy battle cruisers passing Boulogne, speed about 20 knots. Proceed in execution of previous orders', Pizey led his six ships out to do battle with the German giants without hesitation. Their original plans had envisaged only a night attack; a daylight sortie had been considered to be out of the question. But the urgent needs of the situation brushed aside all the wisdom and accepted doctrine of every destroyer attack exercise since Jutland. Off they sped, their old hulls straining the choppy seas as their equally ancient engines worked up to twenty-five or more knots.

The six accompanying Hunts were sent back, as they did not carry the torpedo tubes, which alone could inflict any serious damage on the German heavy ships. Although their AA firepower would have been welcomed later against the combined attacks of the *Luftwaffe* and the RAF, the Hunts just lacked sufficient speed to keep up, and anything less than twenty-eight knots would have failed to make the interception as required. Further risks were taken to 'cut the corner' and Pizey led his flotilla across a reported British minefield. In fact the mines did not exist, but Pizey had no idea at the time that this was the case, and again accepted the risk. Their planned route was far too roundabout to given them any chance of making the interception.

It was 1145 when the destroyers started out and it was hoped to intercept the German fleet off the Hook of Holland at the Hinder Banks before nightfall. The rendezvous point was the North Hinder Buoy and at this spot the destroyers were to form two attacking divisions: *Campbell*, *Vivacious* and *Worcester* as the First Division and *Mackay*, *Whitshed* and *Walpole* the Second Division. They would then attempt to make a classic night-time attack, launching their full complement of torpedoes as near as possible simultaneously at both bows of the enemy heavy ships in the hope that some, at least, might score hits. Whether any of these unprotected little vessels could possibly have penetrated close enough to a modern battle-cruiser's main and secondary armaments sufficient to carry out such an oft-discussed, but rarely-achieved deployment, remained a subject on which few of those concerned cared to speculate!

Even at twenty-eight knots, the older boats had difficulty in maintaining the pace, but as most considered themselves to be on a one-way journey, and defects to the engines were ignored and the destroyers were pushed to, then beyond, the limits. The two Flotilla Leaders, being slightly less ancient and slight larger than the destroyers, could have made an extra knot or two, but only at the expense of splitting the force and concentration was the only, albeit slim, hope of achieving a worthwhile attack. Despite most valiant efforts, however, *Walpole* began to fall behind from 1318 onward, and Lieutenant Commander Eadon reluctantly had to signal that she had burnt out her main bearing. She was released to try and make her way back to safety on her own.

Air attacks commenced shortly after she had departed. Junkers Ju88s dropped bombs close to both *Mackay* and *Worcester* without effect. They also signalled back their contact and at 1340 Admiral Ciliax was receiving news of the British surface deployment as 'One cruiser [*sic*] and five destroyers in grid square AN 8714, course 095 degrees, high speed.' He calculated, correctly, that they were a destroyer force, which had been on patrol off Harwich and had been ordered to attack. He was not greatly concerned; the force was small, and he had two hours in which to prepare to meet them with his mighty guns, even if the *Luftwaffe* failed to stop them beforehand. Furthermore, he hoped that his course and speed would take him clear of their interceptions altogether. The weather was beginning to worsen considerably, which could help the Germans avoid a battle entirely.

By 1400 the mine barrier had been cleared. During the passage of this unknown hazard the bulk of the ships' crews had lain face down on the decks facing inwards, which, it was fondly hoped, would reduce the effects of being blown up by mines. The ships might still have been too late, despite their daring, but, at 1435, *Scharnhorst* struck the first of several mines, which delayed the German fleet's unruffled passage north.

RAF Attack Indiscriminately

Walpole had meanwhile been struggling back to the west, but was still at the edge of the minefield, her engineers trying to repair the damage, when she was sighted by two Wellington bombers. Although she was nowhere near the German squadron's position, was a lone ship with a British roundel painted prominently on her forecastle and bore absolutely no physical resemblance whatsoever to a German battlecruiser, both aircraft commenced determined attack runs against her.

Two sticks of bombs were dropped by the Wellingtons, fortunately well wide of the stationary ship. *Walpole* refrained from returning fire. The bombers turned to make second runs, but the destroyer was saved from further ordeal by the appearance of a group of German fighters, which promptly attacked the RAF planes and chased them away! These German aircraft then maintained a standing patrol over *Walpole* for a short time before making off back to the east, presumably at the end of their endurance. By this time temporary repairs had enabled *Walpole* to get moving once more, and she limped across the minefield to be met by some of the twelve Hunts sent back out from home bases to rendezvous and guard the veterans back if necessary. *Walpole*'s experience at the hands of Bomber Command was to be a far from a unique one.

The remainder of the flotilla, in single line ahead, were buzzed at 1445 by a solitary Hampden. The ships' guns were kept trained fore and aft and the word was passed down from the bridge 'Friendly aircraft ahead'. But the Hampden held its course and swooped low over *Mackay*'s starboard bow, releasing a salvo of bombs, which exploded hard in her wake, drenching the rear gun crews with spray. 'Check, check, check' was ordered, although no gun had opened fire in defence. The aircraft turned and made a second run, this time at *Worcester*, releasing another stick of bombs. This one proved to be a straddle either side of her bridge but, once more, the ships did not fire and the bomber made off. This sort of attack was repeated several times during the course of the day.

German Squadron Sighted and Attack Commenced

Visibility had steadily worsened and it was soon down to about four miles. Seas grew heavier with waves breaking over the forward guns' crews as they stood at their open mountings. It would make spotting the enemy more difficult; it would, conversely, make their chances of attacking successfully before they were themselves seen, much better. Only one of the five remaining destroyers had an up-to-the-mark radar system installed, and this was the *Campbell*, which was equipped with a Type 271 set. Apparently it had been destined for another vessel, but while *Campbell* had been refitting, Pizey had 'acquired' it to replace his old fixed-type bridge radar. It was fitted in place of the old type director at the back of the bridge, and had a range of twelve miles. A dedicated radar rating had maintained it and it worked to perfection. At 1517, two large contacts were showing on the screen at a range of nine and a half miles. They were twenty-two miles from The Hook at the time of the contact, and any doubts that this was, indeed, the enemy, were removed when, fifteen minutes later, gun flashes could be seen in the murk ahead. It was the German battle fleet.

Campbell led in at once to attack the leading enemy vessel. This was *Gneisenau*, as the *Scharnhorst* was still far astern, needing to catch up after her mine damage. *Vivacious* and *Worcester* followed Pizey into the attack and the British ships achieved considerable surprise; so much so that they were able to break through the E-boat screen and turn parallel to the battlecruiser at a range of 4,000 yards and engage her defiantly with their puny 4.7-inch guns. Captain Pizey's report read:

> We were engaged by the enemy's main armament as we went in. It seemed incredible that we were not hit. Our aircraft attacked about the same time and a German destroyer came out of the mist to deliver a torpedo attack against *Vivacious* which passed down her side about 15 yards away.
>
> At 3300 yards the enemy's fire was so heavy that I decided to turn and fire torpedoes. Our luck would not have held out much longer. *Vivacious* turned with me and we fired torpedoes together.

Worcester pressed even close under a heavy concentration of fire receiving hits and suffering severe damage. All ships attacked the leader of the enemy line.

Away to starboard, *Mackay* and *Whitshed* were also pressing home their attacks. They were concentrating on the bows of *Gneisenau* when *Prinz Eugen*, taking avoiding action from air attack, came at them head-on, not realizing at first that they were British. Captain Brinkmann gave them no chance to escape from this wonderful mistake. At 1545 the Germans let fly with every gun they had from point-blank range (under 4,000 yards); but both destroyers, although deluged with spray, escaped any direct hits. In fact, the closest German shell was at least a quarter of a mile away, so wild was their shooting at this critical juncture. Both ships' torpedo crews found it difficult to aim with the water swirling round their ankles, the ships rolling and pitching, with heavy shells screaming overhead and the mist closing, but both got away full salvoes at their enormous adversary before they clawed their way round and steered to safety. Their target vanished almost at once into a rain squall and, although they thought that they had scored a hit, they had failed to damage *Prinz Eugen*. Likewise, although her return fire improved enough to cause them grave concern, they too, escaped without a single casualty.

The other three British ships were now much closer and *Gneisenau* was straddling them regularly. Captain Pizey wrote: '...I felt our luck could not last much longer.' *Campbell* fired a full salvo of six torpedoes, and *Vivacious* three; all she had. They then put their helms hard over and again survived vicious enemy fire, to take refuge in the protecting sea mist. This brave attack went unrewarded, for every torpedo missed its target.

Finally *Worcester* went in. Lieutenant Commander Coates had delayed for three minutes after his two companions had turned and fired, so determined was he to score a hit. At this stage, both German heavy ships were able to concentrate their fire on this one adversary, and by this time they both had the range, which was point-blank for modern naval weapons. Both German ships, in fact, later claimed to have sunk her, a claim that can easily be understood. Captain Otto Fein, of *Gneisenau*, stated that his guns scored numerous direct hits and so convinced was he that the target was doomed, he ceased fire as he saw no point in wasting shells. *Prinz Eugen* likewise rained down concentrated salvoes of 8-inch shells on the slender hull of the old destroyer, three of which smashed into her simultaneously.

Despite this punishment, *Worcester* got away her full complement of torpedoes, only to share the same heartbreaking disappointment of her consorts; all missed. As Coates was later to write: 'When I fired my first torpedoes I saw black smoke coming up from the water. I thought it was a hit from one of my torpedoes, but it was a bomb exploding near *Gneisenau*. I felt shattered and useless as I realized my torpedoes had gone well astern of *Gneisenau* and ahead of *Prinz Eugen*.'

The three 8-inch shells tore away the whole starboard side of her bridge and ploughed through her thin plating, causing great damage. They were followed in rapid succession by two further salvoes. Yet another pair of 8-inch shells from the cruiser, and two 11-inch shells from *Gneisenau*, pounded her into a pile of smoking debris. Both boiler rooms were gutted, her guns disabled, huge rents torn into her starboard hull, and holes drilled into her bows where huge fires ignited. Listing hard over, she rolled helplessly in the heavy swell, a defenceless hulk as the whole German squadron swept past her. Coates was convinced that his command would not long survive such massive punishment and gave the order: 'Prepare to abandon ship.'

Due to the intense noise of shells, bombs, pounding seas, the hiss of escaping steam and the cries of severely injured men, this order was mistaken for 'Abandon ship' and the wounded were lowered into rafts, while other crew members went over the side and were carried by the tide from their listing vessel. It seemed as if her last moment had indeed come.

Survival of the *Worcester* and the Return of the British Flotilla

And yet, incredibly the *Worcester* somehow remained afloat. Not only that, but the remaining crew members continued to battle to save her, despite the seeming hopelessness of their task. Thus it happened that, when *Campbell* and *Vivacious* returned to the scene a little later, they found their companion still on the surface, although with raging fires along her whole hull line. Pizey's first job was to pick up the men in the water. He then considered the possibility of salvaging *Worcester*.

> When most of the men in the water had been brought aboard *Campbell*, and *Vivacious* was handling the rest, we closed *Worcester* to take her in tow. Picking up the survivors was difficult because of rough weather and the inability of men to help themselves due to wounds, intense cold and exhaustion.
>
> Somehow *Worcester* was getting her fires under some semblance of control, and we could not help but raise a cheer when she signalled she was able to raise enough steam to attempt the passage home herself.

They were later joined in turn by *Mackay* and *Whitshed* and all managed to achieve eight knots speed as they steered toward Harwich and safety. During this time the British destroyers were subjected to air attacks from both enemy and friendly forces alike, who seemed equally incapable of recognizing which ships were which! *Campbell* was attacked by Beaufort torpedo bombers while trying to rescue men from the water and was forced to go astern. She lost the rafts, but luckily she was able to relocate them and pick the men up later. Several other air attacks were also driven off by gunfire.

Meanwhile, superhuman efforts aboard *Worcester* finally resulted in her getting under way. The other four destroyers waited until she was on course and then complied with Admiralty orders to return to base, refuel and re-arm for another foray! *Worcester* eventually made her own way home, as she had missed the Hunt class destroyers sent out to meet and escort her.

Summary of the Destroyer Attack

Although it cannot be denied that the passage of the two German battle-cruisers and the heavy cruiser, together with a host of escorting light vessels, was anything other than a humiliating defeat, despite many post-war attempts to minimize it, the almost suicidal bravery of the men of the Royal Navy – the destroyers, MTB and Swordfish TSR aircrews – makes stirring reading, even in the cynical climate of 2007. Certainly, no blame can be attached to these men for the failure of their attacks. As the Admiralty was to write at the time of Pizey's epic sortie:

> It was pressed home very well in the face of enemy gunfire. *Campbell*

and *Vivacious* escaped damage due to Captain Pizey's faultless judgement and handling of the ships, plus a modicum of luck.

It is a thousand pities that such bravery should not have been better rewarded by so much as a single torpedo strike, but it was not to be.

This was merely the last in a succession of such destroyer attacks on these great German vessels. In 1940 *Acasta* and *Ardent* had attacked these same vessels fearlessly and scored a damaging hit on her. *Glowworm* had attacked the *Admiral Hipper* in the same manner and ended up by ramming her. In many other actions since that time the German heavy ships had shown remarkable caution when approached by British destroyers; off Sierra Leone, in the Bay of Biscay and in the Arctic. Always the British ships had gone into the attack in spite of the odds; always the Germans had fled. No matter how gallant their men, how powerful their ships, the routine reaction from both sides demonstrated the respect of the Germans for the Royal Navy, despite local successes and headline-snatching events like the Channel Dash.

The Navy, like all other services, had been cruelly stripped of resources in the inter-war years, and consequently, when war had broken out, just did not have the power to respond to the German challenge.

This episode was, perhaps, the most humiliating day of a war which, up to that point, had been little other than a whole series of humiliations; Norway and Dunkirk, Crete and Singapore; the loss of *Royal Oak*, *Courageous, Glorious, Hood, Prince of Wales, Repulse* and *Barham* with the Indian Ocean fiasco and Dieppe yet to be added to the list. There seemed no end to Britain's woes in this war.

CHAPTER THIRTEEN

See-Saw War

The survival of the *Worcester* was remarkable, considering her age and the great damage she had received. And yet on such ships, and such men as her captain, the fate of Britain depended during the first years of the war. Nor was *Worcester* unique. Consider just one of her many Great War contemporaries that were serving, and would continue to serve, with great distinction throughout the Second World War. Her history was recorded by one of the wartime captains, later Commander Henry Graham de Chair, DSC, RN. He was appointed to *Vimy* in May 1941, and, initially he was disappointed, having hoped for a modern Fleet Destroyer. He wrote:

> The *Vimy* made two sorties to Boulogne on 23 May 1940; first to land a demolitions team and an RM/RN covering party (235 men in all) under artillery, mortar and machine-gunfire. She returned to Dover and was sent across again during the afternoon to bombard German tanks and vehicles, and then into the harbour to assist in evacuation. It was then that Lieutenant Commander C. G. W. Donald was mortally wounded on the *Vimy*'s bridge by machine-gunfire; another officer was also killed. HMS *Keith*, inboard, also lost her Commanding Officer. Both ships returned to Dover under the command of their First Lieutenants.

Lieutenant Commander R. G. K. Knowling assumed command of the *Vimy* on 24 May and late on the evening of 27 May was ordered to proceed with utmost dispatch to the beaches to the east of Dunkirk. Lieutenant Commander Knowling left the bridge at 2355 and was not seen again; he was officially reported as presumed lost overboard. His place was taken at 0300 on 28 May by the First Lieutenant, Lieutenant A. P. W. Northey, who completed this evacuation sortie, as well as another later on the same day, before handing over to Lieutenant Commander M. W. E. Wentworth at 1545 on 29 May.

The *Vimy* thus had four commanding officers in six days. Between them, they undertook at least ten cross-Channel operations between 22 May and 1 June and brought off over 3,000 troops from France. Northey eventually retired as a captain, with the CBE and a DSC and two Bars, the latter awarded for his conduct at Dunkirk and Boulogne. Under de Chair's command the old *Vimy* went on to sink the Italian submarine *Alessandro Malaspina* in September 1941, and badly damaged a second, *Luigi Torelli* the same day and finally helped to sink a third, the German *U-162*. Relieved by Lieutenant Commander Stannard, VC, RNR, the *Vimy* was fitted with a Hedgehog anti-submarine mortar and quickly sank two further U-boats.

Before the war destroyers like the *Vimy* were only considered good enough for the scrap heap; once war was upon us, Commanders-in-Chief fought for them to join their commands, so great was the need for destroyers. De Chair was told by one officer in Operations Division: 'Don't be too hard on us. In the last war we had 400 destroyers, plus Italians and Japs. Now we only have 240 minus both, and a lot more work to do.'[1] He could have added minus the French as well! And so they carried on; veterans, Hunts and the brand-new ships, all to a common cause.

After the shock outcome of the escape of the German squadron, the remainder of 1942 saw a limited period of offensive action, which attempted to restore some of the confidence eroded by the spectacle of German heavy ships parading along our shoreline. Only a few destroyers could be spared from routine convoy tasks, and the heavy losses in the Mediterranean and Far Eastern theatres of war meant that little in the way of large-scale reinforcements could be expected. Limited strikes were mounted, both against German ships slipping and up and down the Channel, and against the German-held coast. Churchill had never accepted the concept that the Allies should allow the build-up of 'Fortress Europe' unopposed, and he was always eager to strike at the enemy, even though his many earlier escapades, mounted with too little strength to make them effective, had all failed dismally. He got his way again in 1942 and there were to be yet two further disasters of this type, Operation *Agreement* against Tobruk in the Mediterranean and Operation *Jubilee* in the Channel, which resulted in the bloody fiasco at Dieppe.

An excellent example of wisdom after the event, was the announcement, on 18 March, that the 1st Destroyer Flotilla was to be reinforced by further Hunts released from the Home Fleet Flotillas at Scapa Flow. Accordingly, C-in-C Portsmouth, was notified that the destroyers *Albrighton* (Lieutenant Commander R. J. Hanson), *Berkeley* (Lieutenant J. J. S. Yorke), *Bleasdale* (Lieutenant P. R. N. Lewis) and *Calpe* (Lieutenant Commander J. H. Wallace) were to join his command. That more escort destroyers were required in the Channel quickly became apparent when E-boat attacks increased markedly during this time. In an attempt to discourage this upsurge, the destroyers *Blencathra* (Commander J. H. Rucke-Keeene), *Calpe, Fernie, Walpole* and *Windsor* patrolled between Beachy Head and Portsmouth, but failed to intercept and engage the enemy.

The Varied Work of the 15th Flotilla, 1942

Like their sisters at Portsmouth, the guardians of the western end of the

Narrow Sea led a varied life, as Admiral Sir Guy Sayer, KBE, CB, DSC, recalled:

> During the greater part of this period, the flotilla consisted of H. M. ships *Cleveland* (my ship), *Brocklesby*, *Atherstone* and *Tynedale*, and the Polish ships *Krakowaik* (the former HMS *Silverton*) and *Kujawiak* (the former HMS *Oakley*) which, when sunk off Malta, was later replaced by *Slazak* (the former HMS *Bedale*).
>
> Our routine and normal employment was escorting Channel convoys between South Wales and Southampton, but our ships took part in a miscellany of other activities. One was present at the Dieppe raid, four took part in the St Nazaire operation, several fought their way to Malta and back as convoy escorts, some were in the North African landings, others on Atlantic escort duty, despite our short endurance – and all had many odd jobs to do at odd moments, such as air/sea rescue, sweeps after fishing boats in the South Western Approaches, patrolling to intercept enemy commerce raiders, U-boat hunts, supporting Combined Operations raids, and so on.
>
> One way and another, these little ships were always busy. They saw plenty of excitement, not a little fighting, and many hours of boring 'ocean slogging'. Those who manned them can be proud of the part they played and look back on service well done.

Offensive Patrols, March 1942

When the Hunts had the time, they began more and more to take part in offensive actions against the enemy. One such sweep, Operation *Cloak*, was mounted in March in an attempt to scoop up the German supply ships in the vicinity of Alderney in the Channel Islands, but no enemy craft were sighted. A more exciting event took place on the night of 13-14 March.

The Armed Merchant Raider *Michel* (*Schiff* 28) (*Kommandeur* von Ruckteschell) had left Kiel on 9 March and arrived at Flushing two days later. Here she was provided with a strong escort to help her break through the Channel. This escort consisted of the 5th TB Flotilla, *Seeadler, Falke, Iltis, Jaguar* and *Kondor*, and nine M-Class minesweepers. The heavy coastal gun batteries, alerted by wireless intercepts that the British were on their way, went to full alert. An attack by six MTBs and three MGBs was therefore easily repulsed.

In the meanwhile the destroyers on patrol off Beachy Head (*Blencathra, Calpe, Fernie, Walpole* and *Windsor*) were ordered in. In the confused skirmishing that followed, the British ships claimed to have scored one torpedo hit out of six torpedoes fired by *Walpole* and *Windsor* on the enemy raider, to have scored shell hits on one German escort, and to have sunk two E-boats. The Germans in return, claimed to have severely damaged two destroyers (*Fernie* and *Walpole*) and received no losses in reply. The truth, as usual, lay somewhere in between. No torpedo hit was made on *Michel* although the British destroyer's attack was later described as, '...a serious threat'. So serious, in fact, that the raider dropped her disguise and opened fire with her main armament of six 5.9-inch guns. There were no E-boats present. *Michel* only took splinter and light flak damage and only one officer was killed. On the British side, the two named destroyers were indeed both hit, but not seriously, and as the Official Historian later was to note wryly: 'Little damage was done in fact, to either side.'

The Hunts on Patrol: an Eyewitness Memoir

Douglas Clare, who served aboard the destroyer *Albrighton*, and who became the much respected secretary of the 1st Destroyer Flotilla Survivors Association, has left us with this summary of the work of the Hunts on the Channel patrol during the period 1942-43.

> Encounters with enemy aircraft – not to mention some none too friendly meetings with our own planes – have in general been omitted as dates are vague. One must also bear in mind that many an offensive patrol was carried out, and many a convoy escorted without obtaining close contact with any opposing forces, but they – and most certainly the former – could nevertheless be almost every bit as tense and exciting as those occasions on which action actually ensued. Just take two examples: HMS *Albrighton* on patrol in the Channel in company with the Fighting French Destroyer *La Combattante*, the latter being 'Senior Officer'. Together we were ordered to intercept several large German destroyers off the French coast, but it was obvious that by taking the normal route we would not be in the required position in time, so the Captain of *La Combattante* decided we must take a chance and make a short cut over one of our own minefields. All to no avail unfortunately, as the enemy was not met. And again, HMS *Albrighton* had spent some considerable time getting 'up moon' of what was thought to be several German Torpedo Boats (ships comparable in size to the Hunts) close to the French coast, her crew keyed up and ready for anything, only to find out in the split second of opening fire that they were friendly forces – our Steam Gunboats in fact. Such incidents were commonplace.
>
> Almost all ship-to-ship engagements took place at night, radar being initially non-existent, and even when it was fitted was a far cry from present day attainments, although obviously a great help. Reliance was almost invariably placed on a visual sight of the enemy aided by binoculars and in some instances by the sound of ships engines/propellers being picked up on anti-submarine listening equipment. This of course meant that engagements with one's adversaries were invariably at quite close range, sometimes virtually alongside one another. Illumination of one's quarry was occasionally by searchlight, but more often by Starshell (a bright magnesium flare on a small parachute fired from the 4-inch guns and the 2-pounder 'bow-chaser', and by means of rockets fired from their launchers which were attached to the outside of the gun shield of the 4-inch guns). To all this can be added the tracer (illuminated)

fire of all weapons less than the 4-inch, though this illuminator was mainly intended as a guide to 'aiming' the guns in darkness. The results of the use of these varied forms of illumination just had to be experienced to be appreciated – if that be the right word for it!

The Germans are on record as having said that of all their adversaries in the Narrow Seas and Coastal Waters of Western Europe the vessels their Coastal craft feared the most were the destroyers equipped with 2-pounder bow-chaser mountings.

The First DF was a mixture of Hunts, based at Portsmouth, but hardly ever, if at all, operated as 'A Flotilla' in the accepted sense, frequently joining up with other ships from either Plymouth or Sheerness or even Harwich for a 'sweep'. *Albrighton, Bleasdale*, the two Norwegian-manned ships, *Eskdale* and *Glaisdale*, and *La Combattante* (the former HMS *Haldon*), about the only ones which spent most of the time belonging to the 1st DF – many other ships, including the Polish Hunts, came and went and much the same can be said of the Hunts at Sheerness and Plymouth.

When leaving Portsmouth for night patrol we always used to test electrical firing circuits to the guns, using dummy projectiles. One particular evening as we were going out someone got it wrong and pushed a live one up the spout, that 'test' resulting in a shell landing somewhere in the vicinity of Ryde in the Isle of Wight. We never did hear the outcome of that. As there was virtually no radar in the early days reliance on seeing the enemy first mainly centred on good old pussers binoculars (a good pair of eyes were essential). But we could never get enough binoculars – however, a good dodge was found by 'writing off' a few pairs after any decent action until a stock was built up!

I can recall little or no rationing on board, in fact it used to make us feel quite guilty when going on leave and seeing what civilians had to live on. I well remember using up to a dozen fresh eggs to make a cake for my Mess. I was a virtual non-smoker, whereas those who did smoke found it very hard when on night patrols in the Channel and unable to leave their post to have a 'burn', many of course nipping away for a 'quick one'. Invariably I had a pocket of dried apricots myself to chew. One usually couldn't leave the bridge during patrol, the 'heads' for the bridge personnel was a couple of buckets at the back of the bridge.

The Portsmouth destroyers were occasionally given a night or two at Southend, anchored off the pier, with all-night leave, as a change and a rest. In fact we were usually far from either, those with families in the south-east invariably broke the rules and nipped off home, and those of us unattached spent our nights at Southend making very merry, as only matelots know how. Invariably the trip meant taking a convoy through the Straits at night and so at action stations or first degree of readiness throughout and, what with being up most of the night living it up at Southend, it was a relief to get back good old Pompey and the pleasures and delights of our 'local' pub.

The ship's company galley was in the after deckhouse, oil fed from a tank above on 'X' gun deck. The tank was so sited that the 'stops' on the 4-inch trainer prevented the gun from being fired near to it. On one occasion of course the 'stop' failed, the tank was split when the gun fired, the oil ignited and reached the 'ready-sue' locker full of 4-inch shells, some of which exploded. The gun crew hastily abandoned ship by jumping over the side. All were eventually picked up!

Though fitted with depth charges, being in the Channel meant that there was very little scope for their intended use. Every so often one had to be fired for test purposes. This was usually done in known 'fishing grounds', which meant fresh fish for all and also for the RN Hospital at Plymouth or Portsmouth depending on which way we were sailing.

Most of the Portsmouth-based Hunts of the 1st DF carried two German-speaking ratings to man the radio for listening to enemy light craft transmissions, particularly the E-boats. The HF/DF and other specialized equipment used for such intercepts was known in the fleet as 'Headache'. Consequently the senior of two operators – a Flemish Petty Officer – was very soon given the name of 'Aspro'. A German Navy Signal Book was also carried aboard.

Operation *Myrmidon*: Planned Landing at Bayonne, 1 April 1942

One of HMS *Albrighton*'s first jobs on joining the flotilla was a search for some of the motor launches that had survived the St Nazaire raid. That attack, which was brilliantly carried out and achieved its objective of making the dock unusable by the *Tirpitz*, falls outside the area covered by this book, but several other operations were planned on a similar scale that do fall within its parameters, in those operations Channel flotillas were allocated, although some of the operations were eventually aborted. One of these was Operation *Myrmidon*, an intended assault by a large commando force upon Bayonne near the Franco-Spanish border.

The warship force for this operation included five Hunt class destroyers, which were to escort the Landing Ships *Queen Emma* and *Prinsis Beatrix*. The latter vessel had been a Dutch Cross-Channel passenger ship, which ran the service between Harwich and The Hook in happier days. They were diesel-driven, fast and good sea-boats. As converted for their wartime role, each carried one Commando of about 450 men. The Hunts allocated were *Albrighton, Badsworth, Calpe, Middleton* and *Wheatland*.

The target for the Commando force was the tidal River Adour, and its military significance lay in the fact that Spanish iron-ore was smelted here for the Ruhr armament works. There were also TNT factories where compliant Vichy workers were busy turning out explosives for their Nazi masters. There were a large number of coasters and similar craft which transported the ore, so the destroyers were assigned to deal with them as well. The whole force sailed from Falmouth on a sunny afternoon in April, and by the 4th, were well out into the Bay of Biscay. The Senior Officer of the escort was *Badsworth* with the other four destroyers allocated a Personnel ship between each pair for close escort.

As the attack group approached the 'run in' areas ready for the assault, they hoisted large Spanish Navy Ensigns. The Personnel ships went ahead, giving the impression that they were independently-routed Spanish vessels, while the Hunts dropped back to just over the horizon. The weather had steadily deteriorated as time went by and, although this shielded them from the enemy, the Hunts were making heavy going of the Biscay rollers. As one of their crew recalled, 'Little happened save that we just rolled our guts out'.

That night the troops embarked in their landing craft and headed for the shore. But bad weather caused the whole operation to be called off at the last minute, even as they were heading in toward the target.

Meanwhile, as a diversion, the destroyers had carried out a bombardment of St Jean de Luz. The only result of this was to bring down on their heads several mild dive bombing attacks the next day, but no casualties resulted on either side and the crestfallen force returned to Falmouth without having accomplished anything at all.

Skirmish off the French Coast, 23-24 April 1942

Albrighton was in action off the French coast at Fécamp on the night of 23-24 April. Doug Clare told me that:

> The weather was absolutely atrocious, accompanied by a pitch-black night, and it was not until *Albrighton* was in the middle of the convoy that the enemy was sighted. An E-boat, obviously mistaking *Albrighton* for one of its own side, tried to come alongside, until his error was pointed out to him! (For some obscure reason the Royal Navy christened the German fast motor torpedo boats E-Boats [E for Enemy] but in fact the Germans themselves called them *S-boots*, or *Schnellboots* – Fast Boats)
>
> It was our first action against shipping and it was truly a very rough night. Obviously the enemy convoy had been picked up by some means for we were at anchor off the Isle of Wight when first ordered to intercept. We set off at best speed with seas coming over the bridge, but we reduced speed when we arrived in a position to intercept. The first contact was when the E-boat tried to come alongside. 4-inch and pom-pom could not depress sufficiently to engage him! The Captain was shouting for *somebody* to open fire and I grabbed the stripped Lewis gun but only fired one round. I found out afterwards I had only unhitched one safety catch). Grenades were kept at the rear end of the bridge but were not available and by this time we had, of course, increased speed and a normal gun battle commenced. I remember sending our first action report: 'Am heavily engaged off Fécamp' to the C-in-C, Portsmouth. I do not know what damage we did but we certainly learnt quite a bit!

Raids and Excursions, May 1942

Such hit-and-run raids were becoming more common. On 4 May *Calpe* was ordered to intercept a 4,000-ton merchant vessel which was believed to have sailed from Boulogne, but Admiralty orders stipulated that the operation must not go further than forty nautical miles from the English coast. Next day, 5-6 May, it was *Albrighton*'s turn again when she attacked enemy light forces off Cap d'Ailly. Doug Clare described it as:

> ...a hectic night. *Albrighton* managed to get right among them by a 'Ruse de Guerre' – as the enemy flashed a signal challenge at *Albrighton* she promptly signalled the same challenge back at them, and their uncertainty as to whether she was friend or foe enabled her to get close. This ruse was frequently used. German shore batteries also joined in the engagement.

On the night of 14-15 May there was further skirmishing. The raider *Stier* (Schiff *23*) *Kapitän zur See* Gerlach) broke through the Channel in the same manner as the *Michel* before her. Once more as her principal escort she had the 5th TB Flotilla: *Kondor, Falke, Iltis,* and *Seeadler*, and as many as sixteen motor minesweepers accompanied her. The Dover batteries shelled her and heavy attacks by British MTBs managed to sink both the *Iltis* and *Seeadler* with very heavy loss of life. This was satisfactory, but *Stier* herself survived. She got into Boulogne and then sailed in short stages until she reached the Gironde and safety. Among the many forces at sea attempting vainly to halt her passage, were the Hunts.

On the night of 14-15 May, *Albrighton* ran into several German armed trawlers off Cap de la Hague. Douglas Clare again:

> My main memory of this one is standing on the bridge with the old stripped Lewis gun cradled, like you see in bad American films, firing away at a trawler close-by as its crew was running along a catwalk to get to its forward gun. *Albrighton* was hit by a large wave or some heavy swell which flung me off balance, set me staggering back, finger tightly round the trigger and .303 from the stripped Lewis spraying all around our own bridge, with all the personnel hitting the deck!

The Battle of Cawsand Bay, 16 May 1942

With the bulk of the *Luftwaffe* busy in Russia and North Africa, bombing attacks were comparatively light and mainly of the hit-and-run type conducted by fast fighter-bombers. On one occasion the German pilots ran into the 15th Flotilla and got a nasty shock, as Vice Admiral Sayer later recalled:

> The 16th May 1942, was a warm, misty day, when just after noon *Cleveland* and *Brocklesby* slipped from No. 1 wharf and proceeded to sea for exercises. *Cleveland* led *Brocklesby* down the Hamoaze, through the boom at Devil's Point and into the Sound, where a small convoy of

merchant ships was at anchor in Jennycliff Bay waiting to sail that evening.

In accordance with long-standing practice, *Cleveland* went to 'action stations' on passing Devil's Point and the clearing away, lining up and checking of the armament were completed before the outer gate was reached, and at this point the ship was at full action alertness.

Brocklesby was not quite so quick, some hitch had occurred when she was still sorting out, when just after *Cleveland* had turned into the swept channel round the western end of the Breakwater we heard, away to seaward the sound of several aircraft engines – very low and moving fast.

The time was 1244. Suspicions were immediately aroused on *Cleveland*'s bridge and the guns alerted. Nothing could be seen owing to the mist, until suddenly there appeared, streaking low over the water in line astern, four fighter aircraft. They were making straight for the Sound from seaward coming in approximately over the eastern end of the Breakwater.

The poor visibility prevented positive identification but their method of approach left us in little doubt of their hostile nature, and I ordered the four-inch guns to open fire. A full-deflection salvo was away almost instantly – it missed – and the shells must have disturbed the gulls and gannets as they burst on the cliff face below Staddon Heights.

A moment later there came the unmistakable 'whoomphs' of a stick of bombs dropping in the convoy area. By great good fortune they also missed – and then our real turn came. With a roar of opened throttles the enemy aircraft – Me109s as we saw them to be – swept round to port to make good their escape. The leading pair passed out of range up our port side and made off to seaward. No. 3 swung close to us and got all that we could give him with our close-range weapons. He was hit hard and was last seen losing height and wobbling badly as he staggered off into the mist. Later we heard that this aircraft had failed to return to base and we were officially credited with him.

No. 4 swept wider still and, diving straight at *Brocklesby*, sprayed her with cannon fire, causing three men to be wounded and a hole in her funnel – but, as this plane flew over *Brocklesby*, *Cleveland*'s multiple pom-pom, shifting target rapidly from No. 3, shot his starboard wing off. The next moment he was on fire, and within a flash the aircraft cart wheeled in flames into Cawsand Bay.

And so, within minutes, ended our brief battle – fought within sound, if not sight, of our home port. Somehow this added to the satisfaction of knocking out 50 per cent of the enemy force – fitting reward for the readiness, alertness and steadiness of a first-class ship's company.

But there is a postscript to this story. The man to whom the greatest credit was due for his excellent shooting was the gun layer of *Cleveland*'s multiple pom-pom. Only that forenoon, just before we sailed, he had been up before me to have his gun layer's rate removed owing to his having failed to pass the periodic eyesight test! It was with great pleasure that I expunged that decision from the record and substituted a recommendation for a decoration – which, in due course, he got!

Mixed Forces attack on German Convoy, 19-20 June 1942

In an attempt to combine the new steam gunboat's speed with the Hunts firepower, *Albrighton* operated with *SGB-6, SGB-7* and *SBG-8* against a small German convoy of two vessels escorted by a destroyer flotilla in the Baie de la Seine on the night of 19-20 June 1942. *SGB-7* (Lieutenant R. Barnet) and her sisters had a short, sharp engagement with one of the enemy destroyers, firing torpedoes which missed, but one of the merchant ships was sunk. The *Albrighton* received a message stating the *SGB-7* had been hit heavily and had stopped. The enemy quickly closed in and the last message received was that the crew of the gunboat were destroying their craft. Lieutenant Barnet and almost all of this crew were taken prisoner.

Major E-Boat Victory off Lyme Bay, 9 July 1942

One of the most severe blows inflicted upon British Channel convoys in 1942 took place when the 2nd E-Boat Flotilla under *Leutnant zur See* Feldt attacked a convoy on the night of 9 July. *S-67* (*Leutnant zur See* Zymalkowski) scored a torpedo hit on the tanker *Pomella* (6,766-tons) which duly sank. In a mass attack the remaining boats, *S-48, S-50, S-63, S-70, S-104* and *S-109* scythed into the convoy sinking the armed trawler *Manor* and some small vessels, totalling 5,426 tons. Not a single E-boat was hit in return during this very one-sided engagement.

Further Engagement off the French Coast, 28 July 1942

Another brief, if inconclusive, action took place some fifteen nautical miles off Cherbourg on the night of 27-28 July, when the destroyers *Calpe* and *Cottesmore* (Lieutenant Commander J. C. A. Ingram) surprised and engaged two German armed trawlers at 0245. During their withdrawal later in the morning the *Luftwaffe* made repeated attacks on the two Hunts and near-misses caused three casualties aboard *Cottesmore*.

Disaster at Dieppe: Operation *Jubilee*, 19 August 1942

In a year which had witnessed so many disasters at sea for Britain, (the most recent, the catastrophic massacre of Russia convoy PQ 17 had only just taken place in the Arctic) yet another combined operations blunder in the Channel area took place. It was the biggest raid yet attempted by Mountbatten's organization but bore all the hallmarks of hurried and poor planning coupled with another under-estimation of the probable enemy response. This time a severe penalty had to be paid, and it was exacted mainly from the Canadian troops flung ashore on the steeply sloping beaches with inadequate fire support. The RAF, who claimed a great victory, but, in fact, received a total drubbing at the hands of the *Luftwaffe*, now re-equipped with the superb Focke-Wulf Fw190 fighter, also paid part of the price. The price paid by the Royal Navy was the destruction of many landing craft and supporting light forces, and one destroyer, bombed, damaged and forced to be sunk. Here we are only concerned with the Navy's part in this calamity.

The principal naval units involved in Operation *Jubilee*, were the Hunt class destroyers *Calpe* (acting as HQ ship), *Fernie* (reserve HQ ship), *Albrighton, Berkeley, Bleasdale, Brocklesby, Garth* and the Polish *Slazak*; the river gunboat *Locust* was the heaviest armed vessel of the force, and the Landing ships, Infantry (LCI) with the troops embarked were the *Duke of Wellington, Glengyle, Invicta, Prince Albert, Princes Astrid, Prinsis Beatrix, Prince Charles, Prince Leopold* and *Queen Emma*; thirty-eight coastal craft (Free French *Chasseurs*, MTBs, MMS etc) and 179 landing craft of all types.

The LCIs were to convey the 4,961 officers and men of the Canadian units involved, the Canadian Essex Scottish, Royal Hamilton Light Infantry, Royal Regiment of Canada and South Saskatchewan Regiment, and the 1,057 men of No. 4 Commando. Their objectives were nebulous but included first, to hit as many valuable military targets as they could; these included a new radar station, heavy gun batteries, and the docks; secondly, to gain expertise into landing on a large scale against prepared enemy defences. The lessons were learnt, and they were harsh ones, which dominated British thinking for the next two years on such matters, although largely scorned by the American top brass (until reality caught up with them at Omaha Beach that is!)

All hope of surprise was lost when, while still en route to the objective, the landing craft on the eastern flank ran into a German coastal convoy. This, despite the fact that a warning had been issued by C-in-C, Portsmouth, that this convoy was in progress, but a confused mêlée developed, during which the steam gunboat *SGB-5* was badly damaged and the German escort vessel *UJ-1404* sunk. Thus fully alerted, the German garrison ashore was waiting and ready and entirely destroyed the bulk of the landing craft force. Of 516 officers and men who managed to struggle ashore, 485 were killed, wounded or taken prisoner. Only the Western Flank landing, and that of the Commandos, fared better.

The main landing force was covered by the gunfire of the Hunts and the old *Locust*. None of these ships mounted a weapon of a larger calibre than 4-inch and thus, the scale of bombarding fire that they could offer was small. It was the considered opinion of several of the senior officers that the inclusion of an old battleship, armed with eight 15-inch guns, would have altered the balance in favour of the Allied force. That was just one lesson later implemented at future landings to good effect. The limited value of even the small weapons of the destroyers and the *Locust* was hampered by the fact that only two of the Hunts were actually able to gain radio contact with their bombardment parties ashore. The support given by those two ships, being directed precisely, was of great value; that of the others was, necessarily, far less so.

The report of *Albrighton*'s Bombardment Liaison Officer, Captain V. K. James, makes illuminating reading: *Albrighton*'s task was to provide gunfire support from the directions given by F1 (Captain R. C. Carswell, MC, RCA of the South Saskatchewan's) and F5 (Captain J. H. Thomas, RA, with the Cameron's of Canada). Captain Thomas was killed on the beaches and Captain Carswell wounded and taken POW during the day's fighting. After contributing to the initial general bombardment, *Albrighton* was to have given supporting fire on Green Beach and to the west of the Casino area.

At 0330 they saw the Commando landing craft on the flanks engaged by tracer fire, which lost the element of surprise planned for the remainder. By 0415, *Albrighton* had followed astern of the landing craft approaching White Beach, and bombarded the beach to the west of Casino as planned. Their fire lifted to the rising ground overlooking Red and White Beaches as instructed, but the smoke-shells fired were not effective in shielding the landing craft or troops ashore. At 0459 F1 ashore contacted them to notify them 'SSR landed' and this was passed on to *Calpe*.

By 0534 F1 was to the east of Green beach and *Albrighton* herself was being engaged by a German Light Battery some 100 yards west of the radar station between Green and White beaches. From the bridge of the destroyer they could clearly see what appeared to be an enemy OP and several individual German soldiers near the gun position. Several salvoes of 4-inch shell silenced these positions and scattered the enemy troops.

By 0609 F5 had signalled 'Landed Green beach' and two minutes later F1 was calling for fire on a machine-gun section to the east of Green beach, but the target was obscured by smoke. *Albrighton* moved clear of the smoke and opened fire on the target a few minutes later. It seems that much of this fire was to good effect. At 0815 for example, *Calpe* ordered her to close the harbour entrance and engage hostile guns shooting from the breakwaters onto Red and White Beaches. *Albrighton* closed by 0900 and duly engaged the breakwaters and lighthouse by deliberate, direct fire. The troops ashore later reported that the fire was effective. At the same time, F1 sent an urgent message to engage a fresh target, a house on the cliff east of Green Beach. *Albrighton* replied 'Message understood, coming across'. By 0911 the destroyer was heavily engaged with this new objective and bombarding along the cliff edge. Captain James then signalled F1 to ask if he could observe the fall of shot, but received the reply that he could not as he was held down by enemy fire. James replied, asking F1 to give him more direct shots, but F1 responded 'Consider direct shots too dangerous at present'.

By 1045 there was no further contact with either liaison officer ashore and intense bombing was being undergone from numerous German formation, which concentrated their efforts on the warships offshore. During these attacks, which were almost continuous, the radio aerials were shot away more than once by the pom-poms. Fire from ashore was also heavy and one anti-tank shell went clean through the destroyer without inflicting any casualties. Despite heavy deployment of RAF fighter aircraft, the *Luftwaffe* was able to maintain a heavy bombardment and *Albrighton* herself was twice straddled by sticks of our bombs. A small shell hit the plating just above the waterline near the forward gun mounting, wounding the signals officer and eight of the ships' company.

Chaos Afloat

The official report of Captain P. W. C. Mellings, DSC, RM, who was with 'A' Company, Royal Marine Commando, give some clues to the chaotic state of affairs afloat during the landings:

> H.M.S. *Locust* arrived uneventfully off Dieppe at about 0530 hours, there had been a certain amount of firing and tracer seen on either bow previous to this. The sky was clear, but visibility was greatly reduced owing to the thick smoke resulting from the earlier landings.
>
> At about 0610 hours *Locust* attempted to enter the mole, but it immediately became apparent that the batteries to the east of the entrance had not yet been silenced. *Locust* received two hits whilst preparing to enter, resulting in two killed and about six wounded.
>
> Commander Ryder, seeing that the east batteries were still in control of the channel did not enter the harbour at the time, a bombardment by destroyers and *Locust* being resorted to. It was very difficult in the following hours to get any clear picture as to what was happening, owing to the thick smoke, destroyers bombarding and aerial battles overhead. It did, however, become apparent that the floating reserve...of I believe, about a Battalion in strength, was landed on Blue beach.

Eventually the Marines were ordered by the General in command to reinforce the Essex Scottish ashore on White Beach.

> The Colonel gave his orders from *Locust*, the idea being to pass through the beach to the town and there re-form and report to the Colonel of the Essex Scottish, the object of the force being to pass around the west and south of the town, and attack the batteries on the eastern cliff from the south.
>
> The Marines of Commando H.Q. and A Company were embarked in two MLCs, the force under Major Houghton from the *Chasseur* consisting of X, A and B Companies embarking in AL, the Mortar Platoon, and demolition [platoon] being left behind in *Locust*. The Commandos started to move toward the shore; it being about 1130 hours, smoke was provided by the *Chasseur*, who accompanied us [to] within 500 yards.
>
> Shellfire was opened on the boats almost immediately, at about 4,000 yards, increasing in intensity as the range shortened. The fire appeared to consist of 3-inch – 4-inch Mortar Bombs, or a similar size, intermingled with low-angle gun fire of about 4-inch and tracer shell of about 2-pdr, which may have come from tanks, up to date the range was too

great for S.A.

The fire was all coming from the Eastern cliffs and the end and base of the mole, firing to the north-west.

The range was shortening and rifle and light machine-gun fire was becoming apparent, the *Chasseur*, being now no longer able to support the force owing to the depth of water.

Chaos Ashore

By 1100 it was very apparent that things ashore were going badly as well. None of the Churchill tanks, which had been landed, was able to clear the promenade and enter the town. One-by-one they were knocked out. Whatever the reasoning back at Combined Operations HQ prior to the battle, German specialist troops, used to dealing with hundreds of Soviet T-34s on the Eastern Front, were not going to be intimidated by a handful of Churchills stuck fast on an open beach unable to move! The Allied infantry cowering on those same fire-swept beaches were also mown down and the beached landing craft provided leisurely target-practice for the German gunners. It was very obvious that things had gone ill and attempts were made to try and evacuate the survivors, under intense fire. *Albrighton* closed to within half-a-mile of Green Beach to pick up any soldiers that could move out from the water, including stranded crews from the wrecked landing craft. Troops could be seen moving, using the sea wall for protection, in attempts to reach the eastern end of the beach, at which point they entered the water. German soldiers could be seen continuously firing upon these unfortunates from the rising ground to the east and west of the beaches.

One of the survivors they picked up, pointed out a house on the west side of the beach, which he said contained snipers. *Albrighton* demolished this building by direct 4-inch fire. Another target was an enemy battery marked on the maps as being one mile inland, which they engaged with indirect fire. They also conducted shoots on the village of Arques. Altogether some 200 survivors were rescued by *Albrighton*, most from the South Saskatchewan Regiment and the Camerons, from off of Green Beach. She was the last destroyer to leave the area.

The loss of HMS *Berkeley*

There were heavy bombings by the *Luftwaffe* throughout the whole day. *Calpe*, for instance, with many survivors on board, was damaged by a near-miss bomb and a quarter of her crew were casualties; she managed to return with 278 army and navy wounded for urgent hospitalization. She spent two months in a dockyard afterwards, repairing. *Brocklesby* and *Fernie* were both slightly damaged by shore gunfire; the former also briefly ran aground.

Bleasdale and *Slazak* were sent up the coast for a while, but when it was reported that the five big German destroyers at Cherbourg were heading for the beaches, they prudently went no further, and both these Hunts returned to the beach head, just in time to witness the final evacuation.

In the interim, yet another heavy air attack had broken over the ships and a Dornier Do17, engaged by British fighters, roared away to sea at low altitude, hastily jettisoning her bomb load as she tried to escape. The bombs fell randomly across the sea and, by cruel chance, the last bomb of the stick chanced to fall close alongside the destroyer *Berkeley* opening up her hull. The explosion rapidly brought her to a standstill and she began to list over to starboard. She was totally immobile, hard off the enemy coast and soon began listing as the water flooded into her from the great gash. There was no chance of effecting a tow under such conditions, and the order was given to take off all her crew and sink her with a torpedo. Before this order could be carried out, however, it was cancelled by a 'Negative'. This was because another survivor had been spotted still aboard the doomed ship, the Torpedo Gunner's Mate. He was a very fortunate man as *Albrighton* was just about to fire her first torpedo when he staggered up on deck from below. The *Albrighton* quickly slipped across and tucked her stern close in under that of her unfortunate sister, and he climbed aboard. The first torpedo struck the *Berkeley* under her bridge and completed the work of the bomb by breaking her in half, the bow section quickly going down. However, the rest of the ship merely rose more upright in the water as a result. *Albrighton* was forced to fire a second torpedo, which hit the aft magazine and the hulk then blew up with an enormous explosion.

The funeral pall over the site of the *Berkeley* was an appropriate backdrop to the ending of the Dieppe disaster. In addition to her, some thirty-three landing craft had been lost, three destroyers slightly damaged and one SGB badly knocked about. There had been many casualties among the troops, and 247 Commandos and 3,363 Canadian soldiers had been killed, wounded or captured. Total German casualties from all three of their services were about 600 offices and men.

The *Daily Telegraph* carried the story on the front page of their 4 p.m. edition, with the headline 'Dieppe Raiders Return Home Singing'![2]

Return of the E-boats, October-December 1942

By autumn, the approach of the long, dark nights increasingly brought out the E-boat packs once more, and in even larger numbers which increased their boldness. They were more confident than ever of their power and of British weakness; that weakness appeared to be confirmed early in October. The 5th Flotilla, with *S-68, S-77, S-82, S-112, S-115* and *S-116*, returned to the waters off Plymouth on the night of 18-19 November to achieve another remarkable victory. This force caught a British convoy south of Plymouth and, in determined torpedo attacks, the escorting trawler *Ulleswater* was sunk, as were the coasters *Yewforest* (815 tons) and *Brigitte* (1,595 tons), all the E-boats again escaping unscathed.

The small auxiliary escorts continued to suffer the bulk of the losses at this time, and the third Royal Navy-manned trawler to fall victim to the E-boats attacks was the *Jasper*, which was torpedoed by the *S-81* (*Leutnant* Wendler) on the night of 1 December. Two nights later, the German light craft had even greater success when *S-81, S-82, S-115* and *S-116* returned and, in a fierce encounter, torpedoed and sank the coaster *Gatinais* (383 tons) while *S-115* (*Leutnant* Klocke) hit and sank the Hunt class destroyer *Penylan* (Lieutenant Commander J. H. Wallace, DSO) which had only been in commission for three months. The graves of two of her crew killed in this action, Leading Seaman C. H. Witts and AB P. J. Caldwell, lie close together in a cemetery at Plymouth and for many years a floral tribute was regularly laid there by members of the 1st Destroyer Association.

Brocklesby's Night Action, 31 October 1942

In case it be thought that the German surface craft had totally unopposed success during this period of British reverses, mention must be made of one particularly successful action fought by the Hunts on the night of 31 October 1942. It was still the policy to send over British MTBs to seek out German convoys in the same manner as they did to ours. These craft, however, being smaller and more lightly-armed than their opposite numbers, were at some disadvantage in these exchanges and so, whenever possible, a destroyer was sent over with them to back up their torpedoes with gunfire.

For this particular sortie, *Brocklesby* (Lieutenant Commander G. Blackler) led a force of MTBs to sea in bad weather, with a strong wind, a choppy sea and frequent rain squalls that reduced visibility to a quarter of a mile. Conditions continued to deteriorate and eventually the light forces had to turn back. *Brocklesby*, however, pressed on alone and was duly rewarded in time with sight of the enemy convoy. This appeared to consist of three merchant ships with an escort of one armed trawler and two torpedo boats. The weather had changed totally during the course of her passage across the Channel and the destroyer sighted her quarry just after midnight, steering toward her. Lieutenant Commander Blackler described the incident later, as follows:

> I altered course to keep out of the direct path of the bright moon and the enemy didn't see us until we were very close. One of the escorts started flashing a signal at us and kept flashing until I opened fire. We scored some direct hits on the biggest merchant ship and a smaller on caught fire.
>
> The Germans seemed to be so confused that they began firing at each other. They were still firing while I worked round their stern and came in for another attack. We lobbed in a few shells and heard them firing at each other again. We were hitting them very hard every time we saw them and making them fight each other in the smoke.
>
> All we got in reply was a shell through the funnel. Just as we were leaving we saw one of the merchant ships had stopped, so we shelled her and left her sinking. In the centre of the smoke was a pale orange glow, probably the merchant ship we set on fire at the beginning of the action. It was burning nicely.

It was a brisk and efficient action. *Brocklesby* had already earned commendation that year when she had been commanded by Lieutenant M. N. Tufnell, DSC. She had been attacked by a pair of Junkers Ju88s. She scored a direct hit on the first one with her main 4-inch guns, and it was seen to crash into the sea. The second was hit several times by the pom-pom and near-missed under her nose by 4-inch shells. It was considered to have been severely damaged. Air attacks of this nature were becoming more and more rare. By this period also, the destroyers were now able to give as good as they got, and losses from bombing were minimal. *Brocklesby* was soon in action again off the French coast.

Sinking of the *Komet*, 13-14 October 1942

The Germans had been more heavily opposed each time they had run one of the Armed Merchant Raiders down the Channel but until now they had always succeeded in getting the ships out. This being so, they grew over-confident and, in October, they were made to pay the penalty.

The *Komet* herself, had returned to Germany after a long cruise in the outer oceans where she had sunk many Allied vessels. She had been completely refitted and rearmed with new guns and a radar set. She had a new captain also, Ulrich Brockein, who had served on the staff of Admiral Marschall during the last commerce-raiding cruise of the two German battlecruisers back in 1941. *Komet* had left Germany again on the night of 7-8 October, and had two of her escorting minesweepers sunk and a further pair damaged by British mines before she even reached Dunkirk. After such an inauspicious beginning she had laid up at that port for a time and then continued on in short hops down channel, losing yet another minesweeper before berthing at Le Havre on 13 October.

At 1900 that same day she sailed on the next stage with again a strong escort of minesweepers and the also the ships of the 3rd Torpedo Boat Flotilla, under *Kommandant* Hans Wike, the *T-4, T-10, T-14* and *T-19*. Torpedo Spotter Reconnaissance aircraft of the Fleet Air Arm were instrumental in locating her that night as she left and they dropped flares at 2100, but, although the German escort commander recommended that they seek shelter in Cherbourg, Brockein pressed on. His stubbornness headed him and his command straight into a carefully laid trap.

Two large groups of British destroyers and coastal craft were at sea. The destroyers *Albrighton, Cottesmore, Eskdale, Glaisdale* and *Quorn* (Lieutenant I Hall) had sailed from Dartmouth, along with eight MTBs. From Plymouth were sent the destroyers *Brocklesby, Fernie, Tynedale* and the Polish *Krakowiak*. Off Cap de la Hague, these forces cornered *Komet* and her escort and a fierce battle ensued, fought at very close quarters. According to contemporary British reports, torpedoes from MTB-*236* (Sub-Lieutenant R. Q. Drayson) hit and sank the *Komet*. The German records, compiled from reports of the escorting German torpedo boats, gave a very different account.

The latter reports state, quite clearly, that the German force was smothered with gunfire from the British destroyers and that, in the ensuing panic, gunners aboard *Komet* fired wildly into their own escorts, hitting and damaging *T-4, T-14* and *T-19*, killing the Torpedo Boat Flotilla commander on his bridge.

At 0215, according to these same German accounts, fierce fires and flames were seen aboard *Komet* and, within seconds, she exploded in a huge ball of fire, which shot up high into the night sky. In that colossal detonation, her masts could be seen canting into the centre and she sank like a stone with the loss of her whole crew of 351 officers and men. Not a single person survived.

The CO of *T-14* made a detailed report and from it, the Germans analysed the real cause of *Komet*'s abrupt and total demise; gunfire had set off aviation spirit stowed in No. 2 hold which, in turn, ignited the forward magazines. The German experts did not believe that torpedoes had caused the ship's loss as none of the characteristic fountains of water thrown up by torpedo strikes were observed, nor did any of the crew serving below the waterline in any of the German escorts hear the typical 'torpedo running' or 'torpedo hit' sounds. It appeared certain that credit for the victory should be awarded to the Hunts. The only British casualties were two men wounded when the destroyers of the Plymouth group came under fire from the German coastal batteries. These scored a hit on *Brocklesby*, but did not cause major damage. Even so, the accuracy of these big guns was remarkable.

Eyewitness accounts from the Hunts themselves indicate that the raider was well hit by shellfire and they testify also to the confusion that this caused to the *Komet*'s own gunners. Lieutenant Commander J. C. A. Ingram, commander of *Cottesmore*, stated that:

> ...the enemy appeared to have been taken completely by surprise, and it was only after several salvoes had been fired that any counter-action was taken and consisted partly of the torpedo boats engaging each other with red and green 'Flak'.

When *Komet* blew up, Ingram commented that:

> ... a violent explosion took place, followed a fraction of a second later by another which dwarfed the previous one. Flames shot up at least four hundred feet, the ship blew completely to pieces and burning oil spread over about a square mile of sea; a great pall of smoke rose to a height of several thousand feet. The explosion was an ammunition one, aggravated by oil fuel and took place at 0116.

This explosion was seen by the destroyers of the second group, some thirty miles to the south. The captain of *Brocklesby*, Lieutenant Commander G. Blackler, later wrote that, from south of the Channel, he witnessed '...a bright flash followed by a huge column of smoke...changing into a deep dull red glow and then to the normal glow of a fire'.

As to the German theory, that damage done to the escorts was caused by their own gunfire, Lieutenant Commander Ingram's report leaves little doubt that the Hunts had a hand in this also:

> The situation now was that slightly to the right of the blazing remains of the merchantman, one torpedo boat lay blazing from stem to stern and to the left one lay stopped emitting black smoke. Fire was shifted to the latter and it finally was covered in flames.

However, the German torpedo boats certainly added to the night of woe, as Lieutenant Yorke of *Tynedale* reported:

> ...ceased fire with the remainder at 0234 and it was then seen that the enemy were engaging one another with good effect.

Notes

1. Commander Henry Graham de Chair, DSC, RN, *Let Go Aft: The Indiscretions of a Salt Horse Commander*, Parapress Ltd, Tunbridge Wells, Kent, 1993.
2. Many, many years later, one of the famous *British Movietone News* reporters on the spot, who had submitted the usual 'our brave boys' commentary on the film of this fiasco, presenting it to British cinema audiences as a great and daring victory, confessed his shame at his own voice-over, 'when, in truth, the very sea was running with the blood of the dead and dying'.

Chapter Fourteen

E-Boats versus the Convoys

The first six months of 1943, saw the initiative in the Narrow Sea pass to the British forces. Overall, on the worldwide scale, the impetus of professional skill and superior equipment employed by the Germans and the Japanese was now being eroded by the weight of production of the American, British and Soviet forces. Italy was a liability rather than a contributor to this tilting balance. In the Channel, on a one-to-one comparison, German destroyers, fighter aircraft, precision bombers and tanks were also superior, but it was no longer a one-to-one war and the heavily-outnumbered German forces now commenced what was to be a three-year retreat. Only in the English Channel did the curious situation arise in 1943 (apart from a curious throwback in the Aegean area in the autumn of that year) whereby British forces were still inferior to those of the Germans. The Allied leaders, especially Churchill, was still blinded by the chimera of strategic bombing winning the war with no necessity of invading; merely an Air Ministry dream and a delusion as it eventually turned out to be.

Having received one heavy setback at Dieppe, the British were somewhat reluctant to take on the defences of Hitler's 'Fortress Europe' until and unless it was absolutely necessary. The few Hunts operating in the Channel were not reinforced; even the ships that were available were often diverted to the grander peripheral campaigns being waged at Sicily, Salerno, Anzio and the like. They, therefore, had to take on a still-stronger surface ship enemy in some tough local battles. That they could continue to do so was due to rare and isolated extra ships that Plymouth Command was able to gain temporary operational use of for specific missions and deploy before they moved on. The Germans still maintained strong surface forces, powerful enough to ensure that British offensive patrols were still a very hazardous business and not to be undertaken lightly. And always, their E-boat command remained as efficient and elusive as ever. The mine war, which had never wholly ceased, also saw a brief resurgence during this period with the inevitable losses. In the Narrow Sea, the end of the war still appeared a very long way off in 1943, but there was a buoyant feeling that, maybe, the worst was over and it was just a matter of time.

Operation *HK*; Destroyer Attack off Alderney, 3-4 February 1943

It was well known that the German garrison in the Channel Islands had been heavily reinforced, Hitler sharing Churchill's obsession with its strategic importance; an obsession that was never actually justified by events. The islands themselves were being turned into veritable fortresses with underground tunnels and numerous heavy gun emplacements. The transport of supplies to the German troops and labourers alike was difficult for the enemy to maintain, and the British considered the regular convoy service between Cherbourg and Alderney a good potential target. In March 1942, a destroyer sweep had been conducted to catch these enemy ships, but nothing had been sighted on that occasion. A second attempt was made on the night of 3 February with two Hunts, one of them Polish, which sailed from Plymouth at dusk.

On sighting the Quesnard Light on Alderney and observing that the harbour lights were also lit, it was assumed, correctly, that better fortune now attended them.

There was a full moon and a cloudless sky and the two destroyers moved into an intercepting position some five miles off Cap de la Hague. Both sets of lights ashore were suddenly extinguished and the force thought that they had been observed, but almost at once the lights at the Cap came on again as the convoy entered that area. Within a few moments, two coasters were seen approaching.

The destroyers closed to within 1,000 yards before opening fire with their 4-inch main armament, there being no sign of any escorting ships. Both targets were hit heavily and set ablaze. They appeared to be small, 500-ton vessels and, rather than waste more shells, the destroyers steamed in alongside them and finished them off with depth charges which blew in their hulls underwater, sending both to the bottom. The victims were the former Dutch coasters *Hermann* and *Schleswig-Holstein.* The shore batteries, usually so efficient, were slow in opening fire and no damage was done to either of the destroyers. The Polish destroyer, *Krakowiak*, was in action again the following night when she intercepted an E-boat attack on a convoy off Start Point and drove them off before they could do any damage whatsoever.

E-Boats Attack Another Convoy

The ubiquitous 5th E-boat Flotilla returned to their usual area in some force on the night of 27 February 1943, with *S-65, S-68, S-81* and *S-85.* They surprised a convoy in Lyme Bay and inflicted heavy damage within a few minutes. Two of the convoy, the freighter *Moldavia* (4,858 tons) and the Tank Landing Craft *LCT-381* (625 tons) were sunk, as were two of the escorts, the trawler *Lord Hailsham* and the whaler *Harstad.* No losses were suffered by the E-boats in this audacious sortie.

Loss of *Eskdale*, 14 April 1943

The E-boats continued their frequent penetration of British coastal waters, and one such attack by the 5th Flotilla under the redoubtable Klug on the night of 13-14 April reaped a rich reward. The German force consisted of *S-65, S-81, S-82, S-90, S-112, S-116* and *S-121*. They surprised convoy PW323, consisting of six coasters, escorted by the Norwegian manned Hunts *Eskdale* and *Glaisdale*, and five trawlers. Despite the strength of this escort, the E-boats penetrated the screen and a fierce battle quickly developed. During the mêlée *S-90* (*Leutnant* Stohwasser) put a torpedo into *Eskdale* bringing her to a halt. A static target was too much of a temptation for the flotilla and two more swung away from the merchant ships and concentrated their attacks on the crippled destroyer. More torpedo hits finished her off, the victor being *S-112* (*Leutnant zur See* Karl Muller). *S-65* (*Leutnant* Sobottka) and *S-121* (*Leutnant* Klocke) each scored one torpedo hit on the freighter *Stanlake* (1,742 tons) and sent her to the bottom. Once again, no E-boat was lost.

Action off lsle de Bas, 27-28 April, 1943

Another typical action in which British destroyers were involved on the enemy side of the Channel was an encounter with a small convoy off Isle de Bas at the end of April. *Albrighton* had just anchored in Cawsand Bay outside Plymouth after handing over a convoy from Portsmouth, when she was ordered to sail and join her sister ship *Goathland* (Lieutenant Commander E.N. Pumphrey, DSO, DSC) and proceed to the French coast. Off the coast of Brittany at around 0130 hours on 28 April the destroyers came upon the enemy convoy, two medium-sized merchantmen escorted by two trawlers and a large minesweeper. The night was clear, but the Hunts managed to avoid being sighted while they decided on their plan of attack. They decided to take advantage of the surprise factor and led in through the screen, rounded ahead of the enemy ships, crossing their bows, and took up a parallel course only some 500 yards away, before opening fire. *Goathland* fired two torpedoes at the largest merchant ship and heard two explosions, then a smaller one, being followed by a terrific flash. The target ship stopped as gunfire poured into her. The protecting escorts, which had finally been alerted, closed in from all sides and returned fire at *Goathland* and each other. Having delivered more hits on them, the destroyer made good her escape.

In the meantime *Albrighton* astern took as her target the second, smaller merchantman. This had already been heavily hit and was glowing with fires. *Albrighton* fired one torpedo, which she claimed as a hit. In the meantime further enemy vessels, including E-boats, had hurried to the scene and *Albrighton* found herself surrounded. With odds at five-to-one a fierce close-range combat developed, which was continuous for almost ninety minutes.

Lieutenant Commander Hanson later reported that:

> We came so close to the enemy supply ship that at first I thought we were going to collide with her. She had been badly shot up, and was glowing with fires, so she could not do much to us and eventually we

got into position to let her have a direct hit.

The version given to the press, above, was a little different to reality. Douglas Clare, who was on *Albrighton*'s bridge, later described what took place:

We slipped right through the screen round the enemy convoy and steamed close alongside our intended victim without being challenged. We fired a torpedo and blew his bridge away with our gunfire, while *Goathland* (Senior Officer) was doing much the same to his target. By then the enemy was all awake and at this inopportune moment *Albrighton* lost steerage, I think because of loss of vacuum to the steering motors. The German supply ship tried to ram us and our forward ammunition supply party had been wiped out by enemy fire so there was no more ammo reaching 'A' 4-inch mounting. The after 4-inch guns had taken a direct hit, so although their ammo supplies were OK there were no longer any guns aft to fire it off. The multiple pom-pom had also been hit and put out of action, both Oerlikon gunners hit and wounded; the only weapons left to our destroyer were two stripped Lewis guns on the bridge. All our radio aerials had also been shot away by the intense fire so we could not communicate with SO.

Goathland left for Plymouth not knowing what had become of us and reported that, when last seen, we had been stopped, on fire and believed to be sinking. (The rules were never to sacrifice further ships in an attempt to salvage one already badly damaged, and to be back within easy range of fighter protection by dawn. Perfectly sensible of course and well understood officially, but unofficially they were rules which caused a good deal of heart-searching and sometimes friction at having to leave one's friends behind).

As early dawn broke we were still close to the French coast. I remember seeing what I thought to be a high-speed target nipping along and reporting it, the guns engaging (we had got ourselves sorted out by then a bit) only to find out it was a lump of white rock! There was so much going on of course, one only gets one's own picture of events – I was busy with a Lewis gun – but I believe we also managed to get a torpedo away at the time we were broken down and so stopped the attempt by the enemy to ram us. One of my signalmen – a New Zealander – was also manning a stripped Lewis. As he knelt down to put on a new pan of ammunition he was badly wounded and says that thereafter his main recollection was of lying in a bunk below decks and watching the battle through a hole in the ship's side!

Albrighton survived, but the damage she received kept her in the dockyard until the end of May. On the enemy side, neither merchant ship was actually sunk, but the escorting trawler *UJ 1402* was sent to the bottom of the Channel some sixty miles NNE of Ouessant.

Resumption of Minelaying by the Germans

Although air attack was a minor irritation, as the spring gave way to summer nights the *Luftwaffe* joined with other arms in resumption of minelaying, and for a time this became quite intense. For example, on the Channel coast between 2 and 12 May three separate air minelaying sorties were made. On 2-3 and 3-4 May some sixteen Dornier Do217 bombers of *Kampfgruppe* 2 laid mines in the rivers Humber and Thames and along the well-worn convoy lane between Dover and the Thames Estuary. On the night of 11-12 May three dozen bombers repeated the process from the Thames northward, losing five of their number in the process.

The 2nd Torpedo Boat Flotilla joined in this wave of minelaying, repeating once more almost for the last time, the exploits of the German destroyers of previous years. On the nights of 5, 6, 7 and 8 May they audaciously entered British waters under the command of *Kapitän zur See* Erdmann. The *T-2, T-5, T-18, T-23* and *T-25* were involved and all escaped unscathed after completing their lays. The 5th E-boat Flotilla was also used on the night of 7-8 May when six of their number laid mines, some thirty-two being put down south of Selsey Bill without hindrance. This offensive, bold though it was, did not pay rich dividends as earlier campaigns had done. The only fatal casualty was the coaster *Catford* which was sunk on 31 May.

The lack of results did not prevent a large scale continuation of the project, with the whole E-boat force concentrating on this one task between 23 May and 12 June. Based at Cherbourg and St Peter Port the 2nd Flotilla under *Kommandeur* Feldt, the 4th Flotilla under Lt-Commander Lutzow and Klug's 5th Flotilla were reinforced by the 6th Flotilla under Lt-Commander Obermaier. With a combined strength of twenty-one ships they made seventy-seven sorties to lay a total of 321 mines and eighty-four barrage protection floats. Their lays were made off the Isle of Wight and Portsmouth on 23-24 May, in Lyme Bay 28-29 May, 30-31 May and 5-6 June and off Start Point on 6-7 June. There was almost no result from these activities.

On the night of 4-5 and 5-6 June more old friends were active during darkness doing the same job. The destroyers *Falke, Greif, Möwe, Kondor* and *T-22* laid mines in the Channel without detection, but also, once more, without results.

There was another lull after this disappointing series of operations and the German small craft returned to their more usual duties. On the night of 4-5 August for example, the 2nd and 6th Flotillas combined in an attack on patrol craft off the Thames Estuary, but despite the large numbers of E-boats involved (seven), their only victim was the trawler *Red Gauntlet*, torpedoed and sunk by *S-86* (*Leutnant* Wrampe) off Harwich.

Two more attempts at minelaying in the old manner were conducted in September by the 5th TB Flotilla under *Kommandeur* Copenhagen, with *T-27, T-25, T-19, Kondor* and *Möwe*. They laid mines in the Channel on the nights of 3-4 and 4-5 September in operations *Taube* and *Rebhuhn*. Thus for the fourth successive year German destroyers operated undetected and unharmed off the southern coast of England.

The final German sortie of this type took place later that month, on the night of 29-30 September 1943. Again it was the irrepressible 5th Flotilla with *Greif, Kondor, T-19, T-26* and *T-27* that carried out Operation *Talsohie* in the Channel. Again they were successful: once more their bravery and cunning availed them nothing and no ship was sunk by the mines they laid.

The next time the flotilla ventured forth, they found sterner opposition waiting for them than patrol craft. For the first time, they had a serious fright.

Offensive Patrols off the North Brittany Coast: October 1943

With the occasional availability of one or two of the modern Fleet type destroyers to back up the Hunts, C-in-C Plymouth began to mount offensive patrols in an effort to catch and destroy the destroyers of the 5th Flotilla. Unfortunately, the failure of the coordinated efforts of the British 5th Flotilla in 1939-40 was repeated three years later by the equally futile efforts of the mixed striking forces. Nevertheless, they came closer to success than any force hitherto assembled. The overall name for the operation, which was planned with attention to the minutiae of details and thus lacked flexibility, was *Tunnel*. We shall shortly examine this plan in some depth, but in its earliest stages, it involved one or two fleet destroyers and a few Hunts and had, up to the night of 4 October, drawn a blank almost each time. On this occasion, however, action of a sort resulted.

Composition of the British and German Forces

The following shows the composition of the two opposing forces on this night:

British	German
Limbourne (Senior Officer)	*T23* (Senior Officer)
Tanatside	*T22*
Wensleydale	*T25*
Ulster	*T26*
Grenville	*T27*

Numerically the two forces were exactly equal. The *Ulster* and *Grenville* matched the T class on a ship-for-ship basis, but the Elbings outmatched the Hunts in speed, torpedo armament and gun power. The German force, composed of ships of identical types, which were accustomed to working together, were more potent a force than the mixed types from differing backgrounds assembled by the British.

Weather Conditions

All other things being equal, the condition of the weather and moon were vital factors in any high-speed night destroyer action. The sky was overcast, but the cloud base was above the bursting point of star shells, so they could be used with good effect by either side. The night was dark but clear with very good visibility, even though there was no moon. The British force picked up the glare of the Isle de Bas Light from a distance of twenty-five miles. The wind was a light south-westerly and there was also a light westerly swell, which was too small to affect the ships' gunnery. The Hunts, although fitted with stabilizers, did not consider it necessary to use them during the action.

The area of the British patrol was between a position some seven miles north of Les Triagoz and the Vierge Lights. The force had reached the former point just after midnight and had turned to a mean course of 248 degrees, when contact was first made with the German flotilla. Thus the British line, in the order *Limbourne, Tanatside. Wensleydale, Ulster* and *Grenville*, some five cables apart and zigzagging at a speed of twelve knots, was in readiness.

The Running Fight

It was at 0100 hours that the first radar contact was made. The British flotilla was then in a position 277 degrees from the Les Triagoz Light, twelve miles distant, and the German ships were picked up at a distance of some five miles on a bearing of 135 degrees by *Tanatside*. The plot quickly revealed a surface echo although some confusion had been caused half-an-hour earlier when a similar report from *Wensleydale* had turned out to be rocks off the French coast.

The British destroyers came round together to 160 degrees and rapidly closed the range to about 4,000 yards, when *Limbourne* illuminated the target with rocket flares at extreme range. This opening salvo was supplemented by many other flare and star shell bursts, and in the light of this excellent illumination the three leading German destroyers could clearly and sharply be made out. The German force replied in kind; their flares were described as giving a 'daylight' lamp as compared to the yellowish-white of the British star shells. The ships stood out starkly on either side, but the British appeared to have the initial advantage of surprise.

The German ships were heading about 240 degrees relative to the British vessels at a speed of about fifteen knots. All five British destroyers opened fire immediately, while the German ships were seen to alter course to the eastward at once and to increase speed, completing a move they were already undertaking, from their own radar reports.

Fire was intense on both sides for a while, with the German destroyers apparently concentrating their fire on the two British 'Fleets'. It was thought that the reason for this was that the 'Fleets' were larger targets and closer to the enemy at this stage; or because their Home Fleet paint scheme was darker than the Hunts' Western Approaches camouflage, and therefore they stood out more clearly in the glare of flares. Be that as it may, most of the enemy fire was directed at these two ships, while the Hunts were hardly inconvenienced at all. The *Limbourne*'s CO later stated that:

> Enemy fire seemed to be about equally divided between those that fell with a splash and those that burst above the water. Though hit by a few splinters, enemy fire as far as *Limbourne* was concerned was not very accurate and in no way disturbed her own fire. I do not recollect seeing any enemy salvoes fall over nor do I remember thinking that the enemy were using a flashless propellant.

Hits were soon scored on *Grenville*, which was observed to be on fire aft. She dropped astern of the rest of the flotilla and all touch with her was lost for the next two hours.

Grenville's Damage

Before being hit, *Grenville* managed to get off a full pattern of eight torpedoes at about 4,600 yards range from a position abaft the beam of the German line. She estimated the enemy's speed at fifteen knots, whereas from 'headache' reports it was at least twenty-four knots by this time. The running range to hit would have been nearly 8,000 yards. It is probable that all torpedoes went far astern. In his memoirs, *Grenville*'s CO states that he closed to 3,000 yards before firing, but later analysis lays the blame squarely on the failure of the British ships to keep an adequate plot of enemy movements: 'An adequate plot would have given a true indication of the enemy's course and speed, and would clearly have shown the Torpedo Control Officer that he was in a position of "Torpedo Disadvantage".'

Grenville and *Ulster* had increased speed individually as soon as they sighted the enemy, with the result that they became separated. The former was hit twice earlier on, and a large fire started when one shell struck the lattice mast and the blast vented down the mast to `X' gun. The men working the gun at the open shield had no rearward protection; one man was killed instantly and fourteen more were badly hurt. In addition, a cordite bag ignited and touched off the rest of the cordite, the resulting fire quickly spreading to the quarterdeck. Fortunately it was brought under control before it reached the depth charges. By the time the fire was put out, the rest of the force had vanished and contact was not re-established with the Hunts until 0300 hours.

Ulster's Damage

The CO of *Ulster* has also written his memoirs, and his accounts of the initial stages of the action differ from *Grenville*'s and *Limbourne*'s official versions. Commander Donald stated that on receipt of the order 'Four Blue Zero', the order for the British line to turn immediately forty degrees to port together with the object of bringing them all approximately in line abreast, steering toward the enemy line, *Tanatside* and *Wensleydale* made a mistake and instead followed *Limbourne* round in line ahead.

He continues:

> Almost at once I sighted the enemy – several dark shapes steering eastward The enemy ships – whose armament, four 4.1-inch guns apiece, was almost identical with ours – were still steering across our bows from starboard so immediately the guns trained round after it onto the target. Then everything happened at once...
>
> It was a magnificent moment – five destroyers on each side banging away at each other, and a few light craft dodging about in between. By this time we had almost completely reversed our original course, and thus *Grenville* led our line – albeit rather straggly now – with *Ulster* second and the other three astern.
>
> After a few minutes the enemy began to draw ahead. I at once increased 'Full Speed' to get ahead of them if possible so that we could fire torpedoes, and *Grenville* did the same. This was the moment that for months we had been waiting and training for: I felt completely at ease, and thoroughly exhilarated as round after round went off with comforting regularity.

When *Grenville* was hit, *Ulster* continued the chase alone:

> We swept past her. A quick glance showed a fire on one of her after gun mountings, but there was nothing we could do about it, so we pressed on at full speed, still firing away. But the situation was not so funny now, as with *Grenville* stopped and the three Hunts fading away astern taken up with their own spot of action, we were the only one left to take on the three leading enemy ships. The range was now down to about three thousand yards, and splashes appeared all around us.

In fact, *Ulster* received two direct hits: one below the stokers' mess deck, which flooded the forward magazine; another just abaft 'A' gun. One man later died and many others were wounded, four of them badly. Nonetheless, before the enemy drew out of range, *Ulster* fired four torpedoes at a range of 3,000 yards and four more fifteen minutes later at a range of 3,000 yards. DTSD, in his report criticizing this, declared that there was no justification for withholding half the torpedoes for a second attack, but Commander Donald explained that all were not fired in the first attack because, in swinging the ship away from reported shoals there had not been enough time to fire all eight. He admitted the second salvo had been a '...thousand to one chance, but there was no point in wasting it'.

The Hunts in Action

Meanwhile, the *Limbourne, Tanatside* and *Wensleydale* continued the pursuit of the fleeing enemy craft after the big destroyers had fallen out due to damage. The three Hunts continued this chase to the south-east and east until, owing to the close proximity of the same shoals off Triagoz which had thwarted *Ulster*, it was 'deemed prudent' to cease further chasing. By this time, the German destroyers, with their eight-knot speed advantage, had drawn ahead out of sight and range, and all fire had ceased. The Hunts then withdrew to the north-west to get clear of the land and re-form. Course was then altered to eastward, to endeavour to find *Ulster* and regain touch with the enemy east of Les Triagoz. Contact with the German force was never re-established, however.

The SO reported that during the action, the central ship of the leading destroyers was seen to have been heavily hit and set on fire amidships for a short time, and to have given off a considerable quantity of smoke afterwards, while the western enemy vessel of the leading three was also observed to have been hit three or four times. This destroyer was seen to turn to the south at one time during the engagement, but she was fired upon by *Limbourne* and shortly turned eastward again under smoke, and was lost to sight. However, the CO of *Grenville* claims that it was in fact his ship, which was under heavy pom-pom fire from the Hunts at one stage of the action! None of the hits did anything to reduce the enemy destroyers' speed and thus they made good their escape.

Criticisms of the Action

There was much criticism of this action, although it had at least damaged two enemy destroyers. The fact that the SO ignored *Wensleydale*'s original radar report at 0016 hours and dismissed the contacts as rocks delayed firm action for forty-four minutes. *Wensleydale* should not have accepted this decision, but should have made amplifying reports as soon as the number, course and speed of the enemy had been determined. The SO was also criticized for closing the enemy for five minutes at only twelve knots, before increasing to fifteen, later to twenty and then twenty-five knots. This gave the Germans time to turn away and work up their own speed before the Hunts could close to the effective range of their smaller weapons. In his defence, the SO stated that he wished to make an undetected approach and kept the speed low in order to avoid making a large and visible bow wave.

The fact that the two 'Fleet' destroyers acted individually and not as a unit or subdivision was highly criticized. The accounts given by the captains of these two vessels give their viewpoint and seem to indicate that they had intended to act as a unit, but the quick hits on *Grenville* made this impossible. The official verdict made no concession to these viewpoints, but stated flatly that:

> Had these two `Fleet' destroyers been operated together as a subdivision instead of individually, they would almost certainly have achieved better results. It appears probable that they had not had sufficient training together to enable them to operate at night as a subdivision on a line of bearing, and that on this occasion they would have been better employed as a subdivision in line ahead. There can be no doubt that they should have worked as a unit.

Another statement read:

> The low standard of plotting of all ships with the exception of *Wensleydale* must impose a severe handicap.

On the German side the operation is dismissed in a few lines, which might seem to indicate that the Germans suffered more heavily than they cared to admit. Two ships on each side had been damaged, but as Commander Donald later reported:

> ...aerial reconnaissance over the French coast showed two German destroyers badly damaged in the small harbour of Lannion into which they had retired after the action. They remained there for six months, whereas our repairs were effected in four weeks. So I suppose you could count it a draw in our favour, though I would have liked to have blown one of the enemy sky-high.

Destroyer Patrols in the Channel, 1943

Before we move on, let us see the work of the Hunts in the Channel during 1943 through the eyes of one of their crew members, Arthur Renshaw of HMS *Stevenstone*. His cameo portraits cover the varying aspects of life aboard a Channel Hunt at this time. For example, shore leave would be given for part of the crew between 1600 and 2000 hours where possible, before the dusk sailing:

> With 'Special Duty Men' closed up, the captain would be standing on the bridge shouting 'We can't wait any longer' and 'Who's missing now?'. Finally the last stragglers lurched aboard and it was 'Gangway inboard' and 'Let go head rope'. Silently the ship would move astern from the north-west wall towards the *Foudroyant*. Then, out from the harbour, with the odd nod from the Gosport ferry boat and perhaps a wave from a couple of Wrens from Quebec House. Passing the Spit Buoy and finally the Nab Tower we would then know whether we were lucky enough to be a standby ship, ready at a minute's notice, or more likely to be on an 'offensive' or 'defensive' patrol. When we moved out from the North West Wall it revealed, painted in large white letters, the word '*Steamingstone*'!
>
> When on leave during a boiler clean people would often ask 'Where are you?'. When told that we were operating in the Channel some would say 'Oh, coasting – you don't actually go to sea?' or 'My nephew is on the *Duke of York*!' Little did they realize the hazards the Channel destroyers encountered. As soon as the ship had passed the boom defence there was always the weather to contend with – not unusual – but in our case the weather always affected us. If it was rough conditions were terrible; if it was calm the E-boats would be out in strength. Other hazards were floating mines, minefields, enemy warships, coastal batteries, enemy aircraft, explosive motorboats and also our own forces.

To survive all these for any length of time would be a miracle. The last hazard on the list should never happen but it did on more than one occasion. During a 'defensive' patrol in 1943, *Stevenstone* was patrolling in an area in which there was no shipping (if any other ship entered this zone it was classed as enemy) when suddenly out of the darkness loomed another destroyer. *Stevenstone* engaged with all guns and the other ship retaliated. Both ships signalled to Captain 'D' ashore – 'Have engaged enemy destroyer'. It was some time before we of the *Stevenstone* received the signal, 'Break off the action, friendly British destroyer'. How this ship came to be allowed to enter our restricted zone we were never informed.

On another night whilst patrolling I happened to be on lookout duty when suddenly an aircraft dived out of the night sky and straddled us with a couple of small bombs. This was quite definitely a British fighter-bomber and our captain's words were unprintable. Nothing unusual in that. Both these actions could have ended with disastrous consequences; many of these mistakes must have been caused by a breakdown in communications.

On one particular night radar contact was made and everyone came to 'Action Stations' in tense anticipation. We were on 'Offensive' patrol off the enemy coastline, sweeping their shipping lane. The order for 'A' gun to fire star shell was given, as we were ready to illuminate the target. The contact seemed to be stationary as we reduced the range. Maybe it was a stopped E-boat? We drew close alongside the contact and the captain gave orders to illuminate with searchlight. To everyone's amazement it was recognized as a small fishing vessel from one of our fishing towns!

Over the loud hailer it took quite a few minutes to awaken the skipper of the boat who sleepily emerged. He was told in no uncertain terms to 'beat it' and he proceeded to do so at his best speed...four knots! He seemed not to understand just how close he had come to being blown apart in a spectacular firework display. Our Hunts had a reputation for being 'trigger happy'; it was just as well we disproved that story that night. Being 'quick on the draw' however had proved successful and paid dividends in numerous other incidents.

In late 1943 we had a quick boiler clean and the authorities ashore decided to install a new radar equipment lantern to our ship. It was located between the torpedo tubes and 'X' gun mounting. It was a very modern set and was being installed on all the Channel Hunts. After the lantern was fitted we put to sea and knew that we would be out for a few days. During this time a heavy sea developed and later, with a following sea, we began to roll quite badly.

It was well known that all the Hunts were top heavy even before the latest additions. We did a gigantic roll and lay over on our port side for what seemed an eternity, although probably it was for no longer than a few seconds. Was she going to right herself? Fortunately the helmsman, AB Bill Slavan from Glasgow, held on to the wheel and gradually we returned to the upright position. This incident had a curious sequel.

For the next couple of days one of our seamen refused to go below again and just walked constantly to-and-fro with the roll of the ship. This experience had been too much for him and he had snapped. The doctor examined him and decided, once we returned to port, that he should be drafted ashore. As he left the ship the dockyard workers were coming aboard to install yet more ballast below to counteract the new radar lantern!

Chapter Fifteen

The Disaster that was Operation *Tunnel*

We must turn to examine one of the unhappiest disasters to befall the Royal Navy in the Narrow Sea during the Second World War. The Official Historian described it later as a 'setback'; one of the destroyer skippers who was there later put in his memoirs his opinion that it was '...the classic ballzup of the war...'. It would appear that the latter description is, perhaps, the most apt! It resulted in the loss of two fine ships, with no material or physical damage inflicted on the enemy in return. The operation was criticized *before* it took place, so hindsight is not the only basis for judgement. Moreover, very few of the many lessons imparted when locating and fighting the German destroyers in the Channel during the previous three years seem to have been incorporated in the British plan. It was known from numerous engagements, many of which have been recorded here, that the standard German destroyer response to interception by the British surface forces was to fire a full salvo of torpedoes and turn away at full speed, avoiding if possible a gun action. It was also common knowledge that German radar stations on the Channel coast were excellent and had, almost since Dunkirk, been instrumental in tracking all British surface ship movements and relaying this information to their own forces. Yet very little flexibility seems to have been granted to the British forces involved. Let us first examine the basic plan again in depth.

Operation *Tunnel*: The Rival Forces

It was well established that the movement of German seaborne traffic up and down the Channel between Ushant and Cherbourg took place at frequent, if irregular intervals, and mostly by night. The route this shipping, both naval and mercantile, took was to the north of Ushant and within four or five miles of the Brittany coast, and to the east of the Channel Island of Sark. During the hours of daylight, the vessels normally anchored off St Malo or in Lannion or Lezardrieux Bays. Their approximate route was plotted as:

a 000° Ile Vierge Light 5 miles

b 000° Triagoz Light 4 miles

c 180° Barnouic Light 5 miles

d East of Sark, to Cap de la Hague

By October 1943, the main traffic consisted of big merchant vessels plying between the French Biscay ports and Germany; blockade-runners and Armed Merchant Raiders en route to Atlantic destinations from the German home ports; coastal convoys, the equivalent of those on the British side and naval movements: the passage of destroyer flotillas and the like for refits etc. The larger merchant ships were given strong escorts arranged as follows:

> A covering force of at least four Elbing class destroyers or similar escorts, which preceded the convoy proper. A *Sperrbrecher*, several of the large 'M' class minesweepers (equivalent to the British Halcyon or Algerine type minesweeping sloops) and sometimes a flock of E-boats if the convoy was a valuable one. The tactics were similar. If British surface forces attempted to intercept the covering force, it made every effort to draw it from the convoy proper, while at the same time trying to avoid close action if possible. If not, then the standard tactic of launching full torpedo salvoes followed by high-speed flight was adopted. The convoy itself would take evasive action, keeping as close inshore as it could, while ashore the coastal lights would be lit to assist them in this. In addition of course, heavy guns were mounted all along the French coast, not just along the Straits. The batteries that were established on the Cherbourg Peninsula and on Guernsey had ranges of 25,000 to 30,000 yards, all ranging by radar and well locked in to their particular sectors. The surface forces available to the Germans at this time were not large overall by British standards, consisting of about four of the large Narvik type destroyers, mounting 5.9-inch guns; twelve of the smaller destroyers of the Elbing and 'T' classes along with some of the older Möwe class. At least sixteen to two dozen E-boats and as many of the big 'M' class minesweepers were also available.

But if they were numerically weak overall, the Germans could choose the moment to sail and concentrate their maximum strength on defence. By contrast, there was no standing force available at Plymouth or Portsmouth of comparable strength from which to form a striking group of equal power. The only regular warships always available were the Hunt class destroyers of the 1st Flotilla (six to eight ships) based at Portsmouth, and a similar number of Hunts of the 15th Flotilla based at Plymouth. In addition, there were the small boats of the 1st, 21st and 23rd MTB flotillas and the 14th MGB Flotilla based on Dartmouth. In fact, in the autumn of 1943, British surface ship strength in the Channel was as weak as it had been in early 1942. The only additions to this limited strength that C-in-C Plymouth, Admiral Sir Ralph Leatham, could count on were the occasional light cruiser detached from the Home Fleet or the odd 'Fleet' destroyer briefly attached to his command (or passing through his area). The weaknesses of such a scratch force are obvious. The Hunts were used to working with others as a team; that was the only positive feature. They lacked the speed and the heavy torpedo armaments of the newest 'Fleet' destroyers and of the German ships, so they always operated at a disadvantage. The 'Fleets' themselves hardly knew each other and were only on station for short periods when they had numerous other functions to perform. The opportunity to work together, or with other ships, was minimal, and in the majority of cases, completely non-existent. The cruisers were in a similar situation; some, it is true, from the 10th Cruiser Squadron had worked together and had an understanding, but others were randomly attached on their way to and from other stations. Most were armed with 6-inch guns and equipped for surface action.

In addition to these major benefits, the Germans had one other inestimable advantage: practice. The Royal Navy had naturally made periodic efforts to interrupt the steady flow of traffic whenever breaks in the routine coastal convoy work permitted the Hunts to be so utilized. But no permanent striking force was set up until January 1944, incredible as this may seem. The German 'A' destroyers, moreover, were well trained as a team and practised and carried out their set evolutions many times. This was not all, for the constant British attempts at interception had given the Germans a thorough insight into the tactics employed and these tactics were never changed or modified to any great degree. So fixed were the instructions that *Tunnel* might better have been named 'Tramlines'. As tactics never varied it was quite easy for the Germans both to evade them and also, given the time and inclination, prepare a very nasty surprise for the British.

The British Plan

The format for *Tunnel* was laid down precisely, so that ships joining from other commands could slot into the routine without causing the others to adjust. That, at least, was the theory; in practice, ships could not just 'slot in' and be expected to perform like veterans.

The plan called for the British forces to be split into two groups: Force 28, which would consist of the cruiser and all available destroyers, and Force 119, made up of the coastal forces. The intention of the plan was defined as '...to intercept and destroy enemy forces and shipping on passage up or down channel'. The method of execution was laid down as follows:

> When the order to carry out *Tunnel* was given, the respective forces were to pass the Plymouth gate at the time ordered and proceed by way of the swept channel. They were then to carry out the sweep through the position laid down at the times specified. The ships were, unless ordered to the contrary, to return to Plymouth and be back within twenty miles of the British coastline by first light. Should there be any delay, the Senior Officer had to report in advance the probable position of his ships and his intended route home. British ships were not allowed to be

drawn to within effective range of the German batteries. Any ship damaged in action was to retire to the north if necessary and the Senior Officer had to locate damaged ships and escort them back to port 'as soon as conditions permit'.

A series of lettered positions was given to be used as references:

(FF) Casquets Light (GG) Les Hanois Light (HH) 325 Heaux Light 7 (JJ) Sept Iles Light (KK) 000 Triagoz Light 7

(LL) Ile de Bas Light (MM) 000 Ile Vierge Light (NN) Stiff Light Ushant (00) 49°30'N, 5°00'W (PP) 170 Eddystone 7 (QQ) 180 Start Point.

The communications net was vital to the success of the operation, especially with so many ships in the company unfamiliar with either the region or the other vessels, or both. Plymouth W/T was to assume guard for the destroyers on Broadcast Coded Network if requested, but the cruiser was to maintain constant watch on that broadcast. The call signs were allocated as follows:

Collective W/T Call Sign for Force 28: 3 NLR

Collective W/T Call Sign for Force 119: 3 NLT

Collective R/T Call Sign for Force 28: Landlord

Collective R/T Call Sign for Force 119: Cribbage

The individual R/T Call Signs were to be allocated by the Senior Officer from local spares 1-100 in SP2530; C-in-C, Plymouth, was informed of the choice. Air reconnaissance would be arranged, but not much reliance had come to be placed on this source; indeed no useful reconnaissance was received. Fighters from No. 10 Group were asked to perform this function during the operation, but aborted their mission soon after take-off.

The German Plan

Based on their normal overall flexible plan, the Germans planned to sail the merchant vessel *Munsterland* from Brest to Cherbourg in easy stages. She was provided with a close escort consisting of the six minesweepers of the 2nd M/S Flotilla and two new patrol vessels, *V-718* and *V-719*, both equipped with radar. The outer escort consisted of five destroyers of the 4th TB Flotilla under the command of *Kapitän* Kohlauf in *T-23*, with *T-22, T-25, T-26* and *T-27*.

The *Munsterland* and the close escort sailed from Brest on 22 October 1943 at 0500 while the outer escort left Brest three hours later to take up position to the north of the convoy route, within visual distance. They were instructed to escort the merchant ship as far as Lezardrieux that night and then enter St Malo. Any surface action, even with enemy coastal craft, was to be avoided if possible. However, the German intentions had already been largely divulged by their preliminary movements. The *Munsterland* had arrived in Brest on 9 October and the subsequent concentration of six Elbings indicated that an attempt to bring her up-channel was a possibility. The expected sailing was delayed, assumed to have been due to the moon, which was waxing to full on 12 October, and also because of bad weather reports for the following week. Photographic reconnaissance revealed that *Munsterland* had still not reached Cherbourg by 20 October, so C-in-C, Plymouth, decided to take advantage of the presence of a light cruiser and two 'Fleet' destroyers on his station, to carry out Operation *Tunnel* on the night of 22-23 October in the hope of intercepting others.

Various Options Considered

Consideration was given as to whether this sweep was to be from east to west, or west to east. From previous experience it was known that German destroyers went ahead of the convoy and that therefore a sweep from west to east would bring our forces astern of the enemy, which would give them a chance to catch the *Munsterland* unawares without getting involved with the escorts. This was greatly dependent upon air reconnaissance being able to establish the exact location of the target in good time, but in the event, this was not the case. As they lacked this intelligence by the time they were due to sail, the low speed of the Hunts made the chances of overtaking the enemy less certain. Nor could moonrise be ignored; this (bearing 066 degrees) was at 0125, westward. However, low cloud and showers were forecast, which would favour the British forces and, on balance, it was decided that an east to west sweep would offer the best chance of success. The conditions reported that night were:

a – Sky overcast with occasional patches of starlight

b – Prior to moonrise it was a clear night, lights being sighted about twelve miles off. Later visibility improved as the moon rose. There was a south-westerly wind, force 2-3, which later died away.

c – There was a long heavy swell.

It was decided to use the cruiser/destroyer striking force rather than a coastal forces' strike or aircraft attack because of the probable strength of the escort, the greater certainty that the weather would not interfere with the operation, and the probability that the attacking force would have to fight its way through the escort to attack the target.

Composition of the British Force

The make-up of the surface striking force left much to be desired. C-in-C, Plymouth, signalled to them 'Carry out operation *Tunnel* as ordered in my memorandum dated 21st October tomorrow'. They were to sail at 1900 hours on 22 October to carry out this instruction. The ships were the anti-aircraft cruiser *Charybdis* (Captain G.A.W. Voelcker), Senior Officer; the 'Fleet' destroyers *Grenville* (Lieutenant Commander R. P. Hill, DSO) and *Rocket* (Lieutenant Commander H.B. Ackworth, OBE); the Hunt class destroyers *Limbourne* (Commander W.J. Phipps, OBE), *Talybont* (Lieutenant E. F. Baines), *Wensleydale* (Lieutenant P .B. N. Lewis) and *Stevenstone* (Lieutenant W. P. Goodfellow). The last ship was from the 1st Flotilla at Portsmouth and had been lent by the C-in-C Portsmouth, Admiral Sir Charles Little, GBE, KCB, to replace the original destroyer, *Melbreak* of the 15th Flotilla.

The best that can be said of this group of warships is that it was a very mixed force indeed. Brief details of the armament and speed of the squadron is as follows:

Charybdis	32½, knots, eight 4.5-inch guns, six 21-inch torpedo tubes.
Grenville	36¾ knots, four 4.7-inch guns, eight 21-inch torpedo tubes.
Rocket	
Limbourne	28 knots, four 4-inch guns, two 21-inch torpedo tubes.
Talybont	
Wensleydale	
Stevenstone	

Charybdis was an anti-aircraft cruiser with four twin 4.5-inch dual-purpose guns, not armed with the 5.25-inch guns of most of her sisters. She had never operated previously as a surface strike force leader, indeed her entire life up to this point had been providing heavy AA cover for aircraft carriers, mainly in the Mediterranean. She therefore had no experience and certainly very little practice, of surface actions. Her armament was designed to combat enemy bombers and was smaller than that carried by most destroyers. It was certainly not the normal cruiser type of main armament, which was expected to engage the German destroyers at long range as planned in *Tunnel*. To send a cruiser was not sufficient; it had to be the right type of cruiser.

The two 'Fleets' carried the normal war-built armament, totally inadequate for engaging a *Narvik* but almost identical to that carried by the 'T' class ships Germans used for this operation, both in calibre and number. The torpedo armament was also good, and both ships had night fighting experience, the *Grenville* in the same waters against the same opponents, as we have seen. The opinion of her commander, therefore, was perhaps the most valid. The Hunts came from two different flotillas, which meant that their similarity of speed and armament was negated by the fact that they had never operated as a combined fighting group. In fact the Senior Destroyer Officer, Commander W. J. Phipps, had only joined his command a few days beforehand and so hardly knew his own crew, let alone his compatriots or the plan. Although he was the Senior Destroyer Officer, he did not even arrive at the conference on the operation until it was half over!

Narrative of Commander Phipps

The narrative of Commander Phipps shows us exactly what pre-operation background he had before taking part in *Tunnel*:

> 20th October. Joined HMS *Limbourne* at Plymouth at 0900 and took over and walked around the ship in the forenoon. Confidential books were not mustered or taken over. My job as Senior Officer of the flotilla of Hunt class destroyers there. In the afternoon I went up to the offices of the Commander-in-Chief, Plymouth, and called on him and his staff. Left billet alongside the wall at 1800 and anchored in Jennycliff Bay. Hankey, who I relieved, took her down harbour for me and I anchored her just to get the feel of her. Anchored until the early hours, blowing very hard from the south-west and very uncomfortable.
>
> 21st October. Got under way with *Stevenstone* and *Melbreak* at 0245 and down to meet *Revenge* off the Lizard at 0700. Connected and formed screen on her. *Revenge* went along pretty well and shot me off well short of the Needles and I turned and [went] back to Plymouth at the best speed into a head wind. Eased a bit on the way and managed 18 knots later. Didn't like the idea of going up harbour at night or fighting my way through the stuff anchored in Jennycliff, so anchored my party in Cawsand Bay. Military made me very angry putting their searchlights on me as I was coming in but not too bad and anchored them nicely at 2130.
>
> 22nd October. Got under way at 0730 and in slowly because of sweepers and other hang-ups and to oiler at 0830. Had to wait for *Melbreak* going inside at the wall so did not leave the oiler until 1045 and didn't get to the conference on operation 'Tunnel' until 1130. Very hurried show run by Voelcker, Captain of the *Charybdis*. I hadn't the least idea of his intentions and could not get anything out of him. Very unsatisfactory conference. Got away at 1820 with *Stevenstone, Talybont* and *Wensleydale* with *Rocket* to join *Charybdis* and *Grenville* outside and over to the French Coast for offensive sweep up the German convoy route. Things went all right and wind dropped and visibility very good. Lights on Sept Isles and Tabroz Islands so obviously something on the move.

Final Plan of *Tunnel* Adopted

Captain Voelcker's final plan was duly signalled to all ships of the force and repeated to C-in-C, Plymouth. The force was divided as follows:

1st Division: 1st Sub-division – *Charybdis*

1st Division: 2nd Sub-division – *Grenville, Rocket*

2nd Division: 3rd Sub-division – *Limbourne, Talybont*

2nd Division: 4th Sub-division – *Stevenstone, Wensleydale*

The force was to form in single line ahead, on a course of 190 degrees, at a speed of seventeen knots, with the ships in the column three cables apart. The following alterations of course and speed were to take place, in rigid conformity at the approximate times laid down, without any further signals:

a. In position 173° Eddystone 7.5 at 2000 course 147° speed 17 knots

b. In position HH at 0030/23 mean, course 267° speed 13 knots

c. In position KK at 0200/23 mean, course 249°

d. At 0330 increase speed to 18 knots

e. In position MM at 0430/23, course 010° speed 23 knots

The Senior Officer stated in his night intentions signal that he intended to keep his force concentrated unless the action developed into a chase to the east and the Hunts proved unable to keep up. In such an eventuality the Hunts would be detached to sweep westward. It was his intention to approach unobserved to within 6,000 yards of the target before illuminating it and commencing fire, but as soon as their approach was observed by the enemy, fire was to be opened immediately. Any torpedo targets were to be engaged by ships individually as the opportunity offered. *Charybdis* might carry out an attack with the 1st Division in such an instance; the correct depth setting of the torpedoes was essential. In the event of the attack developing into a high-speed mêlée, fighting lights were to be used.

Communications were organized as follows: Set watch at 1830 on CN broadcast by *Charybdis* only, with Plymouth W/T taking guard for the destroyers at the same time. The operational wave (W/T) was 2,500 kc/s and the intercom wave (W/T) was 1,875kc/s. Ships so fitted were to set watch on Type 86 Naval Intercom wave from 0030 to 0430 Type 86 or shaded light only were to be used when making reports not important enough to be made by W/T. Silence was to be kept on all radar and IFF sets except 271 and 272 until contact was made, and then there were no restrictions. Similarly, Asdic and hydrophone silence and echo-sounding silence was to be kept until contact. (Thus no warning of incoming torpedoes would be received if the enemy saw them first and fired before they were spotted themselves.) No mention was made in this signal of the special target of the *Munsterland* or of the concentration of Elbings at Brest. From this it might be taken that none of the British captains knew that they had a specific target, what it was, or that it might be heavily protected. The whole hastily assembled operation appeared to be regarded merely as a routine patrol.

Comments on the Plan by the Director of Training

Because the outcome of the operation was to influence staff opinion at the Admiralty for many years ahead, the opinion of the Director of Training and Staff Duties Division of this plan are worth noting:

> There are strong indications that *Charybdis*'s force had been detected by shore radar and reported to the S.O. of the enemy's destroyer force, and it is reasonable to assume that the enemy were able to make a good estimation as to its composition. The echoes must have been too big to be mistaken for MTBs and the much larger echo of the *Charybdis* can hardly have left them in any doubt that a large ship was leading the line.
>
> A mixed force with no collective training, no knowledge of what enemy forces were at sea, and with deliberately accepted disadvantage of light, was about to encounter a highly-trained striking force which almost certainly knew the numbers, position, course and speed and probably had a good idea of the composition, of our own force.
>
> The failure of *Charybdis* to appreciate the tactical possibilities can be attributed in part to his ignorance of the fact that the enemy convoy was at sea; he was further handicapped in that he was not fitted with 'Headache' – nor did he receive adequate Headache reports from his consorts.
>
> His course of action must have been influenced by the action of the night of 3-4 October, which developed immediately into a chase of the German destroyers. On the composition of the force he stated that:
>
> C-in-C, Plymouth gives his reasons for employing so mixed a force. It was his intention that *Charybdis* and the two Fleet destroyers should deal with the enemy's destroyer force, leaving the four Hunts to destroy the convoy. *Charybdis* however, in his night intention signal, states his intention of keeping the force concentrated except in the event of chase; *Talybont* confirms that it was agreed at the conference that the force should be fairly tightly controlled by the Senior Officer. It can be assumed only that *Charybdis* decided to manoeuvre his whole force in one line because the component ships had had insufficient collective training to enable them to operate as separate divisions in close support. It is generally accepted that not more than five ships can be operated effectively in a single column at night.

Sailing of the Force and German Contacts

The British force left Plymouth at 1900 on 22 October, steering northward in single line ahead in the order *Charybdis*, *Grenville, Rocket, Limbourne,*

Talybont, Stevenstone and *Wensleydale*. By 0030 the next day, having reached position HH, the force duly altered course to 267 degrees, and reduced its speed to thirteen knots. During the run westwards visibility ahead was poor, but the sky was clearing to the east.

As early as 2315 on 22 October, *Talybont* had picked up the carrier wave of German radio-telephone transmissions, and *Wensleydale* also picked it up at 0045 on 23 October. Unintelligible speech was heard by *Limbourne* at 0103; this information was duly passed on to *Charybdis* (which was not fitted with radio telephone interception gear) by the following signal: 'Y raw material indicates 3 units close.' Apparently *Charybdis* did not understand the signal and asked for a repeat.

In fact the Germans were well aware of the approach of the British force. At 2150 the 4th Flotilla was in company with the convoy as agreed. At 0027 the radar station at Perros (Ploumanach) picked up a large surface target moving south. At 0035 this contact was seen to alter course to the westward, parallel to and about four miles north of the convoy route and increase speed to about twelve knots. At first two, later several more, individual echoes began to be traced. By 0400 the Paimpol radar was also plotting the British ships and three minutes later a general alarm was given.

German Countermeasures Adopted

By 0052 the plots showed the British squadron steering 270 degrees at twelve to fifteen knots. Kohlauf took his destroyers northward with the intention of taking up position about five miles north of the convoy route and then proceeding eastward parallel to it. The oncoming British force would then be clearly silhouetted against the horizon to the south-east, providing they kept on their present course. He thus hoped to sight them early and launch an uninterrupted torpedo attack.

He was thwarted in this aim by heavy rain clouds, which came up from the south-west and the lightening of the north-west horizon. But a steady flow of radar plots kept him fully in the picture of British movements throughout his course alterations.

British Radar Contacts Not Passed On

The German signal to alter course together fifty degrees to starboard, followed by a further signal some thirteen minutes later at 0130 ordering a further turn to starboard together, was picked up by *Limbourne*. Five different call signs were picked up, and possibly a sixth, indicating the size of the German force.

At the same time *Charybdis* herself obtained a radar contact ahead at 14,000 yards range. Neither the cruiser nor the destroyers exchanged this information and thus the ironic (and tragic) situation was that *Charybdis* was aware that an enemy force was some seven miles ahead and closing, but did not know how strong that force was or of what type; while the destroyers astern of her, with their radar masked by *Charybdis* from a point right ahead to 27 degrees on either bow, knew that there were probably five or six destroyers close by, but did not know their position. The complete picture was available, but not seen.

Contact Made and Fire Commenced

At 0135 *Charybdis* made a signal that she had radar contact bearing 270 degrees at a range of 8,800 yards. In keeping with his plan to close to within 6,000 yards range of any target before opening fire, Captain Voelcker held his course. He was not aware that the enemy had been plotting him for some time, that the ships he was closing were destroyers with powerful torpedo armaments waiting for just such an opportunity. Three minutes after this report, the German destroyer leader located him due east of them.

Within a few minutes, at 0141 German naval 'Y' operators also intercepted a British signal stating that they had been sighted (but only two German destroyers were reported) bearing 270 degrees, distance six miles, steering 098 degrees. German hopes of achieving a surprise attack seemed dashed by this information. Two minutes later the 4th Flotilla, north of Sept Iles, visually sighted a large British unit bearing 350 degrees at 2,000 metres. The German destroyers immediately turned 120 degrees to starboard in a desperate attempt at evasion. They felt that *they* had been surprised and that the situation was very critical. As the German destroyers turned, the large ship (she was of course *Charybdis*) was seen to alter course 60 degrees to port. At once the leading destroyer *T-23* (*Kapitänleutant* Weinleg) fired a full salvo of six torpedoes. At the same time, two British destroyers were spotted astern of the target, now identified as a cruiser.

Meanwhile there was considerable confusion in the British force. At 0142 *Charybdis* made a signal ordering the force to turn together to 280 degrees (thirteen degrees to starboard) at a speed of eighteen knots, but unfortunately this signal was only received by one ship astern of her, the rear of the British line, *Stevenstone*. Lieutenant Commander Hill later reported that the increase of speed was quickly noticed, but the alteration on course not until 0146

In the destroyers much was happening, not all of it very clearly, all at high speed. The *Talybont* plotted three small units bearing 140 degrees at a range of 4,000-5,000 yards between 0141 and 0144. These might have been E-boats, but none was actually present. A number of enemy speed signals were picked up by all the Hunt class destroyers at 0143, and an indecipherable signal was also intercepted.

At 0145 *Charybdis* opened fire with star shell, at a range of about 4,000 yards, and almost instantly two torpedo tracks were sighted approaching from the port side. These were part of *T-23*'s initial salvo. *Charybdis* put her helm hard-a-port but it was too late. There was a heavy explosion as one or both torpedoes struck home and the cruiser quickly slewed to a halt with a twenty-degree list to port. The German flotilla reported two hits on the cruiser target only two minutes after the first visual sighting. The British destroyers commenced fire on the German ships and the flotilla was illuminated by star shell. Meanwhile *T-22, T-26* and *T-27* all fired salvoes of six torpedoes at the enemy without giving away their position by gunfire. Several new explosions lit up the night.

The British Force Shattered

Total confusion now reigned in the British force. *Limbourne*'s official report read:

> The Senior Officer was observed to alter course about 40° to starboard. No signal was received in *Limbourne* and it was not clear whether a red or a blue turn had been carried out. *Limbourne* followed in the wake of her next ahead. Other ships appeared to have made a blue turn and to be on a line of bearing.

It would appear that *Charybdis* increased speed and led round to port as she opened fire on the enemy, of whose position *Limbourne* was unaware. *Grenville* and *Rocket* held their course at first, followed by *Limbourne*. This manoeuvre put *Charybdis* on *Limbourne*'s port bow about 4,000 yards off. She was plotted and taken for the enemy and was duly illuminated by *Limbourne* with several rockets. She thus attracted several more torpedoes, as did *Limbourne*, which was between *Charybdis* and the German destroyers. While this was happening, *Grenville* and *Rocket* were careering along and leading around to port, crossing *Limbourne*'s bows. The latter was forced to put her wheel hard-a-port and she sounded two short blasts to avoid *Rocket*. While *Limbourne* swung to port a torpedo track was sighted on a relative bearing of Red 140 degrees. The wheel was at once put hard-a-starboard and it was thought that this missile would miss ahead. Unfortunately, this was not the case, and there was a terrific explosion forward.

Limbourne had been struck at 0152 and it was only good fortune that the others did not share her fate. Eighteen torpedoes sped through the British destroyer line; one hit *Limbourne*, while another scored a second hit on *Charybdis*. *Grenville* and *Wensleydale* both had near misses. *Grenville*'s captain thought that the torpedo hit was on the next ship astern, *Rocket*, and did not know that superiority had now devolved on him until *Stevenstone* reported that *Limbourne* had been hit some time later. 'For the next 15 minutes', the report read, 'the ship was manoeuvring to avoid collision.' By 0231 no orders having been received; Hill took command by wireless and proceeded to the north-west to re-form. Meanwhile a rain squall had come down, shutting off visibility once more and drawing a veil of mist over the scene of carnage:

In all, the German destroyers had done remarkably well against a superior force and had not fired a single gun in answer. In the short space of five minutes, they had hit both Senior Officers' ships and scattered and confused the remainder of the force. The British had no idea that *Munsterland* was present and never sighted her at all. They later recorded hits and credited them as follows:

a.First hit on *Charybdis* by *T-23*

b. Second hit on *Charybdis* by *T-27* (*Kapitän zur See* Verlohr

c. Hit on *Limbourne* by *T22* (*Kapitänleutant* Blöse)

T-25 was sunk some months later and one of her survivors recounted that *Charybdis* had been picked up by them at a range of 2,800 yards by their Asdic; she had apparently failed to detect the German ships. The whole flotilla passed down her beam firing full salvoes of torpedoes, and by the time it was *T-25*'s turn to fire, the cruiser had 'blown up and disappeared'.

The Sinking of *Charybdis*

The first torpedo had hit the small cruiser on the port side and had flooded No. 2 dynamo room and 'B' boiler room, putting the after unit out of action. She soon assumed a twenty-degree list to port. The second torpedo struck her at about 135 station causing very severe damage; the after engine room was flooded, the director was displaced, all electric lighting failed and the list quickly increased to fifty degrees. There was no communication with the bridge and abandon ship was ordered.

The cruiser went down very quickly; the Dido class were notorious for that, and within a short time survivors saw her suddenly take an angle by the stern until she was almost vertical. She stayed like that for about half-an-hour with a third of her length out of the water, then the bulkheads collapsed and she sank. She vanished at about 0230.

Report of Commander Oddie

Loss of life aboard *Charybdis* was severe. The Executive Officer, Commander E. R. J. Oddie, was the senior survivor. His final report read as follows:

> At 0030 on 23rd October, the squadron was in position 325° Les Heaux Light 7 miles, and course was altered to 267° speed 15 knots. At approximately 0130 *Charybdis* obtained a radar contact right ahead at 14,000 yards. The contact appeared to indicate several small vessels and two larger ones. When range by radar had decreased to about 9,000 yards the Senior Officer ordered the squadron by W/T to turn together to 280° and increase speed to 18 knots.
>
> When the range had closed to 4,000 yards *Charybdis* fired three star-shells from 'B' mounting over the target. I was on the bridge at this time, which I judge to be about 0145. Simultaneously two torpedo tracks were reported approaching the ship from the port side, and the Captain ordered 'Hard-a-port'. The ship was hit by one torpedo on the port side probably underneath the torpedo tube.
>
> I left the bridge and proceeded to the upper deck to take charge there. On my arrival the ship had a list of about 20°, increasing slowly. A few men were on the upper deck and I ordered them to cut loose the lashings

of timber, which had been stowed under the whalers. As I proceeded aft the ship was hit again by one torpedo on the port side at about 135 station. The approximate time of the hit was 0155. It did a lot of damage, which was apparent on deck. The after director was displaced and the deck was blown up aft. The list increased rapidly and soon put the deck under water on the port side as far as the break of the fo'c'sle. In about five minutes the list was approximately 50°.

At this time the ship was settling by the stern as well as increasing her list. I decided that nothing could be done to save the ship and gave orders to man the Carley rafts aft. There was no communication with the bridge. I could not get forward on the deck owing to the list and fell into the sea while climbing along the starboard side. When I had been in the water a few minutes I saw the ship suddenly take an angle by the stern until she was almost vertical.

Conduct of personnel on Carley rafts, float nets and in the water was good and singing was organized. Difficulty was experienced with the overcrowding of Carley rafts. I consider the rescuing destroyers did very well indeed; men from their crews frequently entered the water to assist in rescuing men who had become weak. I think that a good many men were drowned owing to the length of time of necessity spent in the cold water.

The Struggle to Save the *Limbourne* Commences

The *Limbourne* had been hit forward of the low power room; the damage was compounded when the forward magazine blew up. The whole of the forecastle was blown away forward of the CO's cabin and below the waterline from before the low power room. Despite the immense size of the detonation, the forward boiler room bulkhead held, and although the ship had a heavy list to starboard, all felt that she could be saved if her luck held. She still had steam on the main engines and was in no immediate danger of sinking. One steering motor was still in action. However the bridge steering gear, and all communications from the bridge were out of commission and this nullified early attempts at getting under way stern first.

Both the Commanding Officer and First Lieutenant were badly concussed by the explosion, and command devolved upon Sub-Lieutenant Cunliffe-Owen, who rose to the occasion magnificently. Steam was recovered and the link between the tiller flat and the engine room resumed. Hope was high that the ship might steam herself clear of the French coast which was, by dawn, clearly in sight only five miles away to the south. However, as later stated: '...repeated efforts failed to steady the ship on a course either stern first or bows first, and we succeeded only in turning in wide uncontrollable circles, which, if anything, seemed to be taking us nearer to the enemy's coast.'

It was unfortunate that despite all their efforts Sub-Lieutenant Cunliffe-Owen finally decided that he must get ready to abandon ship in case it proved necessary to scuttle her, lest she drift inshore and be taken by the Germans intact. The motor boat was topped up with fuel and lowered and the floats were made ready. At this time five destroyers were sighted and it was thought that the Germans had returned to finish off their good work, but in fact it was their companions, led by *Grenville*.

Subsequent Operations by British Survivors

In the intervening hours Lieutenant Commander Roger Hill had been striving to bring some semblance of order to the British force, once he realized that he was Senior Officer. After proceeding north to clear the chaos *Grenville* had *Talybont* and *Stevenstone* in company. *Wensleydale* had become separated, but later reported her position and they sailed to meet her. The time was 0250. Hill had assumed all along that the attackers had been German E-boats, which had sunk *Charybdis* and *Limbourne* and fully expected them to be lurking in the wrecks awaiting their chance to torpedo any ships, which appeared on a rescue mission. He therefore sent a signal to C-in-C, Plymouth:

> *Charybdis* and *Limbourne* hit by E-boat torpedoes. Consider both sunk. Heavy rain, *Talybont*, *Stevenstone* in company. As E-boats probably waiting by wrecks, should survivors be searched for? My position is now 030KK 10 miles. 0245.

Within half-an-hour both *Wensleydale* and *Rocket* had rejoined the flotilla, and *Stevenstone* reported the good news that *Limbourne* was still afloat. It was now 0315 hours and without waiting for any reply, Hill decided to return to the scene of the action, duly informing Plymouth of his intention:

> My position, course and speed, 0300KK 14, 270°, 15 knots. Propose searching for survivors at daylight. Request fighter protection. 0300. All five ships now in company. Am closing to search for survivors. My position, course and speed, 256KK13, 184°, 24 knots. 0323.

Back at Plymouth, the C-in-C was not at all clear whether or not the enemy convoy had escaped and at 0330 he duly signalled *Grenville*: 'Concentrate force and then sweep westwards in search of the enemy.' This signal reached *Grenville* just as they arrived back at the damaged *Limbourne*. *Talybont* was told to look after her while the other two Hunts were sent to search for *Charybdis*'s survivors. Taking *Rocket* under his wing, Lieutenant Commander Hill increased speed to twenty-four knots and swept westward. They continued for forty miles without a single blip appearing on their radar screens, and then returned to the rescue ships at about 0500

Talybont had taken on board the wounded and superfluous members of *Limbourne*'s crew and had taken *Limbourne* in tow, stern first. However, the drag caused by the wreckage proved too great and as the ship gathered speed, *Limbourne* took on a violent sheer and parted the tow. The second attempt was no more successful. Lieutenant Commander Hill, on his return, ordered that she be sunk after the rest of her crew had been taken off. *Grenville* and *Rocket* then joined the other two Hunts in searching for

Charybdis's survivors. They were pitifully few, after so long in the icy water. Despite delaying their departure until 0630 only four officers and 103 ratings, from a crew of 688, were found; Captain Voelcker was not among the survivors.

After embarking the rest of her crew, *Limbourne*'s engine room running down valves were opened and the after magazine flooded. She was then torpedoed by *Talybont*. Despite all this, the tough little ship still remained afloat; she was still floating three-quarters-of-an-hour later, her stern portion showing above water. *Rocket* put another torpedo into her at 0640 before departing for Plymouth, whereupon she finally sank.

The British force arrived back at Plymouth at 1000. There was no interference from the Germans, either during the rescue efforts or the return voyage, although they kept watch by radar the whole time.

German Observations and Subsequent Movements

For the Germans, the fight was over almost before it had begun. By 0150 they reported large fires and exploding ammunition amidships in their cruiser target, and some thought that she had broken in two. The Senior Officer of the 4th Flotilla reported that, when last seen, the cruiser target was listing with her stern below water. 'Enemy communicating by lamp: calcium flares and burning oil on surface; enemy evidently carrying out rescue operations.' In all, the action lasted seven minutes and all German destroyers except the *T-25* in the rear had fired full salvoes, twenty-four torpedoes in all.

By 0241 the surviving British ships were reported as withdrawing towards England; the intention to follow and attack was abandoned on account of very heavy rain, and there was some confusion concerning the whereabouts of a second enemy group reported. By 0324 the destroyers had rejoined the convoy and escorted it safely to Lezardrieux, the escorts finally anchoring in Dinard Roads at 0730. British photo reconnaissance the next day located the *Munsterland* at Lezardrieux and the five Elbings at St Malo.

Conclusions: Official and Unofficial

The C-in-C, Plymouth, commented that:

> The enemy destroyers were clearly well trained and drilled in night torpedo firing, and they succeeded in effecting the surprise on our forces which we had hoped to effect on them and their quick action in firing torpedoes had the effect of completely disorganizing our forces for sufficient time for them to make good their escape.
>
> It is also to be observed that the art of night fighting with the added new technique of radar has, up to date in this war, had very little opportunity of practical test, and in the Plymouth Command at all events, little opportunity of exercise.

Table 10: British warship losses in the Channel 1942-3

Name	Type	Date	Details
		1942	
Vimiera	Destroyer	9 Jan	Mined, Thames Estuary
Sona	Armed Yacht	4 Jan	Foundered off Start Point
Lord Snowdon	Trawler	13 Feb	Collision off Falmouth
Staghound	Distilling Ship	27 March	Bombed, Torquay
Campbeltown	Blockship	28 March	St Nazaire raid
Chorley	BDV	25 April	Foundered off Start Point
Tranquil	Drifter	16 June	Collision off Deal
Manor	Trawler	9 July	E-boats, Channel
Berkeley	Destroyer	19 Aug	Bombed, off Dieppe
Golden Sunbeam	Drifter	19 Aug	Collision off Dungeness
Waterfly	Trawler	17 Sept	Bombed, off Dungeness
Fernwood	Collier	18 Sept	Bombed, Dartmouth
Lord Stonehaven	Trawler	2 Oct	E-boats, off Eddystone
Inverclyde	Trawler	16 Oct	Sunk in tow off Beachy
Jasper	Trawler	1 Dec	E-boats, Channel
Penylan	Destroyer	3 Dec	E-boats, Channel
		1943	
Kingston	Trawler	12 Jan	Mined, Portsmouth
Lord Hailsham	Trawler	27 Feb	E-boats, Channel
Ut Prosim	Drifter	2 March	Gunfire, Dover Harbour
Caulonia	Trawler	31 March	Ran aground Rye Bay
Harstad	Whaler	27 Feb	E-boats, Channel
Eskdale	Destroyer	14 April	E-boats, off Lizard
Sargasso	Armed Yacht	6 June	Mined, off Isle of Wight
Zee Meeuw	Trawler	21 Sept	Collision, Gravesend
Ocean Retriever	Drifter	22 Sept	Mined, Thames Estuary
Charybdis	Light Cruiser	23 Oct	German destroyers,
Limbourne	Destroyer	23 Oct	German destroyers,
Lily	Auxilliary	25 Dec	Collision, Portland

He singled out the failure of the ships of Force 28 to exchange radar and intercept information during the approach, and the action of *Charybdis* in closing the enemy end on in view of the torpedo menace, as noteworthy mistakes. He also commented on the German tactics that:

> By their masterly use of this tactic against a superior force they reduced it to equality and threw it into confusion, thereby achieving their object – the safety of their convoy – without the necessity of firing a gun.

He recommended that future operations should be carried out against enemy surface convoys by a trained and adequately homogeneous force, and that this force should be composed of Tribal class destroyers with powerful gun armaments. In this the DTSD disagreed. He did *not* share the view:

> ...that the Tribal class would be ideal – partly because of their large silhouette and partly because of their weak torpedo armament; 'J' and 'K' Class destroyers which carry the greatest combined offensive armament

> of guns and tubes, would seem to be the most suitable. It is essential that the Senior Officer's ship should be fitted with 'Headache'.

This despite the fact that earlier efforts by the 'J' and 'K' class under Lord Mountbatten had been failures.

Argument concerning the best type of destroyer was irrelevant at the time, but later, when a powerful striking force was built up, it became a source of friction and argument between the staff and the senior officers afloat. 'Horses for courses' always applied. The 'B' class with powerful torpedo armaments had given way to the Hunt class when air attack had assumed a greater importance than surface attack. Now the reverse was true, but whether gun power or greater torpedo power was the solution, was still subject to debate.

Viewpoint from *Stevenstone*

The accounts of the captains of the 'Fleets' and the SO of the Hunts have been placed on record, as has the bland official statements on the matter. What the lower deck thought of this episode is recalled by one of *Stevenstone*' s crew:

> As we went slowly astern into the survivors, orders were shouted from the bridge to go for the largest groups as time was running out. Amongst the bobbing red lights and thick oil there was a Carley float containing about twenty men; to my surprise they were singing 'Roll out the Barrel'. As they realized that we had returned the singing turned to cheering. After pulling about twenty men up the scrambling net I noticed that the last person to leave the raft was an officer but I did not observe his rank. We managed to pick up about seventy-eight men and as dawn was breaking we retreated at speed. After asking for air support we were in sight of Eddystone Lighthouse before any aircraft were seen. The captain told us the following day that, in his opinion, it was a mistake to have included a cruiser and two fleet destroyers in our force for a typical Channel action. The four Hunts, i.e. *Limbourne*, *Talybont, Wensleydale* and *Stevenstone* could have successfully dealt with this situation on their own – with their experience of close encounters. Five hundred valuable lives lost in vain.

Chapter Sixteen

British Forces Take the Offensive

In the *Official History* for this period of the war,[1] three incorrect statements are made. It is stated that the Hunts carried no torpedoes; but many actually *did* carry torpedoes. It is stated that there were half-a-dozen of them; but there were more than double that number between Portsmouth and Plymouth. It is stated that there is no historical validity in the contemporary British description of the German destroyers as Narviks and Elbings; but then a very good reason why they were so named is given. Although the Germans themselves called the Elbings torpedo boats, just as in the First World War they had similarly called their destroyers torpedo boats, these ships were of the same size and armament as the British 'Fleets', while their Narvik's, or Z-classes, were twice the size of British destroyers and carried guns of light cruiser size. Therefore, contemporary British descriptions had perfect validity, and their practice has been continued in this book. Likewise, the Germans called their fast motor torpedo boats *Schnellboote*, or *S-boote*, and gave them an S prefix and number. British records termed them as E-boats, or Enemy motor torpedo boats and the name stuck; hence it is used here.

Whatever their correct designation, the German destroyers were efficient vessels with well trained and highly skilled crews. They worked in two well-drilled flotillas and suffered few losses despite their continuous employment on the doorsteps of the British premier naval bases, and within a stone's-throw of overwhelming British air power. Nonetheless, despite the fact that thousands of bombers were within very short range, hardly any German destroyers were sunk by air attack until the last months of the campaign in the Channel, and then most were already damaged or at anchor.

As 1943 turned to 1944, the humiliation of the *Charybdis* fiasco gave way to a more efficiently-organized countermeasures procedure, but it was not until a fully trained destroyer flotilla could be assembled and put to work that real results showed through. Then the lessons, so harshly learned and relearned, finally began to be applied, and the long immunity of the German surface forces in the Channel soon began to disappear. Before the full measure of the achievement could be appreciated, it was overshadowed by the greatest maritime event of the war: the British Army returned to the Continent four years after being expelled. It returned, just as it had left, by way of the Royal Navy, but the forces involved were vastly different and the huge assembly of fighting ships gathered for D-Day contrast very sharply with the meagre resources available to the surface forces for the previous four years. If even a fraction of the seven battleships, two monitors, twenty-three cruisers and 105 destroyers used that day had been raised earlier, the Channel could have been cleared long before.

Attack on Convoy CW221, 2-3 November 1943

The CW convoys, like the CE convoys in the opposite direction, had enjoyed a long period of immunity since the headline-dominating days of the summer of 1940. Three years of warfare had seen them drop into a routine with very few variations. The techniques were refined and made perfect, but such a long period without alarm or action resulted in surprise being achieved by the E-boats. Certainly no such attack had taken place in that area of the Channel since August 1941.

In all, some nine E-boats of the 5th Flotilla led by *Kommandeur* Klug took part: *S-100, S-112, S-136, S-138, S-139, S-140, S-141, S-142* and *S-143*. They caught CW221 off Hastings. The attack was well pressed home and between Dungeness and Beachy Head the night was once more aflame with conflict. No E-boats were sunk, even though they were engaged by the escorting destroyer *Whitshed* and some MGBs. By contrast, torpedo hits sent several of the convoy to the bottom. Sunk in this action were the *Dona Isabel* (1,179 tons), *Foam Queen* (9,811 tons) and *Storaa* (1,967 tons).

Further Work by the German 5th Flotilla

Nor was this the end of the work done by these vessels on the British side of the Channel. They returned on the night of 26 November with nine boats to lay a field of fifty-four mines off St Catherine's Point. Earlier, on 4 November, they torpedoed the tanker *British Progress* (4,581 tons) which, although she made port, had to be broken up. On the night of 1-2 December, they sortied from Cherbourg and hit another convoy off Beachy Head. The trawler *Adventure* became their latest victim when she was sunk by *S142*. The C-in-Cs of Portsmouth and Plymouth commented that the only way to halt such successes was the deployment of more destroyers than they had available to them. They pleaded in vain.

Thus when the 5th Flotilla resumed its offensive early in the New Year, it met with sparse defences and again struck some heavy blows without effective reply. On the night of 5-6 January 1944, seven boats of that flotilla, this time led by *Kapitänleutant* K. Muller, hit convoy WP457 off the Cornish coast. The escort, led by the destroyer *Mackay*, was swamped by no less than twenty-three torpedoes and the convoy lost the following vessels: *Polperro* (403 tons), *Underwood* (1,990 tons) and the trawler *Wallasea* (545 tons). A similar attack on a convoy off the Lizard on the night of 16 January was beaten off by the escorting destroyers.

Table 11: Typical Examples of Surface Warships Utilized in the Channel

Name	Type	Tonnage	*Knots* Speed	Principal Weapons
British				
Mauritius	Cruiser	8,526	32	Twelve 6-inch guns Eight 4-inch guns Six 21-inch TTs
Bellona	Cruiser	5,770	32	Eight 5.25-inch guns Six 21-inch TTs
Charybdis	AA Cruiser	5,450	33	Eight 4.5-inch guns Six 21-inch TTs
Newcastle	Cruiser	9,400	32	Twelve 6-inch guns Eight 4-inch guns Six 21-inch TTs
Galatea	Cruiser	5,220	33	Six 6-inch guns Eight 4-inch guns Six 21-inch TTs
Ulster	Destroyer	1,710	36	Four 4.7-inch guns Eight 21-inch TTs
Javelin	Destroyer	1,760	36	Six 4.7-inch guns Four 21-inch TTs
Tartar	Destroyer	1,870	36	Six 4.7-inch guns Two 4-inch guns Four 21-inch TTs
Fernie	Destroyer	907	26	Four 4-inch guns
Campbell	Destroyer	1,530	36	Three 4.7-inch guns Six 21-inch TTs
Wolsey	Destroyer	1,100	36	Four 4-inch guns
Sardonyx	Destroyer	905	37	One 4-inch gun
Halstead	Frigate	1,300	26	Three 3-inch guns
Halcyon	Minesweeper	815	16	One 4-inch gun
German				
Z-32	Destroyer	2,603	38	Five 5.9-inch guns Eight 21 in TTs
Z-26	Destroyer	2,603	38	Five 5.9-inch guns Eight 21-inch TTs
Karl Galster	Destroyer	2,411	38	Five Sin guns Eight 21in TTs
Richard Beitzen	Destroyer	2,232	38	Five Sin guns Eight 21-inch TTs
T-27	Destroyer	1,294	33	Four 4.1-inch guns Six 21-inch TTs
Jaguar	Destroyer	933	33	Three 4.1-inch guns Six 21-inch TTs
Falke	Destroyer	924	33	Three 4.1-inch guns Six 21-inch TTs
M-343	Minesweeper	543	17	Two 4.1-inch guns Two 21 in TTs

Success of British Long-Range Guns, 1943-44

It was during this period, however, that some unexpected successes were achieved by British forces and by those which had hitherto remained somewhat in the background. The big guns mounted around Dover had often ranged and fired upon German shipping creeping up and down the Channel, but had rarely achieved a hit, far less a sinking. Persistence and dedication was ultimately rewarded, when, on 2 March 1943 they sent a 2,382-ton ship to the bottom, followed by a second of 3,094 tons, on the night of 3-4 October 1943. But their greatest victory was achieved on 20 January 1944. The German supply ship *Munsterland* had been quite successful in keeping Armed Merchant Raiders active in 1943, but she needed to replenish in a German port. On 8 October 1943 she had arrived in the Gironde and sailed for Cherbourg, attempting to pass up-Channel in short stages, as usual, with a heavy escort of destroyers and light craft for each step. It was slow work, but by December she had reached Dieppe and on the first day of 1944 she had inched as far as Boulogne. The final and most dangerous stage lay ahead of her. Escorted by the destroyers *T-28* and *T-29*, *Munsterland* put to sea to pass the Dover Straits on the night of 20-21 January. The 6,408 ton vessel had, however, been closely watched and determined attempts were made to prevent her getting any further. It was the heavy batteries, which achieved this object. Let us therefore let Captain J. S. Walsham of the Royal Artillery describe this operation as he saw it.

Sinking of the *Munsterland*, 20 January 1944

Our only resounding success crept up on us imperceptibly. It started with a bit of 'Mess Scuttlebutt', in which those who were in a position to overhear conversations not meant for their ears, said that the Colonel had received a visit from the Intelligence people.

The Intelligence people, so the story went, had said that there were certain German captains who had been awarded the Iron Cross for taking vessels through the narrows between Calais and Boulogne. These Captains took the ship over at one port and piloted it through to the other, and that they relied on *our accuracy*! That gave us food for thought. Certainly in the days that followed there were a lot of plotting Officers conferences and all the old TFD tapes were re-examined. There were lots more drills on the miniature range. In the end they deduced from the tapes and drills that what was happening was as follows: – The Captain would take the ship out of harbour knowing that our radar sets would pick him up at once; he would know also that if the moon was down and visibility bad, Wanstone and South Foreland would engage him as soon as he came within range. He would then sail straight into the narrows keeping as close to the French coast as he could at the same time allowing himself room to manoeuvre.

Wanstone, with the longest range, would fire the first ranging salvo. Let us suppose that the radar sets, observing the fall of shot, with respect to a ship sailing Boulogne to Calais, reported that the salvo (two shells) was in line with the target but plus two hundred yards for range. The Captain would, too, observe that the shots were plus for range. He would do nothing, knowing full well that the next salvo would be minus two hundred yards and the Test Firing Distribution would be keeping the guns locked on to him if he kept his present course and speed. The Captain would continue to do nothing until he saw the flash of Wanstone firing the second salvo. He would then turn hard to starboard, i.e. towards the last fall of shot. Wanstone's corrected salvo was now in the air and would not arrive for another 90 seconds by which time he would be long gone. In fact the Captains, if they kept their nerve, could play this fox and geese game with both Wanstone and South Foreland, all of which accounted for our notable lack of success during the previous months.

What to do about it was the question. By the next dark of the moon, somebody, I cannot now remember who, possibly Major Edmunds, Wanstone's Commander, came up with the idea that if we were to use the 6-inch guns at Fan Bay to make flashes by firing blanks, we could confuse the Captains into turning towards our *next* fall of shot instead of the *last* one. Fan Bay battery was nearer to the edge of the cliff than Wanstone but observed from the sea it would appear almost in line with it.

Then we had a bit of luck, for according to RAF reconnaissance reports, a large vessel was working its way up the French coast from Brest. They even told us its name, the *Munsterlandt* [*sic*] and they estimated it at about 8,000-tons. We had a couple of days before it was the dark of the moon and during that time the whole Regiment perfected the drill they would use

It was almost with relief that we heard the 'Sea Alarm' go and the Tannoys begin their ritual chant, 'Observe hostile target moving left'. The ship behaved as usual by sailing straight into the narrows. We fired our opening salvo, then reloaded and waited about 45 seconds, which was our usual time to reload and fire again. During this period the radar made very careful fall of shot observations, so we knew which way she would turn if our theory were correct. Then Fan Bay fired a salvo of blanks to make a big flash. The target immediately started to turn towards the last fall of shot. Even as the real vessel was turning the plotting room was turning the model ship on the TFD onto the new course. The moment the turn ceased, with the guns laid onto a new future position, Wanstone and South Foreland fired. The vessel was now heading full speed into the future fall of shot, not the last one as the Captain expected; they were heading for a rendezvous with 1,800 - pounds of HE from Wanstone and 1,200-pounds from South Foreland. It worked! After the 4th or 5th salvos the plotting room made the unusual move of announcing over the Tannoys that the target appeared damaged and was steaming in a circle, then several salvoes later, 'Target stationary, echo fading, appears to be sinking. Cease fire!' and a little later still, 'Resume normal routine'.

Munsterland ran aground to the west of Cap Blanc Nez after being hit and further salvoes finished her off. Her destroyer escorts were attacked by two old biplanes of the Fleet Air Arm; even at this late stage of the war, the navy lacked real aircraft. Although they were not hit, *T28* was damaged by leaks in her boiler room. All in all, it was a very satisfactory night's work.

On the night of 20 March, the long-range guns were again on target, sinking the German tanker *Rekum* from the 'Hecht' convoy in the Straits.

Further E-boat Sorties, January-March 1944

The reinforced German E-boats continued to be the major threat in the first quarter of 1944, despite all that could be done against them. On the night of 31 Janury-1 February, for instance, they scored another success when the 5th Flotilla struck at CW243 off Beachy Head. *Albrighton* was the escorting destroyer and the E-boats came in four waves; the resulting combat being described by Douglas Clare later as 'a hectic night'. The net result however was that the convoy lost the merchant ships *Emerald* (806 tons) and *Caleb Sprague* (1,813 tons) as well as the escorting minesweeping trawler *Pine* (543 tons) while the Germans escaped scot-free.

Their relative immunity however was rapidly drawing to a close. More effort was being put into intercepting these raiders both by improved radar and stronger patrols. This policy. long overdue, soon began to bear fruit. On the night of 27-28 February a combined sortie by the 5th and 9th Flotillas against another CW convoy failed miserably, and two of the boats were damaged in a collision. The following night the same force, minus the two cripples, returned but once more a strong and alert defence caused them to abort the mission without any attack being made. The same thing happened on the night of 16-17 March off Lizard Head, and again two of the boats were damaged in a crash.

More alarming to the Germans was the determined efforts being made to engage and destroy them by strong surface forces patrolling from Plymouth. An attack by both E-boat flotillas against convoy WP492 to the north of Land's End found the convoy with the corvettes *Azalea* and *Primrose* for escorts. But a powerful force which had just been created was at sea in an attempt to intercept them. This consisted of the light cruiser *Bellona* and the big Tribal class destroyers *Ashanti* and *Tartar*. A second force, consisting of the Hunts *Brissenden* and *Melbreak* with several MTBs was also steering to cut them off. In the resulting battle, *S-143* was hit and sunk with the loss of her crew. This was the first time that the E-boats had been so seriously challenged; it was a sign that, at long last, sufficient ships, properly trained, and of the right type, were being made available to the surface forces in the Narrow Sea.

Action off Brittany, 5 February 1944

Another of the classic Hunt forays took place on the night of 5 February. A German force was surprised and attacked close inshore in the early hours of the morning. The enemy units were the destroyer *T-29* and the minesweepers *M-156* and *M-206*. The British force consisted of the destroyers *Tanatside, Talybont, Brissenden* (Lieutenant The Hon D. E. E. Vivian) and *Wensleydale*. They achieved complete surprise. In a brisk engagement before the enemy reached the safety of the coastal shoals *M-156* was badly damaged and, although she reached harbour, she fell an easy target to subsequent air strikes, which finished her off.

Force '26' and the 10th Destroyer Flotilla

After the *Charybdis* fiasco much hard thinking was done on how to counter the German destroyer tactics of firing torpedoes and running. Captain Basil Jones described the problems and the final British answers in his memoirs, thus:

> The enemy were skilled with torpedoes, and had permission to turn away, and a coast to run to. In an encounter of this sort, on a well-known 'tramline', the chances of encounter end-on or nearly end-on were the most probable. We had the duty to intercept the enemy and only the night to detect where he was along his route. It seemed that generally we must steam along that route but the formation in which to do so was questionable, and Line Ahead appeared vulnerable. The formation of a well-trained force was therefore put in hand, consisting of the cruisers *Bellona* and *Black Prince* and the newly-formed 10th Destroyer Flotilla.
>
> The force was fortunate in that all ships were equipped with revolving radar aerials and Plan Position Indicators, which enabled the whole scene of action to be presented continuously in their Plotting Rooms. The importance of this technical device cannot be over-emphasized, since it made feasible the adoption of new formations at night, the risk of mutual interference having led hitherto to Line Ahead being generally adopted.

The formation eventually chosen for this type of operation consisted of a sub-division of destroyers 1.5 miles 45° on each bow of the cruiser. The force would be manoeuvred into contact by the cruiser, who would then illuminate the enemy with her more powerful and long-range star-shells and release the destroyers to attack from either bow or quarter of the enemy. Continued illumination by the cruiser allowed all destroyers' guns to be used offensively, while the cruiser's own offensive and longer range guns would tend to slow down, if not destroy, the enemy until the destroyers were in close action. All three parts of the formation had greater freedom of action in avoiding the enemy torpedo attacks to be expected, and the radar equipment allowed continuous watch on all parts of the formation. The

Tribals had only one torpedo mounting, but had four 4.7-inch guns on their forecastles. In the main it was planned to bring the enemy into action with the gun.

These new formations and tactics soon brought positive results. Even prior to that, however, the Germans received some hard knocks early in 1944. It is important to remember that although this type of well-formed, well-ordered striking force was the ultimate answer, there always remained scope for individual ships to show their own particular skills in the intensive, close-range surface fighting of the Channel. Some would say that the crews themselves merited the reward of action by their skill and aggressiveness. The Polish destroyers were renowned for this, and many a Hunt veteran has stressed to the author that one was always quick to respond to any challenge from a Polish destroyer; they didn't ask twice before opening fire! The Free French Hunt *La Combattante* and the Canadian Tribal *Haida* had similar reputations.

Exploits of *La Combattante*

The former HMS *Haldon* was transferred to the Free French Navy on 15 December 1942 and her second captain, *Capitaine de Corvette* Andre Patou took command on 2 February 1943. She had a busy war, and in 1944 came into her own.

On the night of 19-20 April she was on patrol in company with the destroyer *Middleton* (Lieutenant J. N. D. Cox, DSC) south of Worthing. Visibility was extremely poor, but at 0350 on 20 April a report was received from coastal radar that E-boats were operating against a CW convoy off Beachy Head. In fact, it was the 5th and 9th Flotillas trying their luck once more, but they failed to find easy pickings. Instead they stumbled on a tiger. The two Hunts increased speed and, steering an interception course to the east of Beachy Head, *La Combattante* picked up blips on her radar screen at 0455 at a range of 1,500 metres. Six illumination flares were fired on that bearing, the enemy now having been identified as six distinct echoes moving at high speed. *La Combattante* increased speed and attempted to head them off. The German flotilla was retiring as fast as it could towards Calais with the Free French destroyer some 3,000 yards astern. But the enemy was faster than the Hunts. Further contacts were obtained but the E-boats were drawing away all the time, and each minute was bringing the destroyer closer to the waiting shore batteries and aircraft, with dawn not far away. At last, at 0608 *La Combattante* gave up the fruitless chase and, as the sky lightened, she rejoined *Middleton* at 0645. Both ships entered Plymouth at 0830. Although they were displeased because they had failed to catch their fleeing enemy, they had in fact caused that enemy to panic and one E-boat, *S 144*, ran herself aground in the hasty retreat so some damage was done.

The Frenchmen did not have to wait long for a second attack against these enemies, for on the night of 25-26 April the two E-boat units were out again and were detected in the same area. This time *La Combattante* was accompanied by the frigate *Rowley* (Lieutenant Commander F. J. G. Jones) and when the enemy was reported off Boulogne, both ships again steered to intercept. It was at 0200 that signals were received showing the enemy to be to the south-west of Beachy Head. This time they were caught. The action was later described thus:

> At 0146 the guns of the *Combattante* opened up. The range was about 1,500 yards but, at 0148, one of the E-boats was sunk. The track of one torpedo was seen by the *Combattante*, but she slowed down as she ran among the survivors of the E-boat. One man was picked up, and then another torpedo just missed the French vessel.
>
> The captain did not hesitate. Full speed ahead was ordered and an attempt was made to re-engage the other E-boats. The solitary German prisoner in the French warship led to a strange scene. He was young and could not get over the fact that he was a prisoner in French hands. He was taken to one of the mess decks and given some food. He had never seen such good bread apparently and it was not easy to persuade him that bread was unrationed in England.
>
> Before being taken to the interpreter's cabin the German asked for a comb and a mirror. There is no mirror in the mess so we led him to a big picture of General de Gaulle and in the reflection of this he combed his hair. As he did so, he said with some embarrassment, 'France is such a beautiful country'. There was a dead silence among us who knew it so much better than he did.

Their victim was the *S 147*. The post-war account (*Chronology of the War at Sea*, Vol 2, Rohwer & Hummelchen, translated into English) claim that the destroyers *Berkeley* and *Haldon* also took part in these actions, thus giving an impression of overwhelming force. However, *Berkeley* had been sunk two years earlier and *Haldon* was *La Combattante*'s former name!

Nor was the destruction of one enemy ship the end of the story. On the night of 12-13 May *La Combattante* was again on patrol as part of a line of destroyers and frigates stretched along the Channel south of the main convoy routes from St Catherine's Point in the west to Beachy Head in the east. This line consisted, from west to east, of the Greek corvette *Tombazis*, the British frigate *Stayner*, the British destroyer *Stevenstone*, the British frigate *Trollope*, the French destroyer *La Combattante* and the British corvette *Gentian*. Quite an Allied force, but of widely varying speeds, types and armaments, showing that not all the earlier lessons had been incorporated into action. The sea was flat calm, visibility fair; ideal E-boat weather. The boats of the same two E-boat flotillas arrived, prowling along the convoy routes along the south coast between Selsey Bill and Portsmouth. This time the patrol line was waiting for them and they could not penetrate it to get at the merchantmen. It was a frustrating time for the Germans.

La Combattante's radar detected the enemy at 10,000 yards range at 0030 and again she swung round on an interception course. Within a short period a force of four E-boats was made out and the French destroyer was rapidly in amongst them. An eyewitness recalled that:

> There were several E-boats this time. 'Action Stations' was sounded and three minutes later we let fly on all sides. The E-boats were surprised and tried to get out of range at full speed but after 12 minutes we saw that one of them was on fire and then there was an explosion. We chased the others right across the Channel.

The victim this time was the *S 147* and among those killed was *Leutnant* Klaus Dönitz, the Grand Admiral's second son to be lost in the war. This third victim of the French Hunt gave her an enviable reputation, but on her next engagement the outcome was less happy. On the night of 27-28 May, MTBs *732* and *739* were at sea in the same area as *La Combattante*. Two blips were picked up on her radar screen and, as no British small craft were known to be in that sector, the French ship opened fire, quickly hitting and disabling MTB-*732*, which subsequently sank.

Further Defeats of the E-boats, April-May 1944

Although the three boats destroyed by *La Combattante* were the only losses the enemy suffered at this period, time and time again the attacks on the British convoys, so uniformly successful a few months before, were barred and blocked by the destroyers, frigates and lesser escorts of the Royal Navy. It is beyond the scope of this book to detail each skirmish, but a brief summary of the period reads as follows:

12-13 April: 5th Flotilla from Cherbourg with six boats, attack aborted. 13-14 April: 5th and 9th Flotillas (thirteen boats) into Lyme Bay, beaten off. 14-15 April: 4th and 8th Flotillas (fifteen boats) for minelaying, aborted due to early detection.

18-19 April: 8th Flotilla (seven boats) driven off by destroyer *Whitshed* and two E-boats damaged.

18-19 April: 5th Flotilla (six boats) minelaying, driven off by destroyer *Middleton.*

19-20 April: 8th Flotilla, minelaying, aborted due to weather.

19-20 April: 5th and 9th Flotillas, (eleven boats) attack CW convoy, (see *La Combattante* section).

21-22 April: 5th Flotilla (five boats) attack WP convoy. Driven off by *Middleton* and *Volunteer*, one boat damaged.

23-24 April: 4th and 8th Flotillas (eleven boats) off south-east coast, driven off.

23-24 April: 5th Flotilla (six boats) attacks a CW convoy off Dungeness. *S-100* (*Kommandeur* von Nurbach) sinks the tug *Roode Zee*.

23-24 April: 9th Flotilla (nine boats) intercepted off Hastings by *Stevenstone* and *Volunteer*. Driven off.

24-25 April: 5th and 9th Flotillas (six boats). (See *La Combattante* section).

The E-boats' solitary success was on the night of 27-28 April when the 5th and 9th Flotillas (nine boats) sailed from Cherbourg to attack a convoy reported off Selsey Bill. By a cruel chance they happened instead on a convoy of American LSTs on their way to Devon to participate in a rehearsal for D-Day. The only escorts allocated to guard these valuable ships were the destroyer *Saladin* and the corvette *Azalea*. *Saladin* had been involved in a collision earlier and had to go to Plymouth for inspection. No replacement was sent for her and thus the solitary corvette offered little protection when the E-boats swarmed on to the slow landing craft just as they were entering Lyme Bay. Torpedoes struck many vessels; two sank (LST-507 and *LST-531*) and another, *LST-289*, was damaged. Loss of life was tragic; 197 seamen and 441 soldiers died. Subsequent action did little good, for although the destroyers *Onslow*, *Obedient*, *Ursa*, *Piorun* and *Blyskawica* were dispatched and chased the enemy across the Channel, they were unable to sink any of their ships in reply.

It is ironic that, at a time when the E-boats were suffering setback after setback, a single chance encounter should reward them with their greatest victory since Dunkirk.

Action off the Isle de Bas, 26 April 1944

On the night of 25 April the four destroyers of the 4th TB Flotilla under *Kommandeur* Kohlauf with *T-29*, *T-24* and *T-27*, sailed from St Malo to carry out a defensive minelaying operation off Les Sept Isles and then proceed to Brest. In the early hours of 26 April they sighted a large formation of ships on their radar screens and turned about to run for safety, but they were too late.

The ships they had picked up were those of Force 26. This consisted of the light cruiser *Black Prince* (Captain D. M. Lees, DSO), and the Tribals *Ashanti* (Lieutenant Commander J. R. Barnes), *Athabaskan* (Lieutenant Commander J. H. Stubbs, DSO, RCN), *Haida* (Commander H. C. de Wolf, RCN), and *Huron* (Lieutenant Commander H. S. Rayner, DSC, RCN). For this operation the new dispositions were being tried, and thus one subdivision, *Ashanti* and *Huron* were on the cruiser's port bow and the other subdivision to starboard, with the whole force sweeping from west to east as always. At the end of their sweep, the German radar ashore picked them up and the batteries of the Isle de Bas opened fire on them, but without effect.

Aboard the Allied ships it was feared that this premature sighting would mean that no further contact would be made. At 0130 the whole force turned course to 070 degrees and began to sweep back eastwards. At 0200

Black Prince received radar echoes right ahead and within a short time confirmed these as enemy vessels at a range of 18,000 yards. As usual the Germans fired their torpedoes, put about, laid smoke and withdrew towards the safety of their own minefields. The Allied group pursued them steadily and by 0220 the range had come down to 11,000 yards. *Black Prince* illuminated her target with star shell from her 'B' turret, after moving safely out of the way. She then released the destroyers to follow up while her forward 5.25-inch guns took up a long-range bombardment of the enemy.

With range reduced to 10,900 yards *Athabaskan* and *Haida* also joined in with their forward 4.7-inch guns and soon afterwards the remaining Tribals joined in the general gun attack. The approach of enemy torpedoes was expected and the new flexible formation allowed *Black Prince* to take avoiding action and not share the fate of *Charybdis*. She maintained a steady fire while the destroyers closed with the enemy, until her forward turret jammed and she withdrew from the action, leaving the Tribals to finish the job.

This they were quite willing to do, if the enemy could be caught. With *Black Prince* gone, the two sub-divisions provided their own illumination with *Ashanti* firing star shells for *Huron*, who was leading the formation; *Athabaskan* provided the same service for *Haida*. Their fire was quite effective and the Germans had little in way of reply. 'No matter how we twisted and turned the salvoes always straddled us', was the comment of one German survivor. The German flotilla leader tired of all this, and attempted to obtain some relief by doubling back, but *Haida* and *Athabaskan* concentrated their fire on her while the other two Tribals kept up the pursuit of the remaining two Elbings, one of which, the *T-27*, had been badly hit early on and was attempting to reach Morlaix.

Destruction of *T-29*

At 0420, following further salvoes, the *T-29* rolled over to port and went down. She took with her *Kommandeur* Kohlauf, as well as her CO, *Kapitänleutnant* Grund, and 135 men; seventy-three were later picked up by German patrol craft.

Of the other German destroyers, *T-27* had been heavily hit aft; her engine room and upperworks were badly knocked about and hits were scored on her rear gun mountings. *T-24* was also hit and one of her guns, all her W/T equipment and other communication put out of action; she had taken fourteen casualties before she escaped. In their own report the Germans stated that the new British dispositions were effective: 'The British ships, in complete comfort, were hacking us to bits. His oblique position astern made him invulnerable to torpedo attacks.'

On their part, the Allied force escaped almost without damage; the only reply taken was by the destroyers when they imprudently closed in on the sinking *T-29* and were fired on by short-range weapons before they finished her off in retaliation. Further damage was done in this complicated high-speed action when the two divisions became entangled. *Huron* crossed the bows of *Ashanti*, which was forced to take drastic avoiding action; one engine was put to full ahead, the other to full astern, to drag her round to avoid a collision. In so doing, this danger was averted, but *Huron* was still struck amidships. The damage, which could have been final, was thus reduced, but her bow was split with a nineteen-foot gash from her stem. She was still, however, capable of high-speed steaming and the four destroyers returned to Plymouth at twenty-five knots.

Haida's damage was limited to splinter holes through the hull and 'X' gun deck, while the Sick Bay and Captain's day cabin had also been damaged, but only minor injuries were caused. *Ashanti*'s damaged bows were repaired by 27 May, in time for D-Day. Short-range gunfire had killed one man aboard *Huron* and wounded others, hits being taken on the stokers' mess deck and the pom-pom mounting. Her hull damage from collision with the *Ashanti* was quickly repaired so that she too was ready by 27 May. *Athabaskan* was unscathed.

It was a neat action and a foretaste of things to come. It had taken four years to break the supremacy of the German destroyers in the Channel, but now the British were firmly on the offensive. Nor did the pressure ease. The British group, although brilliantly successful on their first mission, were still relatively untried. The Germans had experience and were far from easy to defeat. They were soon to gain more than ample revenge for this defeat.

Destruction of the *Athabaskan*, 28-29 April 1944

It was known that *T-24* and *T-27* were sheltering in a damaged state in the port of Morlaix. They could not remain confined there forever, and it was expected that as soon as it was possible they would make a dash for Brest and enter the dockyard there. Constant watch was therefore kept on them. Meanwhile, of the Tribals only *Athabaskan* and *Haida* were available, thanks to damage. These two destroyers were out on patrol, providing cover for coastal forces employed in laying mines off the Isle de Bas on the evening of 28 April, when word came that radar contact had been made. The two German destroyers were out and racing for the safety of Brest, so the two Canadian Tribals were immediately ordered to intercept. At 0400 on the morning of 29 April, off the port of St Brieux, they caught up with them, and *Haida* commenced the action by firing star shell twelve minutes later.

The response of the two German destroyers was exactly as it had always been; they altered course, fired a full salvo of torpedoes each and continued at full speed. The Allied force fell for it; of the twelve torpedoes fired by the German ships nine went astray, but three remained on course and of these three one scored a direct hit on *Athabaskan* at 0417. It detonated in her gearing room, just aft of amidships. It was not a large compartment, like an engine room or boiler room, and although the damage was extensive it need not necessarily have been fatal.

Aboard the stricken ship, the deck above where the torpedo had hit, and the adjacent deckhouse, had collapsed, causing 'Y' mounting to collapse also. Her steering gear was wrecked and her propellers stopped; for a time she was carried along in the wake of *Haida* by her own momentum. The after pumps ceased to function and the fires spread rapidly aft making the after steering position untenable as well. Steadily she began to settle by the stern. Forward preparations were being made to have her taken in tow, but the seriousness of her damage overtook this and her boats were hoisted out.

By 0430 the raging fires had reached the after magazine of 'Y' gun, the twin 4-inch HA mounting above the blast. The results were final and devastating. The order to 'Abandon Ship' was given and *Athabaskan* finally went down at 0442. The survivors took to the water. *Haida* and the enemy had vanished into the night.

Table 12: Analysis of Torpedo firings during Channel Surface Actions 1943-4

Date	British Forces	Torpedoes carried	Potential firings	Actual firings	Hits	German Forces	German sunk	British sunk
9-10 July 1943	*Melbreak* *Wensleydale* *Glaisdale*	6	6	3	1	*T-24, T-25, M-9, M10, M-12, M-84 & M-135*	*M-135*	
3-4 Oct 1943	*Grenville* *Ulster* *Limbourne* *Tanatside* *Wensleydale*	22	16	16	-	T-22, T-23, T-25, T-26, & T-27		
22-23 Oct 1943	*Charybdis* *Grenville* *Rocket* *Limbourne* *Talybont* *Stevenstone* *Wensleydale*	30	27			T-22, T-23, T-25, T-26 & T-27		*Charybdis* *Limbourne*
5 Feb 1944	*Talybont* *Brissenden* *Tanatside* *Wensleydale*	9	9					
25-26 April 1944	*Black Prince* *Ashanti* *Haida* *Athabaskan* *Huron*	22	16	16		T-24, T-27 & T-29	T-29	
28-29 April 1944	*Haida* *Athabaskan*	8	8		-	T-24 & T-27	T-27	*Athabaskan*
8-9 June 1944	*Tartar* *Ashanti* *Huron* *Haida* *Eskimo* *Javelin* *Blyskawica* *Piorun*	41	32	14	2	Z-24, Z-32, ZH-1 & T-24	ZH-1 Z-32	
	Ursa *Glaisdale* *Krakowiak*	12	12	-	-	& T-28		

12-13 June 1944	*Scorpion* *Stord*	16	-	-	-	*Mowe, T-28*	
14-15 June 1944	*Ashanti* *Piorun*	9	9	5	1	*M-343, M-412, M-422* *M-432, M-442, M452*	*M-343*
27-28 June 1944	*Eskimo* *Huron*	8	-	-	-	*M-4611, V-213*	*M-4611*
7-8 July 1944	*Tartar* *Huron*	8	-	-	-	*M-4601, M-4605*	*M-4601* *M-4605*
14-15 July 1944	*Tartar* *Huron* *Blyskawica*	16	-	-	-	*UJ-1420, UJ-1421*	*UJ-1420* *UJ-1421*
4-5 Aug 1944	*Bellona* *Tartar* *Ashanti* *Haida* *Iroquois*	34	-	-	-	*Hother Weg, Otto.* *M-263, M-486, V-414*	All
12 Aug 1944	*Albrighton* *Assiniboine* *Qu'Appelle* *Skeena* *Restigouche*	18	-	-	-	*UJ-* *UJ-* *UJ-*	
12 Aug 1944	*Diadem* *Onslow* *Piorun*	24	-	-	-	*Sperrbrecher 7*	All
14-15 Aug 1944	*Mauritius* *Ursa* *Iroquois*	28	-	-	-	*Richthofen, T-24* *M-385*	*M-385*
22-23 Aug 1944	*Mauritius* *Ursa* *Iroquois*	28	-	-	-	*V-702, V-717* *V-720, V-729, V-730*	All

The Destruction of *T-27*

When her sister ship had been struck, *Haida* had pressed on after the enemy, in spite of the fact that the odds were now heavily against her. Both of her forward guns were firing at the fastest possible rate and she soon registered hits on both retreating enemy destroyers. In desperation, the two German ships parted company; both were damaged. Commander de Wolf decided to go for *T-27*, which appeared to be the most badly damaged and seemed to be slowing down. Further hits were made on this unfortunate ship and in desperation she swung closer and closer inshore to seek refuge amongst the reefs and rocks of the French coast. This proved to be her ultimate undoing, for she ran hard aground at full speed. At the same time, large fires spread to one of her magazines, which ignited in the same ghastly manner as had the Canadian destroyer's earlier. Completely out of control, *T-27* struck the rocky ledge off the Ile de Vierge and stuck fast, still ablaze. *Haida* pumped a few more shells into her hull and then, fearing that she might also run aground, she pulled out and sped off to seek survivors from *Athabaskan*.

At 0450 they found the spot, with dawn not far off and the hostile coast within five miles. Time was running out, but they made one attempt to pick up survivors. *Haida* lowered her motor boat and an empty lifeboat, as well as lifebuoys and Carley floats. Scrambling nets were rigged alongside and *Haida* drifted in among the clumps of men in the dark water. Heartbreaking work followed; as usual, many men were too badly burned or too exhausted to help themselves; others were on the wrong side of the rescue ship and the current swept them away despite all their efforts. Others were too weak to get onboard; two were swept into the churning blades of *Haida*'s propellers. Typical of their stoical acceptance of their fate is the account given of *Athabaskan*'s captain, Lieutenant Commander J. H. Stubbs, DSO, RCN:

> On the port side a raft had come alongside in the final minutes. There were officers and men in it and others in the water clinging to the lifelines. 'Quickly now', said a voice on deck, 'the ship's getting ready to go'. 'Take the wounded first' said the men on the raft, and the wounded were helped out. It was slow work for they could not help themselves. Many were burned. The last of them was just coming up when the ship started sinking by the head. She went very slowly at first, and the men on the nets worked desperately to get the survivors inboard. From somewhere at the back of the raft a voice was heard to call, 'Get away *Haida*, get clear'. A sailor said it was the voice of the young captain of the *Athabaskan*. Other survivors said he had swum to a raft and rested his arms on it, as if they were burned, and had encouraged them to sing.

In all *Haida* rescued some forty-two survivors. Later *T-24* returned with two minesweepers and they rescued another eighty-three. Three men in *Haida*'s motor boat rescued another seven men and headed for England. They were finally rescued when a motor launch found them and towed them into Falmouth. But 128 were lost, including her captain.

The wreck of *T-27* was finished off some time later by a trio of MTBs. *T-24* continued to have a charmed life. In addition to the gunfire damage she had touched off a ground mine during her flight, which damaged her hull underwater, but for a time she was safe. It was her salvo of torpedoes, which the Germans credited with the destruction of *Athabaskan*.

Further German Losses Prior to D-Day: May 1944

Despite constant patrolling by the 10th Flotilla in the few remaining weeks prior to D-Day no further surface actions of this nature took place. Small-scale skirmishing continued, mainly of escorts against E-boats, which resulted in only minor damage to the enemy. The most noteworthy of these was a minelaying sortie by six E-boats of the 9th Flotilla, which laid mines west of Beachy Head on 23-24 May, while five more from the 5th Flotilla carried out a similar operation south of the Isle of Wight. The latter group was caught by surprise by the destroyer *Vanquisher* (Lieutenant Commander F. M. Osborne, RANVR), part of the escort from convoy WP526. She engaged the E-boats briskly and scored hits on the *S-112*, driving the rest off.

Heavier damage was suffered by the German destroyers when they moved through the Channel to change bases from Brest to Cherbourg during that month: On 20 May *Jaguar* and *T-24* left the former port but only *Jaguar* arrived, *T-24* again being damaged by a ground mine and laid up once more. On the night of 24-25 May, the *Falke*, *Greif*, *Kondor* and *Möwe* along with several large minesweepers took the same route to Le Havre. An attack by fighter bombers sank the *Greif* en route and *Kondor* and *M-84* were both badly damaged by mines. Their morale was already at a low ebb when the invasion fleet sailed.

D-Day, 6 June 1944

After a false start, Operation *Neptune* took place on 6 June 1944 and the Allied armies returned to the coast of France. A huge armada of ships carried them and an enormous fleet of warships protected them, guarding their flanks against destroyer, E-boat, submarine and air attack. An even larger force of warships, from battleships and cruisers down to destroyers, frigates and MTBs, cruised off the beach-heads to provide covering fire.

We can only concern ourselves here with a fraction of that mighty array, which deserves a book to itself. Table 12 gives the list of the principal British warships involved in the bombarding fleet, but in addition to these a whole host of British warships was involved in the many subsidiary facets of this mighty achievement. Many warships of our Allies were also present, most of them American.

Two groups of escorts were escorting the 'follow-up' wave after the initial landings. In the west was Force 'B' under Commodore Edgar, which included the British destroyers *Boadicea, Brissenden, Vimy, Volunteer, Wensleydale* and corvettes *Azalea* and *Bluebell* as well as American and Canadian ships. In the east was Force 'L' under Rear Admiral Parry, including the British destroyers *Cotswold* and *Vivacious*, the frigates *Chelmer* and *Halstead* and the corvettes *Clematis, Godetia, Narcissus* and *Oxlip*.

Two powerful destroyer flotillas guarded the Channel flanks. The west was protected by the 10th Flotilla with *Tartar, Ashanti, Eskimo, Javelin*, the Canadian *Haida* and *Huron* and the Polish *Blyskawica* and *Piorun*. In the east the 17th Flotilla performed the same function with *Onslow, Onslaught, Offa, Oribi, Obedient, Orwell, Impulsive* and *Isis*. Attached to each of these flotillas were groups of smaller vessels and coastal craft by the score.

The British ships used to escort the many convoys to and from the bridgehead included the following destroyers: *Beagle, Bulldog, Campbell, Icarus, Mackay, Montrose, Skate, Saladin, Sardonyx, Vanquisher, Versatile, Walpole, Wanderer, Walker, Westcott, Windsor, Wrestler, Kimberley, Opportune, Pathfinder, Cattistock, Eglington, Avonvale, Belvoir, Garth, Goathland, Holderness* and *Meynell*. The frigates included: *Cubitt, Dakins, Deveron, Ekins, Holmes, Lawford, Nene, Retalick, Stayner* and *Thornborough*. The sloops were: *Hart, Kite, Lapwing, Lark, Magpie,*

Pheasant, Scarborough and *Rochester*. The corvettes: *Armeria, Balsam, Burdock, Buttercup, Campanula, Celandine, Dianthus, Gentian, Heather, Honeysuckle, Lavender, Nasturtium, Pennywort, Primrose, Puffin, Starwort, Sunflower, Wallflower* and many Allied and Commonwealth ships of the same type.

The D-Day Bombardments: An Eyewitness Account

For the ships undertaking bombardment, D-Day operations started early. For example, the battleship *Warspite* (Captain M. H .A. Kelsey) recorded sighting the swept channel marker buoy leading to her force's bombardment area at 0120 on the morning of 6 June. She led in a line which consisted of the battleship *Ramillies* (Captain G .B. Middleton, CBE, ADC); the monitor *Roberts* (Captain R. E. C. Dunbar); and the cruisers *Mauritius* (Captain W. W. Davis, DSO), *Arethusa* (Captain L Dalrymple-Smith), *Frobisher* (Captain J. F. W. Mudford), *Danae* (Captain J. R. S. Haines), and the Polish-manned *Dragon*, all under the command of Rear Admiral W. R. Patterson. By 0525 *Warspite* herself had arrived at her correct position, some eleven miles west of Le Havre; she fired almost immediately upon one of her main targets, the shore battery at Benerville. Five minutes later the fire became general along the whole line as every warship strung out across the bay opened fire with their main armament. It was an awesome moment. Fifteen minutes later, *Warspite* was engaged with Benerville again and so it continued throughout the day.

Commander Kenneth Edwards gave some of the background details behind the success of the British warship bombardments, and also tells of some of the problems that beset them:

> The British bombarding squadron had been assembled in the Clyde area, where it had received some special bombarding training before sailing south to the invasion. The postponement of D-Day owing to the weather was particularly trying to the ships' companies of this squadron. The ships had to sail from the Clyde three days before the originally selected D-Day in order to reach their appointed stations off the Normandy beaches at the correct time. They had therefore been at sea for two days when the postponement signal was received. In order to waste the twenty-four hours and at the same time keep the right distance from Normandy in case the invasion was 'laid on' the following day, the bombarding squadron had to turn north for twelve hours and then turn south again. While it was carrying out these time-wasting manoeuvres it ran into a convoy in a fog, but fortunately there were no mishaps.
>
> The bombarding forces duly reached their correct positions between 5 a.m. and 5.15 a.m. on D-Day and the ships opened fire shortly afterwards, using aircraft spotting provided by the specially trained pilots from Lee-on-the-Solent. For this initial phase of the bombardment one ship had been allocated to deal with each big battery. The ships were

therefore working on pre-selected targets, but they also had a degree of freedom of action in that alternative targets had been earmarked, and they were also allowed to engage targets of opportunity as these presented themselves.

It very soon became obvious that, apart from being temporarily silenced because their crews were forced to take to their deep shelters, the big batteries at Le Havre were proving themselves virtually untouchable by air or sea bombardment. These batteries gave their attention chiefly to the bombarding ships, and the gunnery officer of one of the bombarding ships afterwards said that the virtual immunity of the Le Havre batteries, 'gave us deep concern, and seemed to assume a great significance in our lives'.

The truth of the matter was that the batteries had been protected by more and more reinforced concrete and nothing short of a direct hit on the gun barrel or a shell through the opening of the casemate could do them any permanent damage, and both of these eventualities demanded flukes rather than gunnery skill.

The Main Bombardment – Seen from a Destroyer's Bridge

Lieutenant Commander William Donald commanded the destroyer *Ulster* during D-Day and he has left a graphic account of how he viewed the landings that morning:

> For one hour and ten minutes we fired without ceasing, in one long, magnificent and exhilarating roar. At intervals throughout, the signalman touched my sleeve and held up a signal for me to read. Halfway through, he showed me one that has been made many times in British Naval history ... 'Engage The Enemy More Closely'.
>
> At that signal all the destroyers weighed anchor, and moved closer inshore, each one led by their own individual minesweeper in a single combined line. We were firing as fast as we could now, almost point-blank at the shore defences. The assault craft, full of soldiers, were passing us on their way into the assault; we could see the men in them, crouched down ready to spring ashore. In one boat a man was standing up playing the bagpipes.
>
> For five minutes, just ahead of them and just before they landed there was a tremendous shower of rockets onto the nearby beach defences from craft specially designed to fire them, and then on 'Gold' beach, at half past six on that June morning, in the centre sectors of that great assault, the British armies returned to France. One of the greatest moments in history – one the whole free world was waiting for – had arrived at last.
>
> From the bridge of the *Ulster*, we had a grandstand view of the whole proceeding, and it was a magnificent and impressive sight. We ceased firing just then, and moved out to seaward to await the air attacks that never came.

Table 13: D-Day 6 June 1944. The British Covering Fleet

Type	Name	Assignment
Battleships		Bombardment reserve,
	Rodney	Bombardment reserve, East
	Warspite	Bombardment Sword beach
	Ramillies	Bombardment Sword beach
Cruisers	*Scylla*	Flagship Eastern Task
	Bellona	Bombardment reserve,
	Argonaut	Bombardment Gold beach
	Orion	Bombardment Gold beach
	Ajax	Bombardment Gold beach
	Emerald	Bombardment Gold beach
	Belfast	Bombardment Juno beach
		Bombardment Juno beach
	Arethusa	Bombardment Sword beach
	Mauritius	Bombardment Sword beach
	Frobisher	Bombardment Sword beach
	Danae	Bombardment Sword beach
	Dragon (Polish crew)	Bombardment Sword beach
	Sirius	Bombardment reserve, East
	Black Prince	Bombardment Utah beach
	Enterprise	Bombardment Utah beach
	Hawkins	Bombardment Utah beach
	Glasgow	Bombardment Omaha
	Capetown	Escort Groups
	Ceres	Escort Groups
	Despatch	Escort Groups
Monitors	*Roberts*	Bombardment Sword beach
	Erebus	Bombardment Utah beach
Destroyers		Bombardment Gold beach
	Ulster	Bombardment Gold beach
	Ulysses	Bombardment Gold beach
	Undaunted	Bombardment Gold beach
	Undine	Bombardment Gold beach
	Urania	Bombardment Gold beach
	Urchin	Bombardment Gold beach
		Bombardment Gold beach
	Jervis	Bombardment Gold beach
	Cattistock	Bombardment Gold beach
	Cottesmore	Bombardment Gold beach
	Pytchley	Bombardment Gold beach
	Faulknor	Bombardment Juno beach
	Fury	Bombardment Juno beach
	Kempenfelt	Bombardment Juno beach
	Venus	Bombardment Juno beach
	Vigilant	Bombardment Juno beach
	Bleasdale	Bombardment Juno beach
	Stevenstone	Bombardment Juno beach
	Saumarez	Bombardment Sword beach
	Scorpion	Bombardment Sword beach
	Scourge	Bombardment Sword beach
	Serapis	Bombardment Sword beach
	Swift	Bombardment Sword beach
	Verulam	Bombardment Sword beach
	Virago	Bombardment Sword beach
	Kelvin	Bombardment Sword beach

Muted German Response

The German counter-fire, which was expected to be heavy, hardly materialized to any great degree. The *Luftwaffe* failed to put in an appearance and the German E-boats and submarines failed to make any impression at all. A few of the big ships had near misses from German shells, but no great German response took place and by 0930 most of the enemy guns were silent. The officers aboard the bombarding ships, facing the much-vaunted 'West Wall', found this rather puzzling. One officer aboard the cruiser *Mauritius* was later quoted as stating that the whole episode was a 'crushing anticlimax'.

What of the German destroyer flotillas based at Le Havre? They had a magnificent opportunity, as dozens of huge vessels were anchored a few miles from their base. It was a chance to do or die for the Fatherland. Much was expected, but little resulted. Shortly after the bombardment commenced, there was a flurry of activity. A large smokescreen obscured the port from British ships, and at 0600 that morning the bows of several German destroyers suddenly appeared through the smoke. The great gun turrets of the battleships swivelled round and engaged. Abruptly the enemy vanished again, leaving patrol vessel *V-1506* smashed up and sinking from a direct hit with a 15-inch shell from *Warspite*. The 5th TB flotilla, consisting of the *T-28, Jaguar* and *Möwe*,[2] under *Kommandeur* Hoffmann, had made this brief sortie. An attack by an Allied fighter-bomber put two of the torpedo tubes carried by *T-28* out of action but she carried on. An incident called by one German historian 'ineffective' and which contemporary British eyewitnesses described as appearing to be 'more in the nature of a German mistake than a planned attack' was as follows. Three German destroyers burst out of the smoke and were heavily engaged almost at once. No sooner had they sighted the vast phalanx of shipping before them than their nerve failed them and they abruptly turned about and headed back into port, firing their usual full salvo of torpedoes as they went, convinced that no matter where the torpedoes went, they must hit something and hoping for the best that it might be a large ship. They almost got their wish, for there were a number of near misses as the sixteen torpedoes sped into the crowded roadstead.

At least two torpedoes were visible as they passed between *Ramillies* and *Warspite*. A third was only avoided by the command ship *Largs*, with Rear Admiral A. G. Talbot aboard, as she put her engines to full speed astern. The torpedo passed across her bows a few feet ahead and stopped close to the destroyer *Virago* (Lieutenant Commander A. J. R. White) before sinking into the depths at the end of its run. The only success was achieved by the fourth torpedo sighted, which by pure chance hit the Norwegian destroyer *Svenner*. Although at the extreme limit of its range, it hit with enough force to be fatal, striking in the destroyer's most vital area; amidships in one boiler room. Contemporary accounts state that her midships portion jumped out of the water, her funnel collapsed and she crumpled up in a cloud of steam, breaking her back and sinking rapidly. This was the enemy's only success, apart from the mining of the destroyer *Wrestler* (Lieutenant R. W. B. Bacon). She managed to reach harbour but it was decided to pay her off as being beyond economic repair. On 20 July she was sold to the shipbreaking firm of Cashmore and was towed to their yard at Newport on 15 August. A sad fate for a ship whose fighting record since her completion some twenty-six years earlier had been impressive, and had included some good work in the North Atlantic, the Mediterranean on Malta convoys, the North African and Sicilian landings, the Arctic convoys, and whose record included the confirmed destruction of no fewer than three enemy submarines.

Work of the German Torpedo Boats – a French Viewpoint

A different take on the German torpedo boats' effectiveness was given to the author by historian Pierre Hervieux, an old friend, who was born and lived at Le Havre. He disagreed that they were ineffectual:

> On 6th June they sailed through the harbour jetties at 0442. Both the *Jaguar* and *Möwe* fired six torpedoes each, at a range of 6,500 metres, while the *T-28* fired four. One of these scored a hit on the brand-new destroyer *Svenner* (former HMS *Shark*) and sank her. She had never fired her guns in action. Their attack was a very coordinated one against tremendous odds as the three torpedo boats, two of which dated back to 1929, faced the battleships *Warspite* and *Ramillies*, the monitor *Roberts*, six cruisers and three destroyers! Nobody will deny that the spirit that led to this attack and the way it was accomplished would be an honour to any Navy.
>
> They made further attacks:
> 6-7 June *Jaguar* and *Möwe*
> 8-9 June *Jaguar*, *Möwe* and *T-28*
> 9-10 June *Jaguar, Möwe* and *T-28*
> 12-13 June *Jaguar, Möwe, Falke* and *T-28*
>
> But they could not get through the defences at the assembled transports. The Le Havre boats fought against the biggest invasion fleet of all times and they did it against hopeless odds.[3]

Pierre offered this comparison of the German attack on 6 June, with previous British destroyer torpedo actions.

Table 14 British Destroyer Torpedo Attacks Compared with the 6-6-44 German Attack

Date	Torpedoes Carried	Potential Firings	Actual Firings	Hits
12 February 1942	27	27	27	0
4 October 1943	22	16	16	0
26 April 1944	22	16	16	0
6 June 1944	18	16	16	1

But of course, although Pierre has a point, he does admit that, whereas the British were trying to hit high-speed targets taking avoiding action with their attacks, the German torpedo boats has a huge mass of shipping, hundreds of targets, most of them stationary and nose-in to the beaches at right-angles, almost a solid wall of shipping. It would be hard to fire a torpedo into that mass even at long range with your eyes shut, and not hit something; in fact it was probably easier to score a hit under such conditions than miss!

Bombardment Work Continues: 6 June 1944

Throughout the rest of the day precision bombardments of fixed batteries and mobile guns, which the Germans quickly brought up in support, continued to occupy the majority of the larger vessels while the destroyers, remaining close inshore, engaged targets as they appeared, close in advance of the troops ashore. *Warspite* and *Ramillies* were constantly in action, for although their main targets had been silenced by 0930 they reopened fire occasionally throughout the day and had to be engaged afresh. Thus *Warspite* was repeatedly in action with her main armament against the heavily-fortified batteries of Benerville and Villerville between 0901 and 1335. In the afternoon she switched her attentions to concentrations of enemy vehicles ashore, scoring hits on tanks, trucks and the like. She destroyed an HQ and a four-gun battery and then, from 1551 took on the Villerville battery in two shoots until 1814. *Ramillies* was equally engaged throughout; her main targets were the Benerville and Houlgate batteries. *Roberts* engaged the same targets. The modern cruisers *Arethusa* and *Mauritius* with their quick-firing 6-inch batteries were much in demand, and their chief task was the laying down of covering fire for the Sixth Airborne Division, which had dropped east of the Orne to hold bridges over the Caen Canal and the river. They suffered from a lack of communication with troops ashore during the day; in particular, a planned bombardment of a battery at Sallesnelles was not carried out, despite the fact that *Arethusa* was well placed to wipe it out, as it was uncertain whether it was in British hands or not. In fact it had been captured. The gun battery at Longues was engaged by the cruiser *Ajax* (Captain J. J. Weld, MVO), which made phenomenal shooting. The position contained four 155-mm guns in reinforced concrete casemates. *Ajax* fired a total of 144 rounds of her 6-inch guns at a range of 12,000 yards at these guns. When the battery later fell, it was found that she had scored a hit on the casemate of number 2 gun and damaged it; there had been a direct hit on number 3 gun which had destroyed it and several 6-inch shells had been put right inside the casemate of number 4 gun, wiping it out completely. Her sister ship, *Orion*, (Commander J. H. Ruck-Keene, OBE, DSC) contributed to the initial bombardment, but was then muzzled and placed in reserve in case any other ship was hit in the expected massive counter-attacks, which never developed.

In support of the Americans, the monitor *Erebus*, whose crew no doubt recalled her efforts in the autumn of 1940, and the cruisers *Black Prince*,

Enterprise (Captain J. W. Hoskyns) and *Hawkins* (Captain J. N. Josselyn) added their quota. In the central fire zone, good shooting was registered by the *Diadem* (Captain E. G .A. Clifford), *Emerald* (Captain F. J. Wylie) and *Argonaut* (Captain E. W. L. Longley-Cook, CBE). The destroyers were also much in demand throughout the day; *Tanatside* for instance had fired off her entire supply of 4-inch shells by nightfall. *Cattistock* (Lieutenant R .G. D. Keddie, DSC), *Cottesmore* (Lieutenant W. D. O'Brien, DSC) and *Pytchley* (Lieutenant Commander R. H. Hodgkinson), along with the two bigger 'Fleets', earned high praise in the Gold beach area. In support of the Canadians, the cruisers *Belfast* and *Diadem* fired some 1,996 and 1,748 rounds of their main armaments respectively, while the cruiser *Glasgow* (Captain C. P. Clarke, DSO) helped the American and French ships to suppress the German guns off Omaha beach. To give vital support to the American Rangers in this assault the destroyer *Talybont* (Lieutenant Commander E. F. Baines) closed to within one mile of the coast in spite of the dangers involved.

As to its effectiveness, on which some doubt has been cast, the Joint Technical Warfare Committee found that the 'only weapon which was capable of penetrating the strong concrete protection of the casemated guns was the armour-piercing shell from the main armament of the battleships and monitors. None of the bombs used was adequate... .'

Notes

1. Captain S. W. Roskill, *The War at Sea, Vol 3, part II*, HMSO, London, 1964.
2. The fourth vessel, *Falke*, had been damaged in a collision with the *Greif* on 25 May and remained in harbour.
3. Pierre Hervieux to the author, 18 May 1994.

Chapter Seventeen

Hard-Fought Destroyer Battles

The great invasion was a wonderful achievement made possible only by overwhelming sea power. Once the troops had been established ashore the role of the big ships was to provide them with gunfire support for as long as the enemy were within range, and with battleships such as the *Nelson* and *Rodney*, that meant twenty miles or more. The pounding of their great 16-inch guns brought devastation to the Germans for many days after the initial landings. To protect the enormous amount of mercantile shipping, the thousands of landing craft and the host of smaller vessels that filled the crowded waters of the Narrow Sea after 6 June, required long-standing vigilance on the part of the myriad escort vessels. Despite the enormity of the target, losses were remarkably small.

The German response continued to be muted. The bulk of their air power was heavily involved on the Eastern Front, but their torpedo bomber units and others adopted the tactic of mixing with the huge bomber streams from Britain so that they were almost undetectable when making sneak attacks at dusk. It was almost impossible to counter this type of attack. Luckily, they only had limited numbers of this type of aircraft available. Their coastal batteries continued to be troublesome until they were overrun; this did not take long. Although U-boats were switched to attack this great mass of shipping, anti-submarine flotillas made their task very hazardous, although some losses were taken for a short time, especially when submarines turned their frustrated anger against the escorts. More troublesome along the beach-head and the Mulberry Harbours were the 'human chariots' or one-man torpedo units, the so-called 'K' men. Their attacks were largely in vain from the point of view of valuable targets, but there were so many of them that some successes were bound to occur, due in part to an initial lack of vigilance by the Allied seamen. Several valuable warships therefore fell victim to this form of underwater attack. But by far the most lethal German weapon off the beaches was of course the mine, especially the new 'ground mine' or oyster mine, detonated by the pressure of ships' hulls. Some grievous losses were suffered from this weapon, whose effects were devastating.

Our main concern was of course surface attack. Here the limited German forces found themselves overwhelmed by the huge size of the Allied fleet.

They could never hope to make more than a few sorties before destruction but, in the event, made even less of an impression than had been expected. The strong cruiser/destroyer striking forces deployed to block both ends of the Channel funnel were soon in almost nightly action against the German destroyers and minesweepers. In fact, the actions were largely in the form of interceptions as, with their command cut in half, those German destroyers on the wrong side of Normandy desperately tried to make their way back up-Channel to comparative safety. Few managed it.

Loss of HMS *Boadicea*, 13 June 1944

One of the saddest warship losses of this period was that of the destroyer *Boadicea*, one of the Beagle class destroyers; ships which had formed the original Dover flotilla back in 1939. There were few left afloat by 1944 but, with *Beagle, Boreas* and *Bulldog*, *Boadicea* had survived the intervening five years of warfare and had served in distant climes and exotic waters from the South Atlantic to the cruel Arctic Circle. Now she was back in the waters of the English Channel, which she had known so well, and was one of the innumerable British escort vessels guarding the endless convoys supplying the Allied armies ashore. Unsung and unrecorded, they kept the soldiers going while the headlines concentrated on events ashore. With total air and sea control claimed for the Channel, it was widely assumed that such duties were 'safe and routine'; such, however, was far from the case.

Boadicea (Lieutenant Commander F. W. Hawkins) had sailed from Milford Haven on 12 June with the corvette *Bluebell* and four trawlers escorting a convoy of six merchant vessels, with *Boadicea* as SO of the escort. Standing orders on board at the time were that nobody, other than those actually on watch, was to go between decks until after Dawn Action Stations at 0500. The passage was quiet for most of the evening and night. Overhead, huge numbers of Allied aircraft of all types were passing in both directions, the radar screen was swamped with contacts. Thus a Junkers Ju88 torpedo bomber was able to pull one of the oldest tricks in the book by tagging himself on to the Allied bomber stream to avoid detection and then making a swift breakaway attack against a totally surprised ship.

One survivor was Leading Seaman A. J. B. Randall and he later wrote:

> I was on the morning watch with three other guns' crew on the after Oerlikon gun deck. Dawn was just breaking, we had collected our fanny of 'Kai' from the galley and all seemed quiet and normal in the small convoy. Our own aircraft were still streaming back across the Channel, as they had been for some time, and suddenly I saw one aircraft apparently peel off from the rest and flatten out towards the port side of the ship. I immediately recognized it as a Ju88, shouted a warning to the other lads, and turned to the starboard Oerlikon which was my station. As I swivelled the gun I saw a torpedo running towards the stern but not running correctly – it was bouncing out of the water, and it blew up

some fifty yards astern. At the same instant the ship gave a tremendous shudder and lurch and as I glanced forward I had an impression of just a skeleton of the bridge silhouetted against a sea of flame. As I looked a tongue of flame shot towards me and I ducked, managing to get my hands over my face and head before it hit me with some force.

Whether it was blazing wreckage or burning oil I shall never know, but I was knocked from the Oerlikon deck and pinned under it on the main deck. I remember thinking quite detachedly 'Oh well -this is it – I can't get up', and then I was seized with what I can only describe as an insane rage at what was happening. My only thought was to get back to the gun, and I must have thrown off whatever was lying on top of me and started to climb back up the ladder to the gun deck. I must, however, have been blown along the deck quite a way as I soon realized that I was on the ladder leading to 'X' gun deck. As I reached the top, what was left of the ship tilted straight up and I was thrown into the water accompanied by various items such as most of the depth charges. Fortunately these were set to safe and did not explode, and as I reached out I touched a rolled up cork scrambling net. I clung to this for a moment, and half of a Carley raft floated by into which I managed to scramble despite the oil fuel, which by this time covered me and most of the surrounding area. As I looked round I saw the ship, propellers still turning, slide beneath the surface.

Table 15: British Warship Losses in the Channel 1944

Name	Type	Date	Details
Wrestler	Destroyer	6 June	Mined, off Normandy
Lawford	Frigate	8 June	Bombed, off Normandy
Durban	Light Cruiser	9 June	Used as Blockship
Boadicea	Destroyer	13 June	Torpedo bomber, Channel
Blackwood	Frigate	15 June	Torpedo, Channel
Mourne	Frigate	15 June	Torpedo, Channel
Fury	Destroyer	21 June	Mined and wrecked, Normandy
Swift	Destroyer	26 June	Mined, Normandy
Minster	Netlayer	8 June	Mined, Seine Bay
Cato	Minesweeper	6 July	Human torpedo,
Magic	Minesweeper	6 July	Human torpedo,
Pylades	Minesweeper	6 July	Human torpedo,
Dragon	Light Cruiser	8 July	Human torpedo,
Isis	Destroyer	20 July	Human torpedo,
Quorn	Destroyer	3 Aug	Human torpedo,
Britomart	Minesweeper	27 Aug	RAF, off Normandy
Hussar	Minesweeper	27 Aug	RAF, off Normandy
Glen Avon	Auxiliary AA Vessel	2 Sept	Foundered off Seine

Another survivor was the Gunner (T), now Lieutenant Harry E. Howting, and his memory of the incident is as follows:

At or about 0440 a terrific explosion rocked *Boadicea*, which resulted in everything forward of the funnels disappearing. Eyewitnesses have stated that this was caused by the torpedo hitting the ship near the break of the forecastle. The attack was so sudden that nothing could be done to defend the ship, nor was there any chance to open fire at the attacker. The rest of the ship remained afloat for two or three minutes.

I literally fell out of the HF/DF office, after having been shaken to the deck when the explosion occurred. The atmosphere was full of steam, dust and smoke. At the same time the deck started to tilt downwards. I heard Leading Seaman Randall say 'We've been hit'. He had been thrown from the after Oerlikon deck to the main deck, sustaining burnt hands. It was obvious that the end of the *Boadicea* was near – so I jumped into the water. When I surfaced for air I saw above my head the port screw still turning. I decided to swim away. After a few seconds she had gone, taking with her most of the Ship's Company.

Whilst waiting to be picked up, a lashed hammock brushed me. Remembering my instructor's advice in my youth, 'A well lashed hammock will keep a person afloat for 24 hours' – I also remembered on further thought that, due to the dilution of the service because of the war, some of those caught up in the dilution possibly had not been instructed in the '24 hour survival duty'. Nevertheless, I am certain that they were very well versed in many more important items. Anyway, I found a large, piece of wood and clung to this.

We were eventually picked up by the American merchantman *Freeman Hatch*, who lowered a boat contrary to orders 'not to lower boats to pick up survivors' (this duty was normally carried out by Rescue Ships, such as trawlers). Upon counting, we numbered 12 from a total of 188, some with injuries necessitating immediate hospital treatment, such as a broken leg, broken wrists and burnt hands, and all of us sick of the taste of oil fuel.

Frantic loud hailing conversation between the new Senior Officer of the escort and *Freeman Hatch* resulted in our eventually being transferred to HMS *Vanquisher*, who deposited us on the jetty at Portland dressed like characters from a child's fairy story book. We had on grey/white sweaters, tweedy drainpipe trousers, grey socks and brown gym shoes – the end result of some warm-hearted Association – God bless them. But we were a strange looking bunch.

We finished up at the Portland Prison, incidentally, the first visit to one of those places for us! There we were re-washed, re-kitted and re-fed in that order. The injured survivors had been taken straight to hospital from the jetty, while the rest eventually finished up in HMS *Osprey* (a shore base) where we stayed the night. Early next morning, after a certain amount of 'table tapping' (I was not senior enough for table-thumping!) we left for our homes and fourteen days' leave. Orders were given for us to report back after leave to attend the Inquiry.

While the tally of survivors is variously reported as twelve or thirteen, it is known that apart from these, the whole crew of the *Boadicea* went down with her, including her captain and 175 officers and ratings. The very speed with which the ship went down was stunning. Other ships took longer to die: witness another very hard-working destroyer lost soon afterwards off Normandy during the great storm.

Loss of HMS *Fury*: 20-21 June 1944

The destroyer *Fury* (Lieutenant Commander T. F. Taylor, DSC} had given invaluable supporting fire from D-Day onward, but on 20 June she was mined off the beach-head. She found herself in an unenviable position, without steerage on a lee shore. Since 0400 on the previous day the wind had freshened, until by noon it was blowing at gale force. It was dusk; night was closing in when *Fury* was mined. The captain of the Red Ensign tug *Empire Jonathan*, Captain Wilkinson, later recorded in his log the efforts to save the crippled destroyer in impossible conditions:

> At 2100 we received orders from the *Despatch* to assist the *Fury*, which was being towed into harbour by the tug *Thames*. The *Fury* had been mined and disabled. As the *Thames* towed the destroyer the wind and swell proved too much and took control of the *Fury*. She hit a salvage ship and the *Thames*'s towing wire parted. *Fury* dropped her anchor but continued to drift towards the beach. We connected up to her stern but the wire parted in the heavy swell. Got another wire off her but that parted immediately. *Empire Winnie* connected up at the stern but her ropes parted. I manoeuvred alongside and got our rope and wire connected up forward. Could not get away from the side of the *Fury* to start towing so asked *Danube VI* to get hold of me and pull me round. The first attempt fractured the port hawser pipes. The next one succeeded; and we got within 100 yards of her, but as we came level with the harbour entrance the swell and wind once again were too much and our docking spring parted. Away went *Fury* cannoning off the ships, which were at anchor. By now the tide was with the wind and driving her hard to the beach. We connected up again after a lot of difficulty dodging ships and submerged wrecks. We started towing again toward the *Despatch*; the *Fury* was to lay alongside of her.
>
> At 0100 we managed to get his bow tight up so the *Fury* could get a mooring aboard, but as he touched, his bows cut through our tow rope and they failed to get a mooring strong enough to hold him. Once more she started her voyage through the harbour and shipping. At 0130 I connected up again with another 8-inch manila, but the sharp edge of her bows cut through it and we picked up the rope in our propeller, disabling ourselves. We started to drift through the ships ourselves, even after we had let both our anchors down. Eventually we brought up and helplessly watched the *Fury* drive on to the beach.

Here she lay, high and dry. She was eventually refloated and towed back to England, but such was the pressure of work on the shipyards and the quantity of new destroyers now joining the fleet that she was never repaired, but instead written off as a constructive total loss. She was immediately sold to the shipbreaking firm of T. W. Ward and arrived at Briton Ferry on 18 August where she was dismantled. A sad end to a proud ship.

A few days later, the brand new destroyer *Swift* (Lieutenant Commander J. R. Gower) suffered a similar fate, joining the growing list of destroyer casualties, when she struck a mine at 0730 on 24 June, and sank with heavy casualties.

Human Torpedoes and the Trout Line

Towards the end of June 1944 the western end of the Normandy beach-head was largely secured against enemy intervention by sea from the west, save for the remnants of their surface fleet at Brest. To the east the threat still loomed large and by this time the enemy had recovered enough to launch a series of assaults by new weapons: special attack weapons like the so-called 'human torpedoes', the explosive motor boats and midget submarines. They were met by the newly formed 'Support Squadron, Eastern Flank', which was formed under the command of Commander K. A. Sellar, with the dual role of protecting their flank and bombarding the German forces ashore east of the River Orne. Under the control of the gunboat-turned-HQ ship, *Locust*, were some seventy-six landing craft of the LCG, LCF and LCS type, well armed with light weapons, and several motor launches. They formed two lines of defence at night, six miles north of Ouistreham; the landing ships were anchored in the outer line some 700 yards apart with motor launches patrolling up and down inside this outer defence. The whole area was thick with mines; no other types of warship could operate with safety. The whole system was named the 'Trout Line'. It could only be set up at dusk, otherwise the German batteries would have speedily sunk the whole lot; it had to be abandoned before daylight for the same reason. Despite this, the motley collection of craft operated well and repulsed major attempts by the enemy to breach their line.

Commander Sellar was later to report that:

> The Squadron lived and had its being and operated in a heavily mined area, and were ultimately the only inhabitants of this area, as all the other ships were removed as a result of enemy shelling and mining. Four major attacks were made by night by the enemy, using new weapons. Although losses were suffered, these attacks were decisively beaten.

These attacks can be briefly summarized as follows. On the night of 5-6 July some twenty-seven of the 'human torpedoes', or *Negers* as the German naval command called them, attacked from Villers-sur-Mer. At the time it was thought that only four had been destroyed, but in fact the Germans lost nine. In return they sank two big Fleet minesweepers, *Cato* and *Magic* of the

40th Flotilla with the loss of four officers and twenty-seven men. As a result of this tragedy the minesweepers were ordered no longer to anchor, but to keep under way between the hours of 2200 and 0400. This resulted in extra strain on the crews, while constant explosions kept them awake as small charges were dropped at intervals throughout the dark hours.

On the night of 7-8 July a second wave of twenty-one *Negers* came in; no less than twelve were sunk for certain and many others were damaged beyond repair or salvation. In return the Polish-manned light cruiser *Dragon* was so severely damaged that she was not considered worthy of repair, and she was scuttled as an additional breakwater. The other major victim was the minesweeper *Pylades*. A sister minesweeper, the *Orestes*, gave a good account of herself in this attack, her log reading thus:

0652 – engaged human torpedo. Pilot seen to be hit.

0707 – engaged human torpedo. Pilot seen to be killed or severely wounded.

0718 – engaged human torpedo. Pilot seen to be killed or severely wounded.

0737 – engaged human torpedo. Pilot seen in water and picked up.

Finally, on 3 August the Hunt class destroyer *Quorn* (Lieutenant I. Hall) was hit at 0250 while on patrol at the northern end of the 'Trout Line' and subsequently sank, as did the minesweeping trawler *Gairsay*.

But in the event these novel weapons were powerless to affect the landings and were so severely repulsed in their attempts that the attacks soon died away in failure.

Further Bombardments off Normandy

Bombarding continued during the army advance from the beachhead. To the fore were the British battleships *Nelson, Rodney, Warspite* and *Malaya*, as well as the old French battleship *Courbert*, which had lain idle in harbour at Portsmouth since 1940. Now she finally rejoined the war with indirect bombardments of German batteries. One noteworthy contribution to the naval participation was in fact made by the army. This was the old light cruiser *Despatch* which was utilized by Captain C. H. Petrie as an HQ ship. She was rescued from '...the entrance to the scrap-heap devoid of all guns and stores...'and towed round to Portsmouth. Her main armament for Normandy consisted of sixteen single Mk. III Bofors guns and two single 20-mm Oerlikons.

Mining of HMS *Isis*; 20 July 1944

Mines of all types continued to take a toll among the mass of shipping off the beachhead. Particularly poignant was the loss of the destroyer *Isis* (Lieutenant H. D. Durrell) that was mined with heavy loss of life. Her passing resembled in many ways the loss of the *Acheron* off Ventnor all those years earlier, for nobody saw her go, very few survived the sinking and even fewer a night adrift before help belatedly arrived. Even today, sixty-two years later, no positive origin for her loss has ever been ascertained. The official report on her loss,[1] read:

> The *Isis* was one of the few ships remaining to the 8th Flotilla since the wrecking of the *Fury* and had been on anti-submarine patrol in the Western Area, ten miles off the beaches, close to 'O' buoy on 20th July. She had been ordered to anchor for the night near to 'O' buoy. She was still underway and had not yet anchored when, at 1802, one survivor, on deck at the time, felt a bump and heard a scraping noise, followed, a fraction of a second later, by a big explosion, followed, almost immediately, by two other explosions. The destroyer took on a big list to starboard, almost at once, and the deck became awash. The *Isis* then sank, bows first, in ten to thirty minutes after the explosion, the stern being well out of the water from beginning to end. With the exception of one rating, who was on the mess deck and thinks the explosions were due to depth charges, all survivors seemed certain, although they had no reason for so saying, that the explosions were due to mines. The fact that she was still moving when hit, seems to rule out an attack by *Marder*'s and suchlike craft.

It appeared that the first explosion was abreast No. 1 boiler room on the starboard side; the damage could not be seen, however, as it was under water. A large hole in the port side was visible; opinions varied as to whether it was just before or just abaft the bridge. A difference of opinion also existed as to whether the bows were cut off or badly damaged.

Except for the Engineering Officer and one sub-lieutenant, no officers appear to have been seen after the explosions. One survivor, who was on the mess deck, and at least two other ratings got on deck, the remainder of the survivors questioned seem to think that no one could have escaped from forward of No. 2 boiler room. There were two wireless ratings on watch. No orders were received in the office so, as the transmitter had blown up, both left; a signal was not sent on the emergency set and this had fateful repercussions on the survivors. Attempts to launch the Carley float were hampered because none of the four seamen present possessed a knife to cut the retainers. None of the four ratings had their lifebelts either, and one was drowned in consequence. The sea was not rough, but there was sufficient wind to kick up a sea. In all, five Carley floats and rafts got away and two Denton rafts, but there were so few survivors that there was ample room. Two aircraft passed overhead soon after the ship started sinking, and two destroyers were seen about two or three miles distant but none of these apparently noticed anything amiss! Many of those that did get away, died of exposure during the night. Some twenty survivors were rescued by the minesweeper HMS *Hound* around 0209, others remained and were not picked up by an American cutter until about 0615 the following morning.

Bombardment of Cherbourg, 25 June 1944

To subdue the many heavy guns known to be manned by picked naval gunners at Cherbourg, in order to facilitate the American capture of that vital port, a squadron under the command of American Rear Admiral Morton L. Deyo was sailed. It consisted of the battleships *Arkansas*, *Nevada* and *Texas*; cruisers *Quincy* and *Tuscaloosa*, and several destroyers, to which were added a flotilla of British minesweepers to clear the path and the cruisers *Glasgow* and *Enterprise* (Captain H. Grant, RCN).

Arkansas and *Texas* were kept to seaward in reserve, but the remainder of the force took up station nine miles from the coast and parallel to it, with the two experienced British cruisers leading the line. Their initial run drew no response so they closed to within seven miles. Still there was no response. Just before midday, with the range down to five miles, a third run commenced and the German guns finally allowed themselves to be drawn. A heavy and rapid firing battle now commenced. As usual the enemy fire was very accurate and the warships had to zigzag to avoid being hit; most were frequently straddled by shells.

The first casualties were the destroyers. The American ships *O'Brien*, *Barton* and *Laffey* were all hit and damaged but in each case the shells were 'duds'. The *Texas* was also hit, but again the shell failed to explode. The whole bombardment was timed to last a mere ninety minutes, but the German guns were far from done and the American admiral was forced to continue the action. *Glasgow* was firing full twelve-gun salvoes with great accuracy and thus drew upon herself the heaviest of the counter-fire. The inevitable happened at 1342 when she was hit by a German salvo. Two heavy shells struck her and the third was a close miss alongside. This time the shells were good ones. One smashed through the after bridge structure into the useless hangar deck where it started a large fire. The other shells did little damage, save for considerable splinter damage. Nevertheless *Glasgow* stayed in line and came back again shortly afterwards with heavy fire. By the time the squadron left, much damage had been done to the defences and shortly afterwards the port fell. It is appropriate that *Glasgow* and *Enterprise* should have helped achieve by bombardment the good work commenced as long before as 1940 by *Revenge*.

E-Boats: The Final Battles off Normandy, June-August 1944

All German light craft were thrown into the battle of the beachhead, and to no avail. Despite the mass of light craft available to them and the enormous size and quantity of the targets, they achieved little. As we have seen, the special attack units were slaughtered for the loss of a few destroyers and minesweepers. Army casualties at sea were minimal. The old enemy, E-boats, also emerged for a death-or-glory series of battles, finding mainly the former and gaining little of the latter.

These attacks can be summarized as follows:

7-8 June: Eight boats from 4th Flotilla attacked a convoy with the destroyer *Beagle* as solitary escort. *LST-376* and *LST-314* sunk, enemy driven off by the arrival of destroyers *Saumarez, Virago, Isis* and Norwegian *Stord*. Five boats of the 5th Flotilla from Cherbourg were intercepted by the frigates *Retalick* and *Stayner*, which damaged *S-84, S-138* and *S-142*.

8-9 June: Eight boats of 5th and 9th Flotillas intercepted by the destroyer *Hambledon* and American ships *Frankford* and *Baldwin* and driven back to port. Eleven boats of the 2nd and 4th Flotillas aborted their missions.

9-10 June: Ten boats of the 5th and 9th Flotillas were driven off with no results by the American destroyers. Ten boats of the 2nd and 4th Flotillas attacked small ships and claimed many hits. Despite this, post-war records show quite clearly that no British ships were sunk. The *S-180* and *S-190* were both mined.

10-11 June: Eleven boats of the 5th and 9th Flotillas re-intercepted by British patrols. In the fighting that followed *Halstead* was damaged by a torpedo and the *S-136* and the British MTB-*448* were sunk.

The boats of the 9th Flotilla were more successful and sank the American tug *Partridge* and *LST-496*.

Six boats of the 4th Flotilla were intercepted and driven back to port by the destroyers *Sioux* and *Krakowiak*, the frigate *Duff* and MTBs.

Four boats of the 2nd Flotilla were similarly attacked and chased by the destroyers *Kelvin, Scorpion, Scourge*, and *Stord* after they had sunk *Ashanti* (534 tons), *Brackenfield* (657 tons) and *Dungrange*. They eventually reached Boulogne.

11-12 June: Four boats of the 5th and 9th Flotillas attacked a force of American destroyers, *Kommandeur* von Mlirback putting a torpedo into the U.S. destroyer *Nelson*.

Six boats of the 4th Flotilla were very roughly handled by the destroyers *Onslow, Onslaught, Offa* and *Oribi*.

12-13 June: Four boats from Cherbourg tried to break through but were intercepted by the destroyers *Isis, Stevenstone* and *Glaisdale* which damaged the *S-84, S-100, S-138* and *S-143* in a fierce action.

23-24 June: Six boats of the 2nd Flotilla were engaged by the destroyer patrol *Stord* and *Venus; S-175* and *S-181* were damaged.

3-4 July: Six boats of the 2nd and 8th Flotillas were intercepted off Cap d'Antifer by the frigates *Stayner* and *Thornborough*.

5-6 July: Six boats of the 2nd Flotilla intercepted by destroyers off Le Havre and returned to port.

7-8 July: Nine boats of the 2nd and 9th Flotillas in running battles with the destroyers *Cattistock* and *La Combattante* and frigate *Thornborough*. Despite claims of torpedo hits, no British ships were touched and the E-boats retreated.

26-27 July: Four boats from the 6th Flotilla attacked a convoy off Dungeness and claimed to have sunk two ships. Again no ships were lost that night but the *Empire Beatrice* (7,046 tons) and *Fort Perrot* (7,171 tons) were both damaged. The E-boats were chased away on the arrival of the destroyers *Obedient, Opportune* and *Savage*.

29-30 July: One of the biggest successes was scored when three boats of the 6th Flotilla attacked a convoy off Eastbourne. The *Samwake* (7,219 tons), *Fort Dearborn* (7,160 tons), *Fort Kaskaskia* (7,187 tons) and *Ocean Courier* (7,178 tons) were all hit and damaged. *Thornborough* arrived too late to prevent history from being made in the old manner. It was a tragedy that by this stage of the war should have been avoidable.

The furious battles against the E-boats were to continue for the rest of the war at the same intensity. They were one enemy force, which the British never mastered.

Table 16: German Warship Losses in the Channel Area 1940-4

Type	Ship	Date	Cause
Destroyer	*Bruno Heinemann*	14.1.42	Mined off Ostend
	T29	26.4.44	Surface action
	T27	29.4.44	Surface action
	ZH-1	9.6.44	Surface action
	Z32	9.6.44	Surface action
	Z23	21.8.44	Air attack
	T24	25.8.44	Air attack
	Z24	25.8.44	Air attack
	Z37	24.8.44	Damaged, scuttled
	Wolf	8.1.41	Mined off Dunkirk
	Iltis	14.5.42	MTBs
	Seeadler	14.5.42	MTBs
	Greif	23-24.5.44	Air attack
	Falke	14-15.6.44	Air attack
	Jaguar	14-15.6.44	Air attack
	Mowe	14-15.6.44	Air attack
	Kondor	28.6.44	Scuttled
Armed Raider	*Komet*	14.10.42	Surface action
Minesweepers		30.11.41	Mined off L'Orient
	M-8	14.5.42	MTBs
	M-10	14.3.44	Surface action
	M-13	31.5.44	Mined Gironde
	M-25	9.44	Scuttled
	M-26	15.5.42	Air attack
	M-27	11.8.44	Mined Gironde
	M-39	24.5.44	MTBs
	M-83	14.6.44	Surface action
	M-84	11.8.44	Scuttled

Type	Ship	Date	Cause
Minesweepers			
	M-133	6.8.44	Damaged, scuttled
	M-152	23.7.43	Mined Gironde
	M-153	10.7.43	Surface action
	M-156	6.2.44	Air attack
	M-206	14.8.44	Scuttled
	M-262	25.8.44	Scuttled
	M-263	6.8.44	Surface action
	M-271	5.8.44	Air attack
	M-274	5.9.44	Scuttled
	M-276	5.9.44	Scuttled
	M-292	21.8.44	Air attack
	M-304	25.8.44	Scuttled
	M-325	5.8.44	Air attack
	M-343	6.8.44	Damaged, scuttled
	M-344	9.44	Scuttled
	M-345	15.8.43	Air attack
	M-363	25.8.44	Scuttled
	M-366	8.8.44	Air attack
	M-367	8.8.44	Air attack
	M-383	13.8.44	Air attack
	M-385	15.8.44	Surface action
	M-402	15.6.44	Air attack
	M-412	9.3.45	Commando raid
	M-414	17.5.43	Air attack
	M-422	4.8.44	Air attack
	M-428	8.8.44	Air attack
	M-438	8.8.44	Air attack
	M-444	14.8.44	Damaged, scuttled
	M-463	25.8.44	Scuttled
	M-471	25.9.44	Air attack
	M-483	15.6.43	Mined
	M-486	6.8.44	Surface action
	Jupiter	6.8.44	Damaged, scuttled
	Saturn	6.8.44	Air attack

Massacre of the Minesweepers, 27 August 1944

Before leaving the skirmishing in the Channel, off the beaches and elsewhere, and returning to the epic destroyer battles which punctuated this period, mention should be made of one of the greatest tragedies of the Normandy landings. The attack was an aerial one and it caused heavy casualties. But it came not from the *Luftwaffe*, who flew very few sorties at the time, but from the RAF. The war in the Channel in 1944 showed that air/sea cooperation had not advanced one iota since the days when the RAF bombers repeatedly bombed the *Newcastle* and her escorts in November 1940.

On 27 August the 1st Minesweeping Flotilla was attacked by RAF Typhoon aircraft while sweeping off Cap d'Antifer. HMS *Hussar* and *Britomart* were sunk and HMS *Salamander* was so severely damaged as to be beyond economic repair. Two officers and forty ratings were killed in *Britomart* (Lieutenant Commander A. J. Galvin, DSC), three officers and fifty-four ratings were killed in *Hussar* (Lieutenant Commander J. Nash, MBE, RNVR) and eleven men were wounded in *Salamander* (Lieutenant

Commander H. King, RNVR). The other ship in company, *Jason*, escaped without serious damage.

The flotilla had been engaged in clearing magnetic mines from the coast around Le Havre in readiness for a bombardment of that port by the battleship *Warspite* and monitors *Erebus* and *Roberts*, but they were switched back to the Portsmouth-Arromanches route for that Sunday only. Apparently, however, a subsequent signal ordering the ships to resume their tasks off Cap d'Antifer rather than Arromanches, where they had been chiefly employed since D-Day, was not repeated to the Flag Officer British Assault Area (Rear Admiral J. W. Rivett-Carnac). Although the aircraft leader, Wing Commander J. Baldwin, DSO, DFC, AFC, leading the sixteen rocket-armed Typhoon bombers, twice questioned his orders to attack, being sure the ships were British, the shore staff persisted with the strike in the belief that the minesweepers were enemy vessels trying to enter or leave Le Havre.

Signals made by *Jason*, recognition flares fired by all ships, the fact that the British ships did not fire back until they were already badly hit and sinking, and were being attacked a second time as they went down, all failed to deflect the Typhoons from their orders. Nor did the White Ensigns spread on the decks, the firing of the correct Very lights and signals by l0-inch searchlights deter them. They dived again and again, and within the space of a few short minutes, between 1330 and 1345 the flotilla was cut to ribbons. Two trawlers in company, *Colsay* and *Lord Ashfield*, were also attacked and suffered several casualties, but they and *Jason* managed to pick up the other ships' survivors and wounded.

Destroyer Action off Isle de Bas, 8-9 June 1944

The E-boat attacks, although not producing the results expected of them by the Germans against the mass of Allied shipping off the beaches, had resulted in a large expenditure of torpedoes. To get further supplies through quickly to the boats based at Cherbourg, it was decided that the destroyer flotilla at Brest should attempt to make the dangerous passage and at the same time to escape from what was obviously going to become a trap. If they made the journey successfully, these destroyers were to reinforce the German forces at Cherbourg for further attacks, and could also slip back to Germany if this became essential.

Accordingly, on the evening of 8 June, the four destroyers of the 8th Flotilla, under the command of *Kapitän zur See* von Bechtolsheim, sailed with a deck cargo of torpedoes, which added to his vulnerability. His force consisted of the big *Z-32* and *Z-24*, armed with 5.9-inch guns, the ex-Dutch destroyer *ZH-1*, which was smaller and carried 4.7-inch guns, and one of the smaller so-called torpedo boats, *T-24*, with 4.l-inch guns. All had powerful torpedo armaments. Unfortunately for the Germans, they were quickly spotted and tracked as they made their hurried way northward. Aircraft made the initial sighting just before the cloak of darkness covered them, and plans were made to attack them.

The force sent to intercept them was the 10th Flotilla under Captain Basil Jones. This flotilla was split into the 19th Division, with the experienced *Tartar* as his leader and the Tribals *Ashanti*, *Haida* and *Huron*. This group was placed some two miles to the north of the 20th Division, which was placed to act as a guard, behind and beyond the leading ships of the line. This division consisted of the Polish *Blyskawica* and *Piorun*, and the British *Eskimo* and *Javelin*. The two British ships had somewhat less experience of this type of fighting. The whole force was disposed by the C-in-C, Plymouth, in the familiar Tunnel-type sweep, this time some twenty miles from the coast. The first 'pass' was made between the Isle de Bas and Isle Vierge but nothing was sighted and the expected collision course of 255 degrees drew a blank.

On the second westward run, at 0115 they had better luck, and *Tartar*'s radar picked up firm echoes indicating four large ships at a range of about ten miles almost directly ahead of the 10th Flotilla. Jones at once staggered his line to enable each of his destroyer's radar sets to sweep ahead to its maximum efficiency, and to leave the Asdic operators with a clear sound field unmarred by the wakes of the next ship ahead. It was thus hoped that if the Germans adopted their usual course of firing torpedoes and running, advance warning would be available.

Captain Jones had studied earlier battle reports and made his plans accordingly. He expected the Germans to run true to form, and they did. In anticipation that they would turn and fire their full complement of torpedoes once the range had closed to less than 10,000 yards, he confidently held his course and bearing in staggered Line Ahead until 0122. Both British divisions were then altered by White Pendant 35 degrees to starboard and this was followed by a second turn of 50 degrees to port together, with the ships astern steering straight for their line of bearing positions. This had the effect of bringing the whole force's powerful front gun armament to bear on the enemy line, and at the same time, it would comb the expected torpedo tracks. Sixty-four guns faced the oncoming German line, ready to fire.

As expected, at 0126 the Germans fired torpedoes, which were detected on their way. The range had come down to 5,000 yards and the thirty-two 4.7-inch guns opened fire in unison dead ahead and into the enemy line which was, by now, turning away in the time-honoured fashion. But this time, the British had the advantage of a steady course and full control. Although the massed German torpedo attack posed its usual deadly threat, and the *Tartar* leading the line was closely missed both to port and starboard, all torpedoes were avoided and the range was steadily reducing, making good hitting easier for the gunners. Receiving an unexpected battering, to which they could make no effective reply, the German force disintegrated as each ship sought its own salvation. *Z-32* turned to port and steered northward; *ZH-1* turned to port but went off at a tangent to her leader and finished up heading west, while the rearmost pair, *Z-24* and *T-*

24, turned to port and steered a south-westerly course. The British flotilla was therefore forced to abandon its successful concentration and split up to follow the scattering German vessels as best they could.

Leaving the big *Z-32* to be dealt with by the whole of the 20th Division, which was well placed to the north to deal with her, the *Tartar* and *Ashanti* concentrated on the second ship, *ZH-1*, while the two Canadian vessels went after the remaining pair which were heading south. Repeated hits so damaged the *ZH-1* that her speed was much reduced. She vanished in a cloud of smoke and steam, and fire was switched to the *T-24*. This unfortunate was already fully engaged by *Haida*, who herself had been narrowly missed by enemy torpedoes.

Meanwhile the 20th Division had turned in Line Ahead 35 degrees to starboard and sighted their target, *Z-32*, on a parallel course. However, instead of turning towards her, as planned and practised, to concentrate their fire, the Polish ship held on. *Z-32* immediately went into the normal routine, fired her torpedoes and turned away. The 20th Division came back with the same tactics as in earlier years, opening fire and turning away to fire a 'fan' of torpedoes from the tubes trained on the beam. The inevitable result was lost contact.

Her turn-away, moreover, resulted in undeserved good fortune for *Z-32*, who soon found herself undetected on *Tartar*'s beam and quickly opened fire. She heavily damaged the British leader before she herself was hit hard by the fire from both British ships. Captain Jones later described the damage:

> Four shells burst about *Tartar*'s bridge, starting a fire abaft the bridge, cutting leads to her Directors, bringing down the trellis foremast and all radar, and cutting torpedo communications to aft.
>
> The wheelhouse was also hit, killing the Assistant Coxswain; and on the bridge the PCO and torpedo control ratings were killed and a number wounded. As the mast fell over, the call-up buzzer from the aloft look-out position jammed on, and splinters pierced the upper deck of No. 1 Boiler Room causing loss of air pressure and reduction of speed.
>
> The conditions of fire, noise, smoke and casualties were distracting, but with our immediate enemy silenced, I pressed on in *Tartar*, not realizing how much our speed had been reduced by damage to one of the boiler room 'roofs'.

To the other ships of the flotilla, the damaged *Tartar* presented a sad sight. *Tartar* and *Ashanti* soon came upon the crippled *ZH-1* stopped in the water and pointing to the north. *Tartar* passed close astern of her and raked her through in the time-honoured manner of Nelson's day, at a range of 500 yards with guns in local control. *Ashanti* then fired two torpedoes into the stationary vessel and pumped in further 4.7-inch salvoes, which immediately resulted in a huge explosion and sank the *ZH-1*.

The Canadian ships quickly passed out of sight, intent on their victims, but although a fierce gun duel followed at high speeds the German ships again outpaced their Allied opponents, and the two Tribals were forced to give up the chase due to British minefields. Not before they had hit the *Z-24* with gunfire, however. Shells struck her charthouse, and her W/T office, and her after guns were put out of action, but she managed to get back to French waters. Her reprieve was but a temporary one, for there were no facilities to repair her damage, and in her stranded state she fell an easy victim to air attacks which delivered the final blows, as she lay in the Bordeaux estuary, soon after. The torpedo boat *T-24* escaped undamaged. *Z-32*, after taking considerable punishment from *Ashanti* earlier, desperately struggled south trying to effect running repairs. She passed close to *Tartar*, which was in a similar state, and one wonders what the result would have been had the two cripples spotted each other at close range at this time. *Z-32* was not to enjoy immunity for long, however, as the two Canadian ships, returning from one chase, stumbled across her and once more the chase was on. *Z-32* steered desperately to the east, but despite earlier damage and more hits from the Canadian ships' forward guns, she seemed to be drawing away from them. She ran herself to the edge of the British minefield before turning south. The Canadian ships, joined by the *Ashanti* and *Tartar* at longer range, continued to engage her until, finally disorientated, the big destroyer ran firmly aground on the rocks of the Isle de Bas, heavily afire. She was later abandoned and blown up there. All the Allied ships returned to Plymouth Sound at 0530 to be cheered in by waiting crowds and welcomed by the C-in-C on the quay. On 10 June the Admiralty signalled to the Flotilla: The Board of Admiralty convey their congratulations to Officers and Ships' Companies on the spirited action which has caused a potential menace to the main operations to be removed.

The Germans later praised the action as being a 'significant success' for their forces. Although only four of the Tribals had been effective in the battle against four German ships, they claimed to have sunk two of the six Allied destroyers and three light cruisers of the Glasgow type, which they maintained they had engaged!

Notes

1. Details of sinking of HMS *Isis* – report based on statements made by survivors now in HMS *Drake*; from The Commodore, Royal Naval Barracks, Devonport, dated 12 September 1944, to Secretary of the Admiralty (contained in ADM 199/1645, held at National Archives, Kew, London).

Chapter Eighteen

Final Operations in the Channel

Although there were some ten months of war remaining, the rest of the Royal Navy's part in maintaining the freedom of the English Channel, although often dangerous and full of action was, on the whole, an anti-climax. The bulk of the German surface forces had been so mauled that they no longer presented a serious threat. The few major warships were either destroyed piecemeal in similar encounters to those described, or scuttled by their crews; a fate, which holds neither glory nor determination, but one to which the Germans seem addicted. No death-or-glory last ditch battles for them – from Scapa Flow in 1919, through the *Graf Spee* and other similar episodes – scuttle rather than fight marked the end of most German warships. It mattered little to the British forces, who had fought them for so long. What really mattered was the supply of the great armies, which were to fight their way into Germany. This ran almost unhindered from June until the war's end. It was no uncertain victory, but it had been a hard-fought one. We can briefly record the few remaining highlights.

Summary of the East Coast Convoys

That the war along the East coast was a tough one nobody can dispute, but the fighting was far more intense the closer one got to the Thames Estuary and the Dover Straits, as this eyewitness account from HMS *Wallace* emphasizes.[1]

> While it was true we operated out of Rosyth, I would not like to suggest that the East Coast convoys we escorted were constantly under attack as he [ex-Yeoman Harry Hargraves article in *Daily Mail on Sunday*] suggests. From Methil in the Firth of Forth (where the convoys started and ended for us) down to the Humber it was generally fairly quiet as we were out of range of aircraft and E-boats, although sometimes there were attacks. It was from the Wash southwards to the Thames Estuary where attacks would occur. They were never on the scale of, say, the Malta Convoys, of course, and the bombers generally went for the merchant ships rather than the escorts. Raids could be relatively short-lived but have serious consequences regarding losses and damage.
>
> E-boats created the more serious problems – particularly in the days

before radar – because they were so fast and hard to see at night (even when illuminated by star shells) and because they were shallow-draughted, were able to pass safely over the minefields whereas the destroyers could not. It was only when our own MTBs and MGBs were involved was the struggle more even balanced.

Hargraves refers to the sinking of a Rosyth destroyer and the fact that it occurred in January 1942, and that it had been noticed by virtue of a ships name board floating past. So much of this story contains inaccuracies.

Only two Rosyth destroyers were sunk during the war on the East Coast – *Vortigern* on March 15th 1942 and *Vimiera* on January 9th 1942. The former was torpedoed during an E-boat attack, and the latter was mined in the Thames Estuary.

By coincidence, *Vortigern* was sunk on the same night that *Wallace* was also engaged in an attack by E-boats, but the former was going northwards and we were with a southbound convoy. There is no doubt that the incident Hargreaves describes concerned the *Vimiera* but the facts are rather different.

Wallace and *Vimiera* had been escorts of a southbound convoy and were proceeding line astern to Sheerness where we would stay the night. *Vimiera* was leading as she was the Senior Ship due to the rank of her Commanding Officer, and she hit a mine, which eventually resulted in the ship being sunk. We were ready to go to the assistance and pick up survivors, but were given strict orders to steam *astern*, following the exact course used on steaming ahead, until we were clear of the area. The thinking was that – as we had not hit any mines on the way forward it would be reasonably safe to follow the course astern, and so it proved.

I find the references to the name boards being displayed by the destroyers for the benefit of the merchant ships to be ridiculous, and it was never the case. There was no real need for merchant ships to know the name of the escorts, but the Commodore of the convoy would certainly have that information. He would have attended the convoy conference before sailing and been given the convoy number, code name and the names and pennant numbers of the escorts. I had a 35-mm camera and permission to use it onboard. I took many photographs of other escorts and there are no signs of name boards on any of them. In fact, as far as *Wallace* was concerned, her name board consisted of large brass letters mounted on a wooden board and this could be fitted and removed easily. It was only displayed on the side of the aft superstructure and entrance to the Wardroom when we were in harbour. It was always removed just prior to sailing, and Hargreaves would well have known that!

The German Minesweeper Flotilla Wiped Out, 14-15 June 1944

In an operation to finish off the damaged *Z-32*, the destroyers *Ashanti* and *Piorun* were dispatched to a covering position off the Channel Islands and

St Malo on the night of 14-15 June, while MTBs were sent in to torpedo the wreck. While so doing, the two ships unexpectedly ran into a force of between seven and nine German M-class minesweepers escorting a small convoy.

The German ships were in two groups. The *Ashanti*'s captain decided that such small vessels were not worthy targets for his torpedoes and decided to use solely his guns. The Polish commander of *Piorun* came to a different conclusion and decided to fire his torpedoes on his first run at the targets. *Piorun* took the leading group of three ships and, adding eleven knots left deflection, scored one hit. Meanwhile the enemy ships were illuminated with star shells, and gun salvoes were soon smashing into them. The *M-343* was quickly sunk and by the time the two Allied ships left the scene the flotilla was broken up. In all, five minesweepers were left aground, ablaze or badly damaged: *M-412, M-422, M-432, M-442* and *M-452*; while two others, *M-4615* and the patrol boat *V-203* were damaged by bombing next morning while trying to help the cripples. It was a neat action.

In this case, however, the Admiralty was critical. They later sent a signal complaining about the '...general lack of appreciation of the use of the torpedo'. It would appear that on several suitable occasions, of which this was one, their Lordships thought 'torpedo fire was withheld for no apparent reason, and on some occasions when torpedoes were fired the results were disappointing'.

Captain Basil Jones, whose gun tactics had produced results when all conventional tactics had achieved only disaster, was somewhat taken aback by this attitude at this stage of the war. In a detailed reply, he was to write:

> To the inexperienced this might look one-sided. Actually in the close work of a night action a number of individual offensive targets creates a problem even for heavily-armed destroyers. Unless early targets are eliminated extremely quickly, the remainder have quiet gunlayer's firing at close range with their main gun, on a ship unarmoured as themselves, and offering a larger target, and probably considerable free run with their close-range armament as well. For the above reasons I don't think any CO of the 10th Flotilla would prefer his sub-division to have to fight four M-class minesweepers in lieu of two enemy destroyers.
>
> The enemy approved policy of turning to run away gave him the position of opportunity of torpedo advantage. The four gun forward armament of the 10th DF gives us a gun advantage over the enemy when advancing against his retreat. The fact that the enemy ships were faster than us made any delay in turning towards him generally unacceptable. The positively Elizabethan method of projecting torpedoes at right angles to our own ships' fore and aft line is a cause of delay. Our policy was not to turn away nor intend to waste any time at all in closing the enemy. With the above essentials in view, such opportunity for training as occurred was naturally devoted rather to gunnery than the torpedo.

This would appear both reasonable and accurate from the victor of the battles, but as he recorded to me recently, 'The Admiralty and the Tactical Division and School were the "Stick-in-the-Muds", and still were when I attended the latter well after the war.'

In a similar attack on the night of 27-28 June the *Eskimo* and *Huron* tangled with the same type of enemy.

Further Actions against German Minesweepers, 27-28 June 1944

While on patrol off Jersey, with orders to intercept enemy ships trying to escape along the coast of Brittany following the fall of Cherbourg, *Eskimo* and *Huron* picked up contact with their radar screens and at 0100 star shells were fired to illuminate these targets. By their light, the enemy could be seen as a minesweeper and two armed trawlers, at a range of 6,000 yards. Fire was immediately opened, upon which the enemy made smoke and turned away towards the protection of the coastal batteries. However, the rapid gunfire of the Tribals took good effect before they could escape and the minesweeper *M-4620* was soon heavily afire. Explosions began to break out aboard her, and she later sank. The patrol vessels now came under attack and one, *V-213*, was also heavily hit at close range, although not before she had scored one direct hit with her 3-inch gun on *Eskimo*. Here Captain Jones's telling remarks found full affirmation, for the big destroyer only had paper-thin steel protection and a stray shell penetrated her No. 1 boiler room. A second shell smashed into her No. 3 boiler room and soon *Eskimo* was steaming in circles with all main power lines to her switchboard, steering motor, guns, radar aerials and searchlights cut. Her speed was reduced to six knots and at this speed she crawled back to Plymouth. The Germans, needless to say, claimed that they had sunk her but the incident did prove how vulnerable even the largest destroyers were, in close range mêlées in the darkness, from even small ships like this converted trawler.

Canadian Flotilla in Action: 5 July 1944: Operation *Dredger*

Although the 10th DF, often working with light cruisers in support, took part in several other actions against the remaining German destroyers and gradually eliminated them all, these battles took place further south in the Bay of Biscay, and thus out of the scope of this book. But one more set-piece involved destroyers and German escorts in the Channel zone and in this case it was the ships of the Canadian destroyer flotilla which were involved.

These ships, HMC Ships *Qu'Appelle, Skeena, Saskatchewan* and *Restigouche*, (three of them the ex-British destroyers *Foxhound*, *Fortune* and *Comet*) of the 12th Escort Group, were led by Commander A.M. McKillop, DSC, RN, in the first vessel. U-boats had been sent in large numbers to Brest in order to strike at the mass of shipping which the German destroyers and E-boats had lamentably failed to damage. It was known that these submarines often sailed in squadrons from Brest with an escort of armed trawlers, and the Canadian destroyers were sent in to intercept this movement. The destroyers sailed at twenty-five knots, which was subsequently reduced to twelve to eliminate tell-tale bow waves and make surprise more complete.

They found the lighthouse working and used it to take their bearings. They were thus able to pinpoint their positions down to a few yards. This was essential as the success of the operation depended upon meticulous time-keeping so that they would fall in with the enemy at exactly the right place and right time. At midnight they turned northward inside the Rade de Brest; it was pitch black. Soon after, reports were received that the German convoy was on time as expected.

It was now the early minutes of 6 July and all was ready. From *Qu'Appelle*'s bow, steaming lights could be made out, steering out of the harbour entrance. This proved to be a coastal convoy and it was left alone while the Canadian destroyers moved silently upon their intended enemy. Commander McKillop later described what happened:

> As soon as I was well up between the trawlers and their base I went on to 30 knots and passed the enemy's bearing, course and speed to the other ships. When the range was about 3000 to 4000 yards the enemy challenged by flashing the letter 'W'. We 'acted wet' and made 'W's back until the range had been shortened to 2600 yards. Then I fired my first cluster of rocket flares and the ball opened.
>
> There were four trawlers in diamond formation with two U-boats in the centre of this diamond-shaped screen. The whole lot, and the land in the vicinity was shown up by our rocket flares.
>
> We opened fire and at first it was a target shoot, for the enemy seemed to be completely upset by being met on his own doorstep, and from the direction of his tracer he seemed at first to think that he was being attacked by low-flying aircraft. By previous arrangement *Qu'Appelle* went for the leading German ship and 'A' gun scored a couple of hits before any of his tracer even came in our direction. I saw his 88-mm gun go up in the air and over the side early on.

The vessel they attacked, *V-715*, was sunk. Hits were also scored on a submarine, and a few stray shots struck *Qu'Appelle*, without serious damage.

> We passed fairly close to the U-boat, and *Skeena* hit him once or twice with Oerlikon, but unfortunately not with 4.7-inch.

Further Bombardments at Caen: July 1944

During the British breakout from the beach-head there was much hard fighting and many of the heavy ships gave invaluable supporting fire throughout early and mid-July, including the battleship *Rodney*, the monitors *Erebus* and *Roberts* and the cruisers *Belfast*, *Enterprise* and *Mauritius*. In particular the 16-inch guns of the battleship proved devastating, both in accuracy and in power, against German tanks and troop concentrations, as witness this account:

> In our second shoot we fired seventeen rounds at a mobile eight-gun battery, which had taken up a position at Ifs, two miles south of Caen. We secured a hit with our second round and went on hitting it. The Bombardment Officer on the spot reported that no rounds were more than a hundred yards from the target, and that two salvoes fell bang in the middle.
>
> In our fourth shoot we fired at thirty-six tanks collected to the east of the previous target. We fired fifteen rounds of armour-piercing shell and nine rounds of high explosive, and were told that our shooting was 'extremely effective'.

These massive bombardments were the most valuable aid to the army's advance from the beach-heads, a fact ruefully acknowledged by the Germans themselves.

Second Defeat of the U-Boats in the Channel: July-August 1944

It will be recalled how a submarine offensive in the Channel in the early days of the war had been defeated. Now, with rich pickings on hand, the new schnorkel equipped U-boats returned for a second attempt. In spite of the huge concentrations of ships, and their own numbers, they failed to make much more than a token impact. They were also made to pay for such success as they had. On 5 July the *U-390* was sunk by the destroyer *Wanderer* and frigate *Tavy*. Next day *U-678* was sunk off Beachy Head by the Canadian destroyers *Kootenay* and *Ottawa*, while on 18 July the frigate *Balfour* disposed of *U-672. U-671* sailed from Boulogne on 4 August and was sunk by the frigate *Stayner* and destroyer *Wensleydale*.

A second wave of U-boats arrived in the middle of August, and almost at once the corvette *Orchid* sank the *U-741*; the Canadian destroyers *Chaudiere, Kootenay* and *Ottawa* destroyed another pair, *U-621* and *U-984* and the British destroyers *Forester*, *Vidette* and *Wensleydale* sank the *U-413*. The survivors were then recalled to Norway.

Assault on Walcheren Island, 1-8 November 1944

By the end of August, almost the whole of the English Channel was cleared of enemy ships. Although much fierce fighting still took place in small clashes against the host of small craft that remained pinned down in the war zone, most of the warships on active combat duty were concerned with routine patrols and escorting. After four years of intense effort victory was in sight. Only one other major operation remained on the fringes of the area. In clearing a passage to open the vital port of Antwerp to feed and supply the advancing Allied armies, the fortified island of Walcheren had to be taken. Its many batteries of heavy guns were preventing the clearing of minefields of the Scheldt and the whole operation was highly reminiscent of the Dardanelles. Fortunately, although the fighting inshore was hard, the outcome was a happier one for the Allied cause. This was due, in no small measure, to the covering bombardments from the heavy ships.

Again, the brunt of heavy covering fire was provided by the 15-inch guns of the Royal Navy, carried by the battleship *Warspite*, and the monitors *Roberts* and *Erebus*. It is fitting that the grand old monitor should have taken part in both one of the first and one of the last uses of heavy guns in the Channel in the Second World War.

On 1 November the bombardment commenced at 0820 by *Warspite* and *Roberts*, but *Erebus* was again plagued by turret failures; not surprising, considering her age. The initial targets were the German batteries of which one, W15, was taken in hand by *Roberts* after *Erebus* failed to engage. After an hour the fault was rectified and all three heavy ships continued to engage targets of opportunity. The lack of air spotting, commented upon in 1940, again proved a factor in restricting the effectiveness of the ships' fire, but W15 was silenced for half-an-hour at a crucial juncture, while *Warspite* also temporarily silenced another battery, W17, south of Domburg, which contained four 8.7-inch guns.

Final Actions Against E-Boats, 22 March 1945

Although the German war machine at sea had been defeated in the English Channel by 1945, one group remained to the end, fighting a hard fight, which was never quite subdued. This was the E-boat force. Although the strong escort groups, which the British now used to patrol the Channel had almost totally denied access to these E-boats, and the loss of their bases close to main routes further handicapped them, they fought doggedly to the end. It is fitting, therefore, that one of the last actions to be fought against these foes was controlled by a man who had served throughout the war on the destroyers, which formed the mainstay of the British defence against them throughout this time. He was Commander W. J. Phipps, now commanding the destroyer *Mackay*. On the evening of 21 March, *Mackay* sailed on what Phipps later described as 'My last patrol with the 16th Flotilla'. What took place the next evening and night is best left, once more, to his own words:

> Joined up with the convoy at 2300 but did not like it much as they were very big ships and I had to go out three miles or more to prevent interference with my radar. Aircraft reports of E-boats out of Den Helder and Ijmuiden began to come in at 2230, which looked as if they would be over about 0030.
>
> These boats were in fact the combined 2nd and 5th E-boat Flotillas and were out to attack shipping between the Thames Estuary and the Scheldt.
>
> From all reports they looked to be marking time east of the convoy route and looked like a second XI rather windy, but I think now were waiting for the party from Den Helder who had been attacked by aircraft and two of them reported sunk and they had chucked their hands in and gone home. When this buzz got round things happened. I arranged to be at my southern end at 54G buoy, my favourite place, at

0115, and on the way there by cutting corners at 57 buoy, I saw aircraft drop flares right ahead and worked it out that the enemy were fifteen miles away and if they came in on a westerly course I should hit them nicely. Got over just clear of the eastern edge of the channel and immediately picked them up bearing 155 degrees seven miles.

Endeavoured to park my MTBs on my beam ready to release them to cut off the retreating enemy, but had a little difficulty as there was a determined attack going on at the convoy. Closed my enemy at 27 knots on a steady bearing and aimed to go for the middle of the five E-boats so as to engage targets on both sides. Opened fire on them at 0134 at 1200 yards and close range weapons in action to port and starboard. A most unholy din and I shall never do that again purposely. Enemy sighted at 500 yards and beautifully illuminated by star shell and Thompson more steady and good shooting right for line, and overs and shorts and hits observed, but couldn't kill them. Enemy besides playing their usual tricks with smoke etc which were not very successful as I was to windward of them:

(1) Fired torpedoes at me.

(2) Dropped a charge which exploded 100 yards on my port beam without damage.

(3) Dropped two smoke floats.

The latter fooled me for a bit and I turned to throw a depth charge at it as I thought it was an E-boat burning. Very soon realized my mistake and stopped the starboard Oerlikon which was heavily engaged with it. Target was still being hit but got away with it somehow and though I was doing 27 knots the range opened to 4,500 yards when I ceased fire, plotted them on and considered what next. During this engagement one AB was wounded on the fo'c'sle.

My target got separated from the main body of four others and managed to work round me and shoot off and join his pals when they hung about and re-formed about 0145 and then damn it came back for another shot. I was ready for them. Enemy had re-formed and were I think still five there still. Held them by radar all the time and placed myself nicely, heading to the westward of the leading ship, closing at 27 knots on a steady bearing.

There was no need for any attempt to prevent them seeing me, it was very clear by now in a half moon and I saw them streaking for the channel at 3,500 yards and taking not the least notice of me. Held on until 1,200 yards when I opened fire again on the leading ship with a 6-pounder pom-pom and Oerlikon. To my astonishment the leading ship turned directly across my bow while the others streaked off for home to the north-eastward. Here he was coming apparently slap for me and I thought 'Here he is coming across my bow and will drop a charge under it'. Closing at a combined speed of about 55 knots, I had less than half-a-minute to do anything.

I put the wheel hard-a-port in the hope that I might hit him instead, and also made the speed across less for the guns. The 6-pounder hit him six times, the Oerlikon fired a belt into him and the pom-pom fired 16 rounds before he ran out of their sight, the gunner's mate fired a magazine of Bren into him and I bloody nearly threw my cap at him. Though peppered to hell he got away with it, though I saw his smoke toy on fire as he shot across my bow. No explosion under me but a few seconds on the starboard quarter, so the delay action of the charge had saved me. A bit of return fire but not much, as I think his upper deck was not very healthy. I suppose it was about 40 yards ahead of me but he disappeared under the bow. I flipped her round to try and pick him up again but with a full wheel on at that speed everything was in rather a pickle, and he was opening at about 40 for a few seconds and by the time I was a little tidier after half a minute he was out at 1500 or so again. Though I fired at him for a bit he was at too long a range. He did make me take my eye off the rest of the group, but I think understandably. They had had enough for the night by then so shoved off homewards... .

This terse and laconic account by the captain of one destroyer illustrates perfectly the speed, confusion and tenseness of the fighting between destroyers and E-boats at night. The German account (Rohwer & Hummelchen, see Bibliography) published in this country merely states: 'engine trouble on *S 120* necessitated the breaking off of the operation'. It is just maybe possible that HMS *Mackay* had a hand in it, too!

The Liberation of the Channel Islands, 8 May 1944

And so, finally, the fighting came to an end in the Channel and once again it became a free highway, the busiest traffic route in the world. Fittingly, one of the most symbolic events of those times, the surrender of the German garrisons in the Channel Islands, was received by two of the veterans of the old Dover Patrol, the destroyers *Beagle* and *Bulldog*. No more apt vessels could have been chosen to represent the scores of small craft which had contested that narrow stretch of waterway for so long. The next day another famous Flotilla Leader, HMS *Faulknor*, embarked the German senior officers who had defied us for a whole year and took them to Plymouth. Thus ended the battle for control of the English Channel. One of the survivors of those epic days, who served aboard both regular destroyers and the little Hunts of the 1st Flotilla during the grimmest period of the war, later wrote to me of the memories that stretch of water holds for him now:

Hold the Narrow Sea? Yes we did hold, but at what cost... .

Note
1. Michael Joyce to the author, 28 March 2005.

Select Bibliography

It should be noted the most of the source material for this book comes from the official ADM 199 files held at the National Archives, Kew, London; selected documents held at the Imperial War Museum, Lambeth, London; the Churchill College Archive Centre, Cambridge and eyewitness accounts and memoirs from survivors. The following books are only for general background guidance on related facets of the war in the Channel.

Anon., *British Coaster*, (HMSO, London, 1947). The bland official (MOI) account of coastal shipping during the Second World War, brief and concise, consisting isolated incidents accurately detailed. Good maps.

Batten, John, *Dirty Little Collier*, (Hutchinson, London, 1945).Gives a good idea of the viewpoint of the Merchant Navy sailors themselves.

Beaver, Paul, *German Destroyers and Escorts*, (Patrick Stephens, Cambridge, 1981). Good photographic history; sparse on historical details and actions.

Bradford, Ernle, *Wall of England,* (Country Life, London, 1966). Slim volume with sketchy basic details of the history of the Channel.

Capper, D., *Moat Defensive,* (Arthur Baker, London, 1963). Good background and history, but frustratingly vague on the Second World War.

De Chair, Commander Henry Graham, DSC, *Let Go Aft: The Indiscretions of a Salthorse Commander*, (Parapress, Tunbridge Wells, 1993). Good sketches on life in destroyers in the Second World War.

Divine, A. D., DSM, *Dunkirk*, (Faber & Faber, London, 1945). The very best book on the naval activity, even better than the same author's later book on the same subject *The Nine Days of Dunkirk* from which it was adapted.

Edwards, Commander Kenneth, RN, *Operation Neptune*, (Collins, London, 1946). The best source for naval side of the D-Day Normandy landings and aftermath.

English, John I., M.Sc (Trans), B.Sc (Econ), *The Hunts: A history of the design, development and careers of the 86 destroyers of this class built for the Royal and Allied Navies during World War II*, (World Ship Society, Cumbria, 1987). The best factual account of these ships, with some good original photographs.

Fisher, Rear Admiral R. L. Fisher, *Salt Horse: A Naval Life,* (Privately produced, undated). Good insights into destroyer operations, but done in a casual, throw-away style that wastes a lot of its historical value.

Jones, Basil, *And So To Battle*, (Jones, 1976) Privately produced, fascinating account by the leader of the 10th Destroyer Flotilla.

Lund, Paul and Ludlam, Harry, *Out Sweeps*, (W. Foulsham, London, 1978). Good history of minesweepers, spoilt only by attempting too much for size.

McKee, Alexander, *The Coal-Scuttle Brigade*, (Souvenir Press, London, 1957). Good journalism and perceptive judgements. Badly arranged and hard to follow chronologically.

Muggenthaler, August Karl, *German Raiders of World War II*, (Robert Hale, London, 1978). Excellent and detailed account, interesting for Channel passages of the various raiders.

Rohwer, J. and Hummelchen, G., *Chronology of the War at Sea*, (Ian Allan, Shepperton, 1972). Useful for dates and ships, but typically one-sided from the German viewpoint and containing a large number of inaccurate or ambiguous statements presented as facts. Atrocious English-language editing of factual information.

Roskill, Captain Stephen W., *The War at Sea*, (Chaotic arrangement of three volumes in four books!) (HMSO, London, 1957-66.) Scholarly standard overall history; but with some surprising omissions.

Sclater, William S. B., *Haida*, (OUP, Oxford, 1946). History, trans-Atlantic style. If you can stand the hyperbole contains some interesting detail.

Scott, Peter, *Battle of the Narrow Seas*, (Country Life, London, 1945). The definitive account of the MTB war; often imitated, yet even today, never bettered.

Scott, Rivers, *The Gateway of England*, (Dover Harbour Board, Dover, 1956). Handy background on Dover. Nothing on the war.

Smith, Peter C., *Into the Minefields*, (Pen & Sword Maritime, Barnsley, 2005). The only full account of destroyer minelaying in both World Wars and beyond.

Ward, Peter, *From Africa to the Arctic: A Year on the Destroyer HMS* Beagle *during WWII*, (Brewin Books, Studley, 2003). Not much on the Channel but history of a famous ship that served twice in that area.

By the same author

NAVAL
Action Imminent
Arctic Victory
Battle of Midway
Battles of the Malta Striking Forces
Battleship *Royal Sovereign*
British Battle Cruisers
Cruisers in Action
Destroyer Action
Destroyer Leader
Eagle's War
Fighting Flotilla
Hard Lying
Heritage of the Sea
Hit First, Hit Hard
H.M.S. *Wild Swan*
Into the Minefields
Midway; Dauntless Victory
Pedestal; the convoy that saved Malta
Royal Navy Ships' Badges
Task Force 57
The Great Ships Pass
War in the Aegean

MILITARY
Massacre at Tobruk
The Royal Marines: A Pictorial History
Per Mare, Per Terram
Victoria's Victories

AVIATION
Close Air Support
Fairchild-Republic A10A Thunderbolt
North American T-6, SNJ, Harvard & Wirraway
Lockheed C-130 Hercules
Ship Strike
RAF Squadron Badges
T-6; the Harvard, Texan and Wirraway
The Sea Eagles
The Story of the Torpedo Bomber

DIVE BOMBERS
Aichi D3A1/2 *Val*
Curtiss SB2C *Helldiver*
Dive Bomber!
Dive Bombers in Action
Douglas SBD *Dauntless*
Douglas AD *Skyraider*
Fist from the Sky
Impact! – the dive bomber pilots speak.
Into the Assault
Jungle Dive Bombers at War
Junkers Ju.87 *Stuka*
Luftwaffe Colours – Stukas – 1
Luftwaffe Colours – Stukas – 2
Petlyakov Pe-2 *Peshka*
Straight Down!
Skua; The Royal Navy's Dive Bomber
Straight Down!
Stuka at War
Stukas over the Mediterranean
Stukas over the Steppe
Stuka Spearhead
Stuka Squadron
Vengeance!

Index